The Invention of Infinite Growth

The Invention of Infinite Growth

How Economists Forgot
About the Natural World

Christopher F. Jones

ONEWORLD

A Oneworld Book

First published in Great Britain, the Republic of Ireland and Australia
by Oneworld Publications Ltd, 2025

ISBN 978-0-86154-004-4
eISBN 978-0-86154-005-1

Printed and bound in Great Britain by Clays Ltd, Elcograf S.p.A.

The authorised representative in the EEA is eucomply OU,
Pärnu mnt 139b–14, 11317 Tallinn, Estonia
(email: hello@eucompliancepartner.com / phone: +33757690241)

Oneworld Publications Ltd
10 Bloomsbury Street
London WC1B 3SR
England

Stay up to date with the latest books,
special offers, and exclusive content from
Oneworld with our newsletter

Sign up on our website
oneworld-publications.com

MIX
Paper | Supporting
responsible forestry
FSC
www.fsc.org
FSC® C018072

**For Silas and Margo,
with hope that lessons from
the past can help them
inherit a more just and
sustainable future**

Contents

Introduction

There are . . . no limits to the carrying capacity of the earth that
are likely to bind any time in the foreseeable future. There isn't
a risk of apocalypse due to global warming or anything else.
The idea that we should put limits on growth because of some
natural limit, is a profound error.

Lawrence Summers, chief economist of the World Bank, 1992[1]

A curious idea lies at the heart of American political and
social life. It is an idea that captivates politicians across the
spectrum and is often the most important metric by which
they are judged. Its successes and failures are front-page
news. It touches on people's personal lives, shaping their
expectations of the present and the future. Is it freedom?
Liberty? Democracy? No. It is a narrower subject, one that
the founding fathers did not mention. It is not red, white,
and blue, but gray, almost anonymous.

The idea is this: infinite growth is the key to a better
future.

Delivering economic growth has become the most
powerful imperative in politics over the past seventy-five
years. The formula is clear: rapid growth is good, slow
growth is alarming, stagnation is insufferable, and decline
is disastrous. Policies that claim to enhance growth are
almost always welcomed; those that would impede it are
usually doomed. Nor is this just an American story. Governments worldwide are obsessed with expanding their

economic output, whether to lift their nations out of poverty or to outshine their neighbors.

The pursuit of infinite growth is also the single greatest threat to human sustainability. In the frantic quest to increase output and acquire more goods, people across the globe are emitting vast quantities of greenhouse gases, leaching toxic materials, cutting down rainforests, and pushing countless species into extinction. Despite advances in efficiency, the ever-increasing scale of economic activity continues to accelerate climate change, biodiversity loss, ocean acidification, and soil erosion. The planet's relatively stable ecosystems of the last several millennia are changing more radically than ever before.

For all of humanity's technical prowess, we remain dependent on natural ecosystems for our survival. More than half of the world's population live in regions where annual monsoons provide the fresh water needed for humans, animals, and plants. The relatively mild climate of Europe results from the warming effect of the Gulf Stream current. Coastal infrastructure across the globe is predicated on sea levels remaining steady. And all of us rely on a thin layer of topsoil to grow plants, which use the free pollination services of bees and the nutrient processing provided by insects and worms. If droughts or floods ruin crops, if fisheries are depleted, if pollinators perish, iPhones cannot feed us. The global quest for growth has taken too little account of these realities.

Economic growth versus the environment: it is one of the most important debates the world faces. At the same time, I believe it is a curious one. Why is it so common to pit one against the other? Why is growth calculated with little regard for the natural world? Why haven't the narratives of economic growth changed in the face of overwhelming evidence about climate change and ecological degradation? And is it really true that ever-increasing growth will result in ever-improving lives?

I have written this book because I am concerned and puzzled that "versus" is the main word that springs to mind when economic growth and environmental sustainability are discussed. I am concerned because climate change is a grave danger that will cause great harm if not addressed aggressively. I am convinced by reports from tens of thousands of scientists that loss of biodiversity, melting of ice sheets, acidification of the ocean, and related ecosystem changes will have significant consequences on the quality of life for billions. I fear the impacts of extreme weather events on vulnerable populations. What will happen when countless people have to migrate from regions that can no longer support their populations in a world where borders have never been more fiercely defended? I worry about my children inheriting a volatile climate that causes widespread suffering.[2]

At the same time, I have also been puzzled about why environmentalists and economists have such different visions for the future. In particular, I have wondered why economists have tended to be much more optimistic about the potential for infinite growth than academics of nearly every other stripe. Lawrence Summers, chief economist of the World Bank, summarized this view in 1992 by stating that "there are no limits to the carrying capacity of the earth" and that it would be a "profound error" to limit growth. Things have not changed enormously since then. In 2018, the Nobel Prize in Economics was awarded to William Nordhaus and Paul Romer. Nordhaus was celebrated for his contributions to the economics of climate change, where he is widely acknowledged as the world's leading thinker on the topic. Yet when he accepted his award in Stockholm, he argued the optimal path to decreasing greenhouse gas emissions would allow global temperatures to rise 4 degrees Celsius by 2140. Paul Romer won the prize for his contributions to growth theory, where he was famous for arguing that because ideas drive growth, there are no meaningful limits to economic expansion. Economics is known as the dismal science, for its insistence that there are no free lunches and everything is a matter of trade-offs. Yet when it comes to the future of growth, optimism trumps pessimism.[3]

The situation is even more surprising because there is considerable evidence that infinite growth does not correlate with infinitely better lives. Growth economists rarely ask who is receiving the benefits of growth and who is not. It is too often assumed that everyone benefits from growth, but history shows this has seldom been the case. This matters enormously. Growth that provides resources to those who lack secure housing, food, and medical care can have an incredible effect on quality of life, leading to longer and healthier lives with greater comfort and autonomy. But funneling growth into the hands of the wealthy does little to improve their lives while also harming everyone else through increased inequality and environmental degradation. For the last several decades, America and much of the world have seen too little of the former and too much of the latter. Why, then, is it still so common to talk about growth as a rising tide that will raise all boats despite abundant evidence to the contrary? This is the dangerous delusion of infinite growth.

When I began this book, I expected to write a blistering critique of the economics profession. It is a popular genre, and many have been justified in castigating economists for a host of shortcomings.[4] But I came to realize this was no simple story of heroes and villains. People matter in history, and most of the people in this book were not corporate shills, free market fundamentalists, or enemies of the environmental movement. Consider Robert Solow, the most important figure in the history of growth theory. His work paid little attention to the natural world, and when environmentalists in the early 1970s warned of potential ecosystem collapses, Solow quickly labeled their arguments "worthless."[5] Yet Solow was in favor of pollution controls, collaborated with labor groups, and served on an advisory board to the Sierra Club. He and many of his followers were left-of-center thinkers who consistently pushed back against opponents of regulation and expressed concern for the natural world. I have found no evidence that they took significant corporate funding or that their views were distorted by those hoping to preserve the status quo.[6] Rather than a black-and-white tale of right and wrong, this book offers a tale of reasonable choices leading to an unreasonable place—indeed, an increasingly unlivable one.[7]

This is also not a tale of heroes and villains because, as with all tricky debates, there is no simple answer. Economic growth has delivered much good to many, and billions around the world are desperate to improve their lots. Yet all economic activities, no matter how efficient, have some impact on the natural world, and those collective effects have loaded the atmosphere with warming gases, altered the acidity of the oceans, and led to enormous losses of ecosystems and species. Reconciling the natural world with economic growth is truly a wicked problem, and one that will require many perspectives.[8]

History offers crucial and often overlooked insights into this topic.[9] Studying the past reveals that economists did not always abstract the natural world from their analyses, nor did they always imagine infinite growth to be possible. This offers hope. By considering how today's ideas became dominant, it is possible to reconsider ideas once abandoned and rethink assumptions made in different eras. Studying the past can help us craft a more sustainable future.

The Fetishization of Growth

Economic growth has been called "the most important idea" of the post–World War II era.[10] Though politicians have given lip service to ideas such as freedom, justice, and democracy, no other idea has driven the policy process like growth over the past seventy years in nations as different as the United States, Russia, Germany, Japan, and China. If there is a single litmus test for how well a political leader is doing, it is the growth rate. Ronald Reagan knew this when he asked voters in 1980 if they were better off than they were four years ago as a way to discredit Jimmy Carter. A dozen years later, Bill Clinton's adviser James Carville bluntly declared, "It's the economy, stupid." When growth is good, political parties usually stay in power; when it is poor, they are often voted out.

Growth holds this cherished place because it has been hailed for many decades as the surest path to better lives. It has allowed populations to be better fed, have more comfortable housing, expand educational access, improve healthcare options, and live longer lives. As societies experience growth, work often becomes shorter, less physically demanding, and safer. Wealthy nations tend to have more stable political systems, better democratic participation, and greater protections for human rights than poorer ones. Given that there is very little historical precedent for redistribution of wealth within or between countries, growth offers a pathway for uplift across the globe.[11]

This broad faith in growth has been amplified by its seemingly universal appeal across political divides. Liberals and conservatives who disagree about nearly everything still concur that growth is good. President Lyndon Johnson in the 1960s argued growth could support a "guns and butter" campaign that would allow the US to fight a war in Southeast Asia while also expanding the domestic social security net. Two decades later, Ronald Reagan touted growth as the key to cutting taxes while also pursuing his "Star Wars" defense programs. There have been fierce debates about how to slice a growing pie, but an almost universal belief that bigger is better.

Nor is this simply an expression of American capitalism. The Soviet Union was similarly preoccupied with material expansion, adopting ambitious five-year plans to increase output, in the belief that impressive growth rates would convince other nations to adopt communism. China did the same, highlighted by its "Great Leap Forward" program in the late 1950s; in recent decades, its growth rates have been among the world's highest. Many developing nations have praised growth policies as the best means of securing a good future for their citizens. And even when there has not been an internal push for growth, agencies such as the World Bank and International Monetary Fund have often required such countries to implement growth-oriented policies in order to qualify for loans.[12]

The global obsession with growth centers on one number that stands above all the rest: gross domestic product (GDP). Called "the world's most powerful number" and "one of the great inventions of the twentieth century," GDP emerged in the early 1940s out of calculations of national income designed to assess the Great Depression and guide wartime mobilization.[13] This overarching number has exerted outsized sway on political discourse. GDP has come to be equated in the popular imagination with how well a nation is doing overall. Whenever a new quarterly calculation is announced, it is almost always front-page news with celebrations of high growth rates and alarm bells at any sign of slowdown.[14]

It may be a surprise that the obsession with "the power of a single number" is so new.[15] Before the 1930s, GDP did not exist, nor did the language of economic growth. People had long spoken of expansion or material progress and debated economic policies such as tariffs, taxes, labor rights, and corporate privileges. But the idea of quantified economic growth—and that the government was responsible for delivering it—did not exist.[16]

This is not to suggest that rulers and intellectuals in the past ignored questions of material prosperity or the improvement of financial conditions. The history of economic thought extends hundreds, if not thousands, of years, and government policy has long been concerned with the wealth of nations. But the modern quest for GDP growth is different in key ways. It has risen in prominence above all other priorities, it requires the government to draw continually on economic expertise to manage the process, and most crucially, it is a never-ending goal. There is no finish line or target point at which a nation can rest on its laurels. The growth obsession is like a hamster wheel that must always be kept turning.

It is easy to understand why growth is fetishized. To its defenders, growth is an imperative of the highest moral order. It is much better for freedom and citizens, they argue, to have governments focus on increasing economic output than on military endeavors or exclusionary nationalist projects. Growth is also necessary for employment, as it is posited that only an expanding economy can generate jobs. If one cares about improving the lives of the lower classes or the developing nations, expanding the pie is the surest bet. To be against growth, on this view, is to be an elitist insensitive to the real needs of billions. The case for growth has many strong points.

The Case Against Growth

The praise of growth is so powerful that one might assume there is little reason to question the force of its logic. However, simple stories frequently mask as much as they reveal. Enthusiasts have painted a fairytale sketch of growth in which a benevolent fairy godmother waves her wand and the benefits of economic expansion magically make everyone better off, and only the evil stepmothers are excluded from the gains.[17]

The reality is much more complex. Growth is not an unalloyed good or a timeless virtue. The connections between growth and improved human lives vary enormously across time and space depending on several factors that are too often ignored. Growth's benefits must be assessed in light of the fact that economic expansion, in the words of one economist who still considers growth essential, is frequently "climate-destroying, inequality-creating, work-threatening, politics-undermining, and community-disrupting."[18]

The greatest weakness of the modern growth discourse is that it ignores the environmental consequences of economic expansion. Climate change is being felt across the globe in the form of droughts, floods, heat waves, and extreme weather events; in the coming decades, scientists predict the harms will grow increasingly dire as sea levels rise, agricultural zones shift, and monsoons change. At the same time, we are witnessing the greatest loss of biodiversity since the extinction of the dinosaurs sixty-five million years ago. As many as half of the living creatures on the planet may perish in what some call the "sixth great extinction." By almost any measure, humans are consuming resources, cutting down forests, and emitting pollution at unsustainable rates, rendering the planet less livable for people, plants, and animals. While there have been improvements in the efficiency of the global economy over the last few decades, it has not been enough to offset the increasing environmental impacts. There is no such thing as economic growth without an impact on the natural world, and many of the ecosystems humans rely on are under enormous stress.[19]

Climate change highlights the ecological struggles facing society today, but it is not the only one. Several other earth systems are being impacted by human actions, including atmospheric ozone depletion, degradation of freshwater supplies, loss of biosphere integrity, and dangerous shifts in the phosphorus and nitrogen cycles. There is also the risk of rapid shifts in earth systems that cannot be reversed except over long time periods. These tipping points include the possibility of ocean currents shifting dramatically, melting permafrost emitting massive quantities of methane that further accelerate global warming, and the collapse of ice sheets in Greenland or Antarctica that will raise sea levels by several meters. A sustainable future cannot be reached solely by swapping out renewable energy sources for fossil fuels to slow climate change; it is also necessary to change land-use patterns, reform agricultural practices, and protect nonhuman species.[20]

The problems with a focus on growth increase further when one considers questions of well-being and inequality. When people are asked what makes a good life, they usually mention financial security, but also point to several other factors including family connections, community bonds, satisfying jobs, spiritual fulfillment, and access to leisure. Growth advocates pick up on the first point and ignore the others, reducing the broad category of quality of life to a narrow calculation of economic welfare. Economic welfare is a linear calculation of how well-off someone is, with the assumption that two units of wealth are twice as good as one unit and a person that is twice as rich is twice as well-off. The logic is clear: ever-increasing growth delivers ever-increasing benefits. But this is not how most people experience the world. Growth has a nonlinear relationship with well-being that depends on how wealthy an individual already is. When people are poor, growth improves life immensely. But once people reach a middle-class income level, the improvements to their lives from growth decrease rapidly. For the super wealthy, additional millions or even billions in their bank accounts have virtually no bearing on the quality of their lives. To use a phrase favored by economists, there are diminishing returns to growth. Middle-class Americans today live in larger houses with bigger televisions and more appliances than their peers four decades ago, but they do not report being any happier or having a higher quality of life. The American economy has increased more than ten times over the past half century, yet one would be hard pressed to say that its citizens are ten times as well-off.[21]

Worse, economic growth can actually decrease well-being. In states and nations with higher levels of inequality, life expectancy goes down and a range of negative outcomes such as obesity, drug use, and teen births go up. Democracy suffers as well. Inequality leads to lower levels of voter turnout and declining trust in government. Crime rates appear to correlate with inequality as well, since large wealth disparities undermine social cohesion. When people experience high levels of inequality, they are less likely to trust one another or to feel connected to their community.[22] The dramatic increase in the polarization of politics in the last several years, from the Trump presidencies in the US to Brexit in Britain to the rise of authoritarian leaders across the globe, stems in no small part from several decades of widespread economic stagnation for the working and middle classes. Yet economic assessments of growth rarely concern themselves with inequality, seeing it as an acceptable outcome of free market forces and even as a necessary spur to innovation.[23]

The story of King Midas, who wished that everything he touched would turn to gold, is instructive. His initial delight in turning objects into gold turned to horror as he realized he could no longer eat, drink, or touch his beloved daughter. In a similar manner, the obsession with economic gain across the globe has too often blinded people to how much can be lost through the endless pursuit of growth.

The great delusion of growth discourses, then, is the assumption that all growth is created equal. Economic gains for people in developing nations that are broadly distributed and have minimal environmental impact should be prioritized. Economic growth that is highly environmentally damaging and lines the pockets of billionaires should be recognized for what it is: a harm to the vast majority of the population. All that glitters is not gold, and all that grows is not to be praised.

Economists and Infinite Growth

So how did we get to a place where never-ending growth is so frequently touted despite its environmental perils and questionable benefits? We can begin to unravel this mystery by tracing the history of economics and how the field has analyzed growth and the natural world.

Doing so requires traversing between national and global stories. This account centers the American economics tradition because, since the mid-twentieth century, economists based in the United States have had an outsized global impact, particularly in growth theory. From 1969, when the Nobel Prize in Economics was introduced, to 2023, economists based in America have won sixty-two times; no other nation has earned more than nine.[24] The economics departments at top American universities are widely considered among the world's best, and top international students often travel to the US for doctoral training. I also emphasize the American context because ideas do not exist in a vacuum. Economic theories both shaped and responded to events in American history including the excesses of the Gilded Age, the depths of the Great Depression, and the politics of the Cold War. A national focus helps clarify the links between social context and intellectual development.

Yet American economics and policy cannot be adequately described without a global perspective. Economists from many nations made theoretical contributions to the invention of infinite growth, and the pursuit of growth has become an obsession in most other nations as well. This is, as a result, an American story that seeks to bring in the global context as appropriate, but not an account of the distinctive paths other nations have taken in their pursuit of infinite growth.[25]

It is also important to clarify that economists do not control the modern discourse of growth. They are only one set of actors, alongside politicians, corporate executives, media commentators, and voters. The pursuit of growth has taken on a life of its own because it is a politically convenient belief that appeals to liberals and conservatives and is as alluring to nations in the global North as it is to those in the global South. The latest academic research and the most sophisticated thoughts of economists rarely permeate these debates, particularly because most economic theorizing since the mid-twentieth century has been too mathematical and abstract for those outside the discipline to understand. Shareholders demand that corporations pursue ever-larger market shares, and many government programs are predicated on ever-increasing revenue streams to fund them. Even if the discipline of economics did not exist, the world would likely be on an unsustainable economic trajectory.

Why emphasize economists, then, instead of business executives and fossil fuel lobby groups? Because ideas matter. And in particular, the idea of infinite growth is one of the greatest obstacles to designing a sustainable future. I focus on economists because more than any other group, they pioneered the idea that infinite growth is feasible and retain a privileged position to pronounce on its possibilities. They possess access to power through the prestige of the discipline and their numerous positions in the halls of governments. For decades, scientists and environmentalists have warned of the dangerous effects of economic activities on the natural world and urged greater protection for ecosystems that are necessary for humanity's present and future. Economists have routinely denounced these claims. Their message of optimism has undermined calls for environmental protection and provided intellectual legitimacy for vested interests opposed to addressing climate change. The economic belief that growth can and should continue justifies the status quo. That is why faith in infinite growth is one of today's most powerful and dangerous ideas, and why it needs to be reconsidered.

If economists loudly and fervently pointed to the need to reconsider the global obsession with growth, would corporate leaders or government officials immediately listen? Perhaps not. There are very powerful forces likely to fight tooth and nail to protect their entrenched interests. But it would still matter. A shift in economic thinking would remove a formidable piece of armor from this defense. Unsustainable actions would be harder to justify and an alignment between economic and environmental perspectives could shift the conversation and provide significant pressure to pass policies that limit climate change and protect biodiversity.

Distinguished economist and peace studies pioneer Kenneth Boulding is reported to have said that "anyone who believes that exponential growth can go on forever in a finite world is either a madman or an economist."[26] Economists are overwhelmingly men—women are far less represented in the field than in practically any other academic discipline—but they are not, generally speaking, mad.[27] Many of the figures in this book are quite reasonable. Yet on the whole, economists have been much more dismissive of environmental concerns than researchers in nearly every other field. Why?

The optimism of the dismal science stems from three critical beliefs, each a product of history: a faith that human ingenuity and technological progress can overcome natural limits, a narrow framing of the relationships between humans and the natural world, and a strong belief that the benefits of growth outweigh its potential costs. This third point is particularly critical and often underappreciated. For the pursuit of infinite growth is driven much more by the argument that growth is essential to better lives thàn it is an absence of concern for the natural world. Those who wish to advocate for a more sustainable future need to grapple as much or more with the links between growth and well-being as they do with the links between economic analysis and the natural world.

When economists today assess whether the natural world will limit economic growth, they typically separate this question into two parts: First, are there enough resources to produce more goods and services? And second, will the wastes and pollution from the production process constrain economic growth? Since the 1970s, the consensus of mainstream economists has been yes to the first and no to the second. Regarding resources, economists espouse a faith that even if the world ran out of certain goods like coal or oil, it would be possible to find suitable substitutes. The world did not leave the Stone Age because it ran out of stones; rather, people found better options for making tools and weapons. Similarly, when resources like oil get expensive, market systems will encourage entrepreneurs to increase supply, and people will have incentives to reduce their consumption or find alternatives. "The world has been exhausting its resources since the first cave-man chipped a flint," Solow wryly noted in 1974, but because flints could be replaced by metal tools, he concluded that "the process will go on a long time."[28] The American natural gas fracking boom since the mid-2000s offers evidence of how new technologies, government investment, and market incentives can turn a situation of scarcity into one of abundance, thereby sustaining growth.

But what about the wastes? Economists have historically treated pollution mainly as a local nuisance. Pollution might be unpleasant and disagreeable, but that does not mean it would slow down the growth rate. This reflects what can be characterized as a thin view of how the environment relates to human well-being. Mainstream economic thought "sees" things that are captured in the price system, focusing almost exclusively on assessing questions that can be answered using the "measuring rod of money."[29] Some parts of nature are intensively priced, most notably inputs to production such as barrels of oil, tons of coal, and planks of lumber. But much of the natural world is not: the trees and phytoplankton that generate oxygen and capture carbon dioxide, the life-producing qualities of soil, the hydrological cycles that bring rain to fields, the ocean currents that drive regular monsoons, the bees that pollinate crops, and the beauty of sacred landscapes. Nor are the potential costs of crossing tipping points routinely assessed. The result is a false ledger of economic accomplishments—one that overinflates assets while undercounting debits. The modern economic worldview is deeply limited in its ability to account for the complex ways humans depend on and benefit from natural systems.[30]

Faith in technological advances and market signals, along with a simplified view of human relationships with the natural world, has given economists confidence that growth can continue indefinitely. Moreover, they believe that it should continue to grow, because growth is seen as the best path to better lives. A planet with much greater environmental swings and richer people is preferable to a planet with ecosystem stability and less wealth. The medicine of slowing or stopping growth to protect the natural world is considered worse than the disease.

The argument runs like this: human well-being is shaped by a plethora of factors, most of which cannot be quantified or brought into the sphere of economic calculations. But even if you cannot know what brings a person joy, you can bet that they are in a better position to obtain it if they are financially better off. Moreover, being poor leaves people vulnerable to many things that could diminish their well-being. Ecosystem change is one such threat, but so are lack of nutrition, inadequate access to healthcare and education, and vulnerability to civil war and political strife. In the last several years, the COVID pandemic did more to disrupt quality of life for many than any environmental change, and the war between Russia and Ukraine has mattered far more for those living nearby than extreme weather events. The best remedy for improving people's lives, according to many economists, is to make them richer, as with extra resources, they will be more resilient to the full range of potential harms. When William Nordhaus, the world's leading climate economist, won the Nobel Prize in 2018, he argued in his speech that if reducing climate change "would require deep reductions in living standards in poor nations, then the policy would be the equivalent of burning down the village to save it."[31]

Economists also claim that growth matters in wealthy nations as well. Growth can generate jobs for increasing populations. Many government social programs, such as Social Security, are predicated on ever-larger revenues to cover rising costs. Others argue growth is necessary to preserve social stability. If the pie is growing, everyone has a chance to improve their lot. If it does not grow, then the only way for one person to improve is by taking from another, thereby exacerbating social tensions. Finally, some contend that economic growth is crucial for protecting the environment. Only when societies are richer will they devote resources to reduce pollution and invest in renewable energy. Thus, many economists believe that, even if there are harms from climate change, a cost–benefit analysis favors the continued pursuit of growth.

Each of these arguments underpinning the invention of infinite growth is a product of history. And each has been contested at many points. Economists have not always claimed that growth can and should continue. The natural world has not always been sidelined in the history of economic thought. Tracing this history matters, then, because it reveals that today's ideas are neither natural nor inevitable. It is possible to imagine other ways of calculating the connections between humans, the natural world, and economic well-being that better serve our present and future.

Historians, Economists, and the Future of Growth

The laws of economics are frequently posited as universal and timeless. An increase in supply will lower prices whether the product is grain in ancient Egypt, rice in tenth-century China, or microchips in twenty-first-century America. Rational actors will always aim to maximize their utility. Growth is better than stagnation.

But our world is not universal or timeless. People and societies change and evolve. What is rational in one stage may not be rational in another; what is valued in one time and place may not be prized in a different era or location. In the case of growth, what once delivered a great deal of uplift to many can, at a different time, do more damage than good. Children need to grow to be healthy, but in adults, growth usually signifies obesity or cancer. We need history to situate economic ideas in specific times and places to distinguish growth that is needed from growth that is harmful.

In particular, the story of growth cannot be separated from the quarter century following World War II. This was a time of many remarkable convergences: the adoption of GDP as a measure of governance across the globe, the development of growth theory, the orthodoxy of neoclassical economics, ignorance about climate change, and a period of decreasing inequality in much of the global North. Yet a wider sweep of history reveals how truly exceptional this period was. Growth has not always been prioritized, it has not always been seen to be infinite in potential, and it has not always produced such broadly shared collective benefits.

More than anything else, this book is a call to rethink growth in the context of present realities: climate change, stagnant well-being, rampant inequality, and a planet under duress. It is not a call to do away with abstractions and models of economic theory. Rather, it is a call to broaden our perspectives. It is a call to consider what growth means, to assess its consequences, and to create a balance between human desires, social well-being, and planetary sustainability. It is a call for a more open discussion of economic growth including historians, environmental scientists, politicians, and citizens. It is a call to ask whether economic principles developed in the Holocene can guide us in the Anthropocene. It is a call to recognize that economic growth is too important to leave to the economists.

A first step in opening this conversation is to understand just how variable ideas about economic growth and natural limits have been over the past 250 years. It is to the origins of economics as a distinct topic of study in the late eighteenth and early nineteenth century that this book now turns.

1 ∗ Before the Invention of the Infinite

Thomas Robert Malthus did not seem an obvious villain. A mild-mannered and handsome man known as Robert to colleagues and Bob to friends and family, he was congenial and friendly. Born in 1766 with a cleft palate and a speech impediment, he worked hard to overcome his disability, gaining a position as a parson at a small chapel in rural England and later holding the first professorship in political economy in Britain. In spite of his halting lectures, he was beloved by his students and referred to as "Pop" behind his back. He hardly seemed destined to become the world's most famous pessimist.[1]

If anyone was to blame, it was his father. A well-to-do solicitor, Daniel Malthus's true passion lay in debating the day's radical thoughts. In the mid-1970s, the elder Malthus became particularly fascinated by the utopian tracts of William Godwin and the Marquis de Condorcet, which claimed the human condition could be substantially improved through enlightened governance.[2] Eager for his son's thoughts, Daniel initiated lengthy conversations at the dinner table. But the younger Malthus did not share his father's optimism. Making things better now, he argued, would just make things worse later. Convinced of the clarity of his logic, he recorded his ideas in an anonymous pamphlet that would captivate his contemporaries and reverberate through history.

Published in 1798, *An Essay on the Principle of Population* launched Malthus into international renown. The argument can be stated simply enough: over time, population growth would exceed the food supply and lead to mass deprivation. His beliefs hinged on a few key propositions. The first was that the food supply would grow linearly $(1 + 1 + 1 + 1 \ldots)$ whereas population could grow exponentially $(1 + 2 + 4 + 8 \ldots)$. In addition, food required land, which had two limitations. First, it was finite in supply; once it was all in use, you could not make more. Second, it was subject to diminishing returns, which meant that it got harder and harder to increase output over time with more capital or labor. One additional worker or application of fertilizer added to a field, for example, might increase the output by 50 percent, but hiring one more laborer or fertilizing another time might only gain you a further 30 percent improvement. This meant that food production might not even grow linearly, but show a decreasing rate over time $(1 + \frac{7}{8} + \frac{3}{4} + \frac{5}{8} \ldots)$. The limited supply of land and law of diminishing returns made infinite growth of food production an impossibility.[3]

But population did not have those diminishing returns, at least in the short term. The passion between the sexes, as Malthus phrased it, was constant. When times were good and they could support their offspring, poor people would have more children, and more of those children would survive into adulthood. This growth in population, however, undercut visions for progress. More mouths needed more food, which would raise prices. At the same time, more bodies meant more workers would be competing for jobs, lowering wages. The result would be an inevitable return to a basic struggle for subsistence for most of the population. This led Malthus to oppose efforts for poor relief both in Britain and its colonies on the premise that such

well-intentioned aims would only make the problems worse by encouraging further population growth. It was a dark view of the world
with grim policy recommendations.[4]

Adam Smith, by contrast, is remembered for his optimism. The
epitome of an absent-minded professor, Smith frequently ambled
around Glasgow in the late eighteenth century lost in thought and
talking to himself, sometimes emerging from his daydreams far from
his intended destination. He was even known to smile during church
services as his mind wandered, drawing the rebuke of the clergy. Like
Malthus, he was well loved by his students despite having a nervous
disposition and irregular speech.[5]

Smith's optimism came from a belief that selfishness could produce a better world. Remembered today as the father of political
economy, he was better known during his life for his insights into
moral philosophy. His first book, *The Theory of Moral Sentiments*
(1759), argued that morality emerged from our ability to empathize
with others and to view situations from the perspective of an impartial observer. Because people want to be treated well, if they understood the effects their actions would have on others, it would give
them clear guidance to treat them well in the hopes that good be-
haviors would be reciprocated. Self-interest could be harnessed for
the greater good. Then in 1776, he published the *Wealth of Nations*,
which pioneered the idea of the invisible hand of the market guiding
even selfish interests into social benefit. Smith looked at the world
and saw much to be pleased about.[6]

The misanthropic pessimist versus the upbeat optimist. The contrast between the men and their historical legacies could hardly be
starker. Smith is remembered as the revered father of economics
while Malthus is the gloomy prophet of demography. But this binary
masks crucial similarities between the men. In particular, when the
two looked at issues of the natural world and the limits to growth,
they saw eye to eye. The supply of land was finite and subject to the
law of diminishing returns. As a result, growth could never be infinite, and advanced economies would eventually stagnate into a

stationary state. Many other influential economists, including David Ricardo and John Stuart Mill, agreed, with Mill even claiming that the decreasing returns from land constituted "the most important proposition in political economy."[7] On the topic of the impossibility of infinite growth, Malthus was no outlier.[8] Remembering this history is an important step in recognizing that the idea of infinite growth is a break from the past, not a timeless reification of a natural law.

The Limits of Classical Political Economy

Economic questions have a deep history. Since barter and exchange have been part of the human condition, people have paid close attention to questions of value. Historians have identified trade across borders dating back as far as 3500 BCE and the presence of proto-"multinational" companies in Assyria around 2000 BCE.[9] Money is at least as old as 600 BCE, while insurance and the practice of lending at interest extend more than two thousand years into the past.[10]

But economics as a field of study is a much more recent development. The idea that the economy should be analyzed separately from other aspects of society is less than a few centuries old. In fact, the term "economist" was rarely used in English until the latter half of the nineteenth century. The analysis of topics now understood as economics were mostly viewed as part of broader inquiries into moral and natural philosophy, which is illustrated by Adam Smith developing his economic ideas while holding a professorship in moral philosophy at the University of Glasgow.[11] Therefore, while there is a deep history of thinkers commenting on economic matters from Aristotle (circa 350 BCE) to Thomas Aquinas (circa 1250) in the Western world, to say nothing of Fan Li in China (circa 500 BCE) and Ibn Khaldoun in Tunis (circa 1375), most of these thinkers opined on a range of subjects, not limiting their purview to the economic world.

The study of economics took a major step forward with advances in political economy in the second half of the eighteenth century.

Returning to this time reveals not only an era in which the sophistication of economic thought increased, it also shows that several prominent thinkers considered questions of the natural world and growth to be related. Because the natural world was limited, growth could not be infinite.[12]

This should not be a surprise. Ignoring the natural world is a privilege of a modern world of temperature-controlled buildings, mechanized farms, personal vehicles, and indoor work. In industrialized nations, weather patterns typically merit a quick glance or mention; it takes an extreme weather event—a hurricane, drought, or flood—to remind people today of the interconnections between nature and human life.

In the eighteenth century and earlier, this was not the case. Material conditions provided only minimal separation from the natural world for all but the most elite. The vast majority of people were cold in the winter and wet when it rained. Few could choose to stay indoors when the weather turned bad, and even the wealthy lived in drafty and unevenly heated homes. Droughts and bad harvests did not simply mean a decrease in profits, they meant hungry stomachs and even starvation. Life had seasonal patterns dictated much more by weather systems than by carefully laid plans.

Moreover, a keen observer could tell that almost every economic activity involved the natural world. Agriculture was the clear basis of the global economy, with most of the population employed in raising crops. The grain trade, as a result, loomed large in the economic discussions of the day. In addition, practically any manufactured good required nature's bounty. Making bricks, for example, required clay, straw, and copious amounts of wood for firing them. Making clothes necessitated sources of fiber such as sheep for wool, plants for cotton, or worms for silk. Dyes came from plants such as indigo or insects like cochineal; spinning and weaving machines were made of wood and metal; and cloth factories required external sources of power, such as a waterwheel. As a result, bad harvests, droughts, or blights could be as devastating to manufacturing enterprises as they could to the agricultural sector. The material and economic conditions of the eighteenth century, therefore, suggested it made little sense to ignore the natural world.[13]

This was also an era where stagnation, rather than growth, appeared to be the norm. Before about 1820, the world experienced very little of what we now consider economic growth: a regular increase of economic activity on a per capita basis. From the times of the Romans to about a thousand years ago, the average person did not grow richer. The economy as a whole expanded when there were more people, but each individual still generated about the same amount of income. In the eight centuries from the dawn of the second millennium until about 1820, growth could be characterized as a "slow crawl" with only a 50 percent increase in average incomes during this long stretch.[14] This rate of increase would be so slow as to be hardly perceptible.

It was in this world of limited economic growth and dependence on nature that Adam Smith wrote one of the most consequential works in the history of economics: *An Inquiry into the Nature and Causes of the Wealth of Nations*. Published in 1776, the three-volume tome ran more than a thousand pages, reflecting on topics as diverse as the grain trade of France, the fate of cities and towns after the fall of the Roman Empire, the prodigious population growth in America, and the economic conditions of China.

Today, the depth and breadth of Smith's thought has largely been whittled down to two points. The first is Smith's idea of the invisible hand of the market, which held that individual self-interest operated in the public good. "It is not from the benevolence of the butcher, the brewer, or the baker, that we expect our dinner," he wrote, "but from their regard to their self-interest. We address ourselves, not to their humanity but to their self-love, and never talk to them of our own necessities but of their advantages."[15] If people were left alone to pursue their selfish desires, they would be drawn to those activities for which other humans were willing to pay, thereby leading to mutual satisfaction. The second major point concerns the benefits of the division of labor. He opened the *Wealth of Nations* with a parable of pinmakers, noting that with "utmost industry" a person working on their own "could certainly not make twenty" pins a day. Yet when pin making was broken into eighteen distinct steps—drawing the wire, straightening it, cutting it, forming a head, etc.—and each person was responsible for only two or three tasks, a team of ten "could make among them upwards of forty-eight thousand pins in a day."[16]

While these points were of great importance to Smith, few realize that the phrase "invisible hand" occurs only once in the *Wealth of Nations*, midway through the second volume. And Smith's focus on labor practices as the basis of wealth stands in contrast to modern thinkers who emphasize capital and technology instead. Reducing his thought, therefore, to these two points skews our understanding of his worldview.[17]

In particular, this selective reading misses the fact that Smith believed there were limits to growth, and that these limits were rooted in the natural world. Nature's gifts should not be underestimated: "No equal capital puts into motion a greater quantity of productive labor than that of the farmer," he wrote, because "in agriculture . . . nature labors along with man."[18] He estimated that the free powers of the sun and soil added at least a quarter and perhaps a third of the value to capital in agriculture. This stood in contrast to manufacturing, where labor could never be as productive: in a workshop, "nature does nothing; man does all."[19] As a result, he concluded that "the land constitutes by far the greatest, the most important, and the most durable part of the wealth of every extensive country."[20]

But land was not infinite, nor could its output be expanded forever. It was subject to diminishing returns. If you had a plot of land, you could increase its production by adding more capital (such as fertilizer) or more labor (additional farmhands). The first application of fertilizer would certainly increase your output. But a second application of equal quantity would not be as beneficial, and a fifth or sixth application might actually be counterproductive by damaging the soil. The more you put in, the lower the returns you could expect. Labor was the same. Adding a second farmhand to a field would allow more careful tending of plants, thereby raising output. But as a third, fourth, or fifth worker was hired, each additional laborer would generate a progressively lower benefit. There simply would not be as much productive labor to perform, and too many workers might actually reduce efficiency by getting in each other's way. Ten pinmakers were far better than one, but adding ten more might overcrowd the factory and hamper production. A limited supply of land plus diminishing returns meant the economy must eventually reach a stationary state—a point in time at which growth was no longer possible.

Smith found the idea of limits dispiriting. He fervently believed that the "progressive state" of advancing wealth was when "the laboring poor, . . . the great body of the people, seems to be the happiest and the most comfortable." But "it is hard in the stationary, and miserable in the declining state" because profits and wages would be reduced to minimal levels. "The stationary is dull; the declining, melancholy," he grimly concluded.[21] But there was little to be done, because "both productive and unproductive laborers, and those who do not labor at all, are equally maintained by the annual produce of the land and labor of the country. This produce, how great soever, can never be infinite, but must have certain limits."[22] These words of caution are often ignored; Smith's stationary state has been far more invisible than his famous hand.

By articulating limits to growth, Smith countered a more optimistic strain of thought that had been circulating in Britain since the early seventeenth century. Francis Bacon, one of the pioneers of the scientific revolution, argued in works such as *The New Atlantis* (1627) that human ingenuity could manipulate nature and create abundance. In the next generation, his follower Samuel Hartlib articulated a cornucopian faith that scientific inquiry could generate remarkable advances. In the century and a half before the *Wealth of Nations*, therefore, there had been animated debates in fields ranging from natural theology to political economy about growth and limits.[23]

Yet Smith found more inspiration in the French Physiocrats than Bacon and Hartlib. In 1764, a rich patron hired Smith to tutor his son, so Smith resigned his position and traveled the continent for two years. In Paris, he met the royal physician François Quesnay and his group of thinkers, *les Économistes*. There he discussed with the Physiocrats their central argument that nature was the one true source of wealth. Only farmers, they argued, generated a true profit because they benefited from the free gifts of nature. One seed became two because of the sun, soil, and water. "Agriculture is the only human labor with which the sky cooperates without ceasing and which is a perpetual creation," Pierre Samuel du Pont de Nemours, a prominent Physiocrat, noted in 1764, arguing that "we strictly owe the net product to the soil, to providence, and to the beneficence of the creator, to his rain that beats down and changes it to gold."[24] In the manufacturing sector, though, such surplus did not exist. Plants continued to grow after farmers put down their tools, but a factory did not generate another product once workers went home. The agricultural sector was productive, while manufacturing was sterile because it simply rearranged what had been generated by nature. Quesnay and his colleagues employed the term physiocracy— roughly, "the rule of nature"—to denote their views on economic wealth. Smith did not fully share their pessimism about the sterility of the manufacturing sector, but he was influenced by their attention to the natural world.[25]

Smith's view that limits were inevitable did not permeate the generally optimistic tone of his writings. Though he wondered whether Holland and China were approaching the stationary state, he thought it remained off in the distance for Britain; in the bustling New World, it was even further away. Rather than fretting about the arrival of the stationary state, he was far more interested in the ways that division of labor could produce significant gains in the meantime. But he was no apostle of the infinite.

It was in the hands of the next generation of political economists, including Thomas Robert Malthus and David Ricardo, that the stationary state received greater attention. Malthus and Ricardo were unlikely friends. Malthus was the son of a rural English lawyer trained for the clergy and unlucky with his investments. Ricardo was the son of Jewish merchants who converted to Christianity after falling in love with a Quaker woman and made a fortune trading stocks. Even though both were obsessed with political economy, their styles and conclusions differed wildly. Ruthlessly systematic and seeking to reduce political economy to its barest bones, Ricardo's analysis highlighted the unfair advantages held by landowners. Sprawling in mind and struggling to develop a coherent system, Malthus's arguments about population and limits have been debated for centuries. In long letters, they vigorously attacked each other's ideas while expressing great esteem for one another.[26]

One of the few points Ricardo and Malthus agreed on was that the world at the turn of the nineteenth century was a more dismal place than Smith had depicted in 1776. A series of bad harvests in the late eighteenth century and the horrors of the French Revolution made it harder to believe that a good social order would result from people following their selfish motives. Perhaps that explains why Malthus could not share his father's excitement about utopian ideas. The bread riots of the day pointed to the dangers of having more mouths to feed. With population able to outstrip food supply, limits seemed a lived experience, not a theoretical possibility.

For Malthus, these dynamics meant that the plight of the poor was inevitable and insoluble. Well-intended policies to aid the poor would only create worse problems in the future by allowing more children to be born. Though Malthus later modified some of his positions, the popularity of his original ideas among conservative British elites led to the withholding of aid during famines in India, causing millions of unnecessary deaths.[27] It is little wonder that those reading Malthus dubbed economics the dismal science.[28]

Ricardo had a different perspective on where poverty came from, but also saw unchecked growth as an impossibility. Whereas Malthus largely blamed the poor and their propensity to procreate, Ricardo turned his attention to the wealthy. Primarily concerned with the distribution of wealth between the three major classes of society—rent for landowners, profits for capitalists, and wages for workers—Ricardo argued in his widely read 1817 textbook on political economy that landowners occupied a privileged place in the system and were poised to absorb an increasing share of wealth over time.[29]

By rent, Ricardo did not mean the idea of regular payments for land or housing in the way that one might pay a monthly fee to live in an apartment today. Instead, rent represented the benefits of owning land that was better for growing crops than other land; it was "that portion of the produce of the earth which is paid to the landlord for the use of the original and indestructible powers of the soil."[30] As someone who owned a large farm and studied its operations carefully, Ricardo knew that not all agricultural land was equal.[31] Some land was flat, easy to till, and possessed rich soils while other lands were hilly, stony, or dry—or had thin soil. The same amount of capital and labor invested in the best land would produce a much greater return than the same inputs applied to other lands. This difference represented rent, and it was a gift of nature, not the product of human effort.

Looking to the future, Ricardo argued that rent would absorb an increasing share of the pie until growth was no longer possible. Like Malthus, Ricardo concurred that wages would be set at subsistence levels. Both took a dim view of workers, assuming that whenever wages rose, they would inevitably have more children; these offspring, in turn, would flood the labor market and drive wages back down to subsistence levels. So the real question of wages centered on the cost of living. Capitalists would have to pay workers enough to cover their daily needs, the largest and most variable of which was food. Ricardo thus assumed wages would be low when food was cheap and high when it was expensive. The cost of daily bread, therefore, not only determined wages, it had a major effect on the profits of capitalists as well. When capitalists had to increase wages to allow workers to buy food, it lowered profits.[32]

David Ricardo carefully analyzed production at Gatcomb Park, his estate farm, as part of his studies that recognized soil quality and diminishing returns from the natural world meant infinite growth was not possible.

The limits of the natural world put capitalists and landowners on a collision course, but it was a battle that landowners would inevitably win. The amount of land available was finite and it was subject to the law of diminishing returns. "The laws of nature," Ricardo wrote, "have limited the productive powers of the land."[33] You could coax more out of the land with more capital or labor, but "by doubling the original capital employed on [land], the produce will not be doubled."[34] Once you factored in a growing population, it was clear that the cost of food would increase over time. To feed more mouths, farmers would be forced to till less desirable soils and add more capital and labor to their fields. But due to diminishing returns, the cost of food would still increase. Capitalists, in turn, would need to increase the wages they paid to workers, and that money would come out of their profits. Workers would take those wages and pay them to the landowners in exchange for food, thereby transferring the profits of the manufacturing sector to landowners. "The only real gainers would be the landlords," Ricardo summarized.[35]

These dynamics also meant that the whole system could not grow forever. The pressures on the land and the hungry mouths of workers meant that "The natural tendency of profits then is to fall; for, in the progress of society and wealth, the additional quantity of food required is obtained by the sacrifice of more and more labor."[36] Even the gains of the landlord could not extend forever. Eventually, Ricardo concluded, "there must be an end to accumulation" once "population will have reached its highest point."[37] And well before this stationary state was reached, "the very low rate of profits will have arrested all accumulation."[38] Growth was subject to the limits of the natural world.

Smith, Malthus, and Ricardo all agreed that the stationary state was inevitable and that it was unfortunate. John Stuart Mill was the most noted political economist to challenge this pessimism, arguing that stagnation could be a good thing. A famous utilitarian philosopher and economic thinker publishing in the middle of the nineteenth century, he agreed about the inevitability of the stationary state, but believed the end of growth might usher in a better future.

Like the others, Mill viewed the stationary state as a necessary result of the limits of the earth. "Land differs from all other elements of production . . . in not being susceptible of indefinite increase," he wrote in *Principles of Political Economy*, his influential 1848 text.[39] Finite in supply, the land was also subject to diminishing returns, such that "doubling the labor does not double the produce."[40] The importance of this observation could not be overstated. "This general law of agricultural industry," he emphasized, "is the most important proposition in political economy."[41] It established that "the increase of wealth is not boundless," and the arrival of the stationary state should be expected.[42]

Yet Mill argued that the stationary state "would be, on the whole, a very considerable improvement on the present condition."[43] Once a country neared the end of growth, he believed it would have acquired sufficient wealth that a good life could be made possible for many, if not all, with a reduction of unpleasant labor and increased leisure time "to cultivate the graces of life."[44] In fact, once humans were freed from the divisive competition and drudgery of struggling to get by, they could live much fuller lives, with a greater role for education, art, and community. "A stationary condition of capital and population," Mill optimistically asserted, "implies no stationary state of human improvement."[45]

Though they disagreed about whether the stationary state was dismal, melancholy, or an opportunity for richer lives, these leading lights of classical political economy agreed that it was inevitable. The limits of the natural world meant an eventual end to growth.

This does not mean that Smith, Ricardo, Malthus, or Mill should be viewed as environmentalists. They all believed that it was appropriate and desirable to use nature's gifts for human profit. Just because nature was limited did not mean it should not be exploited. They were more interested in achieving material expansion, whether by the invisible hand of the market, the division of labor, or comparative advantage in trade. The arrival of the stationary state was inevitable, but it was largely seen as a distant proposition.[46]

Still, their works hold an important truth. The idea that economic growth has no natural limits is not a timeless feature of economic thinking. The practice of studying the possibilities of expansion without including the natural world is a recent development.

The Paradoxes of William Stanley Jevons

William Stanley Jevons was a man of paradoxes. There is even one named after him. The Jevons paradox states that increasing the efficiency with which a resource is used does not actually decrease demand. Instead, increased efficiency encourages people to use more of it, which he realized when studying James Watt's improvements to Thomas Newcomen's original steam engines. The amount of coal steam engines required dipped significantly thanks to Watt's innovations, but there was a rebound effect. Now that steam engines were more efficient, it became practical to use them in more places, thereby leading to an even larger use of coal. "It is a confusion of ideas to suppose that the economical use of fuel is equivalent to diminished consumption," he wrote, concluding that "the very contrary is the truth."[47]

Jevons penned these words in his 1865 book *The Coal Question*. It was a time when British industrial power was at its height worldwide, but Jevons did not feel as exultant as many of his peers. The problem was rooted in nature's limits. Jevons knew that coal was the foundation of British industrial power, writing that "coal in truth stands not beside, but entirely above, all other commodities" and reminding his readers that "coal is almost the sole necessary basis of our material power." But coal was not infinite. Though some analysts predicted British coal reserves could last several hundred years, Jevons thought the decline would come much sooner. He argued that exponential increases in demand would drain reserves faster, and rising extraction rates would make it uneconomical to access many coal deposits. This left a difficult dilemma. Britons must make "the momentous choice between brief but true greatness and longer continued mediocrity," he grimly concluded.[48]

The Jevons paradox continues to be an important concept in the study of energy efficiency. Yet there is a second paradox associated with Jevons. In the history of economics, Jevons is much more famous for his pioneering of neoclassical economics than his views on coal. At the same time he was working on *The Coal Question*, he was also developing new ideas about how goods should be valued. Rejecting the prevailing labor theory of value, he developed a system that emphasized consumer willingness to pay rather than the effort a worker put into a good or service. His insights, echoed by a few contemporaries, gave birth to neoclassical economics, which has become the dominant form of economic thinking in the Anglo-American tradition.[49]

Coming to terms with the rise of neoclassical economics is essential for understanding the invention of infinite growth. Over the course of the twentieth century, neoclassical economics became not just *a* way to do economics, but *the* way. And neoclassical scholars did much to exclude the natural world from economic analysis and extol growth. But if we pay attention to Jevons's arguments in *The Coal Question*, they raise a crucial question: How can a man who believed limited natural resources would limit growth also have developed a methodological approach that would reject the pessimism of his coal investigations?[50]

Answering this paradox requires revisiting the development of neoclassical economics. The thumbnail sketch goes like this: by the mid-nineteenth century, some core problems in classical political economy, in particular the labor theory of value, suggested the need for new approaches. Ricardo's labor theory of value held that the worth of a good was linked to the amount of labor that went into it. But was this really true? After all, the value of a painting by a skilled artist was worth more than that of a less skilled one, even if the two had received similar training and spent the same amount of time on their canvases. In the 1870s, three thinkers independently developed a similar breakthrough to this quandary. William Stanley Jevons, Carl Menger, and Leon Walras worked in different countries and intellectual traditions, but each still came to the idea that value was determined not by the amount of labor that went into a good, but by how much consumers were willing to pay for it. They also observed that consumers valued the first item of a good more than the second, third, or fourth, and would be willing to pay less for each additional increment. The point at which the cost of a good exceeded the amount the consumer was willing to pay could be considered the margin, and this determined the price of a good. This insight was the root of the famous chart of supply and demand curves that students today learn in their first economics classes. In 1890, the

British economist Alfred Marshall synthesized these ideas into what became the most widely adopted and influential textbook of the next several decades, *The Principles of Economics*. Neoclassical economics had been born, setting a new trajectory for the field.

To its defenders, the neoclassical approach had much to offer. The calculation of individual utility maximization and demand curves lent itself to a mathematical approach that appeared objective, just like the natural sciences which were widely hailed as the leading edge of knowledge. It also offered an effective repudiation of socialist thinking. In the hands of Ricardian socialists and Karl Marx, the labor theory of value was used to demonstrate that capitalists unfairly appropriated the output of workers. Marginal analysis, on the other hand, seemed to show that in a world of perfect markets, workers and capitalists received their fair shares. Even those who were not necessarily critical of socialism could be drawn to this approach, because it offered a seemingly neutral way to study explosive matters at a time where academics could often be fired if their views offended wealthy benefactors of the university.[51]

At first a technique for understanding the value of goods, neoclassical economics ultimately wrought a profound change in economic thought. By assuming that rational actors maximized their utility in open markets with full information, it emphasized different questions than the classical political economists asked or those who would follow in the historical and institutional schools. In classical political economy, the central questions focused on the distribution of wealth and resources between the three major social groups: capitalists, landowners, and workers. Investigating such questions often brought up discussions of justice and fairness. Neoclassical economics shifted the gaze from conflicts between social groups to the maximization of individual preferences and the efficiencies of market transactions. Here, questions of efficiency and optimization analyzed by the all-knowing and ever-rational *homo economicus* loomed larger than ones of ethics.

Neoclassical economics would also come to diminish the role of the natural world in economic analysis. So much of the natural world and its importance to humans cannot be captured in market transactions of what consumers are willing to pay. And while classical political economists studied three factors of production—capital, labor, and land—neoclassical thinkers in the twentieth century dropped land as an independent category of analysis, choosing to treat it as a subcategory of capital.[52]

But this did not happen in Jevons's day. The dominance of neoclassical economics would take nearly a century to complete. In the decades surrounding the turn of the twentieth century, this new technique for understanding how goods should be valued was considered one approach to certain economic questions, but not the only strategy. Neoclassical strategies might inform one topic while being considered irrelevant to others; they were a powerful new tool for economists, but many believed a proper tool kit included other approaches as well.

Jevons's concern for coal captures this perfectly. When he studied the valuation of goods, he used neoclassical tools. When he analyzed the future of growth, he saw a British economy dependent on a nonrenewable resource that would eventually run out. There was no contradiction in this during a transitional stage of economic thinking in the late nineteenth century. The tradition of political economy running from Smith to Mill was being challenged, and it would eventually be replaced by neoclassical approaches. But this was a slow and uneven process, and no single approach would hold sway until well into the twentieth century. And even among early advocates of neoclassical techniques, Jevons demonstrates this new system did not mean they would inevitably consider infinite growth to be feasible.

The Struggle for the Soul of Economics

In 1884, Richard Ely decided it was time to ruffle some feathers. Less than thirty years old, he was not an imposing man, with a slight build, boyish face, squeaky voice, and tendency to ramble at the lectern.[53]

But as a young professor at Johns Hopkins University in Baltimore, he had the certainty of a missionary, a passion for hard work, and little doubt about the virtues of his cause. Political economy, he was convinced, had become dominated by sympathizers of the powerful and too inattentive to the needs of the people. Its methods had become too abstract and its conclusions too satisfying for the wealthy with its promises that "pursuing their own egotistic designs" would "truly benefit others" and its false comforts that "no sacrifice" was needed to help the poor.[54] Something had to change. Collaborating with a group of fellow young and reform-minded thinkers, Ely called for a "new school" of thinking that would be embodied in the creation of the American Economic Association (AEA) in 1885.[55]

The late nineteenth century marked a pivot in the history of economics, a time when the moniker "political economy" fell out of fashion in favor of "economics." It was also the time when new methodologies flourished, including neoclassical economics, historicism, institutionalism, and evolutionary economics. The decades around the turn of the twentieth involved a "struggle over the soul of economics" with men like Ely fighting fiercely over what questions the discipline should ask and what methods it should use. These debates would have important implications for how economists would treat the natural world and analyze growth, though what is crucial is that no consensus within the field existed during the decades surrounding the turn of the twentieth century.[56]

Ely's effort to create a professional society with the name "economics" instead of "political economy" represented more than just a change in nomenclature. The late nineteenth century witnessed sweeping changes in how and where academics worked, characterized by increasing disciplinary specialization, an expanded university system, and the rising influence of American institutions of higher learning. Political economy revealed by its name an interest in interdisciplinary thought, whereby economic matters were connected with politics and philosophy. Both Smith and Mill made major contributions to philosophy as well as economics, which were not considered distinct fields. But in the late nineteenth century, academics from nearly all fields began to carve out more specific domains of study, with topics such as history, political science, anthropology, and economics all seeking to distinguish themselves from one another.[57]

These changes went hand in hand with the expansion of the American university system. Largely seen by European scholars as an intellectual backwater through the mid-nineteenth century, particularly in economics, the US's expanding university system now provided new homes and professional opportunities. In 1880, there were only three chairs in political economy in America and no major American academic journals devoted exclusively to economics; most Americans traveled to Europe for advanced training. In 1900, however, the nation had more than fifty university chairs in economics and several specialized journals.[58] But American universities often had little protection for academic freedom, which helped spur the rise of professional societies to establish standards for their disciplines: the AEA was just one of more than two hundred professional societies formed in America during the 1870s and 1880s.[59]

These changes shifted who could become an economist and where they were likely to work. It had been common for economic thinkers in the nineteenth century to be self trained, work outside universities, and publish on multiple subjects. By the turn of the twentieth century, most prominent economists received a doctorate, were based in universities and published many of their findings in journals read mainly by their peers. And as the twentieth century progressed, American economics began to be taken seriously in Europe.

But what should economists study and how? Ely's proposal and the corresponding backlash from his critics showed this could be a bitterly contested point. Ely argued that political economy's search for abstract laws and principles left it unable to grapple with the enormous changes seen over the previous century. Smith and Ricardo wrote at a time of relatively small factories and the beginning glimmers of industrial progress. Such a world bore little resemblance to the giant factories and industrialized cities of the late nineteenth century. What did a small group of pinmakers dividing their steps have to say about massive enterprises powered by steam engines, controlled by industrial titans, and operated by the working poor? How could one expect to derive timeless laws in a world of such rapid change?

For Ely, economics needed to begin with history. This reflected his graduate training in the late 1870s in Germany, where he became an adherent of the historical school. Founded by Wilhelm Roscher, Bruno Hildebrand, and Karl Knies, the German historicist tradition emphasized social context over abstract laws. Historicists did not believe that universal laws of economic behavior could be separated from political, historical, and cultural contexts. People did not act in a vacuum. They bought goods that reflected the fashions of the day, they invested in enterprises that took advantage of the specific natural resources available locally, they spent or saved or gave to charity in ways shaped by their religious beliefs, and they paid wages or went on strike according to social expectations of just compensation. German historicists were particularly skeptical of finding constancy in the rapidly industrializing and urbanizing world of the nineteenth century. Instead of abstract theory, economists needed to engage in rigorous empirical study about the interactions between people's social contexts, their choices, and how these changed over time. Economic ideas also had to be specific to time and place. Two societies with different histories and cultures would generate different findings, and what was true of a society at one time might not be true a generation before or after. Economics had to include history, politics, and culture.[60]

Many American economists, such as Simon Newcomb and William Graham Sumner, disagreed, arguing just as forcefully that the natural sciences offered the correct guide, not history. Physics, in particular, represented the ideal for economics because its search for universal laws had generated enormous advances throughout the nineteenth century. Moreover, it offered formulas that would allow economics to become a mathematical discipline, and those formulas aligned closely with new developments in neoclassical analysis. If economics were to advance systematically, it needed quantitative and abstract theory; it needed to be neoclassical.[61]

But could the tidy models of neoclassical thought capture the complex economic world of the burgeoning industrial American economy of the late nineteenth century? Some argued forcefully that the formulas of neoclassical economics relied on unrealistic simplifications that were intellectually lazy and showed too little correspondence to the real world. How could one talk about rational actors optimizing their utility when industrial titans bribed judges and cajoled the state into using force to break up labor protests? Cycles

Many American economists in the late nineteenth and early twentieth centuries believed questions of monopoly power, inequality, and corruption were more relevant to understanding the Gilded Age economy than the efficiency of markets. The political cartoon "The Bosses of the Senate," by Joseph Keppler in 1889 illustrates the economic problems that many in the historical and institutional schools considered essential to tackle. Library of Congress, Prints and Photographs Division, LC-USZC4-494.

of boom and bust characterized by ruinous rate wars and monopoly control surely could not be understood by assuming free markets. These critics suggested that abstract models had too little to say about the crucial issues of the day: monopoly power, worker exploitation, and class struggle.[62]

Consider Thorstein Veblen. While Ely looked to history, Veblen favored anthropology and evolutionary science. Born in 1857, Veblen was the most original economist of his era. A notorious outsider, Veblen was openly agnostic at a time most universities insisted that professors advocate Christian values, open to socialism, a terrible husband, an inveterate womanizer, a disinterested teacher, and a difficult colleague. But his brilliant insights put him at the heart of American economics.[63] For Veblen, the neoclassical world of rational individuals maximizing their utility made little sense. At the same time, he considered the historical school to be theoretically lacking. One of his most famous ideas was "conspicuous consumption," which he popularized in his landmark work, *The Theory of the Leisure Class*, published in 1899. Social norms and values channeled pecuniary activities in ways that had little to do with rationality. The leisure class for Veblen was not full of capitalist investors creating a world of plenty for all; instead, it was a parasitic group that extracted wealth from the laboring masses. Rather than spending money on objects with a direct relationship to their well-being, they poured resources into symbolic acts or objects that had the primary purpose of ostentatiously displaying their social status. The lower classes then bought into this game, scrambling to adopt the manners and customs of their social superiors. Economic wants, needs, and practices were rooted in cultural evolution and social norms, not objective or timeless calculations of rational utility.[64]

The Theory of the Leisure Class made waves across the academy and is a title still familiar to many. Its subtitle—"An Economic Study in the Evolution of Institutions"—is less well known. Yet it is consequential because it helped inspire the rise of the institutional school of economics. Walton Hamilton officially launched this school in

1918, arguing that "institutional economics" offered "the only way to the right sort of theory" because it uniquely addressed "the customs and conventions . . . which determine the nature of our economic system."[65] He critiqued neoclassical approaches for "a failure to recognize the complexity of the relations which bind human welfare to industry."[66] He argued that they could not explain "why some of us are better off than others." To answer such fundamental questions, economic theory needed to prioritize "the conventions of competition, of property, of inheritance, of the distribution of opportunity which make incomes what they are."[67] Many agreed. Over the next several decades, several of the nation's leading economists rallied to the institutional school.[68]

The institutional school drew inspiration from both Veblen and the historical economists, though major figures such as Hamilton, Wesley Mitchell, and John Commons also sought to differentiate themselves from both. None would deny Veblen's brilliance, but there was a lurking concern that his savage criticisms were not systematic and that his obsession with evolutionary stages of society lacked empirical data.[69] Similarly, while the attention to history by economists such as Ely was commendable, they found it too descriptive and too political. Institutionalists wanted to be clear that they were taking a scientific approach to economic theory. Men such as Wesley Mitchell and John Commons used institutional approaches to show that topics such as business cycles and the labor movement could be understood only through a systematic analysis of the social, legal, and political factors that shaped market activities and the ability of workers to organize and achieve fair wages.[70]

These tensions in the methodology of economics have never been fully resolved. What matters here is that these questions remained vibrantly debated through the first decades of the twentieth century. In the marketplace of ideas, thinkers from all methodological backgrounds achieved significant recognition, including being elected president of the AEA, holding top university positions, and publishing in the most prestigious journals. Political economy had become economics, but what economics was to be in practice remained up in the air.

The Paper No One Read

In 1931, Harold Hotelling published the most important article in natural resource economics. There was just one problem: no one knew it.

Economists today celebrate "The Economics of Exhaustible Resources" as a foundational text. The paper laid out many of the issues that came to define natural resource economics in the 1970s, including what is now known as the Hotelling rule—a method of calculating the most efficient rate of extraction for a nonrenewable resource. Hotelling adopted the perspective of a mine owner seeking to maximize profits. The fundamental question was how fast to deplete the stock. Mining aggressively in the present meant more money could be obtained now and invested in capital that would grow over time. But producing too much right away might lower prices, and saving more for later might allow the mine owner to profit more if prices went up. Using the calculus of variations—a branch of mathematics that exceeded the training of the vast majority of economists at the time—Hotelling offered a formula that provided advice to the mine owner based on market prices and the rate of interest.[71]

Neoclassical in approach, Hotelling's rule emphasized optimizing the use of natural resources while expressing little concern for depletion: it was often better to use coal or oil now to generate wealth than to save it for the future. Unlike Jevons, who feared the decline of coal would lead Britain to a state of mediocrity, Hotelling was much more optimistic. He granted the possibility that, at "a distant time, . . . all the resources of the earth will be near exhaustion, and the human race reduced to complete poverty" but downplayed this concern by asserting that "the exhaustion of one or a few types of resources will not bring about this condition."[72] This insight has stuck. Seventy-five years after its publication, one prominent economist argued, "Rarely has a single paper had as much influence on the development of a whole field of economic research as this one has had."[73]

Such an assessment would have been surprising to any economist working in the 1930s. Or the 1940s, 1950s, or 1960s. In fact, when Hotelling suffered a debilitating stroke in 1972, he had no idea that this paper would become an important part of his intellectual legacy. This is not to say he lived in obscurity. A brilliant thinker known for his dry humor and "indefatigable" capacity for work, he had three other eponymous findings: Hotelling's T-squared distribution (a breakthrough in multivariate statistics), Hotelling's Law (an economic principle that suggests competitors had incentives to produce similar goods), and Hotelling's Lemma (a microeconomic contribution to firm theory).[74] He taught Milton Friedman, advised Kenneth Arrow's dissertation, and was honored with not one, but two, festschrifts of his life's work in statistics and economics. Yet neither volume mentioned his 1931 paper, discussed his "rule," or lauded his contributions to natural resource economics.[75]

What does it mean that economists today consider Hotelling foundational when his peers found his article irrelevant? It points to a fundamental tension in how the past is interpreted. Those who look back from today's broad acceptance of neoclassical economics can easily trace a direct line from Hotelling's approach to contemporary practices, while ignoring the plethora of other perspectives on the natural world from his time. But this is a mistake. The fact is that, through the first several decades of the twentieth century, many economists took an interest in the natural world and thought it deserved a prominent role in the field's inquiries. During his lifetime, Hotelling's rule is better understood as an exception.

Economic interest in the natural world at the turn of the twentieth century reflected the rise of the conservation movement. Any intelligent observer of America's rapid growth during the nineteenth century could tell that the nation's vast natural resources had produced great wealth for some. It was also easy to see that large

Yosemite Falls, 1861. Images of the grandeur of places like Yosemite began circulating in the second half of the nineteenth century, helping inspire the conservation movement, which encouraged many thinkers, including economists, to pay greater attention to the natural world.

amounts of waste and pollution accompanied these efforts, with denuded landscapes from clear-cutting, rich soils swept into rivers through poor farm management, and prodigious quantities of fossil fuels used inefficiently. The problems were so notable that in 1907, President Theodore Roosevelt declared "the conservation of our natural resources and their proper use constitute the fundamental problem which underlies almost every other problem of our national life."[76] He subsequently brought leading politicians, business executives, and scientists together and charged them to address the fact that "the natural resources of our country are in danger of exhaustion if we permit the old wasteful methods of exploiting them longer to continue."[77] Working with his close adviser Gifford Pinchot, a

forester and advocate of wise use conservation, Roosevelt's conference highlighted a surging interest in questions of preserving natural resources.[78]

Many economists took up this challenge. Lewis Cecil Gray, born
in 1881 and trained as an agricultural historian, is a good example.
Trained in the historicist tradition but known to employ neoclassical tools, he is almost as important as Hotelling in the history of resource economics.[79] Both techniques were on display in two major
articles: "The Economic Possibilities of Conservation" (1913) and
"Rent Under the Assumption of Exhaustibility" (1914).[80] Today's
economists remember Gray mostly for the latter, which like Hotelling's paper, took the perspective of a mine owner trying to decide
how much to produce and how much to leave for the future. He argued that the mine owner's choices are most shaped by "the rate of
interest, the law of diminishing productivity, and the value of the natural resources under the individual's control."[81] Gray's mathematics
were simplistic compared to Hotelling's calculus of variations, but
the general line of thought was similar.

Yet remembering Gray only for his neoclassical views presents
a distorted view of his thoughts on the natural world. Drawing on
his historicist training, Gray's 1913 article argued that wants were
shaped by the particularities of a culture, and that in many cases,
those wants could be socially undesirable. The frivolous spending
of money on luxury goods for public display ridiculed by Thorstein
Veblen revealed that individual utility should not be the polestar
of sound social policy. And Gray thought the same was true of resources. "A vast amount of consumption is neither based on welfare, nor on enjoyment; it is solely dictated by convention," he wrote,
echoing Veblen. Citing the waste of coal burned for electric advertising, he approvingly cited a colleague who claimed it was a "chemical
orgy of waste, a crime of competitive advertising for which some day
thousands of individuals must shiver for months."[82] Though he acknowledged it would be "exceedingly difficult," he insisted that such
attitudes should be changed, that human wants "be diverted from

objects which require very scarce resources."[83] Conservation "constitutes a type of ethical requirement which is upon a higher level than
any that has heretofore existed," sounding much more like Theodore
Roosevelt than Harold Hotelling.[84] Since discounting the future led
to much higher levels of waste, he urged that policies ensure "the interest rate must be rendered as low as possible."[85]

Gray came to the topic of resources through the study of agriculture. Today, agricultural economics is a relatively minor part of
the field, but in his time, it was one of the largest and most vibrant
fields of study within economics.[86] Its prominence drew from both
a strong sense of social importance and a unique set of data. In the
1920s, alarm bells were ringing across America about the farm problem. Spurred by high food prices in the 1910s during the First World
War, farmers had rushed to bring new lands into production. But
many of these lands had low-quality soils, and in their haste to pay
off debts, farmers worked them too hard. The result was a vicious
circle: more food meant lower prices, requiring more production,
which led to further soil erosion and less profitable agriculture.[87]
Economists responded by creating a series of new organizations, including the National Association of Agricultural Economists in 1915
and the Bureau of Agricultural Economics in 1921. Combined with
sixty years of research by the United States Department of Agriculture, agricultural economists suddenly found themselves swimming
in data. Flush with facts and figures about seed prices, crop yields,
transport costs, land values, debt ratios, harvesting techniques, fertilizer applications, and more, agricultural economists became pioneers in econometrics—the application of statistical methods to
economic data.[88]

Agricultural economics in the 1920s and 1930s, then, encom-
passed an intellectually exciting frontier of economic thought applied to a problem of major concern. This was true within neoclassical thought, as some economists essentially treated each farm as
a "firm" and sought to maximize productivity through optimizing
crop selection, fertilizer application, and other inputs and outputs.

But equally, agricultural economists worked in the institutional tradition to tackle problems such as the predatory power of railroads and grain elevator operators. In nearly all cases, cross-disciplinary insights from agronomists and rural sociologists informed economic analysis. And as was common at the time, both qualitative and quantitative analysis, as well as neoclassical and institutionalist approaches, existed side by side.[89]

Coal was also in turmoil in the early twentieth century. The coal industry faced labor strikes and low prices, then shortages and high prices during World War I, followed by gluts and more labor struggles in the 1920s. Walton Hamilton, the pioneer of the institutional school of economics, thought it provided a perfect exemplar of the necessity to move beyond neoclassical approaches. Collaborating with Helen R. Wright—a pioneering economist and social researcher who would later become a dean at the University of Chicago—they coauthored two works: *The Case of Bituminous Coal* (1925) and *A Way of Order for Bituminous Coal* (1928). The coal trade, they said, showed practically no signs of the ideal order posited by neoclassical assumptions. Prices vacillated wildly as companies engaged in rate wars that left many in bankruptcy, scarcity and glut regularly harmed consumers and producers, miners suffered abhorrent accident rates, strikes were common, and investors faced enormous uncertainty. The gap between what "the community expects from an orderly industry" and "the actual performance of the world of bituminous coal" was vast.[90]

The problems ran deep, and they required the broad perspectives of institutional thinking to grasp. The coal industry's chaos emerged from a complex and historically situated pattern of high overhead costs, insider trading, friendly bankruptcy laws, little labor regulation, and more. These institutional factors meant that even if "people in the industry are doing the best they can," their collective actions would lead to "evil" rather than "good."[91] There was no beneficent invisible hand operating in the coal market. In 1928, the two authors suggested the remedy, an elaborate merging of all coal companies into a single conglomerate that would be controlled by workers and consumers. No such proposal was ever implemented, though Hamilton touted many of these ideas as a participant in several New Deal programs.[92]

Many studying the oil industry found similarly deplorable conditions. John Ise, a native Kansan who got his PhD at Harvard University, minced few words in describing the waste of America's oil industry. Much of this could be seen in Kansas, which was producing about a tenth of the nation's oil in the 1920s. Yet Ise was not impressed. Writing in 1925, he bluntly concluded that "it must be admitted that the history of the United States oil policy . . . is a strong indictment of the policy of private ownership" that "will some day be regarded as one of the worst sins of all history." Citing "feverish and wasteful exploitation" characterized by "immeasurable stupidity," Ise savaged the "insane zeal of fortune hunters" and the lack of wisdom of private owners. "In the oil industry," he concluded like Hamilton and Wright had for coal, "the theory of laissez-faire . . . fails completely."[93] Some form of government ownership and regulation must be implemented to ensure that valuable resources were preserved.

George Stocking was more measured in his language but came to similar conclusions. A native of Texas who had spent a year working in the oil industry before getting his PhD at Columbia University under Thorstein Veblen and Wesley Mitchell, he had also seen firsthand the tremendous waste associated with oil development. In 1925, Stocking deplored the "haphazard methods of competitive, private exploitation." Laying out in detail the problems associated with oil's movements beneath the ground, the dynamics of pressure within oilfields, competing property claims, and poorly aligned incentives, he too concluded the invisible hand was no benevolent force: "Competition in the petroleum industry works at cross-purposes with the economical exploitation and utilization of petroleum." Well regarded by his colleagues, he founded the department of economics at Vanderbilt University in 1947 and was elected president of the AEA in 1958.[94]

Collectively, these thinkers reveal that economic thought about the natural world in the early decades of the twentieth century went far beyond Hotelling's neoclassical advice to the profit-seeking mine owner. Economists tackled topics including waste, exploitation, and labor justice. They challenged the assumptions of efficient markets and the virtues of laissez-faire. And many certainly did not forget that the success of the economy was linked to the availability of the resources that powered the nation's factories.

*

The history of economic thought reveals that economists have not always imagined infinite growth and downplayed the natural world. The opposite is, in fact, the case. Leading scholars of political economy argued the finite supply of land and law of diminishing returns would lead to a stationary state. Even as economics came to replace political economy in the late nineteenth century and neoclassical economics was pioneered, economists still retained a vibrant interest in the natural world.

In the long-run perspective of the history of economic thought, the idea of growth without limit is a remarkably new proposition. Excluding the natural world was a break from the past. And if ideas have changed in the past, they can do so again in the present. The call for economists to more carefully consider the links between economic activities and environmental sustainability is not a call for the field to something it has never done before; rather, it is a call to return to ideas that have been forgotten.

2 ∗ The Discovery of Growth

It should have been an easy task, but Moses Abramovitz was flummoxed. He had agreed to write a "state-of-the-field" article on economic growth. For academics, this is a straightforward task: find what's out there, read it, summarize it, and offer a few conclusions about where the field might be headed. The trouble, Abramovitz discovered, was that there was almost nothing out there to review. Economists had simply ignored the topic. He opened his 1952 essay with a surprising claim: "The problem of economic growth lacks any organized and generally known body of doctrine. . . . In spite of a continuing interest which began very early, the question has remained on the periphery of economics."[1] How could he summarize the state of a field that didn't exist?

Perhaps he should have just declined the assignment. But Abramovitz had been interested in growth for a while. Like many academics, he had served in government intelligence during World War II, and he had come to believe that the war had been won by American industrial capacity more than anything else. Abramovitz wanted to know more. Why was it that the United States had come to have such an advantage, and what explained the different trajectories of the other major nations? And why had so little been published on economic growth?[2]

The simple fact is that economic growth was a new and protean concept in 1950. On the face of it, this is quite surprising. The previous century, after all, had witnessed unprecedented economic expansion. Consider the changes. With railroads a novelty, a person in 1850 rarely traveled faster than a horse; by 1950, the transcontinental railroad system had been supplemented by widespread automobile ownership and commercial aviation. Most people lit their homes with open fires, candles, or whale oil in 1850 and cleaned their homes, dishes, and clothes with the sweat of their brows. A century later, electricity powered lights and a whole suite of domestic appliances. Whereas newspapers and word of mouth were the primary sources of news in 1850, radios, telephones, and televisions transmitted information across the globe. Cities that had once contained tens or hundreds of thousands of residents now numbered in the millions, and most industrialized nations had much larger urban populations than rural ones. Someone like George Washington would have been surprised at many of the technological developments that occurred in the half century after his death in 1799, but he still would have been able to negotiate American society in the 1850s. Resurrected in 1950, the civilization would no doubt have appeared utterly alien.[3]

Yet these profound transformations had not been understood or analyzed with the nomenclature of growth. Concepts like prosperity, abundance, and material progress were much more commonly employed. Within economics, rather than explaining how and why the pie was getting bigger, much more ink was spilled on questions such as why some had bigger pieces of the pie, why the pie contracted or expanded in regular business cycles, and how the pie could stagnate if consumer demand disappeared. And it wasn't just economists who seemed to lack the language of growth. One historian of growth concluded, "There is in fact hardly a trace of interest in economic growth as a policy objective in the official or professional literature of Western countries before 1950."[4]

Things would change, though, and quickly. By 1960, growth was so ascendant in economic and policy circles that Vice President Richard Nixon could admonish his critics for engaging in what he derisively termed "growthmanship," and growth theory had become one of the hottest fields of research within economics.[5] A more meteoric rise of an intellectual framework and policy goal would be hard to imagine. This profound shift began in the depths of the Great Depression and exploded onto the scene in the aftermath of World War II.[6]

A Curious Omission

Today, when economic growth is a central preoccupation of politics, it is startling to realize that it was not so for earlier generations. This is particularly surprising because not only had the period from the mid-nineteenth to the mid-twentieth century witnessed historically unprecedented levels of economic growth, but classical political economists had analyzed the possibilities and limits of economic expansion and discussed the stationary state.[7] The topic had, however, largely disappeared with the transition from political economy to economics in the late nineteenth century. When publishing *The Theory of Economic Growth* in 1955, economist W. Arthur Lewis argued that "no comprehensive treatment of the subject has been published for about a century," referencing Mill's *Principles of Political Economy* in 1848 as the last systematic investigation of the topic.[8] In the early 1950s, the idea of growth remained fuzzy in the economic imagination.[9]

Why? Perhaps it was too hard, as Lewis claimed. After Mill, he suggested, economists "were too sensible to try to cover such an enormous field."[10] But the profession has never lacked practitioners with the confidence to take on big topics. Instead, the problem may have seemed too easy. Economists may have thought growth simple to explain, particularly in the American context. The nation had a booming population, lots of land, abundant natural resources, and few laws constraining business enterprises. The more interesting and complex challenges for many economists concerned the character of growth and the distribution of its effects.[11]

The dispiriting effects of the Great Depression likely played a role as well. Much of the expectation of sustained economic expansion came crashing down in the 1930s. Even as World War II came to an end, there was little reason to think that growth would return. Most economic observers feared the conditions of the 1930s would return once government wartime spending declined, especially as there had been a notable recession after World War I. Moreover, the rampant inflation seen in numerous countries after the First World War made

Memories of the Great Depression and fears that stagnation would return after World War II meant many people, including most economists, were surprised by the rapid growth in the postwar economy. National Archives and Records Administration.

the prospect of postwar growth worrisome, as any gains might be off-set by the decreasing value of money. At best, most observers hoped for a postwar economy characterized by stable economic conditions with full employment and minimal inflation.[12]

Reflecting this reality, secular stagnation became an influential economic idea of the 1930s. Alvin Hansen, most famous for intro-ducing Keynesian economics to America and helping establish So-cial Security, led the charge. He feared that the Great Depression had revealed that rapid growth would no longer be possible. A ma-ture industrial economy—much like the stationary state of the clas-sical political economists—would not have much room to expand.[13] These were notable words of caution from the man who "influenced the nation's thinking about economic policy more profoundly than any other economist in this century."[14]

Another answer lies in language. When reflecting on the coun-try's remarkable progress, observers used words like "productivity," "abundance," "industrial development," "expansion," "expanding frontiers," and "material progress." The word "growth" did not have as capacious a meaning, and was most often linked with population or the size of cities.[15] Analyzing the growth of population or met-ropolitan regions could be quantified and used as a proxy for eco-nomic performance, but this was not the same as trying to assess the overall economy. Textbooks introduced students to topics like cap-ital, labor, value, and tariffs, but had no sections on growth, which also was nearly absent from the titles of articles published in major journals.[16] Prominent economists such as Joseph Schumpeter, Wes-ley Mitchell, and Irving Fisher studied topics such as innovation, business cycles, and capital markets. As Abramovitz noted, all these topics held clues, but none of them consistently used the language of growth or captured the broad ways we have become accustomed to thinking about it today; they were "fragmentary" pieces whose "precise significance" had "not been developed."[17]

This may seem an arbitrary semantic distinction, but it isn't. Even if concepts of material progress or development overlapped with growth, they were not identical. In a crucial decade between the late 1940s and the late 1950s, economic growth would come to have a narrower definition and a broader reach: narrower in the sense that it was understood as a technical measure largely calculated through the framework of gross national product (GNP) and broader in the sense that it became an overarching goal of policy. By claiming that they were the experts best positioned to calculate GNP and advise on the conditions necessary to improve it, economists took advantage of this technical definition of economic growth to improve their professional standing and increase their access to power.

Conceptually and linguistically, economic growth did not appear as an explicit category of analysis for economists, politicians, or citizens until the middle of the twentieth century. It was neither natural nor inevitable: it had to be invented.

The Intellectual Infrastructure of Growth Thinking

The French novelist Victor Hugo claimed human thought has no limit. He may be right, but ideas depend on existing knowledge to gain credibility and influence. Anyone can dream of walking on the moon; those who can tap into the latest advances in rocket science have a much better chance of making it a reality. Powerful ideas depend on intellectual infrastructure.

During the 1930s and 1940s, two intertwined developments laid the groundwork for the emergence of economic growth as a concept: the invention of the economy and the creation of GNP. As Timothy Mitchell has argued, before the 1930s, there was no such thing as "the economy" among Anglo-American economists. Up to that point, "economy" largely meant a personal habit of thrift or efficiency, not an abstract entity that could be governed. If you instructed someone to act with economy, they would know to be frugal; if you instructed someone to act on "the economy," it would not be clear what you were talking about.[18]

This is reflected in the vague ways the classical political economists discussed growth. Thinkers such as Smith or Ricardo pointed to general laws or processes by which growth might occur—division of labor or comparative advantage in international trade—but could only point to suggestive examples, such as Smith's pin factory or Ricardo's analysis of cloth and wine in England and Portugal.[19] They had access to some data about a few particular industries but very limited data about the economy as a whole.[20] Tariff receipts provided some insight into balance of trade, and tax records gave analysts some sense of the overall scope of economic activity, but these were suggestive insights, not a comprehensive picture. Even as late as the 1920s, John Maynard Keynes lamented the lack of detailed statistics in Britain, calling them "deplorably deficient."[21] The case was not that much better in America; when Frederick Tryon analyzed the links between energy and output in the 1920s, he sought to infer the size of the economy through categories such as "physical volume of agricultural production," "physical volume of manufactures," and "physical volume of mining."[22]

Such sporadic points of evidence could provide clues to a nation's economic health, and merchants, farmers, and politicians certainly had a sense of whether a period was prosperous or stagnant. They could see when warehouses were full or empty, when ports were bustling or stagnant, and when factories operated through the night or shuttered for weeks. But there was no way to measure the whole economic system to say whether it was growing or not, and at what rate. The economy was not yet an object of inquiry. The topic of growth was qualitative rather than quantitative and amorphous rather than specific.

Inventing the economy as a quantified object of analysis came in a roundabout fashion. The great economic questions of the first decades of the twentieth century concerned distribution rather than growth. This was an era of vigorous and often violent conflict between capitalists and laborers. Each side claimed the other took more than its just share and defended their arguments with data points such as wage levels, corporate profits, or the ratio of worker pay to food staples. But it was not clear that an impartial observer could actually assess whether things were getting better or worse for workers or capitalists and what constituted a fair share for each side.[23]

The desire to gain a clearer picture of such matters led to the creation of the National Bureau of Economic Research (NBER) in 1920. A nonprofit organization funded by several prominent foundations, NBER's goal was to provide policy-relevant knowledge without policy recommendations. The organization made a splash by choosing Wesley Mitchell as its founding director of research. In his mid-forties, Mitchell was widely recognized as one of the nation's leading economists. Academically gifted, he trained under John Dewey and Thorstein Veblen at the University of Chicago, where he was known as Veblen's star student. Oscillating between classes in philosophy and economics, he quickly decided that pure theory could never be satisfactory and was therefore a critic of the exclusive use of neoclassical methodologies. If one started with abstract principles and simple deductions, the result was akin to sophistry: a clever enough person could logically reach any conclusion. To say something of value required blending theory with empirical information. And more than any other economist of his era, Mitchell was committed to establishing a solid empirical basis for his conclusions. Every day, he could be found at his desk with a pipe in his hand, a slide rule at the ready, and a green eye shade on his forehead.[24]

A prolific thinker and advocate of the institutional approach, Mitchell contributed to many branches of economic thought. His most famous contributions came from his lifelong interest in business cycles: those recurrent patterns of ups and downs that seemed to buffet the economy regularly, such as the American financial panics of 1819, 1837, 1857, 1873, and 1893. In 1913, Mitchell published *Business Cycles*, a 600-page treatise comparing economic fluctuations in the United States, Britain, France, and Germany from 1873 to 1908. Befitting Mitchell's empiricism, the pages were filled with tables and charts tracking wholesale prices of consumer goods, relative prices of farm and mine products, unemployment rates, bank deposits, and more. For Mitchell there was never such a thing as too many statistics, a faith he hoped others would share, writing that "men seriously interested in the workings of the money economy will share my regret that the statistical materials are not more complete."[25] The book was a major success, hailed as a "landmark in the development of economics," strengthening Mitchell's reputation as one of the field's leading lights.[26]

At NBER, Mitchell helped guide its first research project: a study of the size and distribution of the nation's income. The goal was to assess "whether the national income is adequate to provide a decent living for all persons, whether this income is increasing as rapidly as the population, and whether its distribution among individuals is growing more or less unequal."[27] Answering such questions was enormously complex. How could one even determine the national income? What should be included and excluded? Clearly, a product sold to an individual would count, but what about a small company that made automobile parts and sold them to Ford? Should the sale of the part and the car both be tabulated, or would that be double counting? What about the labor of a housewife that was unpaid, or the work of a government employee whose salary was paid by taxes? And there was the challenge of gathering data, which was always an exercise in persistence and creativity. Diving into corporate filings, census reports, litigation hearings, trade journals, and more, Mitchell and his colleagues assembled the first comprehensive statistics on the national income.[28]

Income in the United States found that the national income had more than doubled from 1909 to 1918, from about $29 billion to more than $60 billion, though it cautioned that wartime inflation meant that the real gains were much smaller. Americans had much higher per capita incomes than Europeans—about a third higher than Britons and more than double the average in Germany—and while inequality had been growing strongly before World War I, it had been decreasing recently.[29]

Although NBER's report was well received, it did not immediately lead to regular gathering of data on national income. It took another decade, the depths of the Great Depression, and the hard work of Simon Kuznets. And indeed, there was no guarantee that it would happen at all. Kuznets was reticent to take on the job, and without Mitchell prodding him, he might not have done it.

Shy and unassuming, Kuznets was born in Ukraine in 1901 and emigrated to America in 1922. A wiz with numbers, he quickly gained entrance to Columbia and attracted the attention of Mitchell, who became his adviser. Both shared a deep commitment to empirical evidence, both were committed to using data to improve social justice, and both had an enormous capacity for work. Moses Abramovitz summarized the thoughts of many when he described his feelings toward Kuznets as "love mixed with awe."[30]

While battles between capitalists and laborers in the 1910s and 1920s had illustrated the lack of clarity about the nation's income and its distribution, the scale of human deprivation in the early 1930s brought the issue to new light. Everyone was aware of the economic crisis and that millions were suffering, but no one knew with detail how much had been lost. In Congress, Wisconsin Senator Robert La Follette Jr. led an effort to get the Commerce Department to start collecting and publicizing national income statistics. It took more than two years to get a small amount of funding for the effort. His colleagues balked at spending more money at a time of scarcity, and many subscribed to the view that the Depression was just a business cycle that would naturally correct itself. Interfering would only make things worse.[31]

It was not only La Follette Jr.'s colleagues who doubted the merits of the project. Many economists were skeptical as well. The Commerce Department's well-respected director of economic research, J. Frederic Dewhurst, declined, considering it a waste of his time. Even Kuznets had his doubts about its importance. No one really saw how consequential the work would become.[32]

By 1933, Commerce pressured NBER to take on the job, and

Kuznets agreed, bringing in his former student Robert Nathan and a small support staff. Many of the challenging methodological problems remained—what to do with unpaid labor or black market activities? Should government spending be seen as an asset or a cost to society? To what extent could a measure of income capture changes in social welfare? Drawing on NBER's previous work, Kuznets rallied his team to quickly determine how the nation's income had changed over the past four years.

What they found was bleak. National income had been over $81 billion in 1929, but it had shrunk to less than $50 billion by 1932. This 40 percent decline in three years was three times worse than anything that had been seen that century.[33] At the same time, unemployment was rising to unprecedented levels, with over five million out of work in 1930, nine million in 1931, and thirteen million in 1932. Moreover, the distributional questions were even worse. Returns on property, typically owned by the wealthy, had declined by 31 percent, but the wages for workers were down by more than 40 percent. Furthermore, higher-paid managers on salary saw their wages decrease only half as much as hourly workers. As Kuznets concluded, "the Depression seems to have put its greatest burden upon those who, in view of their already low position on the economic scale, could least afford to lose."[34]

In Franklin Roosevelt's administration, Kuznets's work on national income found a receptive audience. By breaking down several industries and classes of workers, his data clarified which groups were suffering the most and where intervention should be directed. They helped inform several of Roosevelt's New Deal programs, many of which targeted unemployment. Roosevelt was also quick to learn that national income numbers could be used as a political tool. In his 1936 reelection campaign, he touted a near doubling of national income over the past four years as evidence of his accomplishments.[35] The idea of a "national economy" had begun to take hold, and Kuznets's report helped lead this charge by using this language explicitly.[36]

Moreover, the use of these numbers finally convinced the Department of Commerce to collect statistics on an ongoing basis, versus occasional reports at times of crisis. To manage the economy in real time, policymakers needed data to be published regularly. In 1937, Commerce started to issue monthly national income reports, a task headed by Robert Nathan.[37] National income reporting became an expected part of governance within a few short years.

This regular collection of data not only helped make the idea of studying and managing the economy possible, it also bolstered the role of economists in government. Large teams of economists were needed to gather and interpret the statistics, of course, but the change went deeper: economists began to argue that their expertise was continually needed to adjust policy to current conditions. Previously, most discussions of economic matters assumed that you could set a policy once and leave it in place. People disagreed deeply about whether to implement tariffs or to regulate industrial trusts, but they generally held that one policy was right or wrong regardless of economic conditions.[38] With the regular collecting of data, economists claimed that policies would need to shift in response, thereby requiring their constant expertise. Their efforts bore fruit: while there were only about 600 economists employed by the federal government in 1929, five to eight thousand had become government employees by the early 1950s.[39]

Kuznets's Monster

Kuznets knew the power of a single number to capture the imagination. And he worried greatly about how his research would be used. He spent the first ten pages of his 1934 report qualifying its findings. He noted the imperfections of the methods and the incompleteness of the data. And he harped on a theme he would repeat countless times. National income was a poor proxy for social welfare: "The welfare of a nation can, therefore, scarcely be inferred from a measurement of national income," he warned. But he understood the temptation would be strong. "The human mind" had the tendency "to simplify a complex situation in a compact characterization" in ways that were "dangerous" and subject to "abuse."[40] National income statistics were exactly the type of reductive number that could mislead policymakers. And this is exactly what happened.

The growing influence of these measurements occurred subtly in the late 1930s and 1940s, as national income measures became subsumed into a system of national accounts used to calculate GNP.[41] The work of Mitchell and Kuznets remained important, but a couple key differences emerged as Milton Gilbert, a former student of Kuznets, headed the effort, and the Department of Commerce took the project back from NBER. Gilbert shared Kuznets's interest in statistics, but not his focus on social welfare. For Gilbert and many American politicians in the late 1930s, preparation for possible US involvement in World War II loomed as a more pressing problem. Ensuring adequate industrial production, not reducing unemployment or the unequal distribution of income, took priority. Studies of national income became studies of national product.

The phrase "gross national product" may have been first mentioned in 1934 by Clark Warburton of the Brookings Institution, though the idea did not get widely taken up until the early 1940s. By 1942, Gilbert and the Commerce Department began publishing regular estimates of GNP and used it extensively in the war effort. Military leaders wanted as much of the nation's industrial capacity converted to the production of war matériel as possible, but careful planning was needed to make sure such efforts would not lead to unacceptable shortages of civilian goods. Moreover, planners had to grapple with where to place orders for military equipment. If too many orders were placed within a single region, that area might experience shortages of workers, energy, and transportation capacity. Even many free market advocates acknowledged that the invisible hand could not solve these problems in the short period of time available.[42]

The newly established War Production Board (WPB) took on this task, hiring Kuznets, Nathan, and Abramovitz, among others. It proved an exciting time for economists. Kuznets delighted military brass by using his statistics to argue the American economy in 1940 could provide twice as much war matériel as they requested. With several Allied defeats in Europe in 1941 plus the opening of the Pacific Theater, the military promptly tripled its requests. This time, the economists were less agreeable, with Kuznets arguing the military orders had to be cut by a quarter. The generals were furious. Head of WPB Donald Nelson backed Kuznets, however, and convinced Secretary of War George Stimson to accept the reductions. It was a huge win for the economists and for the power of GNP to shape policy.[43]

American economists were not alone in collecting such statistics. The Depression and the preparation for WWII affected many other nations that also chose to invest in the development of economic statistics to manage the crises. These efforts revealed disagreements about what should be counted. In the Soviet Union, economists had already developed an accounting system in the 1920s, predicated on Marx's distinction between productive and nonproductive labor, that excluded services from national income. Countries such as Norway and Hungary included household labor in their calculations. British economists, including Colin Clark, James Meade, and Richard Stone, linked national accounting to Keynesian economic ideas in ways that were later adopted in America. In fact, there were so many ideas about national accounting by 1939 that the League of Nations was already attempting to create a single standard model, an ambition thwarted by the outbreak of World War II.[44]

The broad interest in gathering regular data reflected the influence of John Maynard Keynes and his highly influential 1936 book *The General Theory*. In essence, Keynes sought to overturn the prevailing view that business cycles would automatically correct themselves. He demonstrated that it would be possible for economies to fall into a low-level trap where diminished confidence from businesses and consumers would prevent economic activity from returning to pre-Depression levels. In such a scenario, significant government spending would be needed to break this cycle. In order for policymakers to understand the state of the economy and whether a push of investment was necessary, they needed regular data to understand shifting conditions and teams of economists to interpret the data and make recommendations.[45]

The path to standardized GNP calculations took a major step forward in 1944 when key economists from the United States, Britain, and Canada met to coordinate their approaches. British economists, and Richard Stone in particular, convinced their colleagues to adopt several of their techniques. Over the next few years, most other countries fell in line with this approach. Sometimes the carrot of international collaboration was sufficient; at other times, the stick of postwar financing institutions forced the change. In order to be eligible for American funding through the Marshall Plan, nations were required to report national income statistics. In 1953, the United Nations codified these standards in the System of National Accounts. Within a short time, GNP calculations had become a global expectation.[46]

After helping establish GNP, Kuznets went back to his research position at University of Pennsylvania. Like many other intellectuals, he had been happy to support the war effort, and he agreed that in war, a focus on production made sense. But he harbored deep concerns about the continued use of GNP in peacetime. The switch from income to production, he argued, confused means with ends. The production of goods was a means to a better life for people, but not an end unto itself. Income came much closer to capturing what mattered to people: their ability to purchase goods and services. Focusing on production foregrounded an abstract entity over human needs. But Kuznets's voice would soon be drowned out by a nation— and a world—that quickly became addicted to GNP.[47]

Growth Ascendant

By the end of World War II, the intellectual infrastructure was in place to think about economic growth in a new way. It had been an uncertain path and one that took a while to achieve. NBER's first study of income was not followed up, and well-respected economists like Dewhurst and Kuznets harbored suspicions that a project on national income wasn't worth their time. Even with the Department of Commerce reporting regularly on GNP, there was no guarantee that an obsession with growth would emerge.

In fact, in the immediate postwar period, dreams of growth were heavily tempered by a worry that hard times loomed. It was clear that unprecedented government spending had been the major catalyst in breaking the chronic stagnation of the Great Depression, but what would happen when soldiers returned to the workforce and military contracts dried up? And if the economy avoided recession, hyperinflation might be the result, just as it had been for many countries after World War I. Paul Samuelson, one of America's most influential economists, warned in 1943 that a postwar boom "could be the antithesis of a prosperity period, constituting instead a nightmarish combination of the worst features of inflation and deflation."[48] Textbooks emphasized that stability should be the dominant objective, not growth.[49] The fiscally conservative Eisenhower never jumped aboard the growth bandwagon, emphasizing stability and full employment rather than ever-expanding GNP.[50]

The creation of the Council of Economic Advisers (CEA) played a pivotal role in reflecting, and then casting aside, the caution of the immediate postwar years. The CEA was established as an advisory body to the president as part of the Employment Act of 1946. For economists, the act, which also established a joint committee of Congress dedicated to the economy, provided an important stepping stone for shaping government policy.[51]

Under the leadership of Edwin Nourse from 1946 to 1949, the CEA emphasized policies that would enhance employment and assure stabilization. Born in 1883, Nourse was an agricultural economist and longtime researcher at the Brookings Institution. Moderately conservative, he recognized the potential of growth to solve some problems, but saw it as only one among many aims for the council. The benefits of growth risked being offset by inflation, and Nourse advocated tempered action.[52]

This caution disappeared when Leon Keyserling took over from Nourse in 1949. A quarter century younger, Keyserling was a lawyer with training in agricultural economics as well, and he had advised both Roosevelt and the liberal New York Senator Robert Wagner on the Agricultural Adjustment Act, Social Security, and the National Labor Relations Act. A man with "an undaunted conviction of the correctness of his views," Keyserling staunchly advocated liberal policies, so much so that he was one of the first to come under attack during Joseph McCarthy's Red Scare.[53]

Keyserling launched growth to the center of attention in the CEA's 1949 Annual Report, a document that has been described as "growthmanship's declaration of principles."[54] Decrying the stultifying effects of "moderation, compromise, and reconciliation," Keyserling argued that "a new generation needs new ideas."[55] He claimed it was time to cast off policies based on the assumption of stagnation with "the firm conviction that our whole economy can and should continue to grow."[56] Crucially, for Keyserling, this approach should supersede efforts to limit inequality: "Efforts to promote expansion of the total production and income of the economy are more significant than measures to 'redistribute' the current product."[57]

Keyserling's emphasis on growth and away from redistribution may seem surprising for a committed liberal and supporter of trade unions. In many ways, this was a political choice made from his direct involvement with the increasing antagonism between business, labor, and the New Deal in the late 1930s. His 1949 report argued that "the only thing that could stand in our way—provided that the lasting peace is achieved—would be excessive internal discord."[58] Rather than engaging in an all-out confrontation between government and capital, Keyserling claimed it was better to work together to build a bigger pie from which all would presumably benefit. It was an attempt to transform fights between the left and the right into a more constructive "politics of productivity."[59] As one of Truman's most trusted aides, Keyserling was in an ideal position to place growth at the heart of American politics.[60]

The power of growth thinking soon became embodied in one of the most consequential negotiations between labor and capital at midcentury: the 1950 "Treaty of Detroit" between General Motors and the United Auto Workers (UAW). During World War II, when many automobile factories were modified to produce tanks and other essential war matériel, many industries experimented with a management model that gave government, business, and labor a say in major decisions. Emboldened, the UAW sought to bargain for a host of benefits in the postwar years, including input on strategic decisions. General Motors executives vehemently rejected that idea, but as it wanted to end strikes, the company agreed to a wide range of concessions including pensions, health care, and most notably, cost-of-living adjustments to wages. Workers would share the benefits of increased productivity. The deal aligned the interests of management and labor around growth. What was good for General Motors was not only good for America, it was good for its workers.[61]

The seductive allure of growth thinking helps explain its rapid ascent and persist appeal. While Nourse argued that you could not have your cake and eat it too—a persistent saying in economics—Keyserling rejected this pessimism. Instead of making tough decisions about the distribution of income, one could bypass those debates by growing the pic. It has been an idea that has since proven very attractive to politicians across the spectrum.

Of course, an expanding pie could only quell social tension if the pie actually grew. Here Keyserling got lucky. He made his push to focus on growth as the American economy was entering a quarter century of remarkable prosperity. GNP skyrocketed from $200 billion in 1945 to $300 billion in 1950, nearly $550 billion in 1960, and more than a trillion by 1970.[62] At the same time, a series of social policies from the New Deal era, ranging from the GI Bill to progressive taxation to greater support for trade unions, meant that this massive increase in wealth was spread remarkably evenly throughout the population. The quarter century after World War II has been known as the great compression or great leveling because of how evenly the growing pie was sliced. For millions, this prosperity made an enormous difference by reducing food insecurity, providing access to improved clothing and housing, and placing the dream of a middle-class life within reach. Leaving an urban apartment for single-family homes in new suburbs like Levittown, New York, symbolized for many Americans the new opportunities in an era of widely shared prosperity.[63]

The special nature of this historical period cannot be underestimated. It was truly a golden age for growth because of how much economic expansion improved lives and how broadly that prosperity

The postwar economic boom raised millions of Americans into the middle class, bringing the dream of owning a home in a suburb such as Levittown, New York, into reach. Gottscho-Schleisner Collection, Library of Congress, Prints and Photographs Division, LC-DIG-gsc-5a25985.

was shared. The richest Americans saw their share of relative income decrease slightly while those on the bottom notched important gains. Though Black Americans continued to be underpaid and understood they would often be the last to be hired and the first to be fired, they went from earning about 40 percent compared to their White counterparts before the war to nearly 70 percent in 1960.[64] Inequality remained, but far less so than in the decades before and after.

What was happening in America was echoed across the world. The potential of growth as a way to have it all and avoid conflict attracted politicians from western Europe to Moscow to Japan.[65] In Europe, politicians also sought to dispel tensions between labor and capital through a focus on economic expansion. In practice, this meant dividing the labor movement, as moderate unions were seen as fit to bargain with while radical unions were largely excluded.[66] And the promise of growth appeared fulfilled, with average GNP gains in western Europe of 5 percent from 1947 to 1959 exceeding the robust 3.5 percent growth rate in the United States.[67]

And if the allure of having it all was not sufficiently appealing, there was also a stick. In the wake of World War II, a series of international financial arrangements—the Bretton Woods financial system, the Marshall Plan for European reconstruction, and the institutions that became the International Monetary Fund and World Bank—required countries to report their income statistics publicly if they wished to participate. Receiving loans or aid meant buying into the world of GNP calculations and prioritizing growth.[68]

The Cold War further drove an international focus on comparative growth rates. The United States and Soviet Union did not just worry about a missile gap, they were also obsessed with which economic system would triumph. And that battle was also a contest to entice the nonaligned nations of the world. Was capitalism or communism better for growth? Each superpower sought to demonstrate that theirs was a superior system for the global South to adopt.

Even though the United States economy was serving its population well in the 1950s by reducing poverty and expanding the middle class, its growth rate still lagged other countries. The American economy had been increasing between 3 and 4 percent per year at a time the Soviet Union was boasting rates of 8–10 percent. While many were skeptical of the Soviet numbers, American defense experts repeatedly testified to Congress that the United States was losing its advantage.[69] The 1961 edition of the most widely used textbook at the time by Paul Samuelson predicted that the Soviet Union would overtake the United States as the world's largest economy between 1984 and 1997.[70] Growth became seen as necessary for national security, not just individual pocketbooks.

By the mid-1950s, growth had cemented itself as the prized object of domestic and international politics, trumping previous issues such as stabilization, employment, and inequality. It was easy to see why. Domestically, a focus on growth could unite liberals and conservatives and lessen tensions between workers and capitalists. Internationally, global competition encouraged many politicians to do all they could to avoid falling behind. Whatever the problem, growth offered an answer.

"Three-Quarters of the Human Race Will Be Wiped Out"

Yet there was a fly in the ointment. Could a finite planet support infinite expansion? The massive mobilization of resources for World War II revealed the voracious appetite of the American industrial machine. A small fraction of the world's population, Americans were consuming nearly half the world's resources.[71] And while the nation was blessed with natural abundance, there were several strategic materials that could not be obtained domestically. When the Japanese cut off supplies of rubber grown on plantations in Southeast Asia during the war, for example, American military planners had to scramble to find alternatives; other essential inputs such as tin, nickel, asbestos, manganese, chromite, and cobalt largely came from overseas as well.[72] During World War II, concerns about national security and strategic stockpiles dominated the debate over the "minerals problem"; after the war, growth replaced security as the primary framework for thinking about resources. Was there enough material for the American economy to grow? What about the reconstruction of war-torn Europe and Japan, not to mention the ambitions of newly decolonized nations? During the 1940s, America's steelmakers were fretting over the decline of the Mesabi iron ore range, and Secretary of the Interior Julius Krug predicted domestic oil production would not keep up with demand in the near future.[73] By the end of World War II, the question was no longer abstract, and it was no longer confined within the nation's borders.

These questions rhymed with those asked in the early twentieth-century conservation movement, but they were not identical. When Teddy Roosevelt brought the nation's leading thinkers together in 1908 to discuss conservation, they focused almost exclusively on American resources, and they emphasized questions of pollution and waste. After World War II, scientists began to articulate a new object of study: the global environment. This process had much in common with the creation of the economy. The global environment had always existed as a physical array of planetary systems, but it had not been an explicit object of analysis. Most often, the word "environment" had been used to indicate the background conditions in which humans lived, and it was studied in local contexts. The global turn in environmental thinking directed attention to the idea that humans shared a global environment and that what happened in one place could have significant effects elsewhere.[74]

Similar to the creation of the economy, the idea of a global environment emerged from new ways of seeing and understanding the world. One crucial figure was William Vogt, whose 1948 blockbuster, *The Road to Survival*, birthed a genre: apocalyptic environmentalism. Vogt was an unlikely environmental spokesperson.[75] He had no advanced training in science and had stumbled into the field largely through his passion for birds. Buoyed by a confidence sometimes bordering on imperiousness, he overcame a childhood bout of polio that left him walking with a cane to perform research on guano birds in South America during the 1930s. Traveling throughout Latin America on behalf of the US government during World War II, he saw landscape after landscape devastated through overuse and overpopulation. There were too many humans, he feared, and they were pushing the land too hard. In doing so, environmental effects could no longer be seen as just local. What happened in the savannas of Africa influenced farmers on the Great Plains of America; disturbances in the oceans could affect mountain habitats. If humans did not transform their way of living, the results would be catastrophic: "If we continue to ignore these relationships," he warned, "there is little probability that mankind can long escape the searing downpour of war's death from the skies."[76] The result could be that "three-quarters of the human race will be wiped out."[77]

Vogt's impassioned message was amplified by other writers. Henry Fairfield Osborn Jr., the wealthy son of a prominent paleontologist and eugenicist, devoted himself to environmental causes. In 1948, he wrote *Our Plundered Planet*, a book that beseeched people to see themselves as part of nature, not separate from it. Global in scope and looking deep into the past and the future, Osborn Jr. lamented that man had "failed so far to recognize that he is a child of the earth, and that, this being so, he must for his own survival work with nature in understanding rather than in conflict."[78] The wanton use of resources and failure to protect nature represented a dire threat— "even man's very survival" was at stake.[79] The lawyer and conservationist Samuel Ordway Jr. took up many of these same themes and was among the first to provide an environmental critique of what he called "the modern religion of growth."[80] In a 1953 book, he argued that unsustainable consumption of natural resources threatened both humans and the planet. "Within foreseeable time," he warned, "increasing consumption of resources can produce scarcities serious enough to destroy our American Dream of an ever-higher level of living, and with it our present culture."[81]

The alarm bells sounded by Vogt, Osborn, and Ordway resonated in many parts of the world. It was well known that a drive for resources had helped catalyze World War II as the Nazi Party claimed the need for more land for its people (lebensraum) and the Japanese empire initiated conflict to secure oilfields and other strategic minerals. President Truman and other world leaders worried that future resource shortages might threaten lasting peace. This led to a 1949 conference organized by the United Nations Scientific Conference on the Conservation and Utilization of Resources (UNSCCUR) that included representatives from nearly fifty countries. Held at Lake Success on Long Island, the conference sought to analyze the world's natural resources in categories such as energy, minerals, forests, and fisheries.[82] In his inauguration speech the same year, Truman reiterated a sense that there might not be enough to go around. Point Four, as it came to be known, argued that US policy should be focused on providing technical assistance to the developing world. In particular, he emphasized that the "material resources which we can afford to use for other peoples are limited," and that as a result, the United States should focus on using its "inexhaustible resources in technical knowledge."[83]

Environmentalists including Vogt and Osborn were pleased to see the global environment get attention from policymakers but disappointed that ideas of efficiency and maximum yields trumped talk of preservation and protection. When it became clear that the 1949 UN conference would be focused merely on eliminating waste and maximizing the efficiency of resource consumption, groups such as the International Union for the Protection of Nature hosted a separate conference at the same time to promote ecosystem protection.[84] A new idea of a global environment that humans depended on for their survival was starting to emerge, though it did not yet have the close attention of policy elites.

"We Share the Belief of the American People in the Principle of Growth"

In America, postwar fears of resource shortages proved short-lived, pushed into the background by optimism around free trade and technology. Economists played a crucial shift in establishing this rosy outlook, reflecting two important trends: the growing power of economists in the political arena and their faith that natural limits could be overcome. While ecologists studying the global environment worried that international entanglements could have impacts ranging from species loss to mineral depletion to civilizational collapse, American economists looked with confidence at the bounty of other nations. Even if Americans used more resources than could be obtained within the nation's borders, there was a wide world out there to fill the gap.

World War II marked a watershed for economists in the American public sphere. Their successes in wartime planning, the new policy focus on growth, and the creation of institutions such as the CEA stood in marked contrast to the previous decades. Of the hundreds of attendees at Roosevelt's 1908 conference, only three were economists and they played bit parts; foresters, geologists, business executives, lawyers, and politicians were far more prominent.[85] In 1930, more than a thousand prominent economists wrote to President Hoover pleading with him to veto the Smoot–Hawley Act, which enacted large tariffs on international trade. Arguing that a decrease in trade would exacerbate the dire consequences of an economy in shambles from the 1929 stock market crash, they advocated lowering barriers to trade rather than increasing them. The message was completely ignored by the president, perhaps in part because the year prior, one of America's most distinguished economists, Irving Fisher, had claimed that stocks were reaching a permanent high plateau just days before the crash. Things did not get much better during the 1930s, as it was widely noted that economists had done little to predict the crash and even less to pull the nation out of the Great Depression. It was with great relief to many economists that their ability to assist the nation's wartime preparations and make meaningful contributions to the victory offered a vital lifeline for a profession whose prospects had seemed dim in the 1930s.[86]

Postwar economists also benefited from the widespread interest in growth, claiming it as their distinctive area of study. Two substantial reports, one in 1947 and the other in 1952, exemplified the rising influence of economics as the proper means to study the links between natural resources and growth. The first was pioneered by J. Frederic Dewhurst—the same economist who declined to head the national income accounts project at Commerce a decade before. In 1933, he took a position at the left-leaning Twentieth Century Fund, a nonprofit organization formed at the same time as NBER to supply policy ideas for social improvement. A decade later, Dewhurst and his colleagues began to analyze the nation's ability to deliver prosperity after the war. In 1947, they published their answer in *America's Needs and Resources*, a book of more than 800 pages of charts, tables, and graphs. Drawing on national accounts and GNP, among myriad sources of data, the report struck an optimistic tone at a time many feared a return to Depression conditions. The American economy had the capacity to generate abundance for the large majority of the population and to meet the needs of its citizens well into the future. The prominent economist John Kenneth Galbraith described it as an "important, ... formidable, ... and encouraging book" that "appears at a time when there is an all but pathological conviction that a depression is inevitable."[87]

Avoiding such a slump, however, would require resources. The report made it clear how essential minerals—and fossil fuel energy in particular—had been to the American economy. The "great progress" of the past century came largely from "the great advantages and economies of this cheapest form of energy" and the "lavish expansion in its use." The "phenomenal increase in the use of inanimate energy," the authors stressed, "more than anything else accounted for the high standard of living and the economic primacy of the United States." Whereas future economists would focus on human capital, technological progress, or innovation as the drivers of growth, Dewhurst and his colleagues pointed to coal and oil.[88]

Even while acknowledging the foundational importance of natural resources, the report cast an optimistic take on looming scarcity.

To be sure, the nation was likely to soon run low on minerals like zinc and copper, but improved efficiency and substitution of new sources could offset losses, as could new technological discoveries. As early as 1947, the report was already touting the possibilities of nuclear power. But most critically, the authors emphasized foreign trade and the "vast resources in foreign areas" that were "relatively untouched." "Given a system that permits free access to the world's resources," the report optimistically declared, "there can be no question of a raw material supply adequate to support an expanding American economy for decades to come." As a last resort, should the nation be forced to spend more labor and money to develop its partially depleted reserves, "no reason exists for believing that depletion is so extensive that it would necessarily become a serious barrier to the maintenance of high levels of production and employment in the future." Even though natural resources were the foundation of American prosperity, policymakers could feel confident about their future availability.[89]

A few years later, the issue of mineral scarcity emerged once again as the United States began to mobilize for the Korean War. In 1951, President Truman formed a special panel to assess the nation's "materials problem": the challenge of "assuring an adequate supply of production materials for our long-range needs."[90] To lead it, Truman tapped William Paley, the wealthy and well-connected head of the Columbia Broadcasting Service (CBS). Paley was not an obvious choice, as he had little experience in resource questions and was far better known as a playboy than a government consultant. But as a Republican, Paley offered political balance to the project and had the media savvy to ensure the report got widely distributed.

Like *America's Needs and Resources*, the Paley Commission Report considered natural resources essential to American growth and acknowledged the days of mineral abundance seemed to be coming to an end. "We have skimmed the cream of our resources," the report warned, urging Americans to adapt to "an era of new relationships between our needs and resources" as the country undertook a "slow

The United States' entry into the Korean War raised concern among policymakers about whether the nation possessed sufficient natural resources. President Truman tapped William S. Paley to form a commission to study the matter. Their efforts would lead to the creation of Resources for the Future, a think tank that has played a crucial role in how economists have analyzed the natural world. Library of Congress, Prints and Photographs Division, LC-USZ62-72424.

transition from a raw materials surplus nation to a raw materials deficit nation." The fundamental reality was that "the consumption of almost all materials is expanding at compound rates" while the supply of minerals could not expand so quickly.[91]

Yet despite its many warnings, the report retained an upbeat perspective, rooted in economic analysis. "We share the belief of the American people in the principle of growth," the report declared, even if the authors acknowledged, "we cannot find any absolute reason for this belief." They justified this perspective by noting that "to our Western minds it seems preferable to any opposite, which to us implies stagnation and decay." This led them to reject the idea of hoarding for the future, calling it a "hairshirt concept of conserva-tion" that should be replaced by "a positive concept compatible with growth and high consumption in place of abstinence and retrench-ment." Those who advocated using less were missing the mark, and their mistake lay in "a failure to recognize the economic dimensions of the problem." The insights of the dismal science could serve as a corrective to the "Malthusian doom" purveyed by Vogt and his followers.[92]

The emphasis on economics as the main way of thinking about the problems marked a shift in who had the authority to speak on matters of public importance. Presidential commissions typically in-volved members from a wide range of backgrounds. But for the Paley Commission, economics was the "most common disciplinary back-ground" of commission staff, and economic ideas were the "com-mon language" that revealed "the extraordinary ingenuity of man-kind" to avert catastrophe through careful planning.[93] The earth's dowry may be finite, but many approaches existed to "compensate" for this "unalterable central fact."[94] Like *America's Needs and Re-sources*, the Paley Commission pointed to the benefits of interna-tional trade. The United States lacked reserves of several key mate-rials and many others could be obtained much cheaper overseas. The authors also emphasized the potential to find substitutes for scarce resources. Revealingly, the fourth volume was titled "The Promise of Technology," and it detailed the ways that technological break-throughs could identify new deposits of key minerals, fabricate new materials, enhance recycling, and substitute abundant materials for scarce ones. Finally, the report argued that its most important find-ing was the need to form an organization capable of monitoring the situation over time. This would result in the creation of the think tank Resources for the Future the following year.

Taken together, *America's Needs and Resources* and the Paley Commission Report outlined many of the shifting thoughts about growth, economics, and limits in the American economy. Both shared a new interest in growth understood through the analysis of national income and GNP statistics. Both placed economics at the center of their analysis, and both expressed faith in technology. In fact, whereas the 1947 edition of *America's Needs and Resources* ended with an eight-page paean to the importance of finite supplies of energy, a revised edition in 1955 ended by praising technology as the key factor—"in a very sense the *primary* resource"—of the American economy. Natural resources "are valuable only because technology has made them available and useful." The final sentence of the report declared "Technology is our primary and inexhaustible resource."[95]

Yet for all their data tables and analysis, when surveying growth and its possibilities, the findings were based in hope as much as empiricism. "Faith" and "promise" recur repeatedly, marking a degree of uncertainty about what this brave new world of growth would look like, and what it meant to speak of nature's limits. In the coming decades, however, this uncertainty would largely be swept under the rug as economists grew increasingly certain that there were no meaningful natural limits to growth.

*

Returning to Moses Abramovitz in 1950, it is easier to understand why he was asked to write about the economics of growth and why he found so little had been said. The idea of growth only took hold in the late 1940s, but once it did, it exploded onto the scene, capturing the hearts and minds of politicians across the globe. Not surprisingly, the American Economic Association wanted to make sure the best economic thinking was brought to bear on the topic.

But Abramovitz's problem remained. Economists such as Keyserling advocated growth and politicians wanted it. But what did the discipline of economics actually have to contribute to the subject? Was there a theory of growth? In Abramovitz's mind, the answer was no. Nor was he necessarily sanguine that a clear answer would emerge. He cautioned that useful answers depended on analyzing industrial organization, entrepreneurship, labor mobility, political structure, consumer preferences, demographics, and more. Tackling these topics would require looking "outside the normal boundaries of economics." Abramovitz ended his survey with an appeal for interdisciplinary work, arguing that "if the economics of growth attains the rank it ought to have in our subject, we should expect to see history, geography, psychology, and sociology take a prominent role in the training of economists in the future."[96]

Abramovitz's vision did not come to pass. Rather than turning to interdisciplinary engagement, economists doubled down on the growing influence of neoclassical methods that reduced the complex world to mathematical models. No one did more to establish this approach than Robert Solow, whose pioneering work in the 1950s revolutionized the field.

3 * The Kingdom of Solovia

Robert Solow was bored.[1] He was easily getting top marks
in his classes at Harvard in 1941, but he was not entranced
by the institution. Having grown up in a working-class
Jewish neighborhood in Brooklyn, he did not fit in with the
upper-class elites that made up the majority of the school's
enrollment, particularly since he was two years younger
than most of his peers. He found more common ground
playing horseshoes with the Irish townies than socializ-
ing with his privileged classmates.[2] So when the Japanese
attacked Pearl Harbor, he decided to sign up for the army.

Solow had been following the rise of Hitler and anti-
Semitism in Germany and felt strongly that "Hitler had
to go." He had learned German and Morse code while at
Harvard, so he was assigned to a radio intelligence unit in
Italy. Their job was to get close enough to German positions so that they could intercept and decode low power
radio transmissions. For Solow, it was deeply rewarding.
It was close enough to danger that he didn't have "the guilt
of being safe," but he still had a "good shot at later life."

The real payoff was the camaraderie among a tight-knit unit that followed the Germans all the way up Italy, helping the Allies learn of enemy troop movements and supply chains. "We were buddies," Solow reflected, and he rejected promotion offers because he knew that if his friends had to call him "sir," it would undermine the cohesion. His team was "very, very good" and "it was a marvelous experience."[3]

It was only after his discharge in 1945 that Solow turned to economics. He took to it quickly, becoming one of the most celebrated economists of his generation. Best known for his pioneering work in growth theory, Solow won the John Bates Clark Medal in 1961, awarded to the top American economist under forty, and the Nobel Prize in 1987. Yet his experience near the front lines stuck with him. Throughout his career at MIT and during a stint at the Council of Economic Advisers (CEA) in the early 1960s, he prized the collegial bonds formed by small groups working on pressing problems. And he embraced the idea of reconnaissance, becoming famous for the development of lightweight economic models that helped map new intellectual terrain, a bit like the work of his radio intelligence team in Italy.

Lanky and with a large and angular face that was quick to light into a smile, Solow also had a gift for turning a phrase. When he was giving a paper on inflation at the University of Chicago in 1966, Milton Friedman commented that he had failed to properly appreciate the role of the money supply. In response, Solow blurted, "everything reminds Milton of the money supply. Well, everything reminds me of sex, but I try to keep it out of my papers."[4] When describing Nixon's budget, Solow labeled it "a small step forward for Nixon and a giant leap backward for mankind."[5] His wit and ability to toggle between the cutting edge of economic theory and plain speech made him one of America's most influential economists.

In growth theory, Solow is the towering giant. Much of the field's development has been a reaction to his foundational contributions in 1956 and 1957. His ideas have been so consequential that growth theory has been dubbed the "Kingdom of Solovia."[6] Solow remained an active participant for more than five decades, passing away at ninety-nine years old in December 2023.

Within the history of economics, the story of growth theory can seem pretty simple: before Solow, there was almost nothing; after Solow, growth theory boomed. The reality, of course, is much more complex. Solow himself was quick to note that his ideas were part of a broader conversation among economists and regularly gave credit to others. Moreover, several other approaches to growth—both theoretical and empirical—emerged at the same time as Solow's. Yet because Solow has come to be the most widely recognized theorist of growth and a man who would later comment extensively on the question of environmental limits, understanding the invention of infinite growth requires close attention to his ideas.[7]

"I Will If You Will"

Some people are born to be economists. John Stuart Mill was trained in political economy by his father from an early age. Both of Lawrence Summers's parents were economists, and he had Paul Samuelson and Kenneth Arrow for uncles. Solow's father, by contrast, was in the fur business and neither of his parents had attended college. Precocious, Solow learned to read at age four, skipped several grades, and earned a scholarship to Harvard when he was sixteen. Friendly and social, he got A's easily throughout school, though he preferred playing sports to reading books.[8]

As was true of many who came of age during the Depression, Solow understood the human costs of economic downturns. Though his parents did not lose their jobs, they worried continually about their financial situation, and it was a regular topic of discussion. Moreover, as Jews, he and his family paid a great deal of attention to the rise of fascism and the Nazi Party, thus ensuring that matters of political economy were regularly discussed at home.[9] Just like Richard Ely and the founders of American economics in the late nineteenth century, Solow's formative years came at a time when the failures of the market were more apparent than its successes.

At Harvard, Solow did not immediately arrive at the study of economics. He took a variety of classes in his first two years, flirting first with botany because he heard the Forest Service was a reliable source of jobs at a time when the unemployment rate was still in the double digits. Despite achieving top marks easily in biology, he found the subject not to his liking and moved into social sciences. Uncertain of his path, he left Harvard for the army.

After his discharge in 1945, he returned to Harvard with no clear direction for his studies. He chose economics in good measure because his new wife, Barbara Lewis, a Radcliffe student, had majored in it. He was assigned the distinguished Russian American mathematical economist Wassily Leontief as his tutor. It was a great match. Despite being one of the top economists of his generation, a man who would serve as president of the American Economic Association (AEA) and win the Nobel Prize, Leontief's classes were poorly attended, and he had time to challenge a promising student. Leontief had been born in 1906 into a wealthy Russian family and excelled academically. However, he was a contrarian thinker, and Soviet authorities threw him into jail on several occasions for subversive acts such as putting up anti-communist posters. He soon decided to flee Russia, aided in his escape by the fact that he had a sarcoma on his face; state officials assumed it was terminal and let him cross the border. It turned out to be benign, and Leontief lived another seven decades. In 1933, he came to America, obtaining a position at the National Bureau of Economic Research (NBER) and then Harvard, where he stayed until reaching the mandatory retirement age and moving to New York University. Intensely private and increasingly critical of the economic mainstream, Leontief commanded intellectual respect but little love. Largely a loner who preferred trout fishing to human companionship, he had few friends; his obituaries speak glowingly of his accomplishments but are notably silent about his personality.[10]

Working under Leontief, Solow was introduced to two formative ideas: mathematics and input–output tables. At first, Leontief was repeatedly frustrated, because he would recommend new and exciting work for Solow to read only to remember that the math exceeded his pupil's knowledge. Even in graduate school at Harvard at this time, few students were mathematically trained. Tired of hearing Leontief say, "But no, you can't read this because you don't have any mathematics to speak of," Solow signed up for classes in calculus so he could follow the state of the art. Taking well to mathematical economics, he still was not sold on a career upon finishing his undergraduate degree in 1947. His wife, Bobby, encouraged both of them to apply to graduate school in economics. "I will if you will," he reportedly told her, and shortly after, he resumed his studies under Leontief at Harvard.[11] Though Bobby's graduate training was interrupted for thirteen years to raise their three children, she completed her PhD in economic history and became recognized as an expert in the economic history of slavery and Irish plantations.[12]

Once committed to economics, Solow flourished. He did economics, his colleague Paul Samuelson said, like Ty Cobb played baseball. Both were immensely talented individuals who did "everything with apparent ease," but there was one difference. Cobb would do whatever it took to win, whether it was within the rules or not. Solow had no need to prove himself. Samuelson hypothesized that if Solow were six inches shorter, his publication list would have been twice as long.[13]

Solow worked with Leontief to develop input–output tables, his mentor's focus for the last several decades of his career. Like Wesley Mitchell, Leontief was dissatisfied by the state of economic science. Too much theory, he complained, and too little fact. Neoclassical economists were all too happy to posit a few assumptions, aggregate some data, and come to grand conclusions. Yet he also had criticisms for Mitchell and the NBER approach. The collection of statistics without a theoretical hypothesis led to masses of data without clear meaning. There had to be a middle ground between abstract platitudes and piles of data. He believed input–output tables could serve as the "bridge between theory and facts."[14]

The ideas were straightforward, but implementing them required enormous effort. His goal was to visually represent the exchange of goods within an economy. Each table was a matrix with every sector in the economy included on both the horizontal rows and vertical columns. Read one direction, the table listed all the inputs a sector consumed. For example, a steel manufacturer would need ore, coke, and capital equipment, among other inputs. Read the other direction, it would reveal which sectors absorbed the output; that steel, in turn, would be consumed by car manufacturers, railroads, construction companies, etc. As an idea, it was easy to grasp; the challenge was to figure out the actual interconnections. A table with forty-two sectors had more than 1,500 data points; a table with 500 sectors had nearly a quarter million data points. The calculations were so complex that it only became possible to imagine doing this work in the late 1940s with the invention of the digital computer. Even with access to Harvard's pioneering Mark II computer, running the figures for a forty-two-sector table took fifty-six hours in 1951, as the twenty-five-ton machine tabulated the punch cards.[15]

Processing the data was one requirement. But for the calculations to give useful information, Leontief insisted that they be based on empirical data. Some could be gleaned from the statistics collected by NBER, the Department of Labor, and the Department of Commerce. But many had to be found by poring through trade journals and corporate filings to find industry-specific figures on consumption and production. Leontief particularly believed engineering data to be extremely valuable, noting that if you want to know how much coke you need to make iron, "a perfectly good way is to ask an ironmaster."[16] Solow was a trusted aide, calculating capital coefficients for several industries.

The payoff for this enormous amount of work was potentially very high. If you had an expanding population and wanted to be sure the economy could generate sufficient housing stock, for example, input–output tables could indicate which industries would need to be expanded. In 1944, Leontief used input–output tables to argue that the steel sector would need to expand in peacetime, not contract, which flew in the face of expectations. Steel executives had been very cautious about expanding their capacity to meet wartime demand, fearing it would result in overproduction and low prices after the war. They used this argument to extract generous government support for increasing their capacity, but Leontief suggested little subsidy should be necessary. It turns out he was largely correct: demand for steel reached 96.8 million tons in 1950, well above prewar levels, and near Leontief's prediction of ninety-eight million tons.[17] Such successes led to input–output tables being widely adopted by governments and large corporations for planning.[18]

With his insistence on data specific to each industry, Leontief rejected a common trend among economic theorists of relying on high-level aggregate data. Economists needed data "from below" that came from "a detailed analysis of the technical background of productive processes" and "a reconstruction of technical coefficients from engineering data."[19] This was "costly" to obtain, Leontief acknowledged, but "indispensable" for analysis.[20] Solow was not so sure. "It was Leontief who turned me into an economist," he later recalled, and his mentor's influence meant Solow embraced empirical testing and admonished colleagues who did not.[21] But Solow also became much more comfortable with abstraction as he left Harvard in 1950 for a faculty position at MIT. From that point, he spent very little of his time interviewing ironmasters.

"Everything Else Is Just Pictures and Talk"

Solow's arrival at MIT coincided with a major shift in the American economics profession: the dominance of neoclassical economics. The previous flourishing of alternative approaches since Richard Ely's day rapidly faded away in the postwar world, and neoclassical economics went from a way of doing economics to the way. By the 1950s, a graduate student seeking a top faculty position or an ambitious scholar hoping to publish in a top journal increasingly needed sophisticated mathematics and neoclassical analysis.[22]

No one did more to shape this transformation than Solow's MIT colleague Paul Samuelson. Like Solow, Samuelson had trained with Leontief at Harvard. Brash and brilliant, Samuelson quickly gained a reputation as the discipline's enfant terrible, arguing with his professors and critiquing their approaches. His 1941 dissertation offered a mathematically informed rethinking of the entire field when it was published six years later as *Foundations of Economic Analysis*. Then the next year, he wrote an introductory economics textbook that quickly became the most widely used one in the nation for decades. It was said that faculty and graduate students learned their economics from *Foundations* and undergraduates learned it from his textbook. His influence was so large that he could state with some accuracy, "In talking about modern economics, I am talking about me."[23]

At the heart of Samuelson's approach was the phrase, "mathematics is a language."[24] By arguing that mathematics was the language of economics, Samuelson helped initiate a profound change in the skills economists were expected to master. As Nobel Prize–winning economist Robert Lucas later put it, baldly: "Economic theory *is* mathematical analysis. Everything else is just pictures and talk."[25]

Samuelson's fellow advocates of neoclassical economics were not simply content to espouse the virtues of their approach; they also launched attacks on the historical and institutional traditions. One of the boldest broadsides came from Tjalling Koopmans in 1947, when the thirty-seven-year-old Dutch American took on Wesley Mitchell and the institutional school. Mitchell had continued to work on business cycles since the publication of his 1913 opus. Gathering ever more data, he coauthored another major book in 1946 with Arthur Burns titled *Measuring Business Cycles*.[26] The massive volume was full of data, but to Koopmans it was a deep disappointment. Savaging the NBER approach in a twelve-page review titled "Measurement Without Theory," he lambasted Mitchell and Burns for the limitations of their approach. The work's great failing, Koopmans argued, was that Mitchell and Burns did not integrate economic theory into their analysis. As a result, when they gathered numbers, it was done in inconsistent ways that prevented them from making testable conclusions. "Measurement without theory," Koopmans claimed, could only make weak insights and offer scant advice to policymakers.[27]

Mitchell died shortly after the review was published. His surrogates offered a spirited defense of the NBER program, emphasizing that economics could be a big tent with multiple approaches, but much of the damage was done.[28] It had not helped that the great promise of Mitchell's work never seemed to have been fulfilled. Despite ever-increasing amounts of data, he never managed to distill a theory of business cycles that caught on. Even his defenders acknowledged that the end results were underwhelming. The institutional school faded rapidly thereafter.[29]

Samuelson argued the same could be said of input–output tables. Leontief's mathematical and theoretical work in the 1930s and 1940s, Samuelson acknowledged, was as good as it got and "set me on the way of my life career."[30] He therefore felt "a certain regret" that Leontief spent his remaining decades working on input–output tables. He compared it to Albert Einstein spending his last decades fruitlessly pursuing a grand theory of everything on his own, rather than continuing to engage with the leading edge of physics. Input–output tables just did not have the theoretical sophistication Samuelson thought economics needed.[31]

Methodological debates in academic fields happen regularly, and Young Turks such as Samuelson and Koopmans are to be expected, just as earlier figures like Mitchell and Ely had critiqued their elders. But ideas need to be more than good to take hold: they also need a receptive social context. And in the late 1940s, the legacies of World War II provided the opening Samuelson and Koopmans needed to advance their approach and push aside all other methodologies.

One important consequence of World War II was the development of novel techniques in economics that demonstrated the effectiveness of mathematical analysis and neoclassical insights and helped win the war, such as game theory, linear programming, and operations research. Koopmans, for example, had applied linear programming techniques to transportation questions, helping war planners optimize the shipment of men and matériel to the front lines. The success of these approaches in calculating efficient transportation routes and prioritizing targets for strategic bombing missions burnished the credentials of their promoters. The fact that government agencies, the Department of Defense in particular, provided significant funding for such endeavors was a further draw for many in the profession.[32]

Samuelson's approach to economics further benefited from its resemblances to physics. Many viewed World War II as the "physicists' war" in light of breakthroughs such as radar and the atomic bomb. Physicists capitalized on their rising fortunes to support the creation of the National Science Foundation in 1950, which dedicated significant government funding to the sciences, and physics in particular. Neighboring disciplines looked with jealousy at the universal laws and social prestige of the "queen of the sciences." Since the late nineteenth century, some economists had seen physics as an inspiration for the development of neoclassical methods, even transcribing formulas from physics with a simple replacement of capital and labor for values such as mass and energy. In the postwar period, it became easier for those economists interested in theoretical and mathematical approaches to argue everything else was inferior.[33]

Neoclassical economics received a further boost during the Red Scare. Just as progressive economists such as Richard Ely and John Commons had come under attack for their prolabor views at the turn of the century, Joseph McCarthy used his House Un-American Activities Committee to target economists perceived to be critics of capitalism. Institutional economists who wrote critical tracts about the failures of markets were most likely to draw his ire, and at least twenty-seven different economists were harassed during the Red Scare. By emphasizing the utility of markets and presenting arguments in numerical form, neoclassical economics had the benefit of appearing less partisan or political.[34]

Physicist Robert Oppenheimer and General Leslie Groves at the Trinity atomic bomb test site, 1945. Physicists emerged from World War II with great prestige from their contributions to the war effort, highlighted by the development of the atomic bomb. Many economists believed their discipline should emulate the mathematical search for universal laws that had generated widespread respect and funding for physics. US Army Corps of Engineers via Wikimedia Commons.

Samuelson and Koopmans's vision for economics further won out because it tapped into an American tradition of "trust in numbers." In a contentious political culture where claims to knowledge are often interpreted as being driven by interest group politics, quantitative analyses have often been more persuasive in the halls of government because they have the appearance of objectivity. Economists were much quicker than other social scientists to embrace quantification, and it helps explain how they ended up influencing government more than their colleagues in political science, sociology, or anthropology.[35]

Institutional economics, by contrast, declined rapidly in the postwar period. Many of its practitioners simply reclassified themselves as Keynesians. John Maynard Keynes's 1936 masterpiece, *The General Theory*, offered a compelling new framework for talking about market failures and the need for government spending to correct business cycles. When John Hicks and Alvin Hansen transformed Keynes's ideas into a mathematical model—the IS–LM diagram—in the late 1930s, it encouraged younger scholars who might previously have aligned with the institutional school to rebrand themselves as Keynesians.[36]

Collectively, these developments helped usher in the dominance of an approach to economics that was highly theoretical and mathematical. Pulled by the appeal of new tools and funding to develop them and pushed away from other approaches by the politics of the Cold War and the Red Scare, the methodological pluralism that had long characterized the discipline faded. Neoclassical economics became the discipline's beating heart.

The Rise of MIT and Its Models

Timing is everything, and in 1950, Solow could not have chosen a better time to start at MIT. The economics unit had at best a middling reputation for most of its history. But in 1940, MIT made a coup by hiring Paul Samuelson, and he was in the process of building a global powerhouse with a strong intellectual culture.[37] Members of the economics faculty ate lunch together regularly and collaborated often. Solow embraced the lack of "stuffiness" and "hierarchy," which he gave Samuelson credit for, noting that "if you have the best economist in the world and he's not being stuffy about anything, it must be hard for anyone else to be stuffy."[38]

Politically, MIT economics had the reputation of being left-of-center, and Samuelson and Solow both worked in the Kennedy and Johnson administrations. Though committed to neoclassical tools, they were labeled Keynesians by advocates of laissez-faire because they favored using government to correct market imperfections.[39] Samuelson had helped popularize the neoclassical synthesis in the 1950s in which neoclassical principles dominated microeconomic analysis in the long term and Keynesian ideas of government intervention could be integrated in the short term from a macroeconomic perspective. Some conservatives discouraged the use of Samuelson's famous textbook because it taught students that there were cases where government intervention could be more efficient than markets.[40] When *Newsweek* wanted to give readers a chance to see contrasting opinions on the day's economic issues, they chose Samuelson to represent the left and Milton Friedman of the University of Chicago to represent the right.[41]

MIT also became known for a distinctive style of economics in the 1960s centered on lightweight mathematical models designed to analyze particular sectors of the economy. These "toy worlds," as Solow described them, sought to reduce complexities in order to understand causal relationships. These models were highly adaptable to a range of issues including trade, social welfare, and capital theory. Solow's growth theory would come to be the most famous example of the MIT approach to modeling.[42]

Modeling has a long history in economics and has taken many forms. The French Physiocrats who influenced Adam Smith developed one of the first, the *Tableau Économique*, which sought to understand the effect of monetary flows between landowners, agricultural workers, and artisans/merchants. Many models have been graphical, with the intersecting curves of supply and demand being an elementary example. Some have even been physical, such as when Irving Fisher developed a hydraulic representation of economic equilibrium in the late nineteenth century. For economists, models have become a crucial way not only to describe economic phenomena but to test their theories and understand relationships of causality. For economists, the process of building and refining models is often equivalent to the lab experiments performed by natural scientists. As Dani Rodrik, a noted contemporary economist, puts the matter, "If you wish to grievously wound an economist, say simply, 'You don't have a model.'"[43]

Both Samuelson and Solow had trained under Leontief, but neither were attracted to the modeling approach of his input–output tables. In particular, they found his insistence on empirical data to be overly restrictive. The problem, in their minds, was that Leontief's approach assumed a constant ratio between capital and labor. If making one ton of iron would require ten units of labor and twenty units of capital, then making two tons would require twenty units of labor and forty units of capital; if you had fifteen units of labor and sixty units of capital, you could still only produce 1.5 tons of iron because the capital could not offset the labor constraint. He assumed, in other words, that the ratio of labor to capital was fixed. This meant to that to grasp the interconnections of the economy, you had to understand each industry by reading trade journals and talking to engineers to find the exact ratios.

While Samuelson and Solow agreed this might be true in the short term (a year or two), it did not seem to capture how industries might change over time. In the medium run of two to five years, the situation was much more fluid. In response to market conditions and technological advances, companies could choose to invest in new machines and labor practices that would shift the ratios. If labor got more expensive, companies could replace it with machines, and vice versa. The amount of labor and capital required to make a

DEPENSES PRODUCTIVES.	DEPENSES DU REVENU, l'Impôt prélevé, se partagent aux Dépenses productives & aux Dépenses stériles.	DEPENSES STERILES.
Avances annuelles.	*Revenu.*	*Avances annuelles.*
tt	*tt*	*tt*
600 produisent	600	300

Productions.   *Ouvrages,&c.*

tt	*tt*	*tt*
300 reproduisent net	300	300
150 reproduisent net	150	150
75 reproduisent net	75	75
37..10 reproduisent net	37..10	37..10
18..15 reproduisent net	18..15	18..15
9...7..6 reproduisent net	9...7..6	9...7...6
4..13...9 reproduisent net	4..13...9	4..13...9
2...6..10 reproduisent net	2...6.10	2...6..10
1...3...5 reproduisent net	1...3...5	1...3...5
0..11...8 reproduisent net	0..11...8	0..11...8
0...5..10 reproduisent net	0...5..10	0...5..10
0...2..11 reproduisent net	0...2..11	0...2..11
0...1...5 reproduisent net	0...1...5	0...1...5

One of the first economic models, the *Tableau Économique* (1759) demonstrated the productive capacity of agriculture compared to the sterile domain of industry and reflected the French Physiocrats' belief in "the rule of nature." MIT's models also sought a schematic and lightweight representation of the economy, but they rarely included the natural world. Bibliothèque nationale de France via Wikimedia Commons.

ton of steel in 1940 might be very different in 1945 and certainly in 1950. And with his mathematical skills plus military funding, Samuelson could prove it. Collaborating with Tjalling Koopmans in 1951, Samuelson demonstrated that, if there was a perfectly competitive market, changes in the ratio of capital and labor inputs would have no effect on prices. It was no coincidence that he presented his finding at a workshop hosted by RAND, the military-funded think tank, as it illustrated the links at the time between defense spending and economic theory.[44]

For economists, this was a powerful simplification. Rather than engaging extensively with engineers and industrial managers, economists could take the data they needed from price levels and ignore what lay behind it. Relying on aggregated price levels opened up a new world of models that could analyze the economy with a limited number of variables. Collaborating with Samuelson, Solow quickly demonstrated his aptitude for developing such models.[45] The stage was set for Solow to revolutionize the theory of growth.

Building the Kingdom

It was not surprising that a young and ambitious economist would turn his attention to growth in the 1950s. The topic was "in the air," as he later recalled, and of public concern.[46] Moreover, it was a topic of significant interest at MIT, where the modernization theorist Walt Rostow and the development economist Paul Rosenstein-Rodan were writing about it as well.

But for all its pervasiveness, especially in East Cambridge, Solow was not impressed by what had been written on the subject. To the extent there was a theory of growth at the time, it was the Harrod–Domar model. A synthesis of independent work by the English economist Roy Harrod in 1939 and the Russian American economist Evsey Domar in 1946, the model sought to explain growth through calculating the contributions of capital and the savings rate.[47] For both, the question of growth mattered because of employment.

Seeking to build on the work of Keynes, they argued that full employment required constant growth to accommodate an expanding population. It was somewhat unexpected that their analyses became seen as a theory of growth. Moses Abramovitz didn't even discuss their articles in his survey of growth in 1952, arguing in a footnote that "these theories, though often referred to as theories of growth, are, properly speaking, theories of the requirements of steady growth at full employment."[48] But with growth such an important topic and little else published on the subject, the Harrod–Domar model became the basis of a great deal of work, with one distinguished economist in the 1950s calling it "the most over-worked tool in economics."[49]

Like others, Solow experimented with the Harrod–Domar model, but he was unsatisfied with it. In 1956, he published one of the most famous papers in the field: "A Contribution to the Theory of Economic Growth."[50] He opened by acknowledging that "all theory depends on simplifications which are not quite true," but the key was to ensure those simplifications did not distort the final results.[51] The Harrod–Domar model failed this test because it contained one "dubious" assumption that gave it an unrealistic "knife-edge" property.[52] What was that assumption? It had come from his old mentor. Harrod and Domar drew on Leontief's assertion that "production takes place under conditions of *fixed proportions*."[53] Just as Solow objected to this in the context of input–output tables, he found it insufficient for a theory of growth. Asserting that growth required fixed proportions of capital, savings, and labor implied that the growth process was extremely fragile. If the rate of capital, savings, and labor did not proceed at exactly the same pace, the model implied the economy would veer toward inflation or stagnation. Only a very narrow path generated a desirable steady state—a path as thin as a knife-edge. This struck Solow as incompatible with the real world, which demonstrated that growth could be achieved at different times and places with very different ratios of capital, labor, and savings.

Eliminate fixed proportions, Solow argued, and you got a much

Robert Solow, pictured at his desk in 1973, made pioneering contributions to economic growth theory through foundational articles and mentoring a generation of students who built on and extended his ideas. Courtesy MIT Museum.

more robust model of growth. Like Harrod and Domar, Solow's model assumed that output was a function of capital and labor. But what was the relationship and how would it be calculated? Harrod and Domar had drawn on a production function developed by Leontief, but Solow favored the more flexible Cobb–Douglas production function. This switch—to the outsider a technical and arcane substitution—helped launch modern growth theory.

A production function is a technique for deciding the optimal method of producing goods given the costs of their inputs, which are typically taken to be labor and capital. Suppose a car manufacturer is deciding how many vehicles to produce. A production function can help determine whether it is more efficient to hire more workers (labor), invest in newer manufacturing equipment to increase output (capital), or do neither because the additional costs will exceed the anticipated additional revenues. But not all production functions are the same. Some analyze a single sector of the economy; some aggregate across all of them. Some calculate two inputs; others include a greater number. Some assume diminishing marginal returns; others do not. Some allow substitution between the factors; others assume production will take place in fixed proportions. Devils lurk in the details.

The Cobb–Douglas production function was developed during the 1920s by the mathematician Charles Cobb and the economist Paul Douglas as they sought to calculate the contributions of labor and capital to the American economy. Like Wesley Mitchell at NBER, social justice questions lay at the heart of their work. Was output increasing because workers were working harder and smarter, or was it because capitalists made fortuitous investments in new machines that raised productivity? Did capitalists force workers into low wages, or were the demands of workers so extreme they made profits too hard to obtain? Like Mitchell, Cobb and Douglas hoped to move the debate from fiery rhetoric to clear facts. Their analysis found that labor seemed to be getting its due share over time, though they cautioned that this finding should not "lend an ethical justification to the existing social and economic order."[54] Capital in public hands could be as effective as capital in private hands, so the results could be squared with "socialism, communism, or individualism."[55] This last conclusion reflected Douglas's reformist mentality, an impulse that later led him to be the only former president of the AEA to leave his faculty position to become a United States senator, where he served Illinois for three terms as a liberal politician with a fiscally conservative outlook.[56]

Using the Cobb–Douglas production function, Solow demonstrated that you could model growth without knife-edge properties. The introduction of variable proportions meant that "the system can adjust to any given rate of growth of the labor force, and eventually approach a state of steady proportional expansion." The brittleness of the Harrod–Domar model had been replaced by something much more robust. Growth could be achieved in a variety of ways, a sensible finding given that dozens of countries were expanding their economies with different industries, levels of technological development, and labor markets. In addition, Solow's model revealed an unexpected finding: the rate of growth appeared independent of the savings rate. Saving more might induce a one-time jump in productivity, but it could not generate a sustained improvement in the rate of growth. This suggested that policies to enhance growth needed to focus on other factors.[57]

The fact that growth seemed like it should be the norm rather than an exception reflected how much the world had changed between 1939 and 1956. Writing in 1939, Harrod had witnessed a decade of global depression with little sign that growth was to return; even in 1946, when Domar penned his article, growth was uncertain. So if their model had a knife-edge characteristic (something Domar conceded but Harrod did not), that idea did not necessarily seem inconsistent with the world.[58] But by 1956, after a decade of booming growth, the 1930s appeared more of an exception rather than a norm. Growth appeared robust, and a model of it could be expected to show many paths to maintain it.

Solow's model quickly spread through the economics profession. The Australian economist Trevor Swan published an article later in 1956 that independently arrived at many of the same conclusions.[59] This has led many, including Solow, to argue that the growth model should be called the Solow–Swan model.[60] Yet few today remember Swan's contributions. This is largely because the center of economics in the postwar period shifted from Europe to America, while Swan only published in Australian journals, limiting the reach of his work. Solow also had the ability to write accessibly about his topics, and he trained a generation of graduate students who continued the work on growth theory.[61]

Solow further cemented the uptake of his ideas in 1957 with a companion article, "Technical Change and the Aggregate Production

Function."[62] Much more empirical than his 1956 growth model, it sought to use data on the American economy from 1909 to 1949 to determine the sources of growth. The results included a surprising finding: changes in capital or labor explained very little of the growth process. Instead, growth resulted from a factor outside the model, which Solow labeled "technical change." Others would call it total factor productivity or simply the Solow residual. Regardless of its name, Solow calculated that 87.5 percent of America's growth during the preceding four decades came from technical change, with capital responsible for the remaining eighth.[63]

It might appear this was a disastrous result for Solow's own growth model. He plugged capital and labor into his production functions, but technical change was external to his model— "exogenous" in the language of economics. How could a finding that only one-eighth of the phenomenon the model sought to understand cement its importance rather than diminishing it? His findings mattered because first, it showed that the use of production functions seemed to show a good fit with the actual performance of the economy. Solow liked the ease of the Cobb–Douglas production function, but noted that several others gave comparable results. And second, it told people where to look to understand growth, and just as importantly, where not to look.[64]

Taken together, Solow's articles embodied his approach to modeling, an approach that came to be seen as characteristic of MIT economics more generally: a concise and simple model that could be easily manipulated to provide insight into fundamental dynamics of the economy. Referencing his military experience, Solow likened them to reconnaissance exercises. If you didn't know what a terrain looked like, you could send a few fleet-footed scouts to get a general lay of the land. It would not be detailed enough to develop an entire battle plan, but it could let you know what you needed to know more about. And in particular, it could help you strategically focus on carefully mapping the parts of terrain that were most important to you, rather than wasting effort trying to create a map of lands you were not going to travel over.[65]

Like all maps, Solow's left things out. A map that included every detail of the world would be as big as the world, after all, and of no use. In sketching the terrain of growth, Solow left behind details that concerned some of his colleagues. The fierce competitions between industrialists and the creative destruction of capitalists analyzed by Joseph Schumpeter were entirely absent from his analysis.[66] So too was the knowledge of the factory foremen of how goods were made that Leontief prized. And Abramovitz's belief that the economics of growth would need to include analyses by practitioners of other social sciences had no place in Solow's imagined world.

Still, Solow's model suggested a significant recasting of the landscape, changing the focus from capital investment and the savings rate. It posited that the savings rate did not drive growth; the major driver was technical progress. To be sure, that progress would often be embodied in new machinery, so capital would be necessary, but it needed to be treated as a means and not an end. Policymakers could use multiple tools ranging from tax policy to expenditures to monetary adjustments. His model may have been a toy world, but it encouraged policymakers to think differently about the real world.[67]

Sympathetic to the needs of labor unions, Solow counseled them not to oppose technological progress. Even if the immediate effect might be the loss of a few jobs, increased growth would expand the pie and make higher wages possible.[68] Though Solow acknowledged his growth model could not guarantee policy outcomes, he considered it essential for thinking intelligently about growth, or in another of his memorable phrases, as "mental furniture."[69] It told people where to look to find what they wanted. And those who listened had the power to put those ideas into action.

"The Golden Age of Growth Theory"

Within a few years, Solow's growth theory helped launch a revolution in economics. Growth theory became one of the hottest fields in economics, attracting top graduate students, many of whom flocked to MIT, where "the sixties were the golden age of growth theory."[70] The number of articles in economics journals soared, and economics textbooks were rewritten to include growth theory.[71] The word "growth" rarely appeared in the first edition of Samuelson's textbook in 1948, but by 1964, more than eighty pages mentioned growth.[72] MIT had become "the native land of the 'growthmen'" and the intellectual proponents of "growthmanship."[73]

MIT became the recognized home of growth theory because Solow advanced his original research while serving as a prolific mentor. He oversaw nearly seventy doctoral dissertations during his career, making him the most popular adviser in the MIT economics department.[74] Solow estimated that the work of mentoring likely reduced his research productivity by about a quarter, but he considered it well worth it.[75] The economists he trained did more work on growth theory than he could have alone.

The collection of talented students drawn to growth theory was loaded with star power. There was Peter Diamond, who integrated ideas of fiscal policy and the influences of overlapping generations into growth theory. He got his PhD in 1963 and won the Nobel Prize in 2010.[76] Then there was Joseph Stiglitz, who received his PhD in 1967, the John Bates Clark Medal in 1979, and the Nobel Prize in 2001 after serving as chair of the CEA and chief economist of the World Bank. They were joined by a group of extremely talented students including William Nordhaus (Nobel Prize in 2018), Martin Weitzman, Eytan Sheshinski, Edwin Burmeister, A. Rodney Dobell, and Avinash Dixit, who also made important contributions to growth theory. Sheshinski later recalled the excitement of those heady days, gushing, "We felt we were in touch with the secrets of the universe."[77]

The growth bug spread beyond MIT, attracting many top scholars. Hirofumi Uzawa, a distinguished Japanese economist who taught at Stanford and University of Chicago, expanded Solow's one-sector model into a two-sector model of growth in 1961.[78] Kenneth Arrow, who trained under Harold Hotelling and rivaled

Samuelson as the most influential economist of the twentieth century, published a 1962 article on "learning by doing" that sought to explain how technical change generated growth.[79] Tjalling Koopmans added insights on the maximal growth rate drawing on the work of mathematician John von Neumann in 1964, and economist James Tobin of Yale University integrated monetary policy into the neoclassical growth model in 1965.[80] David Cass, Karl Shell, and dozens of other promising scholars joined the fray as well. The topic was so exciting that the prestigious *Economic Journal* allocated more than a hundred pages in 1964 to a review of the latest developments in the field.[81]

Of equal importance, this was a golden time for growth theory in the public sphere. The Kennedy and Johnson administrations made growth a foundational priority, and Solow was there to spread his ideas, serving as the top adviser to the CEA in 1962. That year, he wrote the chapter on optimal growth in the CEA report, which helped justify tax cuts in 1964. Combining Keynesian concepts with growth theory, these were the first tax cuts directly intended to stimulate the economy.[82]

By the 1960s, politicians sought growth, business groups like the Chamber of Commerce touted prosperity as the defining feature of American greatness, journalists wrote breathlessly about the accomplishments of the United States' economy, and many even began to devise new curriculum for K–12 students that would teach them economic fundamentals.[83] Some of these efforts reflected the ideological debates emerging in the Cold War between capitalism and communism, with conservatives touting the benefits of a free enterprise system. But much of it also reflected the palpable sense that a new world order was possible. American growth was appearing so strong that the abolishment of poverty seemed within reach for the first time.[84]

With a society increasingly drawn to growth, Solow knew he had gotten lucky by getting his timing just right.[85] By offering a model that fit the cutting edge of economic theory and addressed a topic of broad interest, his approach quickly rose to the forefront of the field. It was "one of those rare pieces that quite literally changed the face of economics and launched a thousand theoretical ships."[86] The Kingdom of Solovia had become a mighty realm.

"As Long as Arable Land Can Be Hacked Out of the Wilderness"

Yet within all of this attention to growth and its factors, there was a notable omission: the natural world. Bright young economists directed their energy to multi-sector models, optimal growth theory, and learning-by-doing, but gave hardly a second thought to what role natural resources played in stimulating growth or how the consequences of booming economies might influence the habitability of the planet. The amount of capital a society had to invest in new machinery might limit growth, but not terrestrial endowments.

Solow excluded the natural world from the beginning of his 1956 article. "Output is produced with the help of two factors of production, capital and labor," he wrote, thereby reducing the three classical factors of production—*land*, labor, and capital—into two.[87] He was not alone in doing this. By the 1950s, most neoclassical economists assumed land no longer required its own category.[88] In 1894, the Austrian economist Eugen von Böhm-Bawerk explicitly rejected Ricardo's focus on rent as a distinct category of analysis and argued land should be included with capital.[89] Five years later, American John Bates Clark did the same.[90] And in his 1957 article, Solow made clear that he favored this latter approach, stating that "For present purposes, 'capital' includes land, mineral deposits, etc."[91] Land, that central object of analysis for the classical political economists, the tracts of territory kings waged war to obtain, the hereditary possession that families fought to maintain, no longer had any special standing in neoclassical thought.

Solow mentioned but quickly dismissed the idea that scarce resources needed to be modeled in 1956. Production could occur with constant returns to scale, he argued, acknowledging that "this amounts to assuming there is no scarce nonaugmentable resource like land." Such an assumption, he went on to say, "seems the natural assumption to make in a theory of growth" though he did not specify why, except to note that "the scarce-land case would lead to decreasing returns to scale in capital and labor and the model would become Ricardian."[92] He opined in a footnote that "one can imagine the theory as applying as long as arable land can be hacked out of the wilderness at essentially constant cost."[93] But what would happen when you could no longer do such hacking? Solow was not concerned to find out: "It would take us too far afield to go wholly classical . . . and [analyze] a fixed supply of land."[94] Capital and technological progress were the proper objects of study for growth theory, not the natural world.

The exclusion of the natural world was not forced upon him by the Cobb–Douglas production function. Cobb and Douglas had written explicitly about their interest in further integrating the environment into their calculations, ending their 1928 paper with this revealing note: "Finally, we should ultimately look forward toward including the third factor of natural resources in our equations and of seeing to what degree this modifies our conclusions."[95] But it does not appear they pursued this idea.[96]

Solow's colleagues did not have much more to say about the natural world. Uzawa's two-sector model of economic growth added complexity but maintained Solow's focus on capital and labor as the only factors of production; only several decades later would Uzawa witness the environmental costs of growth in Japan and come to lament, "As I went around to examine in detail the processes by which social and natural environments were torn apart and the degree to which ordinary people were suffering, I could not avoid the feeling that something serious was amiss in the orthodox doctrine of economy theory with which I had been working hard for so many years."[97] Arrow's learning-by-doing model ascribed growth to the increase of practical and theoretical knowledge with no interest in the natural world. Koopmans used the term "resources" in his growth analysis, but these resources were manufactured. While Diamond and Tobin expanded their models to explore the financial system, the natural system drew no attention. And the more-than-100-page review of the latest work in growth theory from 1964 included no references to natural resources and less than five citations to land as a factor of production.[98]

There were two minor exceptions to this pattern, though even they seem to reinforce it. First, Trevor Swan, who independently came to a similar model of growth as Solow did in 1956, considered the ideas of the classical thinkers explicitly. While Solow wrote that he was being "as neoclassical as possible," Swan's article included several references to Smith, Ricardo, Mill, and Malthus.[99] After introducing a model of growth with just capital and labor, he added a case with "the limited powers of the soil" that had concerned the classical economists. In the absence of technical progress, Swan noted, growth would eventually become impossible. Technical progress, however, could offset shortages of land. And if the growth rate of the population was influenced by each generation desiring the next generation to have a better standard of life (rather than multiplying unchecked in Malthus's vision, which Swan saw as the greatest failure of the classical worldview), then even better rates of growth could be obtained. The concerns of Ricardo and Malthus, therefore, were rejected by Swan.[100]

A similar analysis was undertaken by James Meade, an analyst of international trade in Cambridge, UK, and a future Nobel laureate. Interested in synthesizing the new ideas around growth in 1961, he published *A Neoclassical Theory of Economic Growth*, in which he sought to help students connect classical concepts of the economy with modern theories of growth.[101] Including land as a factor of production provided a link to past thinkers, but it did not fundamentally change the outcome. Meade posited that, in most cases, labor or machines could be substituted for land, and like Swan, he highlighted the role of technical progress. Even if land was fixed in supply and could not be substituted, he argued, "growing technical knowledge would enable more to be produced by the same amount of factors."[102]

Even in the rare cases where land was included in theories of growth, then, it did not radically adjust the results. Nothing appeared to stand in the way of infinite growth.

*

Solow's success was a surprise even to himself. "I knew it was nice," he recalled, and "was having the time of my life, because I hit on something that was obviously good." But even he had no idea "that this would become a whole industry" and that many of his core insights would remain central to growth theory to the present day.[103]

The influence of Solow's papers owed much to their elegance and ability to tap into the latest developments in mathematical economics. He shared "Samuelson's way of making mathematics sing economics" in a way that captured the zeitgeist.[104] But his ideas did not conquer the field overnight. Several other economists had been giving growth their attention as well. They disagreed with him on many points, but their work also reveals that even those who disagreed with Solow's neoclassical model of growth did not think the problem was that he had excluded the natural world from it.

4 * Growth Without Nature

The year 1963 has been remembered for many things. In the United States, the civil rights movement pressed the fight for racial justice, punctuated by Martin Luther King Jr.'s "I Have a Dream" speech during the March on Washington. It was a year of violence, with the killing of civil rights activist Medgar Evers, the deployment of thousands of troops to Vietnam, and the assassination of President John F. Kennedy. There were uplifting headlines as well. The United States, United Kingdom, and Soviet Union agreed to a partial nuclear test ban treaty, the cosmonaut Valentina Tereshkova became the first woman to travel in space, and a new polio vaccine was released. Beatlemania spread across western Europe and America, ushering in a new age of music.

Though it finds no mention in history textbooks, 1963 also marked a milestone in the invention of infinite growth. For by this year, a broad consensus had emerged among economists that the natural world presented no meaningful constraint to economic expansion. The idea of growth without limits had become widely accepted.

The journey from the discovery of growth in the 1940s to agreement about its infinite potential happened rapidly. It was shaped by a hunger for growth across the world: the Cold War battle between the United States and Soviet Union for economic supremacy; industrialized nations competing with one another for prestige measured in growth rates; and newly decolonized countries in Africa and Asia seeking better lives for their populations. Resource abundance during the 1950s and 1960s fueled visions of growth without limit, particularly Middle East petroleum. Production in the region doubled from 1950 to 1960 while the discovery of new reserves tripled, and the price of oil decreased by 25 percent adjusted for inflation between 1948 and 1973.[1] Nor was this just a story of petroleum. The opening of many decolonized nations to international trade saw a boom in resource production in many sectors that often outpaced the growth in demand. The fact that the supply of many resources kept increasing burnished optimism that the feast would not run out.

Among economists, the allure of infinite growth extended well beyond the Kingdom of Solovia. Growth was a pervasive topic, and economic discussions of it ranged far beyond Solow's model. Four other groups of economists turned their attention to growth during the 1950s and 1960s: competing growth theorists, development economists, growth accountants, and the researchers of Resources for the Future (RFF). These economists disagreed about much. They disagreed about methodology and what counted as theory. They disagreed about the validity of key assumptions. They disagreed about the utility of modeling. They even disagreed about who counted as a true economist. But there were two points they could agree on: growth was good, and the natural world did not represent a meaningful constraint. It was not just Solovia that was unmoored from terra firma; it was the entire edifice of postwar growth economics.

"Beyond the Confines of the Earth"

Solow's use of neoclassical production functions to model the growth process found particular favor among a new generation of thinkers committed to theory and mathematization, a trend that was particularly powerful in America in the postwar period.[2] But not everyone agreed this was the right approach. Consider Simon Kuznets, who continued to work on questions of growth after laying the foundations for GNP calculations. For Kuznets, the key to understanding growth lay in international comparison. Doing so was essential, he argued, because similarities between countries' final growth rates often concealed huge underlying differences. Countries varied in the extent to which their growth was based on manufacturing versus services, in the relationships between businesses and the government, in the power of trade unions, in the rate of population change, and in cultural attitudes toward work. This variability meant a one-size-fits-all model would mask more than it would reveal. The work of the growth theorist was to assemble data to compare different trajectories and identify meaningful convergences and patterns.[3]

More focused on empirical data and international comparisons than most other growth analysts, Kuznets was, if anything, even less concerned about the natural world. He repeatedly dismissed any notion of limits to growth, seeing never-ending expansion as possible and desirable. "Difficult as it is to imagine unlimited growth in any social process, there are no inherently compelling reasons for the rate of growth of per capita product to decline," he argued in 1959.[4] Acknowledging elsewhere that infinite growth "would seem, on the face of it, an absurdity," he pointed to the power of "the continuous play of the free mind" to develop new ideas and technologies.[5] And should Earth's dowry be tapped, there was always the "vastness of the observable universe." "In these days of interplanetary travel discussions," he opined, "we cannot dismiss the possibility of extending processes of economic production beyond the confines of the earth."[6] The classical economists saw limits because they were too blind to the possibilities of technological change, and he advised reading Jules Verne and H. G. Wells rather than Malthus when thinking about the future.[7] Technology, ingenuity, and ultimately an escape from the planet made infinite growth a possibility for Kuznets.

Colin Clark, Kuznets's British collaborator in the development of national accounting methods, also continued to work on growth topics after helping pioneer GNP. Like Kuznets, Clark saw little reason to worry about limits to growth. A committed Catholic opposed to contraception, he argued against Malthusian concerns by emphasizing that human ingenuity could feed growing populations.[8]

The heart of British economics lay at the University of Cambridge, home to the two most influential Anglo-American economists of the early twentieth century: Alfred Marshall and John Maynard Keynes. During the 1950s, two leading Cambridge economists—Joan Robinson and Nicholas Kaldor—developed growth theories that were alternative models to the neoclassical approach. This caused them to disagree with Solow on many fronts, in ways that will be explored more thoroughly in the next chapter. What matters here is that, even though they offered different ideas about how to calculate growth, they also excluded the natural world.[9]

Joan Robinson was the most famous female economist of the mid-twentieth century. With a smile that her allies found warm but her opponents considered wicked, her denial of a Nobel Prize in spite of her many accomplishments offers strong evidence of the gender discrimination that has been rife in the economics profession. Quick-witted and piercing with the pen, Robinson was deeply skeptical of neoclassical economics and interested in Marxism. While Solow was developing his neoclassical model, she was designing one that emphasized the contributions of workers.[10]

In 1956, Robinson published a major work on capital that also dealt with growth. Working in the classical tradition, Robinson included land as a factor of production, but it was the dynamics between capital and labor that captured her imagination. If capital and labor grew in tandem, it could lead to a golden age of growth with full employment and sustained capital accumulation. But a golden age could also be "limping" if growth in the labor force exceeded capital accumulation, or a "bastard" golden age could result if factors such as inflation limited the expansion of capital and led to high unemployment and low growth. Alternatively, there could be platinum ages of growth—bastard, creeping, or galloping—each of which resulted from a different mix of capital accumulation and labor growth. Her discussions of land were largely limited to one section of her book on the law of diminishing marginal returns, and she did not theorize that it would limit growth.[11] In a more concise sketch of her theory of growth in 1964, she acknowledged that "there is a sort of hubris in setting up a model in which all output is produced by human labor with the aid of man-made equipment, forgetting the kindly fruits of the earth." But her model never factored in such considerations, simply mentioning the topic as an example "of the complications that must be introduced into the model, without attempting to develop them."[12]

In 1957, her colleague Nicholas Kaldor was setting out his own model of growth. Building on classical approaches like Robinson and Keynes, he began with a set of facts that he believed any growth theory would have to explain. These included such statistical regularities as the fact that output and labor productivity appear to grow in tandem and that the capital output ratio was steady in advanced capitalist societies over time. Yet Kaldor argued that no existing theory of growth could explain these features because the main factors driving growth—capital investment, technical progress, and population growth—were too often treated as independent variables. Kaldor's model attempted to set out the interrelationships between these categories, a project that required adding an investment function that tracked the conditions under which entrepreneurs would invest profits in new enterprises and a reintegration of ideas about population growth from the classical economists.[13]

Yet in revitalizing the ideas of the classical thinkers and rejecting "the theories which start off with the Cobb–Douglas type of production functions," Kaldor did not give greater heed to the natural world than other growth theorists.[14] He mentioned the possible existence of diminishing marginal returns to land, but relegated the discussion to footnotes and did not follow up on it.[15] In 1961, he stated that he was following Ricardo except his arguments about the limits of the natural world. In fact, the first assumption of his model was that the "natural environment does not impose any limitation to expansion."[16] So while Kaldor sought to restore some of the wisdom of the classical political economists, it was not their recognition of limits.

Solow was not out of step with his colleagues in his disregard for the natural world. Even theorists rejecting neoclassicism or starting with different premises ended up in a similar place: a theory that had little role for nature.

Development Economics

If one had to pick a place where economists could be expected to take seriously the natural world and its role in growth, a good bet would be development economics. Emerging shortly after World War II, this branch of economic thought turned its attention to the world's nonindustrialized countries in an effort to help them build their economies. As it focused on countries in which the majority of the populations were engaged in agriculture and many industrial development opportunities involved the extraction of natural resources, it is easy to imagine that development economists would pay close attention to the natural world and its potential limits. By and large, they did not. The six founding figures of development economics—Paul Rosenstein-Rodan, Hans Singer, Ragnar Nurkse, Arthur Lewis, Gunnar Myrdal, and Albert Hirschman— gave little attention to the topic in the 1940s and 1950s, nor did their successors.[17]

As far back as the beginning of the Industrial Revolution and the development of classical political economy, there has been interest in how to achieve growth for undeveloped nations. Yet a new stage of thinking began after World War II in response to changes in economic theory, the Cold War, and the breakup of colonial empires. Newly independent nations looked to economic growth as a pathway to autonomy. Not surprisingly, economists were willing to offer their services to those willing to listen. And thanks to the Cold War, their voices were amplified by Western governments eager to demonstrate the superiority of capitalism over socialism. Economists soon had access to powerful patrons.[18]

In addition to studying parts of the world where agriculture and mining were major preoccupations, development economists were also distinguished from other growth thinkers because they largely eschewed neoclassical assumptions. There was already a heady debate in America and Europe about whether it made sense to talk about *homo economicus*—the completely rational actor with perfect foresight. But in developing nations, such an idea fell flat on its face. Markets were fragmentary, capital did not flow smoothly, property rights were not always trustworthy, and an overabundance of workers meant wages were determined more by the level of subsistence than by labor's marginal contribution to profits. Because Solow had been "deliberately as neoclassical as you can get" in his 1956 article, he acknowledged his model was limited to advanced industrial countries.[19] As a result, Albert Hirschman argued in 1958 that "the economics of development dare not therefore borrow too extensively from the economics of growth." He declared: "Like the underdeveloped countries themselves, it must learn to walk on its own feet, which means that it must work out its own abstractions."[20] Gunnar Myrdal was perhaps the most ardent critique of received theory, arguing that it reflected the "dominant interests in the industrial countries" and failed to acknowledge its lack of realism.[21] And W. Arthur Lewis argued the task of development economics was "to bring [the classical framework] up-to-date . . . to help us understand the contemporary problems of large areas of the earth."[22] Development economists were much more likely to cite classical economists such as Smith, Ricardo, and Marx; when discussing modern thinkers, Schumpeter and Keynes loomed much larger than Samuelson or Solow.

Yet the feet that development economics walked on did not make much contact with the earth, even though most of the people they studied did. Though agriculture was the most common occupation in their regions of study, most development economists saw farming as an impediment to growth. Growing crops without mechanization represented an early stage of development that needed to be overcome to obtain economic success. Paul Rosenstein-Rodan made this point in a foundational 1943 article.[23] Studying the poverty and lack of industrialization in eastern and southeastern Europe, he argued there were simply too many farmers—an "agrarian excess population" of more than twenty million people who were not generating growth.[24] To raise the standard of living required "transforming Eastern European peasants into full-time or part-time industrial workers."[25] Creating industrial jobs, of course, required capital, and Rosenstein-Rodan advocated that a "big push" of investment from wealthier regions could shift peasants off farms and into wage labor, thereby initiating a self-reinforcing cycle of growth.

Following Rosenstein-Rodan, capital investment became the dominant focus of development economists. As Lewis put it, "the central fact of economic development is rapid capital accumulation."[26] But how much? How should it be invested? Should it, as Ragnar Nurkse believed, aim at balanced growth that built up several sectors of the economy at once?[27] Or was balanced growth impossible, as Albert Hirschman argued, with a more realistic strategy focusing on a big push in a few industries that would pull the rest of the economy along?[28] Either way, the key question was how to get people off farms and into factories, which meant largely ignoring the regular interactions with the natural world that characterized life for most people in the developing world.

Development economists also downplayed the environment because the presence or absence of natural resources did not appear to directly correlate with rates of growth. Eastern and southeastern Europe had suitable natural resources for development yet remained poor, Rosenstein-Rodan noted.[29] Lewis agreed, arguing that the proper focus of analysis was human behavior, because even if natural resources were necessary for growth, they were not sufficient. A

Construction on the Volta Dam in Ghana, 1962. St. Lucian–born development economist Arthur Lewis was a chief economic adviser for Ghana after it obtained its independence in 1957. One of the nation's major development projects was a large dam on the Volta River intended to supply power for industrial develop-ment. Such development projects often depended on natural resources such as rivers, yet development economists rarely made the natural world a focal point of their studies. NSAG (Nederlands studenten Afrika Gezelschap), CC BY-SA 4.0, https://creativecommons.org/licenses/by-sa/4.0, via Wikimedia Commons.

theory of growth, he wrote, "concerns itself with natural resources only insofar as they affect human behavior. . . . There are great differ-ences in development between countries which seem to have roughly equal resources, so it is necessary to enquire into the differences in human behavior which influence economic growth."[30] Hirschman concurred, stating that "experience demonstrated conclusively that . . . countries poorly endowed with natural resources can achieve high levels of per capita output and income."[31] And for Nurkse, the problem was not the presence or absence of natural resources, it was a question of whether there was sufficient capital to develop them.[32] In a world with international trade and foreign aid, it was assumed resources could always be obtained with sufficient capital.

Hans Singer took this even further, arguing that the development of natural resources in developing regions could be counterproductive. When foreign capitalists invested in the extraction of raw materials, they rarely transferred technology or knowledge to local populations. As a result, these industries did not stimulate the creation of new enterprises. They were, as he noted, "really an outpost of the economies of the more developing investing countries."[33] Of equal or greater importance, however, were the terms of trade. The prices of food and raw materials compared to manufactured goods had been declining for nearly a century. Since the developing nations mostly generated food and raw materials while importing manufactured goods, it meant that the rich nations were progressively benefiting more from international trade than developing nations. As a result, resources had historically been a poor avenue to growth. As consumers of raw materials and producers of manufactured goods, "the industrialized countries have had the best of both worlds . . . whereas the underdeveloped countries had the worst of both worlds," he concluded.[34] It was enough to give credence to "the widespread though inarticulate feeling in the underdeveloped countries that the dice have been loaded against them" and to cast serious doubt on "the pure theory of exchange."[35]

By relegating agriculture to an earlier stage of development, emphasizing capital investment, and arguing that growth did not require resource endowments, the pioneering thinkers in development economics set a pattern of ignoring the natural world that continued for decades. When Nicholas Stern reviewed the history of development economics in 1989, the first omission of the field he cited was the lack of work on "natural resources and the environment."[36] Two decades later, Partha Dasgupta noted little had changed. While he could point to several works on the agricultural sector, "*ecological* capital has been absent from the formal models mainstream development economists have used to discuss policy. It is absent too from influential surveys and texts on the economics of development."[37] He argued this was "puzzling," given that for most poor people, what are now called ecosystems services matter greatly, as they depend on local sources for drinking water, forage opportunities from common lands, flood protection from wetland ecosystems, and more.[38] "Official development economics reflects the rest of our discipline," Dasgupta noted, "in that it too neglects nature's place in economic development."[39] Terms of trade, capital formation, labor rates, and government policy all drew much more attention than natural resources or the environment.

A similar story can be told of modernization theory. MIT was a critical player in this endeavor, establishing the Center for International Studies in 1951. Headed by economist Max Millikan with Cold War funding explicitly designed to push American economic interests overseas, the center believed development required multiple disciplinary perspectives: economists, of course, but also sociologists, anthropologists, psychologists, political scientists, and historians. In 1953, Rosenstein-Rodan came to MIT along with Walt Rostow, who in 1960 would write one of the most widely read treatises on growth: *The Stages of Growth: A Non-Communist Manifesto*.[40] Like the development economists, he focused on capital accumulation and had little to say about the natural world. In addition, Millikan worked to bring in anthropologist Clifford Geertz, sociologist Daniel Lerner, and others. Published works associated with the center tended to involve minimal mathematics and had a notably interdisciplinary style that was in stark contrast to the formal mathematical models of Solow and Samuelson in the economics department.[41]

The result was a bifurcation in growth thinking. By 1955, a year before Solow's model was published, MIT had established development economics as a doctoral field of study.[42] Solow and Rostow knew each other, but their worldviews did not overlap greatly, and they moved in different circles.[43] They were, in many ways, ships passing in the night. Perhaps the most revealing comment came from Paul Samuelson, who after hearing a talk by Rostow that he considered theoretically lacking, remarked, "Walt, you may be an economist among historians, but you are a historian when you are among economists."[44] This was a damning critique from the nation's most prestigious economist. As a public intellectual, Rostow was known as an economist; for the new generation of mathematical modelers, his analysis was sloppy and unsatisfying. For Samuelson, the critique held for all of development economics, which he considered to be voluminous, repetitive, and underwhelming.[45]

MIT was exceptional in having leading figures in economic growth theory (Solow), development economics (Rosenstein-Rodan), and modernization theory (Rostow). But the findings regarding growth and the environment were typical. Even though these figures rarely saw eye to eye and thought different tools and approaches were appropriate to studying growth, they held one thing in common: the natural world could be ignored.

The Measure of Our Ignorance

Moses Abramovitz called it the "measure of our ignorance"; others bemoaned treating it like "manna from heaven."[46] Any way you looked at it, the Solow residual was a problem. His determination that the vast majority of American growth had come from factors beyond capital and labor—what he called technical progress—left a great deal to be explained. Though the finding provided ample evidence that capital accumulation by itself would not generate a takeoff, it did not say much of anything about what actually did generate growth. If Solow's model was, as he liked to say, a reconnaissance mission undertaken by a few scouts to get a rough lay of the land, the more detailed work of comprehensively surveying the terrain remained to be undertaken. Growth accountants sought to fill the void.[47]

Growth accounting was a synthesis of work on national accounts and growth theory that kicked off in the late 1950s. Its main task involved parsing the ambiguous category of technical progress into discrete factors that could be quantified and acted upon. Compared to growth theory, it was a much more empirical and policy-directed set of inquiries. It also reflected the fact that governments in the United States and abroad were increasingly interested in policies to enhance growth and hiring teams of economists to advise them.

Given the more empirical orientation of growth accounting, one might expect its practitioners to study the influence of the natural world on growth processes. By and large, they did not. Their accounting revealed a small and declining role for the natural world in the modern economy, and they therefore focused on other topics like education, embodied technological progress, and correcting datasets. For the growth accountants, the natural world was mostly a rounding error.

When Moses Abramovitz wrote his state-of-the-field essay in 1952, he argued that meaningful work on growth would have to be more empirical and messier than the toy worlds of neoclassical abstraction. "Economists," he reported in words Wesley Mitchell might have penned, "so far have preferred the easier job of discovering the necessary implications of arbitrarily chosen premises. . . . The study of economic growth will not permit them to indulge these proclivities."[48] To actually understand growth, economists would have to collaborate with historians, geographers, psychologists, and sociologists to adequately understand economic life, even if "experience suggests that we cannot be sanguine about the strength of these allies."[49]

Four years later, Abramovitz returned to the topic to study the growth of the American economy since 1870. Published a year before the discovery of the Solow residual, Abramovitz's essay came to a similar conclusion. Neither capital nor labor explained much of the growth of the American economy over the previous nine decades: "Almost the entire increase in net product per capita is associated with the rise in productivity."[50] This finding, he argued, might be "sobering, if not discouraging, to students of economic growth."[51] But it was essential to "pose this problem as clearly as possible" since pinpointing the causes of changes in productivity "will, no doubt, remain the central problem in both the history and theory of economic growth."[52]

Abramovitz did not offer an answer for this "central problem" though he did note that standard measures of capital investment likely overstated the extent of technical progress by excluding things like education and health care from the analysis. Even income spent on clothing and recreation, he argued, could perhaps be seen as partial inputs to production "since in a thoroughly commercializing economy . . . very few expenditures are wholly without the aim and effect of increasing income."[53] Moreover, he cited the potential advantages of the natural world when he noted that increasing returns to scale would be much more likely "when raw materials are plentiful resources."[54] But he did not follow up on this idea in a systematic manner. And even though he continued to believe that raw materials mattered to America's success, he did not provide specific evidence backing this claim.[55]

Edward Denison took the next step. He had worked since the early 1940s in the Department of Commerce calculating national income before leaving in 1956 for the Committee for Economic Development, a think tank that promoted market-based policies.[56] Denison was frustrated by the vague understandings of the actual processes of growth. It was simple for anyone to assume that their favorite factor—be it education or capital investment or scientific research—was the primary cause of growth. Yet how could there be rational policy without a more specific understanding of how much each factor mattered? He bemoaned the "meagerness of well-founded, quantitative conclusions" from economists about "either the sources of past growth or the probable effect upon future growth, and the cost, of adopting any of a wide range of possible courses of action."[57] So he decided to do something about it.

That something was the 1962 publication of *The Sources of Economic Growth and the Alternatives Before Us.* By his own admission, it was only a speculative first word. But anything was better than nothing, and he thought his central findings held up: the Solow residual could be broken into subcategories and any individual policy could only have a very limited effect on the overall growth rate. He broke down the sources of growth into a series of categories such as economies of scale, reduced waste, and advances in knowledge. He also showed that a series of policy options—ranging from increasing the average work week by an hour, adding a year and a half of schooling for each worker, or increasing private investment—might shift the growth rate, but only by at most a tenth of a percent. No single policy could be considered a magic bullet. Any realistic growth policy would have to take a portfolio approach, and it would have to have modest expectations.[58]

Given Denison's skepticism that any single policy could dramatically shift the growth rate, it should not be a surprise that he did not think the natural world had a large role to play either. He determined land was a declining factor in the American economy, decreasing from 9 percent in 1909 to 3 percent in the 1950s.[59] Moreover, more than two-thirds of the value from land came from the real estate sector in cities, not natural resources such as agriculture, timber, or fossil fuels. He also observed that the mining industries, including coal and oil, represented less than 1 percent of national income, and therefore were not a consequential factor for growth. His conclusion was that "policies followed with respect to natural resources are not likely to make much difference to the rate of economic growth."[60] He drew directly on the work of RFF, citing their faith in substitution: "the demonstrated ability of modern society to substitute one material for another" meant that scarcity need not limit growth.[61]

Five years later, Denison wrote a follow-up book that analyzed comparative growth rates between the United States and nine European nations. *Why Growth Rates Differ* offered a similar assessment of the nonimportance of the natural world to growth. Land and minerals were a negligible category compared to capital investment, advances in knowledge, and total employment. Moreover, the contributions of the environment were decreasing over time.[62] While he noted that in a world of autarchy, the availability of land and resources could be a major factor in shaping growth rates, he argued the existence of international trade meant that differential costs were not particularly significant. Therefore, he concluded that national income in the United States might be slightly higher than in the European countries due to the availability of cheap land and abundant resources, but this had no notable effect on the rate of growth.[63]

Denison's work was widely lauded as a helpful, though imperfect, step in growth accounting. Abramovitz offered healthy praise when assessing Denison's work, though he noted the conclusions were "unavoidably built on shaky foundations"[64] and that "there is a certain air of reliability and precision about his estimates which the state of our knowledge today simply does not support."[65] Or as he put it more directly, "I think the figures fall apart at almost every important point."[66] But Abramovitz or other critics did not dispute Denison's assessment of the relative unimportance of the natural world.

Just as the new guard advocating mathematical sophistication in economics thought growth theory took a major step forward when Robert Solow introduced his model, the same thing occurred in growth accounting in 1967. Dale Jorgenson and Zvi Griliches—both of whom would receive the prestigious John Bates Clark Medal for top economist under forty and go on to have long and distinguished careers—argued that growth accounting had failed to adequately track inputs because it relied on errors in the theory of production.[67] Incorrect theory had led to errors of measurement, which had caused growth accountants to overstate the role of technical progress. Diving deep into the data, they claimed that errors in aggregation, in the calculation of prices of investment goods, in relative utilization of capital equipment, and the like, skewed the results. Rather than technical progress explaining the majority of growth, the vast majority of growth could be traced to capital and labor inputs. The measure of our ignorance, they essentially stated, largely disappeared when you took ignorance out of the measurement.

Jorgenson and Griliches were to growth accounting what Solow was to growth theory. Comparing their work to Abramovitz and Denison is much like placing Solow's research next to Wesley Mitchell and Simon Kuznets. They were asking similar questions, but playing a different game. The work of Abramovitz and Denison could largely be understood by a layperson comfortable with tables of data;

Jorgenson and Griliches's work relied on advanced mathematics. Befitting the higher prestige of quantitative and theoretical work over qualitative analysis, it is little surprise that Jorgenson and Griliches's approach won out. Their ideas were soon integrated into national accounting systems around the world, including statistical organizations in the United States government, the European Union, and the Organisation for Economic Co-operation and Development.[68]

Jorgenson and Griliches included land as a subcategory of capital, though they did not highlight it as a significant factor or one that might be subject to limits. After the oil crisis in 1973, Jorgenson began to integrate energy more directly, though he never expressed concern about scarcity. Instead, he was interested in calculating how much the cost of energy might affect growth. If energy was cheap, he reasoned, companies would have more money to invest in capital improvements that would enhance their growth rate; if energy was expensive, they would have less capital, and growth would decrease. He found that the typically cheap cost of energy from 1950 to 1973 helped drive the era's impressive growth rates while as much as two-thirds of the slowdown in growth during the 1970s could be attributed to higher energy costs.[69] Natural resources affected growth, in this view, but only insofar as they constrained capital investment. Fears of scarcity did not merit attention.

The natural world, therefore, was not absent from growth accounting.[70] But it never had anything resembling pride of place. In most calculations, land was quickly subsumed into the broader category of capital. And when energy was analyzed, it was largely to assess the effects of higher prices on capital formation. Labor and capital, not the natural world, were the accounts that mattered.

The Most Important Think Tank You've Never Heard Of

There was one place in America in the 1950s and 1960s where economists paid serious attention to the role of natural resources and economic growth: the think tank Resources for the Future. Formed with funding from the Ford Foundation after the 1952 publication of the Paley Commission Report, RFF gathered a group of economists for long-term study of America's resources and how they might affect growth. Described as "the most important think tank you've never heard of," RFF would play a central role in advancing economic analysis of the natural world.[71] And its overall message was one of optimism. Nowhere was this clearer than in its 1963 publication, *Scarcity and Growth*, which argued growth could continue unabated. In fact, the authors even heralded growth as the key to overcoming scarcity, arguing that by increasing capital and technology, "the process of growth thus generates antidotes to a general increase of resource scarcity."[72]

A good deal had changed in the eleven years after the Paley Commission Report. For one, economics had taken a preeminent role in thinking about natural resources. Scientists and business executives far outpaced economists as participants in the early twentieth century conservation movement, while the Paley Commission research staff was about half economists. RFF's research team was staffed mostly by economists from the beginning. This was essential, economists Harold Barnett and Chandler Morse argued in *Scarcity and Growth*, because the pronouncements of limits by conservationists were consistently "mistaken" and "inappropriate" due to the fact that their analysis "was without comprehension, or even recognition, of the relevance of economic principles or facts."[73] Admitting that their focus on "economic doctrine . . . reflects a professional bias," they still maintained that "serious consideration of the social, and more qualitative, aspects of the natural resource problem must be secondary—that is, must follow understanding of the more quantitative economic aspects."[74] Problems that once engaged lawyers, university presidents, journalists, and others were now claimed to be first and foremost the domain of economists.

And those economists could largely be found at RFF, or collaborating with RFF economists on research grants. Many of the early and prominent names in the early history of environmental and natural resource economics worked at RFF: John Krutilla, Allen Kneese, Sam Schurr, Hans Lansberg, Marion Clawson, Harold Barnett, Chandler Morse, and more. On the whole, it was a young and active group—when the fifty-year-old Clawson was hired in 1955, he was the oldest researcher on staff besides the director, and he recalled that RFF had at least six entrants every year in the Potomac canoe races.[75] While assessing whether the nation had adequate access to natural resources to support growth drove the initial founding of RFF, the varied interests of the researchers led to work on land policy, watershed management, pollution control, and valuation of wilderness areas. In addition, RFF invited collaborations from academic economists across the nation and funded research projects on questions of natural resources. As Robert Solow told a congressional committee in 1973, much of what was known about the relationships between growth and natural resources came "through the painstaking work of . . . Resources for the Future."[76]

A second change that was clear in 1963 was that growth was no longer a protean concept that had to be justified as the Paley Commission Report had in 1952. With growth having captured the global imagination through the 1950s and a wide variety of approaches to studying it, there was no longer any need to confess that they "cannot find any absolute reason for this belief" in growth.[77] Growth was the logical aim of policy, and it was expected to continue.

These shifts meant that RFF economists had cast off much of the organization's early pessimism. And the more they looked at natural resources, the more optimistic they became about the possibilities for sustained growth. Yes, an increasing economy required more resources, but it also generated the money, minds, and technology to overcome any limits.

The year 1963 was a landmark for RFF's publications, though not in the way the organization intended. While *Scarcity and Growth* became RFF's most famous book, the leadership was most proud of *Resources in America's Future*. A hefty tome of more than a thousand pages and hundreds of charts representing years of collective research, it was known internally as "the big book."[78] Encompassing dozens of studies, hundreds of thousands of dollars of research, and no small amount of cajoling from an impatient William Paley, *Resources in America's Future* sought to determine whether the nation would have sufficient natural resources to power its economy to the year 2000.[79] The short answer was a qualified yes: "Neither a long view of the past, nor current trends, nor our most careful estimates of future possibilities suggest any general running out of resources in this country during the remainder of the century."[80] They cited the potential of tapping lower-grade stocks, substituting

Economists at Resources for the Future downplayed concerns about resource scarcity because they believed that international markets could compensate for any shortages in American production. The enormous oil reserves discovered in the Middle East in the decades around World War II, illustrated by a large oil refinery in Iran in the 1950s, seemed to demonstrate that international trade could overcome local scarcity. Nevit Dilmen, via Wikimedia Commons.

abundant resources for scarce ones, importing minerals, and wise use as a "sufficient guarantee against across-the-board shortage."[81] But they did acknowledge uncertainty and the possibility of acute shortages in particular regions and around particular resources, which they thought justified their ongoing research agenda. Major wars, interruptions of international trade, disinvestments in scientific research, and wasteful consumption could all undercut future growth. "By looking ahead systematically," they hoped to "encourage more intelligent and far-sighted responses, primarily better public policies and better private management of the nation's resources."[82]

While *Resources in America's Future* was the centerpiece of the organization's outreach campaign, *Scarcity and Growth* came to have the greater impact.[83] In less than a third of the space of the "big book," Barnett and Morse took direct aim at the idea that finite natural resources would limit growth. Surveying contemporary theories and the history of the conservation movement, they disagreed with the concerns espoused by Malthus's heirs, finding notions of limits "neither self-evident nor easy to formulate in meaningful terms."[84] The basis of their disagreement was both empirical and theoretical. Empirically, the work drew on the research behind *Resources in America's Future*. They argued that the United States from the 1870s to 1950s should offer an ideal test case of whether resource scarcity was increasing, because the nation had experienced enormous growth at the same time the geographical frontiers of the country had been filling in. But surveying a very large number of extractive industries, they found that the price data in nearly all cases showed that it was getting cheaper and cheaper over time to extract necessary materials such as coal, oil, iron, and copper. Lumber products were one of the only exceptions to show increasing costs over time, along with lead, zinc, and bauxite. If decades of wasteful production decried by conservationists had not resulted in these materials getting more expensive, then the idea of a looming shortage seemed unsupported.[85]

Theoretically, Barnett and Morse rejected the focus of most thinkers on diminishing marginal returns, arguing that decades of economic expansion demonstrated that it was not applicable. They lamented the lack of attention to technical progress and substitution as ways to overcome shortages, and they pointed to the power of price signals and international trade to develop new resources. "A society would have to be both primitive and largely isolated," they concluded, "if it is to be persistently subject to Malthusian scarcity."[86] In writing about the potential of technological progress, they dreamed of visions "when power is available in unlimited quantities" and other "potentialities yet undreamed of."[87] Citing the ability of heavy industry and chemical engineering to manipulate atoms, refine ores of low quality, and transform substances from one form to another, they opined that technology was "automatic and self-reproductive in modern economies" and that it delivered "increasing returns" rather than the diminishing ones theorized by the classical economists.[88] Due to this faith in technology, present generations had little reason to hoard natural resources for the future. Using materials now to grow wealthy and build knowledge was the best way to serve future generations, since the most important inheritance to leave was "knowledge, technology, capital investments, economic institutions. These, far more than natural resources, are the determinants of real income per capita."[89] Human ingenuity and science were "turning the tables on nature, making her subservient to man."[90] The only meaningful limits lay in the human imagination.

Scarcity and Growth may have been more gushing in its optimism about technological progress than many other RFF publications, but it captured well the organization's main findings: the absolute quantity of resources on earth may be finite, but human ingenuity offered so many ways of meeting social needs and responding to short-term scarcity that growth could continue indefinitely. And as the organization with the largest collection of economists working on questions of natural resources and the environment—practically no universities had recognized programs in these areas at the time, let alone offered regular courses—the findings of RFF carried significant weight in the economics profession. Their works were typically reviewed favorably in journals and their members were well respected by their peers.

RFF researchers knew ideas did not necessarily travel on their own. As a result, they spent a good deal of time engaging with policymakers, where they often promoted taxes or market-based solutions to environmental problems rather than regulations. Many served on government bodies, wrote white papers, and spoke before congressional committees. RFF also sought to share its findings with the broader public through a magazine, *Resources*. In 1963, they began to publish books aimed at high school and college students on environmental policy and held three-day teacher training workshops in four states to help high school educators integrate economic analysis into the curriculum.[91] By the 1970s, they were moving into television broadcasts.[92]

Through this multipronged strategy, RFF's message of "cautious optimism" was spread far and wide.[93] When Edward Denison looked for values of land and questions of scarcity in 1962, he turned to RFF. When Robert Solow looked for data on natural resources and growth during the 1970s, he turned to RFF, later claiming that "valiant little old Resources for the Future is practically all that stands between you and abysmal ignorance" on matters of natural resources.[94] When policymakers asked about natural resource questions, they often brought RFF economists in for answers. Wherever they went, RFF economists assured others that resources were unlikely to constrain growth.

*

In 1945, the idea of growth without limits would have made little sense to intelligent economic observers. Looking at the devastated industrial economics across Europe and Asia and remembering the depths of the global Depression of the 1930s, few foresaw decades of robust expansion. Moreover, with rationing of key supplies in many countries due to war mobilization, the importance of strategic stockpiles was on the minds of many policymakers. A stable economy that provided high levels of employment seemed the best goal.

By 1963, the picture was much rosier. Economists interested in growth disagreed on many points—how to calculate the causes of growth, what could and should be done in the developing world, how to explain technical progress, whether a big push of capital was needed and if it should be balanced or unbalanced. But men with approaches as different as Robert Solow, Simon Kuznets, Edward Denison, Walt Rostow, and Gunnar Myrdal could agree that growth was both possible and desirable. And they could agree that the natural world held no meaningful limits to that growth.

And why shouldn't they? In the world around them, they saw little evidence of scarcity. Prices for raw materials were low and declining, developing nations were opening their borders to foreign investors, and the types of scarcities that had occurred during World War II seemed a thing of the past. Some resource-rich countries were poor while some resource-poor countries were rich. Moreover, scientific breakthroughs appeared poised to deliver humanity new power to control the natural world. The splitting of the atom suggested the possibility of power too cheap to meter, and advances in chemical engineering gave the tantalizing allure that materials could be manipulated at the molecular level to create new products.

Faith that science and human ingenuity could build a better future could be found across the academy. With the exception of ecology and related research on earth sciences, few academics gave considered attention to the natural world before the 1970s, including in the social sciences.[95] Economics may have been distinct for its emphasis on growth and its methodological approaches, but not in its environmental orientation.

A political emphasis on growth further drove these trends. The Kennedy and Johnson administrations in the 1960s made increasing growth rates a top priority. Domestically, this was pitched as a way to expand social programs and increase the size of the middle class. Internationally, fears that the Soviet Union was outpacing the

United States and the perception that American military interventions were needed to constrain the spread of communism further fueled the imperative for growth. Across the globe, similar dynamics took place. Countries pursued growth both to provide more resources for their citizens and to increase their international standing. To many observers, the benefits of growth seemed far more tangible than any concerns about its sustainability. For millions that had experienced deprivations during the Depression of the 1930s and rationing during World War II, the economic abundance was more than an abstract set of numbers: it was experienced directly in better meals, clothing, and housing.

Considered by the standards of the day, then, the optimism of the dismal science had many justifications. The problem is that too much of our present thinking remains hostage to the logic of that era. The idea that the natural world could be excluded from discussions of growth has outlived its usefulness. Understanding its history, therefore, is not about casting blame on those who pioneered these ideas; rather, it is to remember that these ideas were born at a time of resource abundance, ignorance about climate change, and bounding optimism about the ability of science to solve problems without unintended consequences. Now, it is time to craft new economic ideas about growth and the natural world.

5 * Growth Contested

Robert Solow decided he had finally had enough. He had found 1964 to be an "interminable" and "pointless" year of debates with Joan Robinson that stood as "a living counterexample to the proposition that where there is smoke, there is fire. It was all smoke and no fire."[1] It was time to try something new.

Now forty-two years old, Solow had taken a sabbatical year away from MIT to travel to the "other" Cambridge in England. These were heady times for Solow: his growth theory was at the discipline's forefront and the MIT economics department had gone from a nondescript place to one of the most exciting programs in the world in the last two decades, with Solow and Samuelson promoting a vision of economics that was mathematically sophisticated and built on neoclassical foundations.

While American economics was on the upswing, the University of Cambridge remained a powerhouse. Home to Alfred Marshall, Arthur Pigou, and more recently John Maynard Keynes, the University of Cambridge exerted an outsized influence on economic ideas. Economists in both Cambridges tended to be left-of-center politically and opposed to the free market ideologies of places such as the University of Chicago, giving them some common ground. But crucial differences remained, particularly about the suitability of neoclassical economics. Diving deep into the weeds of production functions and calculations of capital, these economists grappled with foundational questions of their discipline.

No one was more vocal about the devils lurking in the details than Joan Robinson. Since the mid-1950s, Solow and Robinson had been going back and forth about economic methodology. Solow hoped that in-person conversations in England could produce a middle ground that journal articles could not. But that had not happened. Desperate for a new tack, Solow found Robinson in her office one afternoon.

"Imagine," he said, knowing her fondness for communism, "that Chairman Mao calls you in and asks a meaningful question. 'The People's Republic has been investing 20 percent of its national income for a very long time. There is now a proposal to increase that to 23 percent. How should we calculate what will happen?'" Robinson, Solow reported, did not want to be pinned down, "balking, bridling, and dodging" the question. Solow insisted on an answer. Eventually, Robinson said something to the effect of "Well, I guess a constant capital output ratio will do." Solow rejoiced, noting it "made my day . . . I was smiling all the way home to tell my wife that Joan had buckled, and violated her own metaphysics."[2]

To nearly any outsider, this victory might appear trivial if not incomprehensible. It concerned, after all, technical details of capital output ratios that could hardly be understood by the average person, let alone set their pulses racing. But buried in these details was a much bigger prize: the future of economics.

While Solovian growth theory was one of the hottest fields of economic research in the postwar world, not everyone was enamored of it. Three strains of critique began to be articulated in the 1950s, and they gained strength in the 1960s. One focused on the analytical validity of growth theory. Robinson led this line of attack by assailing growth theory—and neoclassical economics more generally—for being built on flawed foundations. Others, such as Amartya Sen, castigated growth theory for having too little policy relevance, a critique that often extended to a general complaint about the field's recent obsession with mathematical models. A third came from those who questioned whether growth was always a good thing. The 1960s witnessed an escalation of protest across the world that demonstrated a growing pie was not sufficient to address problems such as racial justice, women's empowerment, and political freedom. These protests came to a head globally in 1968, as it became clear that rising GNP rates could not paper over a deep dissatisfaction with the status quo. This led some to attack a focus on growth on the grounds that it took too limited a view of what constituted a good life.

Reviewing these critiques reveals that, even from the founding days of growth theory, many of its assumptions and calculative practices were questioned. Calls to rethink economic theories of growth are nearly as old as the theories themselves.

Instruments of Miseducation

From her office in Cambridge University, Robinson could read the tea leaves from America. And just as Koopmans had little tolerance for Mitchell's measurement without theory, Robinson had little positive to say about the obsession with neoclassical analysis and production functions coming from the United States. The politics of this were bad enough, because she saw neoclassical economics as avoiding questions of labor, class, and power. But there was also a gaping fundamental analytical error, she argued, that undermined the whole edifice of neoclassical economics. She fired the first salvo in the winter of 1953–1954. "The production function," she bluntly stated, "has been a powerful instrument of miseducation." It contained an "ambiguity of the conception of a quantity of capital" that generated "a profound methodological error." So grave was this error that it "makes the major part of neoclassical doctrine spurious."[3] The boldness of this claim can hardly be understated: she was essentially saying the fastest growing and most prestigious branch of economic thought had no analytical validity.

Fifty years old, Robinson had already made a name for herself in the 1930s with her pioneering work on imperfect competition, coining the term "monopsony" for a situation in which a single buyer held nearly monopoly purchasing power, thereby being able to distort markets. A core part of the Cambridge Circus—a group of economists who met weekly with John Maynard Keynes—she was at the center of debates about how to address the global economic Depression of the 1930s. And during World War II, she had revitalized the ideas of Karl Marx, while also critiquing the flaws in his labor theory of value. By 1953, she was deep into writing her 1956 magnum opus, *The Accumulation of Capital.*[4]

The more she looked at capital, the less patience she had for the sloppy thinking of neoclassical economists. The core problem lay in measuring it. What was capital? It seemed to be all things to all people, a notoriously promiscuous category potentially including everything from investment funds to raw materials to machine tools. This was not just mixing apples and oranges, it was tossing together toast, cider, and ice cream.

More worrying was the issue of circularity. To accurately calculate whether an investment in capital would be wise, one needed a sense of future output, interest rates, and levels of profit to determine costs accurately. But according to neoclassical theory, interest rates depended on the prevailing levels of profits, as money markets would not lend funds at a lower rate. This created the circle. Changing investment patterns would change profit rates, but if profit rates were changing, how could you accurately calculate interest rates and the cost of capital? You couldn't. Capital could not be both a stock of goods and the basis for calculating the rate of profit. Production functions, therefore, mixed input and output factors that needed to be kept separate. For Robinson, this fuzziness rendered the neoclassical approach null and void.[5]

Robinson's paper opened a long-running debate that became known as the Cambridge capital controversy, pitting Solow and Samuelson against Robinson and her colleagues Piero Sraffa and Nicholas Kaldor. It roiled for more than a decade, expanding to include other issues, such as capital switching.[6] As in many methodological debates, the technical details were really proxies for much broader questions of politics and the proper role of economic inquiry. Through the banality of calculating capital output ratios, critics of neoclassical economics argued that issues of power and inequality were being ignored. At stake in the controversy, therefore, was whether economics would include social and class critiques. Would the thought of Karl Marx and Thorstein Veblen be considered relevant or consigned to history? Would economics be about power and class, or optimization and efficiency?[7]

In particular, capital loomed so large because Robinson saw neoclassical thought as a thinly veiled defense of the capitalist system. If capital investment was the major driver of growth, this implied that capitalists were the primary generators of growth and therefore deserved to keep the lion's share of the profits. Labor, by contrast, was typically portrayed as a passive actor in neoclassical analysis. And neoclassical analysis did seem to offer a reassuring message to the powerful. When John Bates Clark pioneered neoclassical analysis in America at the close of the nineteenth century, he argued these techniques revealed that capitalism was a fair system, allocating to both capitalists and laborers the marginal benefits of their contributions.[8] John D. Rockefeller and Andrew Carnegie may have agreed, but doubtless many of their workers and competitors would not. When Cobb and Douglas in the 1920s created their production function that Solow later drew on, they were interested in examining whether capital or labor was favored in the current system; like Clark, they came to a conclusion satisfying to those in power.[9] Surely the leadership of labor unions who consistently found courts ruling against their efforts to bargain collectively and state militias crushing strikes would have a hard time deeming the American economy a fair playing field.

Robinson and her allies thought it was a mistake to abandon the project of classical political economy, which highlighted questions of distribution rather than efficiency. From Smith to Mill, the great challenge of political economy was to understand the relationships among landowners, workers, and capitalists, and who would benefit or suffer as the system shifted. Yet these questions receded in much of neoclassical analysis, as its tools emphasized individual optimization rather than the power dynamics in which those choices were made. Robinson saw the whole endeavor as the worst of all worlds: bad politics and bad economics.[10]

Defenders of neoclassical approaches were not swayed by Robinson's critiques, arguing that she was making a mountain out of a molehill. Solow responded to Robinson in 1955, claiming, in essence, that perfection was the enemy of good enough. He agreed that the assumption of perfect foresight about costs and interest rates was "something foolish [for] a theory of capital" but the real problem was one of alternatives: "we have no equally precise and definite assumption to take its place." Simplification had its merits, and economists needed techniques that allowed them to say something meaningful in a concise way. "If God had meant there to be more than two factors of production," he wryly noted, "he would have made it easier for us to draw three-dimensional diagrams."[11] The analytical power of economic models came from stripping the complexities of the world out, not in spite of it.

In addition, Robinson may have overstated the centrality of production functions to neoclassical thought. Production functions were one tool among many others, and throwing out an entire toolbox because a screwdriver was not good at pounding nails made no sense. Others argued that the critique only applied to aggregate production functions of the sort used in growth theory to analyze the whole economy. In a production function for an individual firm or sector of the economy, changes in the profit level would not meaningfully shift the prevailing interest rates. As a result, the charge of circularity did not hold except when applied to the economy as a whole. This might be a flaw for a macroeconomic topic such as growth theory, then, but not neoclassical economics as a whole.[12]

Numerous journal articles, conference talks, and trips across the Atlantic during the 1950s and 1960s did little to cause either side to budge. American scholars emphasized the practical utility of mathematical models while English thinkers emphasized the inadequacies of production functions. Robinson and her colleagues did achieve one notable victory: getting Paul Samuelson to acknowledge that capital switching could occur, something he had denied for years. "This causes headaches," he concluded reluctantly in 1966, but "we must remind ourselves that scholars are not born to live an easy existence. We must respect, and appraise, the facts of life."[13]

But such victories were rare. The reality was that after a little more than a decade of debate, almost nothing had been resolved. The Cambridge, UK, scholars still believed their American colleagues relied on analytically flawed tools that were subject to the same critique Richard Ely had offered several decades before: a system of thought that justified the status quo and reassured capitalists that their wealth was an appropriate reward for their economic contributions. Solow and Samuelson saw production functions in a narrower light: as tools that analyzed the economy as it was, without casting normative judgment. They responded to philosophical arguments with an appeal to pragmatics. As one analyst of the controversy put it, British thinkers were "more realistic in some of their basic assumptions" and "logically consistent," but their views were not "simpler, . . . not more elegant. They are totally incapable of producing testable predictions."[14]

By the late 1960s, no one seemed to have much resolve left to fight, and the Cambridge capital controversy simply faded away. Even now, critics argue that neoclassical economists have never satisfactorily answered the questions about capital definition and circularity, but there is little active debate on the topic. Mainstream economics textbooks do not mention the issue and new generations of students are almost never exposed to the topic.[15]

The Cambridge capital controversy may be mostly forgotten, but it reveals two crucial things about economic practice in the 1960s. The first is that Solovian growth theory was contested from the outset. The second is that neoclassical economics had become sufficiently dominant in the American academy that critiques could be ignored rather than addressed. By labeling it as a nonissue—all smoke and no fire, as Solow put it—neoclassical economists made it so. By the 1960s, neoclassical economics had been enshrined in most of the American academy as the proper way to do economics, with a near unanimity among the field's leaders about which types of analysis were appropriate and which were not. Unlike most other fields, particularly in the social sciences, graduate training in economics became highly similar at most institutions, even using a small number of textbooks.[16] This consensus that there is a right way to do economics has meant that the field has largely ignored critiques of neoclassical assumptions, even by distinguished economists.[17]

A Poor Man Wasting His Money on Alcohol?

There is a certain irony in Solow's sense of triumph in Robinson's office that day in 1964. He claimed victory because his model offered a handy device for policy-relevant knowledge that Robinson's "metaphysics" could not match. Yet for a large number of observers, policy relevance represented one of the greatest weaknesses of growth theory, a charge that could be extended to many aspects of theoretical and mathematical work more generally. We have already seen how those concerned with advancing the cause of developing nations found practically nothing of merit in neoclassical growth theory and created the subfield of development economics in response. Even within industrialized nations, critics bemoaned the tendency of growth theorists to prioritize abstract mathematical games over the messy realities of policymaking. And this was not simply sour grapes from those hostile to neoclassical economics. Instead, many were among the most prominent economists of the day: scholars supportive of neoclassical ideas and adept at advanced mathematics who still worried that growth theory exemplified a worrying trend in economics toward policy irrelevance.

The first strike against growth theory's usefulness stemmed, of course, from the field's central empirical finding. Nearly 90 percent of growth, Solow's canonical paper of 1957 argued, came from the mysterious category of technical progress, about which the model had nothing to say. The abstract nature of the exercise was difficult to ignore. In a comprehensive 1964 review of work in growth theory over the preceding quarter century, the economists Frank Hahn and Robin Mitchell acknowledged the remarkable breadth of research but also noted its lack of policy relevance due to the "rather extreme level of abstraction employed and the very artificial nature of the problems considered."[18] They pointed out that the field had a tendency to be "drawn into directions which severely limit its direct empirical applications or usefulness."[19] As a result, despite the "important" theoretical findings, many of which were "by no means obvious or trivial," growth theory was not yet in a position to yield "testable, nontrivial 'predictions.'"[20]

The distinguished economist John Hicks, famous for turning Keynes's macroeconomic insights into a formal model, similarly found growth theory biased toward theory rather than results. In 1965, he argued that modern growth theory was good for "classroom exercises" but "not real problems." He noted further that the topic was too divorced from "something that could conceivably happen." Ultimately, he concluded, growth theory was too enamored with "shadows of real problems, dressed up in such a way that by pure logic we can find solutions for them."[21]

Amartya Sen, a student of Joan Robinson's who did not share her aversion to mathematical neoclassical analysis and would become one of the late twentieth century's most influential economists, put the matter starkly in 1970. He noted that the rise of growth theory corresponded with the incredible postwar interest in growth among rebuilding nations in Europe as well as developing nations in the global South, and that GNP rates were now being used rhetorically to measure the success or failure of capitalism versus communism. This background, he suggested, meant "it would have been natural for growth theory to take a fairly practice-oriented shape." But this had not been the case, with economists focused on "rather esoteric issues" with "remote" links to public policy. "It is as if," he bluntly argued, "a poor man collected money for his food and blew it all on alcohol." The subject retained considerable interest for theoretical reasons, he granted, and due to the complexity of growth, practical results would always be difficult to obtain. Even with this caveat, though, he concluded that the major players in the field were "guided much more by logical curiosity than by a taste for relevance."[22]

These critiques of growth theory were connected to a broader set of questions about where the economics profession was headed now that neoclassical economics grounded in complex mathematical formulations had become dominant. By the early 1970s, many prominent economists skilled in mathematical analysis were sounding alarm bells about this trajectory. Mathematics was a powerful tool, they agreed, but it risked being the proverbial hammer that turned the entire world into a nail.

Consider Romanian-born Nicholas Georgescu-Roegen. Trained in mathematics first and only later becoming an economist, he made a name for himself with several articles in the neoclassical tradition during the 1930s. Despite his excellence in mathematics, by the 1950s he had begun to emphasize its limitations as a methodology. Speaking to the American Economic Association (AEA) in 1969, Georgescu-Roegen implored his audience to think critically about when mathematics helped and when it hindered. "Not every element of the economic process," he stressed, "can be related to a number."[23] He went on to warn of the "harm caused by the blind symbolism that generally characterizes a hasty mathematization."[24]

Wassily Leontief, who trained Robert Solow and Paul Samuelson, among others, argued similarly. As president of the AEA in 1970, he lamented the exaggerated focus on theory within economics and the corresponding inattention to the data needed to determine whether such models could be reliable guides to policy: "The weak and all too slowly growing empirical foundation clearly cannot support the proliferating superstructure of pure . . . economic theory."[25] This was made worse by an "uncritical enthusiasm for mathematical formulation," which masked the feebleness of claims "behind the formidable front of algebraic signs."[26] The discipline needed more "observed facts," a task for which "mathematics cannot help."[27]

As president of the Royal Economic Society in Britain, Ernest Henry Phelps Brown chimed in as well in the early 1970s. He noted that the latest research findings in growth theory, along with work on resource allocation, decision-making, and advances in econometrics, had little to say about how to benefit developing countries, improve the balance of trade, control inflation, halt environmental damages from industry, or advise on the proper balance between the market and government intervention. What was most striking, he noted, was the "smallness of the contribution that the most conspicuous developments of economics in the last quarter of a century have made to the solution of the most pressing problems of the time."[28] Greater attention to history and the other social sciences, he contended, offered a better path for economists to address real-world problems.

Within economics, therefore, lay serious concerns about what a field like growth theory represented. Even sympathetic observers could hardly avoid concluding that the connections of growth theory to policy were weak at best. For a field still aspiring for greater social influence and policy relevance, were abstract models and advanced calculus really the way to proceed?

Questioning Growth

A different set of critics turned their attention to the question of whether growth was as desirable as it seemed. If growth was simply "a synonym for good things in general," James Tobin warned, then it had no real meaning. "Let growth be something it is possible to oppose as well as to favor," he urged his fellow economists.[29] As Tobin suggested, growthmania risked fetishizing growth and turning what should properly be considered a means to good things into an end. Neoclassical theory held that it was. If incomes grew, consumers could directly increase their utility, and this was as good a proxy for well-being as could be obtained. But was more always better?

From a dollars and cents perspective, the large majority of individuals in the industrialized nations were significantly better off in the mid-1960s than they had been three decades before. The remarkable postwar economic boom had swelled the ranks of the middle class and brought more secure food, clothing, and housing to millions. In the United States, the growing pie was shared more equally than at any time in the half century before or after.[30] Yet in spite of, or perhaps in part a result of, this abundance, the 1960s were characterized by an upsurge in protest movements. Activists marched and boycotted for civil rights for Black Americans in the United States, the women's movement sought equal rights and opportunities, the sexual revolution pushed against old-fashioned social values, and political dissidents demanded greater voice. Collectively, these movements gave rise to the counterculture of the 1960s.[31]

The counterculture had an ambivalent relationship with growth. Would progress result from buying into the system and improving it, or was it better to opt out? Buying in was the more common strategy. Many activists, particularly in the civil rights and women's movements, supported the idea of growing the pie but argued forcefully for more equal distribution. Black Americans made important economic gains in the two decades after World War II, but they still lagged significantly behind their White counterparts in pay, knew they were the last to be hired and the first to be fired, and rarely were promoted to leadership positions.[32] When Martin Luther King Jr. spoke of his dream of freedom, he was at the March on Washington for Jobs and Freedom. The protest had been spearheaded by the labor leader A. Phillip Randolph, and issues of economic justice loomed larger than discussions of racial harmony.[33] Those who sought equal pay for equal work and the end of workplace discrimination typically saw growth as a benefit for achieving these objectives.

Other parts of the counterculture challenged the prevailing idea that more was better. The antiestablishment fringes argued that an obsession with growth led to pointless wars, a stultifying culture, and the diminishment of the human soul. Anti-war activists castigated the American government for its atrocities in Vietnam committed under the banner of defending the world against communism. Hippies and others interested in alternative lifestyles experimented with communal living, recreational drugs, sexual freedom, and new age spiritualities. Though belittled by critics as simply a desire for sex, drugs, and rock and roll by long-haired youth, the broad appeal of the movement represented a growing discontent many felt about the emptiness of the rat race. Corporate profits were fueled by advertising and selling consumers products that did not actually make them happier. A better life entailed rejecting consumerism.[34]

The counterculture drew inspiration from a number of critiques that pointed out disconnects between having more things and having a better life. While some of these critiques highlighted environmental limits and will be explored in the next chapter, many in the 1950s and 1960s emphasized the potential disconnects between growth and the quality of life. They were not, of course, the first to make this claim. Recall that Simon Kuznets foresaw the dangers of an obsessive focus on GNP as early as 1934, when he warned that "the welfare of a nation can . . . scarcely be inferred from a measurement of national income."[35] Kuznets was well aware that not all transactions involved equal benefit, and he sought to promote the distinction between "necessary evils" such as military armaments and advertising and "net services" that delivered direct value to consumers, such as food, clothing, cultural amenities, or labor-saving devices. A system such as GNP that did not distinguish between dollars spent on necessary evils and net services could scarcely capture human welfare.[36]

Many in the counterculture objected to mainstream middle-class values, including the obsession with growth, and led protests at sites such as the US Capitol in the 1960s and 1970s. Library of Congress, Prints and Photographs Division, *U.S. News & World Report* Magazine Collection, LC-DIG-ppmsca-50431.

The lawyer and conservationist Samuel Ordway also believed that modern patterns of growth often did not enhance well-being. A colleague of the environmental writers William Vogt and Fairfield Osborn, Ordway cautioned in 1953 that economic expansion could leave people worse off—frazzled and unsatisfied by the breakneck pace of modern life. He bemoaned that devices designed for leisure time such as radios or televisions "do not provide relaxation or spiritual peace" and that "with technological growth, more of us spend less and less of our leisure time in the nonconsuming forms of recreation such as hiking, gardening, sailing, handicraft, or making music." Growth was spiritually sapping.[37]

John Kenneth Galbraith was one of America's most influential public intellectuals of the mid-twentieth century. Born in 1906, he studied agricultural economics before rising rapidly through the government bureaucracy during World War II. Brilliant and politically adept, he was put in charge of the price section of the Office of Price Administration in 1943 with a staff of a dozen; by the end of the war, he oversaw more than fifteen thousand employees seeking to avoid inflation and ration goods for the war effort. After the war, he served as an editor at *Fortune* magazine before becoming a professor of economics at Harvard.[38]

In 1958, he put his thoughts into what may have been his most consequential work: *The Affluent Society*. Galbraith argued that Americans had entered a new historical moment—one in which the problems of abundance were looming larger than the problems of scarcity. This meant that the "conventional wisdom"—a phrase Galbraith introduced—was no longer an adequate guide. When the classical economists laid out their theories of scarcity, they did so in a world that struggled to produce enough to meet basic needs. But production now exceeded human needs. What else could explain the fact that an enormous industry of advertising had arisen to figure out how to get people to buy things they had never even thought to want in the first place?[39] He further wrote that economics needed to distinguish "that part of our food production which contributes not to nutrition but to obesity, that part of our tobacco which contributes not to comfort but to carcinoma, and that part of our clothing which is designed not to cover nakedness but to suggest it."[40]

Only by reorienting itself toward abundance could economics properly understand well-being. Fetishizing consumer sovereignty, the conventional wisdom was blind to a dollar spent on advertising versus a dollar spent on a nourishing meal. Just as bad, the obsession with production directed attention toward private goods and away from public ones. Chrome tail fins on cars and fancy attire could find ready markets, while investments in public transit, livable cities, and clean air were ignored. America needed to eliminate poverty and improve its social services—education, above all, in Galbraith's view—far more than it needed growth in private consumption. An affluent society would enhance well-being only if it prioritized human needs over market transactions. A blind faith in growth needed to be rethought.[41]

Galbraith was not a conventional fit in an economics department, as he bucked neoclassical analysis. Favoring the institutionalist tradition, he may well have been the only president of the AEA after the 1960s who considered Veblen more informative than Samuelson. Good friends with Leontief, the two agreed that by the early 1970s, the vast majority of their colleagues would no longer vote to grant them tenure.[42] Solow, who was sympathetic to Galbraith's politics, castigated his 1967 book *The New Industrial State* by claiming it was "anecdotal," lacked a model, and contained "sophomore errors."[43] Yet Galbraith's influence on popular discussions was very broad, as he had the ears of politicians and the ability to reach audiences with popular books, newspaper columns, and even stories in *Playboy*. But within the field of economics, he was often seen as an outsider.[44]

In 1967, the British economist Ezra Mishan took up many of Galbraith's points. *The Costs of Economic Growth* argued forcefully that the pursuit of growth would not automatically improve human welfare: "The chief sources of social welfare" Mishan declared, "are not to be found in economic growth." A good life, he contended, lay in noneconomic matters such as knowing one's neighbors, being able to walk on safe streets breathing fresh air, and finding contentment in work. Growth not only failed to deliver these amenities, it often made them harder to obtain. Industrial advances generated pollution, while automation replaced skilled artisans with drones who tended machines. He held particular scorn for the automobile, which he described as "one of the great disasters to have befallen the human race" given its role in suburban sprawl, the decline of walkable streets, the rise of air pollution, and time stuck in traffic. If the goal of government policy was to enhance social welfare, then many other policies would do a better job than promoting growth, which "succeeded only in making life increasingly complex, frantic, and wearing."[45]

Mishan had a wide range of intellectual influences. Receiving his doctorate from the University of Chicago in 1951 under the guidance of Milton Friedman before teaching for many years at the London School of Economics, he was not a laissez-faire conservative committed to free markets like his mentor. His critiques of growth and wealth inequality demonstrated that markets and individual autonomy were not sufficient to generate beneficial outcomes. But he did share Friedman's delight in being a contrarian and was skeptical of big government. In part an elitist like John Stuart Mill who thought the good life consisted in intellectual engagement, sojourns in nature, and family life, he was also a social conservative favoring organized religion and opposed to sexual experimentation or the hedonism of some in the counterculture. Respected among economists for his pioneering work in welfare economics and cost–benefit analysis, like Galbraith, he also embraced writing books for popular audiences. Yet he had trouble finding a publisher for *The Costs of Economic Growth*, since it spoke against the spirit of the time; the fact that the work went into multiple printings must have granted him some satisfaction.[46]

The natural world featured in most of these critiques, but rarely as a source of limits. Ordway was the major exception, as the subtitle of his book, "A Theory of the Limit of Growth," indicated. But for Mishan and Galbraith, the problems with growth were not that they necessarily outstripped the capacity of natural systems, but rather that it reduced the pleasure humans could obtain from natural spaces. Mishan, for example, bemoaned "a rich heritage of natural beauty being wantonly and systematically destroyed" to make more money. Worried about the "erosion of the countryside," "the 'uglification' of coastal towns," and "the destruction of wildlife," he and Galbraith argued that growth should not continue because of its ecological effects, not that it could not due to nature's limits.[47]

But these critiques had very limited impact, as the momentum for economic growth proved much stronger. Though reviewers often favorably received the ideas of critics and policymakers occasionally paid lip service to the need to move beyond GNP, actual policy changes were few and far between. Alternative measures lacked the sophisticated data-gathering operations that had been set up for national income accounts, and an obsession with growth rates both domestically and internationally captured the attention of decision-makers. Still, from the very beginning of the drive for ever-increasing economic growth, detractors have been noting that more is not always better.

In Defense of Growth

Growth theorists, along with advocates of the new approach to economics, pushed back against these critiques. At best, they were glancing blows, not fatal jabs. While acknowledging a penchant for theory over practice and a certain level of abstraction, they defended the practice of modeling and asserted that growth theory retained an important role in thinking through policy choices. Solow offered some of the field's clearest defenses.

Critiquing models for abstraction, Solow noted as early as 1957, made little sense. "It is abstraction that makes science possible at all," he asserted.[48] Only by stripping away as many variables as possible could one isolate particular factors to determine their influence on economic outcomes. These models were not designed to capture the full complexity of the real world; instead, they were designed to test out the relationships of various parts in the hope of providing insight into connections. Progress in economics, Solow argued, came when practitioners could "specify the main causal factors and hunt for their connections and interactions. The end product of this kind of theorizing is something like a wiring diagram for an electrical circuit. It tells you what goes where."[49] As the historian of economics Mary Morgan has shown, models for economists are not simply representations of the world, they are investigative devices. Models are, in many ways, to economists what labs are to natural scientists: means of experimentation that facilitate discoveries.[50]

Many economists also defended abstraction as a necessary part of scientific inquiry and pointed to Milton Friedman's argument that the predictive power of a model was all that mattered. Writing in 1953, Friedman had little patience for those who dismissed models because some of their assumptions did not directly match facts on the ground. Of course a simplification such as *homo economicus*, the rational actor with perfect foresight, did not exist in the real world. But if a model based on that assumption made useful predictions about the future, then it was analytically valid. You can ignore the sausage-making process, Friedman claimed, as long as the result tasted good.[51]

Solow was, therefore, somewhat in the minority of mainstream economists in pushing back against this extreme version of functionalism, a stance that only grew stronger in his writings over time. In 1985, for example, he cautioned economists not to overplay prediction as the sole determinant of a good model. "It is a widespread but misleading belief in our profession that the ability to predict is the only true test of the validity of a model," he noted, but forecasting "is not everything, nor even the most important thing."[52] After all, he noted, the history of economic forecasting was littered with errors and economists risked losing public faith because more failures than successes would be the inevitable result of seeking to predict the future.[53] What mattered most was to use models to test assumptions and find causal relationships between variables that could not otherwise be determined. "The large macroeconomic model is an indispensable tool," he wrote. "Economists are distinguished from other primates because we account for indirect effects that they never see. The complete model is how we do it."[54]

Within this more subtle understanding of policy relevance, Solow argued growth theory retained an important role. The real world was so complicated that expecting clear predictions from a theoretical idea that could translate into policy proposal guaranteeing tangible outcomes was doomed to fail: "Exactness in this kind of calculation is not attainable," Solow acknowledged, continuing, "I doubt anyone will ever be able to say accurately that this program of research and development will add x percent to national product per work or that another program will add y percent to year to the preexisting rate of productivity increase."[55] There were simply too many random and unpredictable events that could happen, including wars, recessions, and shifts in consumer preferences. Even changes in weather patterns could send ripples through an economy by altering agricultural yields, vacation plans, and clothing purchases. Such factors not only shaped growth theory, they could wreak havoc on any other economic policy domain including labor, housing, and the money supply.

Casting aside the goal of prediction, Solow favored the less glamorous idea of "mental furniture," noting that growth theory models "serve as an indispensable device for organizing our thoughts."[56] In 1987, he reflected that "the neoclassical model of growth was an essential and useful starting point for understanding the longer-run behavior of advanced industrial economies. Even now, if it did not exist, we would have to invent it."[57] Theory could reveal structural characteristics of the economy which were essential to designing policies to act on it, even if short-term contingencies meant direct predictions were unlikely to pan out.

Beyond reframing the idea of what constituted policy relevance, Solow and his colleagues could point to two more findings. The first, Solow admitted, was pessimistic. Sustained growth over time, the model predicted, would be hard to achieve. This was because the vast majority of measures that could increase the growth rate were temporary. Consider a major technological breakthrough in steel-making that increased output and lowered costs. Steel would become cheaper, and other industries that used steel would benefit, thereby creating growth in several sectors at once. This would move the whole economy to a new level of productivity. However, these gains would soon become part of the new normal, and the growth effects would then subside. As a result, growth required continual technical progress. As Solow noted, this represented a significant challenge, which could be interpreted as a pessimistic result. Realistic policymaking goals, he believed, had to acknowledge this fact.[58]

The second insight was that, even if his growth model could not explain technological progress, one could still assume a nontrivial relationship between capital investment and the growth rate. Technological progress, he reasoned, usually had to be "embodied" in new machines, which required the expenditure of capital. While it was possible that some advances in knowledge or technique could increase output without physical changes, Solow was convinced that new plant equipment or layout was almost always needed to achieve an increase in the growth rate. In 1962, he modeled this insight with the assumption that "new technology can be introduced into the production process only through gross investment in new plant and equipment" even as he acknowledged that "this is certainly not literally true." But in assessing the relative weight of embodied versus unembodied change, he argued "that embodied technological progress is by a substantial margin the more important kind."[59]

Embodied technical progress required capital. And this allowed Solow and others to assume there was still a close—albeit imperfect—link between capital investment and technical progress. Capital investment, in turn, was a function of how much people were willing to save. Would people forgo the immediate benefit of purchasing something now in exchange for the hope of a greater return in the future? Here was a clear avenue for government policy. While free market fundamentalists argued that interest rates and returns on capital investments perfectly reflected the collective desires of individuals, economists with a Keynesian bent such as Solow and James Tobin thought it plausible that social utility would not be maximized by laissez-faire. In 1963, Tobin claimed there were good reasons to think government policy to accelerate capital investment would do a better job than simply trusting the market. "I believe the evidence suggests that policy to accelerate growth would pay," he concluded.[60]

This linkage underpinned Solow's perception of his victory over Robinson in the Cambridge capital controversy. Even if the messiness of the world meant specific growth measures would be hard to implement with a high degree of confidence, increasing capital investment was likely to be a good way to get there. Getting Robinson to concede that point indicated to Solow that his growth theory offered a better path to relevance than anything offered by the Cambridge, UK, thinkers.

Yet the main defense of growth often did not lie in methodological details or the intricacies of economic theory. It was the lived experience of growth since the end of World War II that helped make it a clear priority. By 1970, growth had expanded the middle class and improved the lives of Americans and others across the global North. Millions of Americans could look back and see their fortunes dramatically improved compared to their parents and grandparents. Owning a home and a car had become a realistic ambition for large swaths of the population that could have only dreamed of such an opportunity a few decades before.

The promise of growth also created new political opportunities, particularly in the Kennedy and Johnson administrations. Johnson in particular touted growth as the key to expanding the social safety net in his Great Society programs while also bankrolling the war

As president, Johnson embraced growth because it promised to supply the revenues needed for a "guns and butter" campaign to fight the Vietnam War abroad while investing in his Great Society programs at home, including measures to enhance voting rights, fight poverty, and improve education. He is pictured here signing the Voting Rights Act of 1965. Yoichi Okamoto, via Wikimedia Commons.

in Vietnam. Growth meant you could have guns and butter to fight communists abroad while improving social conditions at home.[61]

Growth was also praised as the primary hope for social advancement domestically and internationally. Solow, for example, argued that increasing the lot of the poor in a stagnant economy would require middle- and upper-class citizens to give away their own resources, which he found politically unlikely, noting that "it is inevitably less likely that a middle-class electorate will vote to redistribute part of its own income to the poor than it will be willing to allocate a slightly larger share of a growing total."[62] And if domestic redistribution was an enormous political challenge with a fixed pie, the international dynamics were even bleaker. "The *only* prospect of a decent life for Asia, Africa, and Latin America," Solow declared, "is in more total output."[63]

To its defenders, then, growth theory offered the conceptual framework needed to ask intelligent questions about policy, recognize the difficulties of sustaining growth over time, and calculate whether policies to increase capital investments would generate net benefits over time. To expect more from the exercise was unrealistic, and to abandon growth models would be to miss out on their valuable insights. Growth theory may not be able to answer every question, they admitted, but it was an important step in the right direction.

To others, it was hard to shake the feeling that such arguments were underwhelming. In a world of intense conflict between capitalism and communism over comparative growth rates and on a planet where billions lived far below the poverty line, growth theory simply did not seem to have a great deal to say about what should be done.[64]

*

The rise of growth theory in the 1960s cannot be separated from broader shifts in economic thinking. Part of what made Solow's approach so successful was that it captured the zeitgeist, a prospect that thrilled its proponents and worried its detractors. The stakes were significant. Would economics be a profession of abstract models manipulated by complex mathematics that only a select few could understand? And if so, would such an approach have anything of value to say to the messy arena of policymaking and the most direct challenges facing economies in both the developed and developing worlds? Or would economics retain its prewar polyvalent nature, where quantitative and qualitative methods existed side by side and the contents of economic journals could be understood by lay audiences? Was there still room for analyses of power, inequality, and other social concerns that could not be quantified?

The American economics profession moved quickly to embrace advanced mathematical modeling by the 1960s. The top journals gave priority to articles using these methods, elite departments disproportionately hired faculty members with mathematical proficiency, and many of the discipline's top prizes went to modelers.[65] Critics of growth largely failed to win the day. Still, they provide a clear record that the assumptions underpinning the analysis of growth without limit have never achieved universal acceptance.

6 * Debating *The Limits to Growth*

"One of the most important documents of our lifetime," Pulitzer Prize–winning journalist Anthony Lewis wrote in *The New York Times*. "If this book doesn't blow everybody's mind who can read without moving his lips," opined business guru Robert C. Townsend, "then the earth is kaput." "It may be as important to mankind as Martin Luther's ninety-five theses," exclaimed a review in *The National Observer*.[1]

The year was 1972, and the dire warnings from *The Limits to Growth* had captured worldwide headlines. Humanity, the report cautioned, was on the brink. If the world continued its current trends, within the next century, "the most probable result will be a rather sudden and uncontrollable decline in both population and industrial capacity."[2] Without swift action, collapse loomed. The laws of exponential growth and interconnections between human and natural systems meant that "one can move within a very few years from a situation of great abundance to one of great scarcity."[3] Such a result was so inevitable that it mattered little what data one began with. Computer simulations revealed that "precise numerical assumptions about the limits of the earth are unimportant when viewed against the inexorable progress of exponential growth."[4] Global societies needed to act immediately, as "every day of continued exponential growth brings the world system closer to the ultimate limits to that growth. A decision to do nothing is a decision to increase the risk of collapse."[5] The message spread quickly, and the report received widespread and favorable coverage.[6]

Except among economists. While large numbers of citizens, politicians, and academics from the natural and social sciences supported the ideas in *The Limits to Growth*, practitioners of the dismal science denounced it, mincing few words: "An empty and misleading work . . . [illustrating] the oldest maxim of computer science: Garbage In, Garbage Out" wrote a group of economists in *The New York Times*.[7] When speaking to Congress, Robert Solow disparaged the report as "ignorance masquerading as knowledge."[8] Halting economic growth was such an "ill-conceived proposal," according to economist Mancur Olson, that "it is tempting for those of us who are economists to dismiss opposition to economic growth as unworthy even of serious discussion."[9]

In the early 1970s, economists were forced to grapple with and defend the idea of infinite growth in ways they never had before. Public interest in the environment was surging, leading to sweeping new legislation and millions of Americans participating in events such as Earth Day. Yet warnings of the dangers of infinite growth had little tangible effect on mainstream economic thought. Economists argued that growth could and should continue, and those arguments still hold considerable sway today.

The Unlikely Environmentalist

On December 28, 1973, Richard Nixon signed the Endangered Species Act into law. One of the world's most powerful environmental measures, the act not only provided protection for threatened animals, it explicitly stated that such efforts should be undertaken without regard to cost. It was nothing short of a coup for environmentalists. Nixon, on the other hand, likely had to force a smile for the cameras. He loved visiting national parks, but the environment was hardly a political priority for him. He almost never mentioned it during his campaign, telling his manager, "Just keep me out of trouble on environmental issues," so that he could focus on things like foreign policy.[10]

But in one of the more unexpected twists in American presidential history, Nixon did more to protect the environment than any other president. Theodore Roosevelt and other heads of state may have cared more, but it was Nixon who enacted into law the most consequential acts for environmental protection. In 1970 alone, the man who privately told industry executives that if environmentalists got their way, they would make Americans "go back and live like a bunch of damned animals," signed the National Environmental Policy Act requiring environmental impact analyses of major projects, inked into law major amendments to the Clean Air Act, and approved the creation of the Environmental Protection Agency. When Congress passed a more aggressive Clean Water Act in 1972 than he had proposed, Nixon vetoed the bill, but Congress overrode him. Despite his misgivings on the Endangered Species Act, therefore, he decided it was smarter to sign it than suffer another public defeat. When told by John Whitaker, one of his main advisers, that his environmental accomplishments would be remembered as among his chief legacies, Nixon gruffly replied, "For God's sake, John, I hope that's not true."[11]

How did a man apathetic about pollution abatement and with a palpable distaste for environmentalists end up signing the nation's most important environmental laws? Partly this was a result of lobbying by his aides such as John Ehrlichman and John Whitaker, for whom the environment was a higher priority. But mostly, it was smart politics. The man some called Tricky Dick knew a political opportunity when he saw it and had few qualms about stealing the

The environmental movement had so much popular support in the late 1960s and early 1970s that Richard Nixon signed into law many major acts even though he was not particularly supportive of them. He is pictured here signing the National Environmental Policy Act of 1969. National Archives and Records Administration, via Wikimedia Commons.

spotlight. The day he signed the amendments to the Clean Air Act, for example, he excluded Democrat Edmund Muskie, the bill's main sponsor, from the ceremony. In the early 1970s, the environment was a winning issue, and Nixon liked to win.[12]

Nixon's surprising legacy resulted from a distinct new phase in the environmental movement that arose in the 1960s and 1970s. To be sure, Americans had long cared about the protection of the natural world, and measures to protect forests, waterways, and soils had been passed as early as the 1600s. Evocative writers such as Henry David Thoreau, George Perkins Marsh, and John Muir inspired readers in the nineteenth and early twentieth centuries to give greater heed to the environment, thereby inspiring the conservation movement. World War II encouraged a new generation of thinkers such as William Vogt and Fairfield Osborn to discuss the environment in global terms. But environmental protection was rarely at the heart of politics or a grassroots issue that captured the attention of millions of Americans until the 1960s.[13]

More than any other figure, Rachel Carson helped catalyze a change in environmental attitudes. Her blockbuster 1962 book *Silent Spring* opened with a haunting image: a bucolic town in harmony with nature until a "strange blight [cast an] evil spell" leading to the sudden death of plants, animals, and people.[14] The blight was DDT, a popular insecticide with no color, taste, or odor. But its effects, Carson warned, lingered and represented a vital threat to life on the planet. Chemical contamination should be treated as "the central problem of our age."[15]

Carson transformed environmental politics into a referendum on public health, thereby inspiring a much wider coalition of middle-class Americans to demand environmental protections. Suddenly, suburban housewives joined with outdoorsmen. When a dramatic offshore oil spill tarnished beaches and killed wildlife in Santa Barbara in February of 1969, outraged local residents used their considerable political capital to draw attention to the need for better regulations. After the Cuyahoga River in Cleveland caught fire a few months later, activists seized on the images to further call for political action. All this fed into the first Earth Day in April of 1970, a remarkable event in which approximately twenty million Americans participated, roughly 10 percent of the population.[16] The surging support for the environment was sufficiently strong that Nixon realized it was better to support the sweeping series of new laws coming from Congress between 1969 and 1973 than to stand in the way.

The Limits to Growth

The broadest swath of the environmental movement in the late 1960s and early 1970s focused on the links between environmental degradation and public health, but many were also interested in the issue of planetary limits. In 1968, the biologist Paul Ehrlich published *The Population Bomb*, a widely accessible book describing the perils of continued increases in human numbers. Four years later, a group of thirty esteemed British scientists lent their signatures to *A Blueprint for Survival*, a report arguing that humanity needed to live much more in concert with nature for the sake of its long-term survival. During the early 1970s, then, popular attention focused not simply on alleviating pollution, but also on fundamental questions about whether infinite growth on a finite planet was feasible.[17]

These developments set the stage for *The Limits to Growth*, the period's most influential statement of planetary limits. The report stood out in part because of its stark warnings, but also because of the mysterious organization behind it and its use of computer modeling. *The Limits to Growth* was sponsored by the Club of Rome, a new society founded by the Italian industrialist Aurelio Peccei. Dubbing itself an "invisible college," it included an elite group of international scientists, business executives, engineers, and diplomats who collectively shared a concern for the "world problematique": a set of complex and interrelated problems common to all societies concerning poverty, overpopulation, environmental degradation, urban growth, and economic insecurity.[18]

In July 1970, a delegation from the Club of Rome met with Jay Forrester, a pioneer of computer science and systems modeling, at MIT. They were quickly transfixed by his recent computer model of the world system, as it seemed to embody their desire to find solutions that combined the technical with the social and that recognized feedback loops between social and natural systems. Also known as "vicious circles," the central idea behind feedback loops is that actions can have much more powerful impacts over time when they trigger changes in other systems. A warming climate that begins to melt permafrost, thereby releasing stored methane into the atmosphere and exacerbating climate change and further melting more permafrost, is one example. Excited to see how systems modeling could provide insight into environmental conditions, the Club of

Rome provided funding for a project. Dennis Meadows, a former student of Forrester's, along with his wife, Donella, spearheaded the effort. Over the next several months, they began to use the computer models to test assumptions about the interlinkages between natural and industrial systems.[19]

In 1972, Forrester and the Meadowses decided to publish their initial findings. The picture was bleak. Continued growth was a grave threat because it stimulated negative feedback loops that would undermine the natural systems necessary for human survival. Even if there were errors in their models or assumptions, they were confident that the outcomes would vary only slightly.[20] They showed scenarios where land productivity doubled or even quadrupled to demonstrate that such advances only delayed collapse by a few decades because of the pressures of population, economic growth, and pollution.[21] They also cited the example of chromium, which they anticipated running out after ninety-five years. Even if the initial stock was five times higher than conventional estimates, the useful lifetime would not even double, only lasting 154 years.[22] While they acknowledged the "preliminary state of our work," they argued that because the logics of feedback loops and exponential dynamics "appear to be so fundamental and general . . . we do not expect our broad conclusions to be substantially altered by further revisions."[23]

Draped in the graphs and aura of the latest computer modeling and backed by a well-funded publicity campaign, *The Limits to Growth* received widespread media attention in newspapers, magazines, and television.[24] While its conclusions and recommendations did not vary in great detail from earlier works, the technical mystique of the report lent it the same air of credibility that abstract quantitative models of growth had often garnered. It was one thing to say the collapse was coming; it was another to provide a computer printout predicting the date.

Global events quickly gave further credence to the report. When the Arab members of the Organization of Petroleum Exporting Countries (OPEC) cut off oil supplies due to American support of

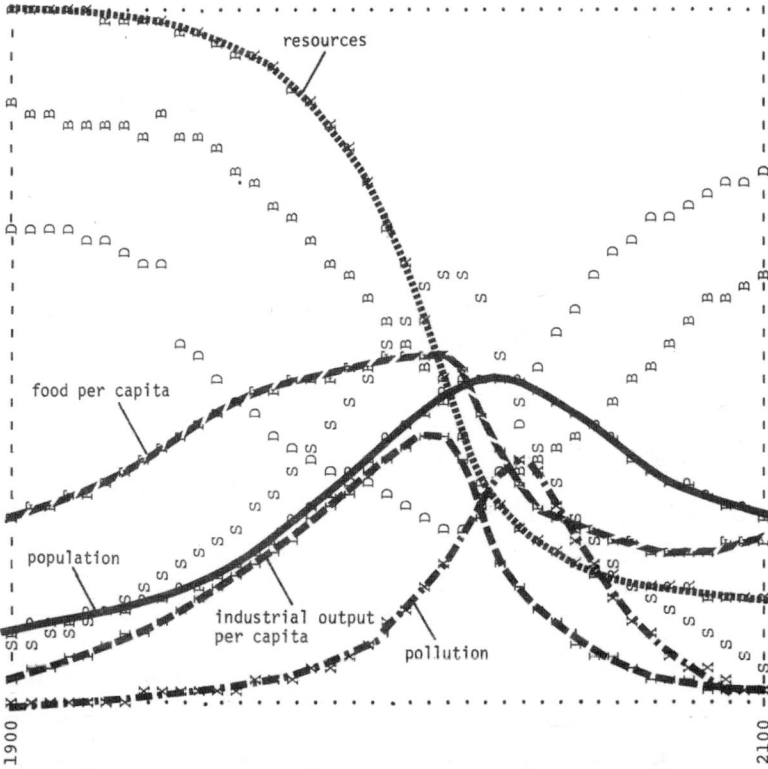

The 1972 publication of *The Limits to Growth* contained numerous charts show-ing how the interactions between resources, population, pollution, and output were interrelated and would ultimately result in devastating social consequences if current trends continued.

Israel in the 1973 Yom Kippur War, gas prices quadrupled. Inefficient rationing led to high-profile gas shortages and public outrage. For many, this was evidence that resource shortages had already arrived.

"The World Can, in Effect, Get Along Without Natural Resources"

Solow was not impressed. Reviewing *The Limits to Growth* for *The Proceedings of the National Academy of Sciences*, he pronounced that it was "worthless as science and as [a] guide to public policy."[25] Stopping growth to achieve pollution goals, he believed, would be akin to "cutting off your face to spite your nose."[26] And at a congressional hearing on "Resource Scarcity and Economic Growth," he said that while there was considerable room to improve environmental outcomes, no immediate sense of catastrophe should drive the policy process.[27]

The fact that Solow, one of the nation's most preeminent economic thinkers, took such a dim view of *The Limits to Growth* boded poorly for the work's reception among other mainstream economists. Solow was known as a progressive economist open to government intervention, unlike some of his conservative colleagues such as Milton Friedman. His objections did not result from a blind faith in free markets or even the common tendency to assume that economic methodology alone could be trusted. Throughout his career, Solow noted the limits of economics and encouraged his colleagues to engage with other disciplines including history and philosophy.[28] Finally, Solow also believed in the importance of environmental protections, frequently arguing that policy measures were needed to curb market externalities.[29] Open-minded and concerned for environmental conditions, Solow still found little of merit in *The Limits to Growth*.

He was not alone. In rejecting what he labeled the "doomsday models," Solow was joined by a small handful of colleagues who engaged with the rising interest in environmental limits. Largely tied to Solow and the think tank Resources for the Future (RFF), they represented the mainstream of the economics profession and saw little reason to think the natural world would limit growth. The theoretical and empirical arguments they developed to express their skepticism resonate to the present.

First and foremost, mainstream economists assailed environmentalists for failing to understand how price signals could stimulate technological innovation and substitution: "The most glaring defect of the Forrester–Meadows models is the absence of any sort of functioning price," Solow wrote in 1972.[30] The law of supply and demand argued that prices should rise when goods become scarce. These higher prices, in turn, would act in several ways to alleviate scarcity. As Solow expressed it to a congressional committee: "The rise in price does at least four things. . . . It reduces the demand for the resource by making things that contain a lot of it relatively expensive; it provides an incentive for manufacturers to substitute cheaper materials for scarcer and dearer ones; similarly, it provides an incentive for exploration; and finally, it guides scientific and engineering effort to those technological areas that are now likely to generate large savings in cost. These things actually happen."[31] Therefore, economists contended, *The Limits to Growth* was fundamentally flawed because it suggested no social adaptation to new conditions. James Tobin and William Nordhaus expressed the matter pithily: "Price appreciation protects resources from premature exploitation."[32]

Empirical analysis of price signals for many resources further indicated that scarcity was not imminent. If a resource was growing scarce, economists noted that there should be change in at least one of three measures: its market price, the quantity of proven reserves, or the cost of extraction. (If smaller and harder-to-extract deposits needed to be tapped, extraction would become more costly). For the vast majority of exhaustible resources, the historical record showed that this was not happening. RFF researchers had demonstrated that, from 1870 to the 1950s, most minerals showed stable or declining prices even as their consumption increased, due to the discovery of additional reserves and improved recovery techniques. Technological innovations and new discoveries more than offset the decline of established reserves.[33]

Solow acknowledged that much of what was known about the future for natural resources came "through the painstaking work of groups like Resources for the Future."[34] For example, in an influential 1972 paper titled "Is Growth Obsolete?," Nordhaus and Tobin answered their own question in the negative. They drew heavily on RFF's 1963 book *Scarcity and Growth* as well as Edward Denison's 1962 book *The Sources of Economic Growth in The United States*, one of the pioneering works in growth accounting. Denison, in turn, relied on RFF data to substantiate his claim that natural resources represented a small and declining percentage of America's overall economic growth.[35] As a result, Nordhaus and Tobin concluded that there was little evidence to support fears that resources would halt growth. "Indeed, the opposite appears to be more likely: Growth of output per capita will accelerate ever so slightly even as stocks of natural resources decline."[36] Empirical data from RFF underpinned key studies arguing that resource shortages did not appear imminent or likely to threaten growth.

Nordhaus further cemented the belief that growth could continue by positing the idea of a backstop technology. If coal and oil got expensive enough, it would justify the development of new technologies such as nuclear breeder reactors that reused their fuel or breakthroughs in solar power that would provide renewable energy.

William Nordhaus pioneered the idea of a backstop technology that could produce unlimited energy if costs rose high enough. He cited breeder nuclear reactors that could generate their own fuel as an example of a technology that was currently too expensive, but might become practical if oil and coal became scarce and expensive. This artist's rendering of a proposed breeder reactor in the 1970s in Tennessee reveals that such technologies rarely made it past the planning stages. US Department of Energy, via Wikimedia Commons.

Such technologies could be assumed to be available as long as the prices of conventional energy sources rose sufficiently.[37]

Beyond the virtues of price signals, substitution, and data showing declining resource costs over time, three other points contributed to the economic critique of environmental limits to growth. First, several economists noted that focusing on growth was a mistake. Even in a steady-state or declining economy, production could take place in a highly polluting and unsustainable manner. Growth might exacerbate such problems, but eliminating growth would not solve them. It would be better to focus policy and attention on the harmful results of economic activity rather than growth itself. As Nordhaus and Tobin concluded: "The mistake of the anti-growth men is to blame economic growth for the misdirection of economic growth.... Zero economic growth is a blunt instrument for cleaner air, prodigiously expensive and probably ineffectual."[38] Pollution and waste, not growth, should be the focus of environmentalists.

Some economists also noted the dangers of stopping economic growth for the developing world, where large percentages of the population lived in poverty. In *The New York Times*, Solow asked, "Can you expect billions of Asians and Africans to live forever at roughly their standard of living while we go on forever at ours?"[39] The Pakistani economist Mahbub ul Haq argued that the alarmism of *The Limits to Growth* sat uncomfortably next to complacency about the fate of developing nations: "The industrialized countries may be able to accept a target of zero growth as a disagreeable, yet perhaps morally bracing, regime for their own citizens. For the developing world, however, zero growth offers only a prospect of despair and world income redistribution is merely a wistful dream."[40] Economists therefore critiqued environmentalists for appearing insensitive to the needs of the global South, even as they conveniently ignored the litany of failures of economic policy to alleviate the gaps between poor and wealthy nations.[41]

Finally, a few economists argued environmentalists erred by using overly long timescales. Envisioning conditions fifty or a hundred years or more into the future was an act of hubris, they suggested.[42] At best, projections could operate usefully over a few decades, perhaps a half century. Anything more than this would be doomed to failure, because it would be impossible to predict what resources societies would need or the technological progress made in satisfying those desires. In later discussions about growth models and the environment, Joseph Stiglitz emphasized finite time horizons: "[Growth models] are intended to help us answer questions like, *for the intermediate run—for the next fifty to sixty years*, is it *possible* that growth can be sustained?"[43] Economic modelers, therefore, often favored shorter timescales than their environmental counterparts.

Mainstream economists expressed these critiques of limits in a range of formats, with varying levels of exasperation. Many economists supported a range of policy measures to address pollution and did not believe in laissez-faire. But on the particular topic of ending economic growth, they were vigorous in their opposition. In *The New York Times*, a team of economic correspondents assailed the report as an "empty and misleading work" of "pseudoscience and polemical fiction."[44] Within academic circles, the response was no more encouraging. In 1973, the economist Mancur Olson opened a special volume of a journal on "The No-Growth Society" by complaining that zero economic growth proposals were "logically inadequate" and "seriously unbalanced."[45] His epilogue, cowritten with RFF economists Hans Landsberg and Joseph Fisher, observed that "it is surely not accidental that rejection of economic growth has emerged simultaneously with preferences for astrology, mysticism, tarot, witchcraft, Eastern religions, and 'mind-blowing' or consciousness-changing drugs."[46] Favoring no-growth policies, in their view, was akin to being an irrational hippie with a fondness for LSD.

These arguments were echoed in two other prominent forums for economists. Solow devoted his January 1974 Richard Ely lecture at the annual meeting of the American Economic Association (AEA) to the economics of exhaustible resources and assured his audience that while the topic included some interesting intellectual problems for economists to work out, collapse seemed unlikely. As long as capital could be substituted for natural resources, "the world can, in effect, get along without natural resources . . . at some finite cost, production can be freed of dependence on exhaustible resources altogether."[47] A clearer statement of the possibility of infinite growth would be harder to imagine.

Solow then collaborated with several other economists in a special issue of *The Review of Economic Studies* in 1974 on the economics of exhaustible resources. The papers described some of the latest developments in economic theory to accommodate nonrenewable resources. None of the pieces expressed concern that depletion would ultimately halt growth; instead, their focus lay primarily in using complex mathematics to calculate the optimal rate at which a nonrenewable resource should be consumed. As Solow put it, "the introduction of exhaustible resources into this sort of optimization model leads to interesting results . . . but to no great reversal of basic principles."[48] For economists, finite resources represented a good opportunity to demonstrate their mathematical sophistication, not a dire threat to humanity.

Collectively, mainstream economists strongly downplayed concerns over limits to growth and the legitimacy of the no-growth position. Whether assailing no-growthers as eco-freaks or characterizing their approach as pseudoscience, they, more than any other group of thinkers, rejected the idea that environmental constraints should reshape perspectives on growth. Infinite growth was both feasible and desirable.

Madmen and Heterodox Thinking

Kenneth Boulding was not so sure his economic colleagues had it right. "Anyone who believes exponential growth can go on forever in a finite world is either a madman or an economist," he was reported to say.[49] Boulding and a small group of other distinguished thinkers sought to bring the natural world more deeply into economics and amplify concerns over environmental sustainability. While their work would inspire many followers and articulate a vision of economics compatible with environmental sustainability, the mainstream economic tradition paid little attention. Like the Cambridge capital controversy, these critiques were largely ignored within the economics community.[50]

Boulding's career demonstrates these dynamics clearly. Born in Liverpool in 1910 to a working-class family, he took quickly to economics during his university days. He published multiple articles in top-tier journals as a twenty-four-year-old, earning him academic positions in America, where he built his career. In 1941, he wrote a textbook that was eventually hailed as a leading example of the neoclassical synthesis of marginal microeconomics and Keynesian macroeconomics. This work, done largely in the mainstream tradition, was so highly regarded that he was the second person to win the John Bates Clark Medal, and he later served as president of the AEA.[51]

But Boulding never believed neoclassical analysis should represent the totality of economic thought. Throughout his life, he was interested in the integration of the social sciences and considered it necessary to analyze the full context of settings that shaped why people made the decisions they did. Reviewing Samuelson's textbook with its tagline, "mathematics is a language," in 1948, Boulding worried that purely mathematical economics would "remain too flawless in its perfection to be very fruitful."[52] He castigated the idea that there could be solutions that were economically optimal but politically impossible, noting that "it is not legitimate to separate the economic from the political."[53] He thought ecology, rather than physics, offered the best approach for economics because it emphasized the interconnections between all aspects of life rather than their divisions.[54]

His interest in a holistic approach to human affairs and engagement with other sciences meant Boulding was a skeptic of growth from early on. Nothing in the natural world grew forever, and periods of rapid growth were followed by stagnation or even collapse. In a 1945 book on economics and peace, he noted bluntly in the preface that "accumulation cannot proceed forever."[55] He argued the economy was like a bathtub whose capacity was limited and doubted that the rapid growth of the past two centuries could continue much longer.[56] In 1953, he sought to establish a general theory of growth across social and natural systems. In all systems, growth seemed to follow an S curve where after a period of expansion, it would eventually slow and cease: "Continuous growth at a constant rate, however, is rare in nature and even in society. Indeed . . . within the realm of common human experience all growth must run into *eventually* declining rates of growth."[57]

In the 1960s, the natural world came to take on a greater role in his work. Boulding's 1966 article "The Economics of the Coming Spaceship Earth" offered his most succinct and forceful statement regarding the interconnections between the environment and economic activity.[58] His central argument was that it was necessary to transition from a "cowboy economy" based on open frontiers, profligate resource consumption, and excessive waste, to a "spaceship economy" prioritizing efficiency, recycling, and a careful balance of inputs and outputs. Whereas the cowboy economy favored growth as measured in crude calculations such as GNP that did not distinguish between the use of renewable versus nonrenewable resources, the spaceship economy considered consumption to be undesirable, as it required the use of scarce resources. Economists, he noted, had "failed to come to grips with the ultimate consequences of the transition from the open to the closed earth" and the requirement to satisfy needs with the lowest input of goods.[59]

The idea of Spaceship Earth took hold in the burgeoning environmental movement, and Boulding became an important spokesperson for sustainability. Over the next decades, he frequently touched on topics of environmental preservation, though as a polymath, he never dwelled long on a single subject. More than any other topic,

Boulding's concept of "Spaceship Earth" grew in popularity so much that it became the name of the signature ride at Disney's new EPCOT theme park when it opened in 1982. The futurist Buckminster Fuller helped spread the idea of Spaceship Earth, and the ride was built inside one of the geodesic domes he popularized. Katie Rommel-Esham, CC BY-SA 4.0, https://creativecommons.org/licenses/by-sa/4.0, via Wikimedia Commons.

peace studies became the foundational issue of his later career, and he became considered one of the field's most important founders. Yet Boulding's attempts to broaden economics to include the natural world and moral sentiments like love and fear gained little traction among his mainstream colleagues, who increasingly saw him as outside their professional orbit.[60]

Nicholas Georgescu-Roegen's career had many parallels to Boulding's. Both came to America in the 1920s. Both made noted contributions to neoclassical economics with mathematically informed insights in the 1930s. And both were polymaths who saw the limitations of neoclassical economics, particularly when it came to questions of growth and the natural world.

Born in 1906 in Romania, Georgescu-Roegen had a difficult childhood marked by the death of his father at age eight, his family having to flee their hometown in World War I, and a militaristic private school education that sharpened his mathematical abilities but stunted his social development. During the 1920s and 1930s, he studied at the Sorbonne in Paris, University College in London, and Harvard University before returning to Romania to serve in the government for a tumultuous decade starting in 1937. Eventually running afoul of his political enemies, he and his wife had to escape in the hold of a Turkish freighter using forged papers. Settling in America, he got a job teaching economics at Vanderbilt in 1949, where he remained the rest of his career.[61]

Brilliant, demanding, and cantankerous, Georgescu-Roegen spent the first half of his career making important contributions to neoclassical economics and the second half seeking to reveal its flaws. By the 1950s, his lifelong interest in the philosophy of science led him to question parts of neoclassical analysis. When he gave the distinguished lecture at the AEA conference in 1969, he argued that economic quantification had gone too far: the field had been "carried away by mathematical formalism to the point of disregarding a basic requirement of science; namely, to have as clear an idea as possible about what corresponds in actuality to every piece of symbolism."[62] Moreover, Georgescu-Roegen became convinced that in taking physics as its inspiration, economics had chosen the wrong science. Biology, with its emphasis on evolution, adaptation, and nonlinear change over time, better fit the actual operations of the economy. As Schumpeter's theory of creative destruction revealed, economic activity did not reflect the linearity or determinism of physical laws; it was based on entrepreneurship, chance, and adaptive responses to a broader ecosystem.

Georgescu-Roegen elaborated these insights most powerfully in his 1971 magnum opus, *The Entropy Law and the Economic Process*.

A wide-ranging, erudite, and dense book, it argued forcefully that the standard practice of abstracting the natural world from the economic process was fundamentally wrong. Economists led themselves and their readers astray by forgetting that all economic processes involve the transformation of physical substances. As a result, each economic transaction must therefore be subject to the second law of thermodynamics—the entropy law—which holds that disorder (entropy) increases in every material transformation. Thus, every bit of economic activity accelerates the pace of entropy. Infinite growth was impossible because at some juncture, there would no longer be sufficient energy to sustain the economy.[63]

The Entropy Law drew widespread notice, though few readers likely managed to wade through the several hundred pages of dense science and philosophy. Georgescu-Roegen provided a more accessible version in a series of public talks in the early 1970s that he published a few years later as an article titled "Energy and Economic Myths."[64] He took central aim at the faith his fellow economists placed in the power of price signals and the infinite potential of technological progress, arguing these were fanciful pronouncements based in a false belief that the economy existed separately of the natural world. He railed against "the myth that the economic process is a circular merry-go-round which cannot possibly affect the environment of matter and energy in any way."[65] In addition, he noted the considerable irony that economists were the most vociferous critics of *The Limits to Growth* report considering their own fetishization of abstract models, like Solow's, which often did not include price signals as an explicit category. He thus concluded: "one gets the impression that the critics from the economics profession proceeded according to the Latin adage—*quod licet Jovi non licet bovi*—what is permitted to Zeus is not permitted to a bovine."[66]

Many of Georgescu-Roegen's articles in the 1950s and 1960s appeared in the discipline's top journals, but by the 1970s, his insistence on including the natural world left him on the outside. "Energy and Economic Myths" was published in a mid-tier journal, and he was bitterly disappointed that an article on energy and economics in 1978 was rejected by *The American Economic Review* on the grounds that it was insufficiently theoretical. A 1974 grant application to the Ford Foundation on topics of entropy and limits was rejected because the program officer argued Solow and Nordhaus had already addressed the theoretical aspects of natural resources in economic theory.[67]

The Entropy Law and "Energy and Economic Myths" continue to be cited as foundational documents by those interested in integrating the environment into economic analysis, and Georgescu-Roegen is seen as one of the core founders of ecological economics.[68] In addition, Georgescu-Roegen contributed to the critique of infinite growth through his mentorship of Herman Daly, who became the most prominent advocate of no-growth, or a steady-state economy. Born in 1938, Daly helped create the subfield of ecological economics and remained among the most strident critics of mainstream growth theory until his death in 2022. After teaching economics at Louisiana State University, he worked at the World Bank from 1988 to 1994, pushing them to integrate sustainability into their investment processes. Afterward, when he returned to the academy at the University of Maryland, he joined the School of Public Policy, not the economics department. As he stated bluntly, "[the economists] would not have me, and I would not go."[69] Heterodox thinking had no place in a mainstream American economics department.

Daly entered graduate school with the hope of using economics to improve conditions in Latin America. At Vanderbilt in the 1960s, he came across a couple of Georgescu-Roegen's classes and became interested in both advancing his knowledge of mainstream economic theory and learning its limitations. Shortly after, he shifted his research focus to environmental questions. Already by 1971, he was vociferously advocating for economic theory to take the environment much more seriously. He edited a volume that year titled *Essays Toward a Steady-State Economy*, reprinting work by Georgescu-Roegen on entropy, Boulding on the spaceship economy, and his own argument outlining the benefits of a stationary-state economy. He lambasted the simplistic calculations of growth that were represented in GNP and their failures to account for social costs or the depletion of natural capital. As he noted, even destructive activities were dubiously counted as positives within mainstream economics: "Is the water-table falling? Dig deeper wells, build bigger pumps, and up goes GNP! Mines depleted? Build more expensive refineries to process lower-grade ores, and up goes GNP!"[70]

By insisting that the economic system be considered a subset of the ecosystem, Daly argued that visions of growth should be replaced with careful planning of a sustainable and just transition to a steady-state economy. For Daly, a steady state meant maintaining population and wealth at a constant level over time with as little dissipation of natural capital as possible. Like in Boulding's spaceship economy, Daly emphasized the virtues of keeping "physical and consumption rates . . . at the lowest feasible level," suggesting that medical technology, which had as its aim the durability and well-being of human bodies, offered a better guide than the planned obsolescence of consumer culture.[71] Like John Stuart Mill, Daly thought the stationary state would allow a focus on improving human well-being. In particular, he touted the benefits of shifting attention from growth, which he associated with finite material inputs and outputs, to development, a qualitative measure that could be enhanced without additional pressures on ecosystems.[72]

Georgescu-Roegen, Boulding, and Daly demonstrate that not all economists believed in infinite growth, and they were joined by a few others, such as E. F. Schumacher, whose 1973 book *Small Is Beautiful* became a bestseller by arguing against the dominant culture of consumption.[73] With the surging popular interest in the environment in the early 1970s, their ideas received broad attention with one notable exception: the mainstream economics community. Once they stopped working within the neoclassical tradition and started questioning its assumptions, these thinkers were no longer able to publish in the discipline's top journals and their ideas were largely ignored by their colleagues. There was no room within mainstream economics to question the logic of infinite growth.

*

From today's perspective, it is clear that mainstream economists won the debate over limits to growth. Policymakers rely ever more heavily on economists, and growth remains the apple of most politicians' eyes. But during the 1970s—a period of immense social change highlighted by new demands for radical justice, gender equity, democratic freedoms, and environmental protection—this outcome did not seem inevitable. Even if most economists considered *The Limits to Growth* to be fundamentally flawed, millions believed its message should be heard. At congressional inquiries about economic growth and environmental matters, heterodox thinkers received frequent invitations to present their views. Georgescu-Roegen and Daly testified about as often as Solow did, despite the latter's greater prestige. In 1973, Daly argued that "ignorance of physical limits" constituted a "failing of growth economics" and that the presumption that increased growth would overcome problems of inequality was morally "absurd."[74] A few years later, Georgescu-Roegen noted "the fact that our terrestrial dowry is finite and can be used only once is the crux of mankind's ecological problem; for this, economics can be of no help."[75]

In the second half of the decade, environmental advocates found a powerful ally in President Jimmy Carter, who declared solving the energy crisis to be the "moral equivalent of war."[76] The sense of uncertainty was so palpable that when Heinz Arndt sought to trace the history of economic growth in 1978, he titled his work *The Rise and Fall of Economic Growth*, indicating a widespread sense that unbridled growthmanship was a thing of the past.[77]

In this period of change, economists did not think their tools needed fundamental reconsideration. Including natural resources in growth models was "interesting" to Solow, but existing frameworks demonstrated they would not cause an end to growth.[78] This optimism was a product of a selective history. Solow and his peers rejected ideas of limits because they had inherited a particular way of thinking about growth and the natural world. They did so because from the mid-nineteenth to the mid-twentieth century they had eliminated land as an independent factor of production, replacing classical political economy's focus on land, capital, and labor with production functions that only analyzed capital and labor. They did so because they cast their lot in the post-WWII era with neoclassical approaches, abandoning methodological pluralism. They did so because the researchers at RFF presented data undermining claims of impending resource scarcity. They did so because, rather than respond to the criticisms of Georgescu-Roegen, Boulding, or Daly, they labeled these thinkers as heterodox and ignored them. They did so, in short, because of a series of choices about which ideas to keep and which to discard.

Those choices continue to resonate. Mainstream economists' rejection of challenges to infinite growth became hardened with the development of natural-resource and environmental economics. As the crises of the 1970s faded into a resurgent economy in the 1980s, economists felt increasingly justified in treating the natural world as an object to be optimized. Though the field birthed multiple subfields to analyze the natural world, these research trajectories included no palpable sense that limits to growth were on the horizon or required serious attention from policymakers.

7 * Optimizing the Natural World

Less than a fortnight into his presidency, Jimmy Carter donned a yellow cardigan and sat in front of a fire to talk with the American public. It was early February in 1977, and Carter sought to rekindle the spirit of Franklin Delano Roosevelt's fireside chats at a time when the nation was facing several crises: energy shortages stemming from the bitterly cold winter, unemployment, and rampant inflation. Speaking slowly, he encouraged citizens to embrace "sacrifices" and to "learn to live thriftily." He asked Americans to lower their thermostats to 65 degrees during the day and 55 at night, explaining that the nation's "failure to plan for the future or to take energy conservation seriously" could not continue.[1]

Energy scarcity and high prices were a persistent theme of Carter's presidency. He advocated that Americans take limits seriously, particularly in the case of energy. Freeing the nation from dependence on foreign energy supplies was "the moral equivalent of war," he declared in the summer of 1977.[2] One of the defining moments of his

Jimmy Carter donned a sweater and encouraged Americans to reduce their energy consumption during a fireside speech in the winter of 1977. His message of restraint would not prove as politically successful as the optimism espoused by Ronald Reagan. National Archives and Records Administration, via Wikimedia Commons.

presidency came on July 15, 1979, when he addressed the nation at the height of the second oil crisis. The problem was not simply that Americans consumed too much and saved too little. The nation was suffering a deeper "crisis of confidence." Decrying "paralysis and stagnation and drift" and an unwillingness to accept "a little sacrifice for everyone," he urged Americans to use energy reform as a "test of our ability to unite this nation," calling it a "battlefield" in which "we can seize control again of our common destiny."[3] Carter's message echoed the broader environmental concerns of the 1970s and the findings of *The Limits to Growth*.

It was a disaster for his presidency. Even though Carter often used military metaphors to describe his policy goals for energy independence, a growing segment of the American population interpreted his rhetoric and ideas as weak. This sense was magnified by the economic slump throughout his presidency and his widely critiqued handling of the Iran hostage crisis that began in November 1979. His "crisis of confidence" speech became popularly known as his "malaise" speech. What his supporters considered his wise recognition of limits and the need for sacrifice was rebranded by his opponents an un-American passivity.[4]

Ronald Reagan seized on Carter's concern with limits to articulate a different vision of America and a future that was centered on optimism and abundance. If an enduring image of Carter is him sitting by a fire in a sweater, Reagan is more often depicted riding a horse in a cowboy hat. Born and raised in Illinois, he came to love the western landscapes of his adopted California and, as governor, approved of many environmental protections. But during the 1970s he increasingly believed that environmental laws such as the Endangered Species Act went too far and protected animals at the expense of people's livelihoods. He celebrated the pioneer spirit of America and the role of free enterprise in stimulating growth, arguing that government regulation was too often the problem.[5]

Reagan won the 1980 election handily, and quickly began to reverse many of Carter's environmental initiatives. He appointed pro-development officials to leadership positions, such as James Watt as head of the Department of the Interior. An advocate of energy development and ally of many fossil fuel executives, Watt sought to stimulate extraction on public lands. When the solar panels Carter had installed on the White House needed to be removed for roof maintenance, Reagan chose not to reinstall them.[6]

The gap between Carter's cautious advocacy of limits and Reagan's enthusiastic embrace of abundance captured the waning influence of the environmental movement in the late 1970s and early 1980s. Even if the specter of Malthusian collapse had receded in the popular imagination, however, the environment had become a much more prominent theme of study across many academic disciplines. The science of ecology saw a surge of funding, and environmental thinking also permeated the social sciences: anthropologists, sociologists, and historians also began to integrate the environment in new subfields.[7] Economics was no exception, and in the late 1970s, two new subfields emerged: natural-resource and environmental economics.

Yet if economists fit the pattern of other academic disciplines in seeking to systematize their understanding of the natural world, they were distinctive in treating it as a minor issue. Natural-resource and environmental economics were largely upbeat lines of inquiry. Yes, resources might become scarce over time and yes, pollution was a problem. But these issues could be optimized with the right economic incentives. Moreover, the benefits of a growing economy far outweighed the environmental costs. As the prominent Resources for the Future (RFF) environmental economist Allan Kneese put it, there were environmental "problems" but not "disasters."[8] There was no reason to think that growth could not, or should not, continue.

The choices economists made about how to study the natural world reinforced their broader faith in limitless growth and have continued to shape environmental policies. Not everyone agreed with this rosy assessment, and many of these critics banded together in the 1980s to form an alternative subfield of ecological economics.

But despite their efforts to argue for a more integrated understanding of the complex interactions between humans and the natural world, their findings have been largely dismissed by the mainstream. The economists who pioneered environmental and natural resource economics may not have embraced all of Reagan's policies or have even voted for him, but their findings lent much more support to his positions than to Carter's.

Hotelling's Lemmings

Robert Solow was honored to deliver the prestigious Richard Ely keynote lecture at the 1973 American Economic Association meeting, but it was a challenge. How could he find a topic that "is absolutely contemporary, but somehow perennial . . . broad without being superficial or vague . . . with some technical interest"?[9] Solow's answer was the economics of natural resources. He claimed that economists had done little to theorize the question of exhaustible resources, and the literature "was not very large."[10] Having already responded to *The Limits to Growth*, he was up on what had been written before the 1970s. This was changing rapidly, though. Solow humorously noted that he was not as far ahead of the curve as he had hoped: "About the time I finished a first draft of my own paper and was patting myself on the back for having been clever . . . it seemed that every time the mail came it contained another paper by another economic theorist on the economics of exhaustible resources. It was a little like trotting down to the sea, minding your own business like any nice independent rat, and then looking around and suddenly discovering you're a lemming."[11]

Within the small literature Solow found relevant to the topic, he argued one figure stood out: Harold Hotelling. For his audience, this was likely quite a surprise. Most would have been familiar with Hotelling's law, his lemma, and his t-squared distribution, and it is likely word of his death a couple weeks earlier had spread at the conference. But almost no one was aware of Hotelling's 1931 article on exhaustible resources. In fact, Hotelling himself likely would have been surprised since the paper had largely been ignored since its publication.[12]

Highlighting Hotelling had important consequences for what would become natural resource economics. In his talk, Solow introduced the principles of the Hotelling rule, declaring it to be "the fundamental principle of the economics of exhaustible resources."[13] The Hotelling rule calculated the optimal rate of extraction of a natural resource—such as from a mine—based on prevailing prices and interest rates. Scarcity did not concern Hotelling, who argued that it would not be a large problem for humanity to run out of some of its resources, because they could be replaced by others.[14] Depletion was not a disaster; it was a process to be managed efficiently. Solow agreed, noting that "if it is very easy to substitute other factors for natural resources, then there is in principle no 'problem'" and "what little evidence there is suggests that there is quite a lot of substitutability between exhaustible resources and renewable or reproducible ones."[15]

By resuscitating Hotelling's ideas, Solow helped define the field of natural resource economics as one of optimization. But this was not the only choice available to him. Whether the literature really was "not very large" depended on the eye of the beholder. Solow's vision did not encompass the Physiocrats' focus on agriculture, Adam Smith and his colleagues' recognition of finite supplies of land and the law of diminishing marginal returns, or the concern with avoiding waste common during the first decades of the twentieth century. If prior work was not mathematical and in the neoclassical tradition, it did not count.

Nor was Solow alone. Those papers that arrived in his mailbox were sent by a small group of economists who were shaping the intellectual outlines of natural resource economics. They included his former students William Nordhaus and Joseph Stiglitz, who shared their mentor's methodological assumptions and lack of concern about scarcity.[16] A 1977 essay by Frederick Peterson and Anthony

Fisher defined the theory of the mine explicitly as "the theory of optimally depleting a stock once and for all."[17] Only at the end did they tackle the question, "Are we running out of resources?" and largely dismissed it. They acknowledged that "it cannot be denied that we are running out in a physical sense" but argued the real question was "are we running out in an economic sense?"[18] The answer, based on "virtually all the evidence" was a firm no: "Technical change, economies of scale, and product and factor substitution have largely prevented erosion of the resource base of the economy." In fact, they claimed, "it appears that extractive commodities have become *less* scarce, in terms of the sacrifices required to obtain them, over the past hundred years or so."[19] With the concerns of *The Limits to Growth* quickly dispatched, the proper study of natural resource economics would be maximizing the efficiency of depletion.

This perspective was further entrenched with the publication in 1979 of an influential textbook by Partha Dasgupta and Geoffrey Heal. *Economic Theory and Exhaustible Resources* taught a new generation of graduate students what natural resource economics was and how it should be practiced. Dasgupta and Heal agreed that "the efficiency with which a market system allocates exhaustible resources" represented "the most important single aspect" of natural resource economics.[20] Though they cautioned against the "overly simplistic view" that scarcity could always be overcome by market forces, their analysis showed little reason to think growth could not continue. "The fact that certain exhaustible resources are necessary for production is in itself not a reason for alarm," they concluded.[21]

As natural resource economics developed, the veneration of Hotelling only grew stronger. Two economists in 1981 noted: "There are only a few fields in economics whose antecedents can be traced to a single, seminal article. One such field is natural resource economics, which is currently experiencing an explosive revival of interest."[22] A quarter century later, Gérard Gaudet celebrated the seventy-fifth anniversary of Hotelling's article, arguing "the word *seminal* takes all its sense when we write or speak about this article."[23] The Hotelling rule, another economist argued a couple years later, "forms the theoretical core of the economics of nonrenewable resources."[24]

Beyond rejecting the critiques of *The Limits to Growth*, defining natural resource economics as the pursuit of optimal depletion had another important implication. It meant that many of the traditional tools of neoclassical theory could be easily adapted to the natural world. "Although economic theory as elaborated in recent years contains very few explicit references to the role of natural resources," Dasgupta and Heal argued, "it does . . . provide a very productive framework."[25] Economics did not need to change to study the natural world, nor did economists need to learn ecology. They simply needed to use the tools already at hand to address questions of scarcity.

Natural resource economics, as a result, was largely an amalgam of growth theory, firm theory, and capital theory, with a side dose of welfare economics. This helps explain why many of the founding figures in the field had a strong background in growth theory, since its use of production functions to model scenarios became central to natural resource economics. This fit with the view that economics was a discipline of tools, not empirical content. The aspiring natural resource economist did not have to learn the engineering details of subterranean water pressure in oilfields or the chemical composition of different coal seams or the geology of copper mines. They simply needed the theoretical assumptions of economic analysis and skill in mathematics to manipulate models.

The Hartwick rule epitomized the economic approach to natural resources. John Hartwick posited that the solution to exhaustible resources was to take the gains from their exploitation and invest them in other forms of capital that would not be exhausted. He thereby reduced a problem that has occupied philosophers for thousands of years—what we owe future generations—into three pages of text mostly devoted to Cobb–Douglas production functions. The simple maxim to "invest all profits and rents from exhaustible resources in reproducible capital" was a tidy quantitative solution that reflected the sense these problems could be easily addressed.[26] Yet Hartwick did not delve into the potential problems of whether all capital could be substituted by other forms or whether the pollution produced by mining raw materials for solar panels meant some technologies might not be truly reproducible.

The development of natural resource economics may have represented an increase in the amount of attention mainstream economists paid to the natural world, but it did not usher in a change in overall outlook. The subfield's conclusions were far more optimistic than those coming from practically any other discipline. Though economists like Solow, Dasgupta, and Heal were careful to avoid sounding like Panglossian optimists by including occasional qualifiers, their analyses noted no reason to take reports like *The Limits to Growth* seriously. Limits might exist in the long run, but for the foreseeable future, they would not be a significant concern. Moreover, the tools of economics did not need a major overhaul to deal with questions of resource scarcity. With small modification, the insights of mainstream theory could illuminate the underlying dynamics of resource markets. Efficiently extracting nonrenewable resources presented an interesting opportunity for calculation, not a profound threat for humanity.

"Having a Problem Is Not the Same Thing as Having a Disaster"

The optimism of natural resource economics drew heavily on the work of RFF and the ideas distilled in 1963 with the publication of *Scarcity and Growth* and *Resources in America's Future*. RFF's empirical data showed that proven reserves of most resources were increasing, the prices of nearly all goods excluding lumber were decreasing, and there was little evidence that extraction costs were growing. Market signals, substitution, and technological innovation meant there was little concern about running out of critical products, particularly in a world of international trade. "The cumulation of knowledge and technological progress is automatic and self-reproductive in modern economics," Barnett and Morse optimistically concluded, arguing that "the process of growth thus generates antidotes to a general increase of resource scarcity."[27]

If there was one source of pessimism in *Scarcity and Growth*, it concerned the topic of environmental quality. The same dynamics that ensured new resources would be found to stimulate economic growth were not guaranteed to ensure healthy ecosystems. Technological advance and substitution might not necessarily prevent pollution, avoid denuded landscapes, or preserve scenic wilderness. The book's final chapter raised the possibility that continued growth could impair "total welfare."[28]

These questions helped give rise to environmental economics, a sibling subfield to natural resource economics. Instead of studying the stocks of materials that went into the production process, environmental economics emphasized the resulting impacts on the natural world—the sinks into which pollutants were dumped. As with natural resources, there was a long and rich history of previous scholarship economists could draw on to address questions of pollution, including much work in agricultural and land economics. As with natural resource economics, prior work that used the framework of neoclassical economics was brought in while other approaches were largely dropped. In another parallel, the field drew heavily on existing branches of mainstream economic thought, particularly welfare economics.[29]

Because foundational principles of welfare economics have done much to shape how economists value growth versus environmental protection, it is helpful to review some of the field's core developments. Arthur Cecil Pigou is often cited as the modern founding figure of welfare economics. Born in 1877, he was trained by Alfred Marshall and took over his chair at University of Cambridge before it passed to John Maynard Keynes upon his retirement. An extrovert as a youth who loved mountain climbing, Pigou's ill health and political disappointments left him a recluse in his later years. A prolific economist who contributed to many subfields, he is known today for introducing the idea of an externality—the notion that some activities generate costs or benefits that are not calculated into the market price. These can be positive, such as when new forms of knowledge are distributed free of charge or when a beekeeper's bees provide pollination services for nearby farms. But the more concerning externalities are the negative ones, such as when people living near a factory suffer health consequences from its pollution or when so many people drive cars on roads that traffic gets congested, thereby leading to lost time and wasted gasoline. Such examples revealed that the invisible hand was not always benevolent. As a result, enhancing social welfare sometimes required manipulating markets. Though many methods could be used to correct market imperfections, from incentives to bargains to technical standards, the most widely adopted measure is what became known as a Pigouvian tax: a levy designed to raise the cost of a product to reflect its true social price. "Sin taxes" on cigarettes or alcohol to offset higher health care costs are one example of a Pigouvian tax, as are carbon taxes to address climate change.[30]

From the outset, welfare economics had a close relationship with cost–benefit analysis. In the first decades of the twentieth century, the US Army Corps of Engineers took the leading role in developing cost–benefit analysis. Tasked with helping develop major water projects for irrigation and hydroelectricity, the corps found itself under continual pressure from partisan advocates to build certain projects and reject others. With huge quantities of money at stake, the incentives for pork barrel politics and favoritism loomed large. Using a branch of thought called "engineering economy," the corps claimed it would only support projects where the benefits clearly exceeded the costs. Cost–benefit analysis became legally required in the Flood Control Act of 1936 and has spread to many aspects of governance since.[31]

A core principle of cost–benefit analysis was the idea that, if the social benefits of a project exceeded the costs, society as a whole would be better off. But how could benefits be determined? Like the issue of what we owe to future generations, this is an enormously contentious question that has long been debated. What is a benefit? To whom? How could it be measured?

For welfare economists, the first move was to restrict the scope of investigation. Pigou opened his magnum opus by articulating the differences between the broad category of human welfare and the narrower category of economic welfare. Human welfare was too complex to study in its entirety and should be left to philosophers, he argued. Economists should focus exclusively on "that part of social welfare that can be brought directly or indirectly into relation with the measuring rod of money."[32] He granted that there was no guarantee that human welfare would be improved by advances in economic welfare. A person that took a grueling job as a menial laborer in a factory that earned a bit more than someone working their own farm likely had a lower quality of life, but he thought this to be the exception rather than the rule. On the whole, improvements in economic welfare would be "*probably* equivalent in direction . . . to the effect on total welfare."[33] As a result, economic welfare was closely enough linked to human well-being that it offered a "powerful guide" to crafting a better world.[34]

With this distinction in mind, economists had a straightforward path to understanding costs and benefits. Social benefit could be inferred from utility, which could be derived from the price system. When consumers chose to spend money on something, they sent a clear signal that they valued that good. The more they spent, the more they valued it. The less they spent, the less they valued it. It didn't matter why they valued something, just that they did. A dollar spent on organic health food was equivalent to a dollar spent on fast food. A dollar spent on aspirin was equivalent to a dollar spent on heroin. An hour spent in meaningful conversation with a friend or a relaxing walk stroll by a river could not be assessed.

This framework provided a way to assess benefits as long as money exchanged hands. But what about the negative side of the equation? Who should bear costs, and what was acceptable to ask of them? One idea came from the Italian economist and engineer Vilfredo Pareto around the turn of the twentieth century. Pareto argued that distributions of benefits were justified as long as the gains to some parties did not require another party to be made worse off. A situation could be considered Pareto optimal if there was no way to distribute resources in a way that some could gain without taking from others.[35]

Pareto's scheme was blind to the question of equality, which mirrored his strong embrace of laissez-faire and opposition to socialism. A single party could capture all of the additional benefits of a proposed change as long as resources were not taken from another party. By contrast, a distribution in which ninety-nine people gained a thousand dollars each would not meet his requirement if the hundredth person had to lose a dollar to facilitate the transaction.

Pareto's guidance suggested that economists need not consider the equality of the distribution of benefits, only whether it would inflict costs on any party. But even this requirement began to be challenged in the 1930s by the British economists Nicholas Kaldor and John Hicks. They argued that the fundamental test of a project was whether it generated a sufficient surplus whereby the winners could compensate the losers. But in a notable twist, they declared that such redistribution did not need to take place. This claim hinged on the distinction between positive and normative economics. The proper level of distribution between social groups, they posited, was normative. It involved subjective questions of worth, value, and justice that were better left to philosophers, kings, or democratic processes. The job of economics was simply to identify which pathways were most efficient. If a measure created a surplus, then the test of efficiency had been met.[36] As Kaldor put it, "it is quite impossible to decide on economic grounds what particular pattern of income distribution maximizes social welfare."[37] Hicks agreed, arguing that careful analysis required jettisoning such complications: "If measures making for efficiency are to have a fair chance, it is extremely desirable that they should be freed from distributive complications as much as possible."[38] While Pareto's requirement did little to encourage equality, it at least insisted that there should not be losers. For Kaldor and Hicks, the fundamental test was whether improvements in economic welfare were possible, not actual.

The popularity of this new way of thinking was connected to a more fundamental debate about the proper domain of study for economists. Up through the first decades of the twentieth century, it had been common to define economics as the study of material welfare. This framing often involved normative questions actively debated by classical political economists and institutional economists. In 1932, the British economist Lionel Robbins proposed a new definition, arguing that economics should be understood as "the science which studies human behavior as a relationship between ends and scarce means which have alternative uses."[39] For Robbins, this put questions of means squarely at the center of economics while ignoring their ends. It was a move embraced by Kaldor and Hicks and later famously by Milton Friedman, who offered one of the most popular defenses of economics as a positive science in 1953.[40] Though it took until the 1960s for Robbins's definition to become widely adopted, it ultimately carried the day. The field of welfare economics came to emphasize efficiency and aggregate economic welfare rather than patterns in the distribution of wealth or the extent to which increases in wealth led to better lives.[41]

When economists began to think more systematically about environmental quality in the 1960s and 1970s, therefore, it was logical that they would draw on welfare economics. But they soon found a significant challenge. Pigou's focus on "the measuring rod of money" provided little insight when price signals did not exist. Natural resource economists had the benefits of market prices for raw materials and labor costs for their extraction or refining, but people did not typically pay for clean air, nor were there market exchanges for scenic beauty. How could economists weigh in on these matters?

One early suggestion came from Harold Hotelling. The National

Parks Service was struggling to determine the economic benefits of its offerings, particularly since it strove to keep entrance fees low to encourage visitation. In 1947, Hotelling argued that it could get a proxy measure for the value people placed on seeing wilderness areas by calculating the time and expense they incurred to get there. If a family were willing to drive eight hours to a park, refuel their car twice, and eat multiple meals at restaurants, all that time and money could help you understand how much they valued the park. Knowing the maximum distances people would go to visit a park allowed an economist to infer a demand curve.[42]

Researchers at RFF followed up on this idea, and the think tank soon became the center of American environmental economics. Marion Clawson, an agricultural economist who had been the director of the Land Bureau, came to RFF in 1955, and led the efforts to refine Hotelling's travel cost method.[43]

RFF included a strong cohort of young and "physically active" economists.[44] For example, John Krutilla, who was in his early thirties and had recently received his PhD at Harvard, also began at RFF in 1955. He had cut his teeth on analyzing the costs and benefits of water development projects, such as the competing plans for Hells Canyon along the Snake River in Idaho. That project had largely excluded nonmonetary uses of the river basin as "extra economic." But Krutilla thought more could be done, and in 1967, he published "Conservation Reconsidered," which became one of the most important papers in the history of environmental economics. Krutilla argued that there was economic value in the preservation of irreplaceable wilderness spaces, as shown by the fact that many people would be willing to pay to preserve them. In addition, economists needed to consider factors of time and irreversibility. Once a wild space was developed, you could not reverse the process. Moreover, wilderness spaces were likely to grow scarcer over time, making them increasingly valuable. He thus posited that there existed an "option value" for preservation that economists should include in their accounting, and that this value would increase over time.[45]

RFF economist John Krutilla theorized that you could integrate wilderness sites, such as the Grand Canyon, into economic theory by inferring an "option value" that society was willing to pay in order to preserve access to natural spaces. As wilderness spaces grew more scarce, he believed the value of remaining beautiful locations would increase over time. National Parks Service, CC BY-SA 2.0, https://creativecommons.org/licenses/by-sa/2.0.

Krutilla and Clawson were joined at RFF in 1961 by Allen Kneese, who led a new program on environmental quality. The primary government response to pollution at the time centered on creating regulations to force emitters to adopt certain technologies or abandon certain practices. This approach began with a moral impulse. Pollution was bad, and no one had an inherent right to foul the air or the water. But Kneese and his team began to make a different argument that was jarring to many: some level of pollution was in the public interest. If economic activity produced goods that people wanted and entailed some level of pollution, ending pollution would be a bad thing because no pollution meant no goods. The real goal of environmental policy, they argued, was to find the most efficient ways to minimize pollution while maximizing the goods delivered to consumers. There was an optimal level of pollution that balanced the benefits of material production against its ecological costs, and it was the job of the economist to find that optimum.[46]

Environmental economics drew on other threads as well. As the once prominent field of agricultural economics began to decline rapidly in the 1950s and 1960s, many people trained in the field refashioned themselves as environmental economists or, if they worked in international arenas, as development economists. The prominent Berkeley economist Siegfried Von Ciriacy-Wantrup brought institutional analyses to questions of resource conservation in the 1950s and 1960s.[47] Ronald Coase argued in 1960 that, in cases where transaction costs were low, independent parties could negotiate agreements on pollution issues without the intervention of the state.[48] And during the 1950s and 1960s, a series of economists, including Scott Gordon and Vernon Smith, performed pioneering work on fisheries management that fed into both environmental and natural resource economics.[49]

The work done at RFF proved highly influential. Kneese was the inaugural president of the Association of Environmental and Resource Economists when the society was established in 1979. When Volvo sponsored a global environmental prize for pathbreaking research in sustainability, Kneese and Krutilla were the first recipients, hailed as founders of environmental economics.[50] The vast majority of economists working in the field came through RFF at one point or another.

During the shift in the 1960s from studying questions of natural resource availability to analyzing environmental quality, RFF maintained a relatively optimistic outlook. Most RFF economists cared about the natural world a great deal: Krutilla was an avid outdoors-man and Kneese loved the New Mexican mountains.[51] But they typically rejected the existential concern that animated many in the environmental movement. Kneese captured the essential differences: "There are some *very* severe problems but most, if not all, of them are amenable to effective and quite efficient policymaking. Having a problem is not the same thing as having a disaster, although much of the environmental literature that stems more from the biological–ecological end of things would have you believe that it is."[52] "I yield to no one in my concern for effective environmental policies," he continued, "but, in my opinion, the environmental movement has had an unfortunately large population of publicity hounds who specialize in alarming the public and proposing no-brainer solutions like stopping economic development."[53] Even among economists with a deep appreciation for nature, there was little patience for questioning growth.

Placing Nature at the Heart of Economics

Herman Daly did not think he was a publicity hound shilling no-brainer solutions. The laws of physics showed that infinite growth was impossible. The findings of ecologists revealed that ecosystems were under enormous strain. And in the 1980s, climate scientists began offering clearer statements about global warming and its dangers. The idea that small tweaks to business as usual were sufficient to solve these problems struck him and others as woefully inadequate.

In 1987, Daly and a group of colleagues established a rival school of thought: ecological economics. Beginning with the premise that sustainability challenges "are *very* serious" and required interdisciplinary collaboration to solve, ecological economists sought to rework the relationship between economic thought and the natural world.[54] Conventional economic analysis largely reduced the environment to a set of stocks entering the production process and a set of sinks for waste products. Ecological economists saw this as backward. The economy should be seen as a subset of the environment, not the other way around. It made no sense to talk about the production of goods and services without an adequate supply of air, water, land, plants, animals, and energy. If the planetary systems that sustained human life were threatened, the economy would suffer as well.[55]

Like natural-resource and environmental economics, ecological economics drew on a long history of thought. While the mainstream subfields limited their historical purview largely to neoclassical thinkers such as Hotelling and Pigou, ecological economists drew from a much wider range. Among economists, they have included Malthus, Ricardo, and Marx and more recent figures including Georgescu-Roegen, Boulding, and Daly. But ecological economists also embraced scientists as core thinkers, harkening back to figures such as Serhiy Podolynsky and Frederick Soddy as well as modern thinkers such as Paul Ehrlich.[56]

The creation of ecological economics was an international and interdisciplinary affair, with social and natural scientists in Europe arranging many of the first important gatherings: Stockholm in 1982 and 1986, Prague in 1985, and Barcelona in 1987, where the International Society for Ecological Economics (ISEE) was founded.[57] This geographic orientation reflected the greater strength of the environmental movement in Europe during the 1980s and the less rigid hold of neoclassical economics. Whereas few American economics departments at the time would hire a non-neoclassical scholar such as a Marxist economist or a socio-economist, the practice was much more common in Europe. To this date, most of the top graduate training centers in ecological economics are in Europe.[58] In addition, while some ecological economists received training in mainstream economics, many more have come from allied natural and social sciences including ecology, biology, and sociology.

With their commitments to sustainability and interdisciplinarity, ecological economists have found it easier to achieve consensus about goals rather than methods. The field "represents a commitment among economists, ecologists, and other academics and practitioners to learn from each other,"[59] the first president of the ISEE, Robert Costanza, wrote, while Clive Spash, another notable early ecological economist, argued that "ecological economics is currently more of a movement than a discipline" in light of the fact that no single issue or set of methods could unite the various perspectives practitioners brought to the table.[60] In many ways, ecological economics has been comparable to the plurality of American economics in the first half of the twentieth century: a mix of approaches ranging from political economy to scientific modeling to updating neoclassical tools. For ecological economists, achieving unity in methods has often been seen as less important than exploring new possibilities, though even insiders have acknowledged that the lack of internal agreement has weakened the field.[61]

One strong point of consensus among ecological economists has been a rejection of the idea of infinite growth. When Solow wrote in the early 1970s that "the world can, in effect, get along without natural resources," it provoked strong backlash.[62] Georgescu-Roegen argued that this was impossible due to the entropy law. Railing against the "myths" of neoclassical economics, Georgescu-Roegen claimed Solow's model worlds "ignored the difference between the actual world and the Garden of Eden."[63] Daly posited the only feasible path for a sustainable future was to plan for a steady-state economy.[64]

Like the Cambridge capital controversy, these debates in the 1970s never got resolved, but simply faded into the background. In the 1990s, Daly attempted to revive the debate. Inviting Solow and Stiglitz and other commentators to return to the topic, Daly insisted that it was time to "put an end to 'conjuring tricks'—to mathematical fun and games with infinity" and integrate the natural world into economic analysis.[65]

The debate hinged on what has come to be known as weak versus strong sustainability. When considering limits to growth, Solow and Stiglitz theorized that as long as human and financial capital grew, they could substitute for natural capital. In this weak sustainability, what mattered was that future generations were left with sufficient overall capital to meet their needs, not a set amount of each type. Solow reiterated this view in 1992, defining sustainability as leaving future generations not "every single thing or any single thing" but rather the "capacity to produce the things that posterity will enjoy."[66] Daly rejected that manufactured capital could always suffice for natural capital using the analogy of cooking. He critiqued Solow and Stiglitz for offering a "recipe that calls for making a cake with only the cook and his kitchen. We do not need flour, eggs, sugar, etc., nor electricity or natural gas, nor even firewood. If we want a bigger cake, the cook simply stirs faster in a bigger bowl and cooks the empty bowl in a bigger oven that somehow heats itself."[67] Daly's view of strong sustainability held that certain amounts of natural capital remained necessary and could not be replaced by other forms of capital.

The exchange of ideas did little to reconcile disagreements that had been entrenched for more than twenty years. Solow complained about Daly's "dense cloud of righteousness" and argued that while the entropy law may be true, it was "of no immediate practical importance for modeling what is, after all, a brief instant of time in a small corner of the universe."[68] Stiglitz concurred with Daly that environmental questions "*are* of concern" but reiterated that substitution could overcome shortages for the foreseeable future, which is what mattered.[69] He also sought to minimize the long-term consequences of their models by stating that "We write down models as if they extend to infinity, but no one takes these seriously."[70] This was, indeed, news to some. The ecological economist J. B. Opschoor commented, "No one ever told me that."[71] Replying to Solow and Stiglitz, Daly complained that they had simply "repeated their well-known positions" and failed "to engage Georgescu-Roegen's arguments."[72] Neoclassical scholars saw little reason to integrate the entropy law into their analyses and ecological economists continued to find the narrow models of mainstream economics unsatisfactory.

A second point of fundamental disagreement between ecological economists and neoclassical thinkers concerns whether the proper and rational object of study is individual maximization or collective action. Ecological economists interested in behavior and evolution have emphasized the ways altruism and collective action outperform selfishness. Under the label of multilevel selection theory, they have drawn on the work of evolutionary biologists to argue that collaborative species achieve much better outcomes than individualistic ones. Only once a community has been formed through cooperation can individuals get ahead by prioritizing themselves. This means that neoclassical economics, with its bedrock focus on individual maximization and competition, cannot account for or explain the true logics that have led to human advance, which are based on cooperation. There is, therefore, "a fundamental moral incompatibility" between mainstream neoclassical economics versus an ecological economics focused "on fitness at the group level."[73] Because "ecological sustainability and social justice are unavoidably group-level goals," achieving them requires perspectives beyond the maximizing individual.[74]

While a deep skepticism of the broad framework of neoclassical economics abounds among ecological economists, there is considerable debate about whether neoclassical methods should be included in the field's tool kit. For some, the whole point of ecological economics is to reject a worldview based on rational foresight, efficiency, and individual maximization and replace it with one that prioritizes the health of ecological systems, sustainability, and community well-being. Once you head down the path of Pigouvian taxes, you have already committed to a world where price signals and efficiency are paramount, leaving little room for biodiversity, wilderness, and sustainability. Others have been less concerned about using the tools in an opportunistic manner. If neoclassical tools help reveal the importance of environmental protection in particular contexts and are convincing to policymakers, then they should be used freely.[75] Those trained in economics, like Herman Daly, have often been the most ardent critics of neoclassical approaches, while those trained in other fields, such as natural scientists, have often been content to use neoclassical tools when convenient and discard them when not.[76]

These ideas offer a small selection of more than three decades of work by thousands of scholars. During this time, ecological economists have put forward numerous ways to rethink the relationships between the natural and economic worlds in a more nuanced manner than neoclassical analysis. They have elaborated Daly's steady-state economy, collaborated extensively with environmental scientists and engineers, and critiqued a focus on individual maximization. They have been among the most prominent critics of the faith in infinite growth. Over two thousand scholars are now members of the ISEE and multiple journals publish research by ecological economists.[77]

Yet even as the climate crisis deepens, ecological economics has made little impact on mainstream economic thought. Even natural-resource and environmental economics are considered minor subfields, and Solow acknowledged in 2002 that "very few of the elite university departments of economics train serious resource economists and environmental economists."[78] The ideas of ecological economics are even less visible in the economics profession, rarely appearing in textbooks or the field's top journals. Neoclassical scholars seldom deign to reply to critiques by ecological economists and mainstream economics departments neither teach ecological economics nor hire faculty members with that specialty.

Ecological economists have also had trouble getting access to the corridors of power. In no small part, this is because their message is often not welcome. Whereas mainstream economists offer reassuring words about the possibility of infinite growth, the caution and concern for the future among ecological economists has been unpopular in a political context that prioritizes growth. Like trees falling in a forest with few people around, the ideas of ecological economics have had a limited audience.

*

The economics profession could be said to have "discovered" the natural world in the 1970s through the creation of natural-resource and environmental economics. But if anything, the development of these fields reinforced the optimism of the dismal science. Natural resource scarcity could be optimized, and market signals would stimulate new discoveries or substitutions. Pollution was a necessary cost of economic growth and should be mitigated, not eliminated. Existing ideas from growth theory, welfare economics, and capital theory could be applied to the natural world with no need to rethink them.

These conclusions rested on the history economists decided was relevant. The rediscovery of Hotelling's 1931 article placed the optimal depletion of resources at the center of natural resource economics. Its fellow subfield of environmental economics drew heavily on welfare economics, which argued that consumer utility should be maximized and that the potential to grow the pie mattered more than who got slices. As with nearly all branches of economic thought during this period, what could be quantified and analyzed with the tools of neoclassical thought was emphasized, and those ideas that did not fit this framework fell to the side.

Most crucially, these fields taught that as long as the right price signals were introduced, more inputs could be found and the problems of environmental quality could be mitigated. Infinite growth could and should continue.

8 * A Climate of Optimism

It was 1980, and Julian Simon had finally dangled the bait that would haul in his prized catch. The white whale in question was Paul Ehrlich, the celebrated butterfly scientist turned Malthus incarnate. For more than a decade, Simon had been badgering Ehrlich with little success, enraged that the doomsayer faced so few consequences for almost always being wrong.

So Simon reached into his deep past to find a new strategy. His father had been a blowhard, prone to making outrageous statements without evidence. One of the only responses Simon could make that would shift the tenor of the conversation was, "Do you want to bet?" Ehrlich had also used the phrase, saying in 1969 that he would wager even money that England would not exist at the end of the century.

Simon suggested Ehrlich put his money where his mouth was. Place a thousand dollars on five natural resources, he offered. If the prices went up, it would be evidence that population pressure and natural resource scarcity were, in fact, threats to future growth; if they went down, it would demonstrate that market forces and human ingenuity could overcome natural limits. Seeking to quiet the pesky Simon, Ehrlich agreed, selecting chromium, copper, nickel, tin, and tungsten in the belief that their prices would rise. It was "the scholarly wager of the decade."[1]

Intellectually, Simon and Ehrlich could not have seen the world more differently. Yet their life paths had much in common. They were born less than four months apart to Jewish families in 1932, and both were raised in nearby New Jersey suburbs. Both became academics and took an interest in problems of population. Ehrlich had drawn on his training in ecology and population biology to consider humans as just one more species subject to the same laws of overshoot and collapse that governed the animal kingdom. Simon had studied experimental psychology at Harvard before entering a career in advertising and then completing an MBA and PhD in business economics from the University of Chicago. As a professor of advertising at the University of Illinois Business School, he helped population control organizations sell the benefits of contraception. Like Ehrlich, he assumed that population growth was a dire threat to humanity.

But by the late 1960s, Simon had a change of heart. The more he looked at the data, the less he became convinced that population growth was a problem. Did population and economic growth deplete natural resources? The voluminous publications of Resources for the Future (RFF) showed it did not. Did population growth lower economic output? National accountants such as Simon Kuznets demonstrated the opposite. What had happened in the past when humans confronted limits? Danish agricultural economist Ester Boserup revealed that people innovated in response to population pressures with breakthroughs like settled agriculture. What about famines? Those were caused not by a plethora of hungry mouths or a lack of arable land but by war, excessive taxation, and despotic governments. Moreover, there was a fundamental ethical imperative at stake that drove Simon: "What business do I have trying to help arrange it that fewer human beings will be born, each of whom might be a Mozart or a Michelangelo or an Einstein—or simply a joy to his or her family and community and a person who will enjoy life?"[2]

Simon converted with the zeal of a prophet. Like his intellectual idol Milton Friedman, who had spent time as a socialist before dedicating all his energies to praising capitalism, Simon preached his gospel of optimism in stark terms. People are "the ultimate resource," he wrote in his magnum opus of that title in 1981.[3] Simon was so bullish on the benefits of more humans that the conservative commentator William Buckley called him "the happiest thing that has happened to the planet since the discovery of the wheel."[4]

Yet Simon knew he had a marketing problem. He lacked a public presence to match Ehrlich, who had launched himself into the national spotlight with the 1968 publication of *The Population Bomb*. Working closely together with his wife Anne, Ehrlich published widely in top academic journals and national periodicals, including *Playboy*. Quick-witted and charismatic, with good looks and a deep voice, he appeared more than twenty times on Johnny Carson's *The Tonight Show*. Ehrlich was the academy's darling, Simon an ignored stepchild.[5]

This began to change in 1980, when Simon published an article in *Science* highlighting many of Ehrlich's failed predictions and bemoaning the fact that "bad news about population growth, natural resources, and the environment that is based on flimsy or no evidence at all is published widely in the face of contradictory evidence."[6] His article led to an exchange of letters and op-eds between him and the Ehrlichs and ultimately the wager. For Simon, the personal upside was enormous, and it brought him to the attention of conservative organizations. In 1983, he moved from Illinois to the nation's capital, where he took a position at American University supplemented by generous funding from the Heritage Foundation and Cato Institute. Even Friedman began to respond to his letters. Simon had "hit the jackpot," as he recalled.[7] Now it was just a matter of time to see the results of the bet.

On September 29, 1990, Simon had his moment of triumph. The price of each metal had fallen over the previous decade, and Ehrlich was forced to mail Simon a check for $576.07. The money was nice, but the public relations victory was priceless. An extended review of the bet in *The New York Times Magazine* cast it as a victory for the era's Dr. Pangloss (the exuberant optimist in Voltaire's *Candide*) over its Cassandra.[8] When economic and environmental worldviews were put to the test, the economists won.

For Ehrlich and his many followers, the lost wager was a bruising blow that magnified the decade's disappointments. "The bet doesn't mean anything," Ehrlich claimed, but this spin could not mask the fact that the tide seemed against him.[9] After the great excitement of the 1970s and the passage of numerous environmental laws, the 1980s saw a steady erosion of public concern with environmental limits under the presidencies of Ronald Reagan and George H. W. Bush. The fears of impending oil shortages highlighted in the oil crises of 1973 and 1979 had given way to flush production and low prices in the second half of the 1980s. Ronald Reagan's upbeat characterization of a shining city on a hill had replaced Jimmy Carter's earnest exhortations to turn down the thermostat. Talk of limits had largely been replaced by a renewed faith in growth.

Simon's victory was welcomed by economists, even if many sought to distance themselves from the extreme nature of his stances. With his brash style, lack of qualifiers, and position in a business school—considered less prestigious than an economics department—he was an uncomfortable apostle for the profession. Simon was not invited to join editorial boards of top journals or give prestigious keynote lectures to economists.[10] Still, most mainstream economists agreed that economic growth could continue indefinitely.

From the 1980s into the 2000s, economists doubled down on the idea that infinite growth was both possible and desirable. The development of endogenous growth theory in the 1980s, pioneered by Paul Romer and Robert Lucas, almost completely rejected diminishing marginal returns or physical limits to growth. Expansion came from the human mind—from people getting smarter, inventing new things, and working more efficiently. Though more technical and less polemical than Simon, Romer and Lucas's research came to similar conclusions: there were no natural limits to growth. And even as scientists began to document with greater certainty the dangers of climate change, economists such as William Nordhaus argued against taking aggressive action and saw little reason to reconsider the discipline's core assumptions. Doing nothing to abate greenhouse gas emissions might be bad, they granted, but overreacting to the problem could be even worse. Growth's benefits were too important to sacrifice for climate stability.

Growth Without Limit

Though growth theory had been all the rage among economic theorists in the 1960s, by the late 1970s, the topic had lost its pride of place. This was partly a response to the dismal economy of the decade. Whereas the quarter century after the end of World War II was characterized by robust growth and improved living conditions for most Americans, the good times stalled in the 1970s as stagflation took hold. An unexpected combination of a low growth economy with high inflation meant hardship for millions and baffled most leading economists. Keynesian economics argued that the proper remedy for a recession was to increase government spending. But doing this increased the rate of inflation, which was already too high. This meant thinkers like Robert Solow did not necessarily have a solution for the most pressing economic issue of the day. There was also a sense within the field that the big questions of growth theory had been addressed. Even Solow reported in 1979 that the subject was "just about played out" and that "anyone working inside economic theory these days knows in his or her bones that growth theory is now an unpromising pond for an enterprising theorist to fish in." It would take "a good new idea [to] transform [the] subject" and make it a hotbed of new research again.[11]

Though it wasn't what Solow had in mind, the most consequential new idea in growth theory came from a dissatisfied MIT PhD student. Paul Romer had begun his graduate work there in 1977, passing his qualifying exams before deciding to leave for the University of Chicago. Son of the three-term Democratic governor of Colorado, Roy Romer, Paul had long hair, a preference for blue jeans, an eclectic mind, and a penchant for moving around. Often he considered leaving the academy to enter political consulting or start a company; after Chicago, he took a faculty job at Rochester in 1983, returned to Chicago in 1988, then abruptly resigned a year later to move to California, where he would later join the Berkeley faculty; stints at Stanford, a start-up company, New York University, and the World Bank would follow.[12]

Even if he moved often, Romer's mind stayed focus on growth. Solovian growth theory was well established by this time, but Romer considered it flawed. First, he rejected the idea that diminishing marginal returns could explain a century and a half of steady—and even accelerating—growth. Solow's model suggested it would be hard to maintain growth over time, but this just didn't seem correct to Romer, who wrote that he was motivated "primarily by the observation that in the broad sweep of history, classical economists like Malthus and Ricardo came to conclusions that were completely wrong about the prospects for growth. Over time, growth rates have been increasing, not decreasing."[13] At the same time, growth was not increasing everywhere. The rich were getting richer while the poor were hardly gaining. This was the opposite of what Solow's growth theory predicted. His model suggested eventual convergence, with capital flowing to poor countries and raising their growth rates above the wealthier nations, but clearly this had not happened. The one exception was the rise of the "Asian tigers"—Hong Kong, Singapore, South Korea, and Taiwan—but ratios of capital and labor did not seem to explain their success. How could growth be more explosive in some places than Solow's model predicted while also allowing certain nations to retain pride of place?

The answer, Romer decided, lay in the human mind. Surely it had something to do with the ways humans learned to do things better over time. And clearly, there was something about knowledge that seemed outside the law of diminishing marginal returns. Once an idea is created, anyone can use it with minimal additional cost. Knowledge was, to use Pigou's terminology, the ultimate positive externality. So in a 1986 paper, Romer argued that knowledge displayed "increasing marginal productivity." As a result, it led to different conclusions than Solow's model, namely that "growth rates can be increasing over time."[14] Indeed, "per capita output can grow without bound" because "knowledge will grow without bound."[15] This, he claimed, was a bold "reversal" of accepted wisdom in growth theory.[16]

But at the same time, Romer realized that there must be something uneven about knowledge. On the one hand, it was impossible for an individual or firm to possess ideas exclusively as "knowledge cannot be perfectly patented or kept secret."[17] But on the other hand, some firms and some nations consistently outperformed others, maintaining and even expanding their leads over time. Somehow, they must be exerting enough control over knowledge to maintain this advantage. Four years later, he specified this further by defining knowledge as "a non-rival, partially excludable good."[18] By non-rival, he meant once an idea was in the public domain, anyone could use it. Consider a design for a tool. When that tool was sold in a market, anyone could copy it. But the ability to design was something different. This depended on the development of human capital that could not be replicated in the same way. A person had to be trained in the design and development process, and that took a great deal of time. By investing in the training of people, firms and nations could retain a higher level of human capital that was "partially excludable" and would allow them to increase their growth rates. Romer's approach became known as endogenous growth theory, because the power of ideas was brought into the model, as opposed to the way technological progress was exogenous to Solow's model.

While Romer was working out his ideas, one of his dissertation advisers, Robert Lucas, was thinking along similar lines. One of the foremost economic theorists of the 1980s, Lucas was famous for integrating rational expectations into macroeconomics during the 1970s. His 1985 turn to growth theory, then, surprised many. Like Romer, Lucas was struck by the wildly diverging economic fortunes of the world's nations. India had a per capita income of $240 in 1980 and its economy had grown only 1.4 percent over the preceding two decades, while incomes and growth rates in the developed nations were forty times and 2.5 times higher, respectively. "The consequences for human welfare" were "simply staggering," he noted, and "once one starts to think about them, it is hard to think of anything else."[19] In Lucas's model, human capital was the key addition, unlike knowledge in Romer's approach, though their theories were more similar than different. Growth came from ideas, and ideas did not obey the law of diminishing marginal returns.

Surprisingly, both Romer and Lucas had ties to the University of Chicago. Under Milton Friedman, Chicago economics had become known for its embrace of free markets. But he had left in 1977, and Romer and Lucas's findings revealed several inadequacies of the market to stimulate growth. On the one hand, firms or nations could monopolize kinds of knowledge. On the other hand, since knowledge was the foundation of growth, you could not trust private actors to invest sufficiently in primary education. Improving growth required government intervention into the economy, particularly in the domains of education and patent protections, not faith in the invisible hand. If anything, these new "endogenous" growth theories presented an even stronger argument for public sector investment than Solow's models.

To the present day, endogenous growth theory remains a contentious subject. Its advocates claim that it represents a much more satisfying attempt to understand growth, because it better fits facts about the world and brings more factors into the model. Defenders of the Solow approach argue there is no inherent contradiction in integrating knowledge into his model and that the fuzzy definitions of knowledge make endogenous models analytically sloppy. Others, particularly economic historians, have resented that the mathematical models of Romer and Lucas made them look more scientific than the details could support. Despite these critiques, endogenous growth theory has won acceptance from many, and both Romer and Lucas have been awarded the Nobel Prize in Economics.[20]

What is most important for the invention of infinite growth is the fact that endogenous growth theory swept away the last of the tenuous connections between economics and the natural world. Knowledge "will grow without bound," Romer confidently declared, leaving no reason to forecast an end to growth. Even the finite supply of exhaustible resources would not end growth, since, as Romer and a colleague asserted, new ideas would develop faster than resources would run out. The price of an exhaustible resource, they concluded, "can remain constant or decline monotonically for all time."[21]

For all time. This was a level of optimism exceeding even that of RFF or the natural resource economists, who tended to limit their purview to the next few decades. The infinite potential of the human mind enabled the infinite growth of the economy. Julian Simon would have agreed.

Rolling the DICE

It was a hot day to be wearing a blazer and tie, but James Hansen donned them to speak to the Senate Committee on Energy and Natural Resources on June 23, 1988. A physicist who was head of NASA's Goddard Institute for Space Studies, he had a clear message: global warming was happening, and it was almost certainly due to the greenhouse gas effect and the burning of fossil fuels. Summers were already getting hotter and droughts more likely, and this trend would only continue if the threat was not taken seriously.[22]

While Paul Romer was extolling the potential of knowledge to produce growth without bounds, natural scientists were speaking with increasing alarm about global warming. The issue was not exactly new. The potential of carbon dioxide and other greenhouse gases to trap solar radiation had been theorized as early as the mid-nineteenth century, and the Swedish scientist Svante Arrhenius created the first model of climate change in 1896. Hansen had come to the issue in the late 1960s as he studied the atmosphere of Venus. It was known that surface temperatures on Venus were much hotter than on Earth and that the thick atmosphere must be contributing. Hansen helped refine the understanding of how Venus's heat got trapped, which then led to a research project on the surface temperatures of Earth. By 1987, their data showed a distinctive pattern of warming.[23] Many other researchers were reaching similar findings, and in 1988, the United Nations authorized the creation of the Intergovernmental Panel on Climate Change (IPCC), a body committed to synthesizing and reporting the latest findings on climate change.[24]

As with *The Limits to Growth*, economists were not convinced of the need for urgent or aggressive action. The most prominent economist to research climate change has been William Nordhaus. He was born in New Mexico in 1941 and grew up fly-fishing, skiing, and exploring the arid Albuquerque basin, giving him an appreciation of the great outdoors and an awareness of the fragile balance of nature. Mild mannered and extremely bright, he thrived at Yale as an undergraduate, then studied for his PhD at MIT with Solow and Samuelson. He so impressed his mentors that Samuelson invited Nordhaus to coauthor the later editions of his enormously influential textbook and President Carter appointed him to the Council of Economic Advisers (CEA).

Like many enterprising graduate students at MIT in the 1960s working with Solow, Nordhaus's doctoral work focused on growth theory. And when the environmental movement gained steam in the early 1970s, he joined his mentor to assess whether ecological limits to growth were real. Like Solow, his answer was largely no. In 1972, he and his fellow Yale economics professor James Tobin cowrote an article titled "Is Growth Obsolete?" in which they denied the likelihood of growth ending. In 1973, he savaged the computer model underlying *The Limits to Growth* for sloppy thinking and grandiose claims. The following year, he argued the empirical evidence did not suggest resources would be a constraint on growth. His article included an early reference to the specter of global warming, though his conclusion was that "waste heat could conceivably be a problem—but not for a while."[25]

The idea of global warming stuck with Nordhaus, who traveled in 1974 to the International Institute for Advanced Systems Analysis (IIASA) for a fellowship abroad. Founded just two years before as an effort to ease Cold War tensions through scientific collaboration between East and West, IIASA was located near Vienna in a restored Hapsburg summer castle. Nordhaus was randomly assigned to share an office with the climatologist Allan Murphy, and their discussions encouraged him to think about how to integrate climate, energy, and growth.[26] By 1977 Nordhaus was arguing that the problem was a "classical example of a market failure" or of an externality in the Pigouvian sense.[27] Putting a price on emissions, therefore, represented the most logical response. But he claimed prices should rise slowly and not very high. Doing nothing may be unwise, but acting too aggressively would be worse if it stalled growth. A very modest price phased in over several decades represented the socially optimal approach. It made sense to be "relatively optimistic" about the technical and economic feasibility of addressing climate change.[28]

In 1992, Nordhaus launched the Dynamic Integrated Climate Economy (DICE) model, which would become the world's most influential economic model of climate change.[29] At its core, DICE sought to apply the insights of growth theory to climate change. The fundamental premise was that society had to choose between consumption now, growth in the future, or a stable climate. This meant that Nordhaus approached climate change as a "question of balance" between these competing goals.[30] Business as usual would generate harms from climate change in the long term, but spending too much

William Nordhaus has been the world's most influential climate economist for several decades, highlighted by being awarded the Nobel Prize in Economics in 2018. He has consistently argued that the benefits of growth frequently outweigh the costs of addressing climate change. Bengt Nyman, CC BY 2.0, https://creativecommons.org/licenses/by/2.0, via Wikimedia Commons.

on mitigation efforts would lower social welfare by limiting growth. "Any rational strategy," he confidently told readers of *Science*, had to grapple with the economics of optimal growth.[31]

And what did growth theory tell people about climate change? Its most important lesson was that aggressive action to tackle climate change was worse than doing nothing. During the 1990s global political leaders and climate scientists began to converge on the idea that emissions should be stabilized at 1990 levels and that the global rise in temperature should not exceed 2 degrees Celsius. But Nordhaus's model argued that such an approach would impose costs that far exceeded their benefits. The optimal path was a very modest policy of abatement—equivalent in 1992 to a tax of about $5 per ton of carbon. Such a path, Nordhaus calculated, would result in average increase of temperature of more than 3 degrees Celsius by the end of the twenty-first century.[32]

Simon loved the spotlight and to gall environmentalists by declaring, "there are no meaningful limits" to growth.[33] The mild-mannered Nordhaus, by contrast, avoided hyperbole and did not seek headlines. But their conclusions hardly differed. Growth was more important than environmental protections. Being richer was better than keeping sea levels stable.

Does Growth Make Life Better?

Nordhaus's conclusions rested on a bedrock assumption of mainstream economic thought: increasing economic welfare through growth is the best path for improving lives. But this is not true in all times and places. The correlation of growth and quality of life depends enormously on how wealthy one is to begin with and how equally the pie is distributed. Yet these crucial questions have garnered little interest among mainstream economists. This has led to an overestimation of growth's benefits that offers a dubious guide to crafting a sustainable and thriving human future.

The most common assumption within the economics profession has been that growth as measured by GDP, despite its limitations, is a suitable proxy for human welfare. This viewpoint has origins at least as far back as the early twentieth century when Pigou declared that economics should focus on economic welfare rather than human well-being. The former could be an object of scientific study using the price system, whereas the latter was so broad it should be left to philosophers. While he acknowledged that under specific circumstances, improvements in economic welfare might lower overall welfare or vice versa, such situations were likely to be exceptions. He argued that "we may regard" improvements in economic welfare "as *probably* equivalent in direction, though not in magnitude, to the effect on total welfare."[34] Walter Heller, who had served as head of President Kennedy's CEA, agreed in 1972: "Large advances in per capita GDP are associated with significant differences and advances in well-being."[35] William Nordhaus thought similarly, acknowledging that while GDP gains may overstate growth's benefits somewhat, a strong correlation still existed.[36]

In the decades after World War II when infinite growth was invented, these claims seemed validated. Not only was the pie getting bigger, it was being shared relatively equally across the income spectrum. Millions were able to improve their economic position and enter the middle class. But since the 1970s, the story has been very different. Skyrocketing inequality and stagnation for average Americans has diminished the social value of growth, though this has hardly shifted economic thinking.

In 1974, the economist Richard Easterlin issued a major challenge to this consensus: growth and welfare were strongly linked at low levels of income, he demonstrated, and weakly linked after people attained middle-class incomes. A student of Simon Kuznets who shared his mentor's commitment to empirical research and skepticism that any single measurement should be relied on, Easterlin based his conclusion on survey data of happiness over time in several countries. He saw that when average incomes were low, a growing economy generated significant surges in the quality of life. But once nations achieved a certain level of wealth—about a middle-class standard—growth and happiness ceased to be correlated. Income continued to rise, but people no longer described their lives as getting better. This has become known as the Easterlin paradox.[37]

Easterlin explained this by looking at what advances in economic welfare could achieve for different people. For those in poverty, more money could improve quality of life via food security, better housing, quality health care, and better education opportunities. Having these social goods could lead directly to healthier, longer, and happier lives.

But once basic needs are met and people have some disposable income for emergencies or leisure, getting richer has only a very moderate effect on well-being. The key thing, Easterlin pointed out, is that much of well-being is relational. Because we live in societies, our happiness depends not simply on what we have, but on how that compares to our neighbors. As Karl Marx had observed more than a century before, when everyone lived in a small home, people were largely satisfied. But once a large home was built nearby, the small houses began to feel cramped and undesirable.[38] As a society gets richer, people's ideas of what constitutes a good life rise with them. "An increase in the income of any one individual would increase his happiness, but increasing the income of everyone would leave happiness unchanged," Easterlin observed.[39] This makes the achievement of a state of happiness a goal as elusive as reaching the end of a rainbow. Growth creates "an escalation in human aspirations," he concluded, that "negates the expected positive impact on welfare."[40] Easterlin's research provided a scientific backing to the folk wisdom that money cannot buy happiness.[41]

Yet Easterlin's findings have not made major inroads among mainstream economists. Economists in general are skeptical of survey data, preferring whenever possible to measure people's choices through market transactions. Others have argued the data do not support Easterlin's conclusions and that there is a robust connection between income growth and well-being. Still others have claimed that well-being is too imprecise a goal and should therefore not be a focus of government policy.[42] In response, Easterlin has pointed out that studies by many critics focus on too short a time period where events like recessions cause people to report lower welfare when growth slows, rather than capturing long-term trends. In particular, Easterlin has cited happiness surveys showing no significant gains among Americans from 1972 to 2014 despite GDP more than doubling. It is this long view, he declares, that matters most.[43]

The economic historian Robert Gordon came to a similar finding by different means. Analyzing the technological transformations in America from the end of the Civil War to 1970, he argued that economic growth drove increases in quality of life that far exceeded the gains in GDP. Consider what life was like for the average American in 1870. Such a person would own two or three sets of clothing, live in small quarters that were cold in the winter and hot in the summer, have no access to indoor plumbing, rarely travel faster than the speed of a horse, work long hours, and eat a plain and minimally varied diet. Major technological innovations drove not only a rapid expansion in GDP but even greater shifts like the development of electrical grids that made factories safer and homes more pleasant and access to automobiles for personal transport. Other changes were humbler yet equally crucial: the ready-made clothing industry that lowered prices of outfits so that cleanliness and variety were not privileges of the wealthy. The rise of indoor plumbing was not simply a convenience but a breakthrough for sanitation and health. By 1970, Americans lived longer and in much greater comfort, worked shorter hours, and had more access to leisure time. These gains, Gordon posited, outstripped the story of GDP growth.[44]

But like Easterlin, Gordon cautioned that economic growth does not always deliver such social benefits. Since the 1970s, major technological transformations have largely come in the field of information and communication technologies. Economic growth continued, but it was much less clear that Americans were getting better off. People certainly benefited from large reductions in the cost of long-distance calling and have enjoyed a proliferating array of entertainment choices. But these innovations have not made workdays shorter or changed the quality of the housing stock, and few would claim that people are ten times happier when they can choose from 1,000 television channels versus one hundred or have twice the enjoyment when they watch a movie on a screen that is twice as large. The technological transformations of the last half century, he concluded, did much less to improve quality of life than those in the century before.[45]

Scholars of inequality have provided further arguments to question the link between economic growth and better lives. Inequality, many studies have shown, causes significant social harms. And it has been the major trend since the 1970s in the United States and much of the rest of the global North. The bottom half of wage earners saw their share of national income drop nearly a third from 1971 to 2016 while the top 10 percent increased their share by more than half.[46] And increasingly, the story has been one of enormous gains by the wealthiest. From 1980 to 2014, the bottom half of wage earners saw their income grow by a paltry 1 percent while the top 1 percent increased 204 percent and the top 0.01 percent grew by 453 percent.[47] This has essentially been a shift of about 8 percent of the nation's income from the bottom half to the top 1 percent.[48] The average American family is scarcely better off than it was forty years ago, and the size of the middle class has shrunk.[49]

Growing inequality has decreased the quality of life for many Americans outside the top 10 percent. In part, this is linked to the relational value of wealth identified by Easterlin. But it is more than

Since the 1980s, inequality has grown rapidly, with the wealthiest individuals gaining the most while the wages of middle-class workers in much of the global North have stagnated. The Occupy Wall Street protests in 2011 captured growing dissatisfaction with the harms of inequality, which include worse health outcomes, lower social cohesion, and increased political strife. David Shankbone, CC BY 3.0, https://creativecommons.org/licenses/by/3.0, via Wikimedia Commons.

just jealousy. Inequality undermines social cohesion, leading to decreased trust in fellow citizens and public institutions. When inequality increases, voter turnout often declines along with trust in government. The dramatic increase in the polarization of politics in the last several years, from the Trump presidencies in America to Brexit in Britain to the rise of authoritarian leaders across the globe, is also evidence of how decades of increasing inequality can erode social bonds. Large wealth disparities even affect health measures, contributing to lower life expectancy and increases in obesity, drug use, and teenage births.[50]

At the same time, making the top 1 percent even wealthier has almost no effect on that group's well-being. For millionaires, an extra $10,000 in one of their bank accounts does not make a tangible difference, while for those with tens of millions, even an additional million dollars will not gain them access to any goods or services not already available to them. A growing economy that channels the bulk of its gains to those who are already well-off—as the American economy has for the last several decades—delivers at best minimal improvements in well-being for elites while causing significant harm for the bulk of the population.

Despite this evidence about the decreasing social benefits of growth since the 1970s, most mainstream economists have not been willing to give up the idea that improvements in GDP offer a suitable proxy for lives getting better. In part, this is because most have downplayed concerns over inequality. Pareto's idea that a change is justified so long as none is made worse off remains a core concept in economics, even though that test does nothing to discourage unequal distributions of wealth. Moreover, inequality is seen as an acceptable outcome of free market forces and even as a spur to innovation: having some people be richer than others generates capital for investment and incentivizes people to work harder and smarter. As an example of how economists have minimized concerns over inequality, the author of the most widely used introductory economics textbook in America, N. Gregory Mankiw, wrote a 2013 article titled "Defending the One Percent."[51]

In 1997, Nordhaus concurred that growth makes lives better by arguing that gains in GDP might understate the gains in human well-being rather than overstating them. His starting point was that when technological progress made things better and cheaper, GDP would not account for the benefits consumers gained from lower prices. To demonstrate, he turned to the history of lighting, assessing the cost of various light sources compared to the illumination they offered, ranging from open fires to candles to electric lightbulbs. He then calculated the income a worker would receive from an hour of labor and translated that into how much illumination those earnings could purchase. The conclusion he came to was stark: "An hour's work today will buy about 350,000 times as much illumination as could be bought in early Babylonia."[52] This suggested a tale of remarkable progress that was hidden in GDP, because as light got cheaper and better, it represented an ever-smaller part of people's expenditures. Humans were not just getting richer as GDP increased, they were getting access to a much better array of products and services that cost less than they ever had before. Things were getting better. Much, much better. *"The true rise in living standards in this sector has been vastly understated,"* he emphasized.[53]

This conclusion has been echoed by others, such as Diane Coyle, an economist who has written about the strengths and weaknesses of GDP. Even while noting some of the number's limits, she has still maintained that "GDP growth is closely linked to social welfare."[54] Following Nordhaus, she concluded that due to the increasing array of products and services consumers had access to, "GDP growth actually increasingly *under*estimates increases in welfare."[55]

The enduring faith among economists that growth always generates better lives ignores history. Ample evidence reveals that growth's social benefits in America were much higher during the golden era of growth after World War II than they have been since the 1980s. This can be seen in surveys that show Americans are many times wealthier than they were fifty years ago but do not report themselves to be happier. And it is apparent from stalled measures of health outcomes and life expectancies, barely decreased working hours, and a shrinking middle class. Growth is not a timeless good, except in the abstract world of most economic models.

Discounting the Future

Some numbers derive their power from their visibility, like GDP, whose movements are front-page news.[56] But other numbers exert great influence in obscurity.

Consider the discount rate. The idea behind it is relatively simple, but how it is calculated makes an enormous difference. Within economics, it is common to assume that a dollar today is worth more than a dollar in the future. One reason is that humans like immediate gratification, and if everything else is equal, people would rather have something now rather than wait six months for it. There is also the matter of uncertainty. If a person waits a year to make a purchase, it is possible the object will no longer be available, or it might have risen in price; there is also the possibility that the person may have died. Finally, there is a general faith that society is likely to be richer in the future than it is today. Since the last two centuries have witnessed a great deal of economic growth, the purchasing power of the average individual has increased regularly. This pattern implies that the benefit of one more dollar in a future bank account is less than it will be for a person today.[57]

The discount rate, which is essentially an inverted interest rate, is how economists calculate what to do in the present for the benefit of the future. Like interest rates, discount rates are compounded over time, so small adjustments can make enormous differences. For example, if you invest $10,000 today for fifty years, it will be worth $20,040 at a rate of 1.4 percent, $145,000 at 5.5 percent, and more than $1,150,000 at 10 percent. The same logic holds for discount rates. If you wanted to avoid a million dollars of damage fifty years from now, it is worth paying nearly half a million dollars today if you use a discount rate of 1.4 percent. But if you calculate it with a discount rate of 5.5 percent, it is only worth spending less than

$70,000 today, and at a rate of 10 percent, the number drops to under $10,000. These few percentage points have massive implications for cost–benefit analyses of present-day actions.

In 2006, the British economist Nicholas Stern brought the use of discount rates in climate calculations to the fore with a major study that was far less optimistic than Nordhaus's DICE model. He had been tasked by the British government with reviewing the state of climate economics and offering policy guidance, and his team came to a clear conclusion: strong action on climate change was needed and economically rational. Stern and his colleagues saw the prospect of doing little as dire—it could ultimately generate damages as high as 20 percent of global GDP annually. But by investing 1–2 percent of GDP in combating climate change now, society would be much better off.[58] The Stern Review was quickly hailed within the scientific and environmental communities.[59]

The economics community was much less impressed. As with the publication of *The Limits to Growth* more than three decades before, economists downplayed the need for urgent action. Many looked to see Nordhaus's reaction. He was, as the director of the Columbia Earth Institute, Jeffrey Sachs, pointed out, "about the most reasonable person I know." But Nordhaus largely rebuffed Stern's findings. The heart of the debate centered on the discount rate.[60]

The Stern Review had argued for much stronger action in the present in part because it advocated for discount rates as low as 1.4 percent in some of its calculations. This was based on an argument that future generations would highly value climate stability and that the value of environmental amenities would be higher. Nordhaus disagreed, arguing that discount rates should be derived from a market measure, such as the rate of interest, the cost of borrowing money, or the return on capital; such rates were typically between 5 and 10 percent.[61] For Nordhaus, Stern's choice of a low discount rate had little analytical foundation and was at best "vaguely justified by estimates of the probability of the extinction of the human race." Nordhaus concluded that "the Stern Review's unambiguous conclusions about the need for urgent and immediate action will not survive the substitution of assumptions that are consistent with today's marketplace real interest rates and savings rates."[62]

Stern responded by noting the impossibility of using market measures for topics for which no markets existed: "There is no market which reveals the preferences of a community considering responsible action over generations." The choices people made about interest rates could not be used to understand how much they valued bequeathing a stable climate to their grandchildren. Applying market rates was an act of "discrimination on the basis of birth dates" that was "ethically arbitrary" and was a "failure of the imagination." He also questioned the logic of applying discount rates to environmental goods, which instead of getting cheaper over time could be expected to grow scarcer and more costly. He chided economists for trying to treat an ethical problem as a mathematical one.[63]

Mainstream economists overwhelmingly sided with Nordhaus. Robert Mendelsohn found the Stern Review to largely be "smoke and mirrors" and "hand waving."[64] Partha Dasgupta agreed that climate change was a major challenge, but critiqued the Stern Review for the numbers it used to embody ethical principles. The matter required far more humility, he argued, and noted that "where the modern economist is rightly hesitant, the authors of the review are supremely confident."[65] Even sympathetic economists had their issues. Martin Weitzman agreed that aggressive action was needed on climate, but he believed the economic choices in Stern's model did not pass muster. The better way to justify upfront investments to address climate change was to think about insurance: individuals and businesses regularly paid to protect themselves against the uncertainty of catastrophic loss. Given the uncertainties in predicting the impacts of climate change and the possibility that damages could be worse than modeled, it was a rational and self-interested decision to insure against such worst-case scenarios through climate mitigation in the present. Such an approach could "recast" the Stern Review's "informal emphasis" into "sound analytical arguments."[66]

Discount rates operate in the background, like the choice of production functions in growth models. But they matter enormously. The difference between a discount rate of 5 percent and 2.5 percent leads to a sixfold difference in the measurement of the social cost of carbon.[67] The higher the discount rate, the less urgent it appears to address climate change. The resistance among mainstream economists to consider low discount rates has reinforced the belief that growth is too important to risk stalling, no matter what happens to the natural world.

"A Century of Climate Change is About as Good/ Bad for Welfare as a Year of Economic Growth"

The conviction among many mainstream economists that growth is more important than climate abatement has shown very little sign of slowing. In 2018, the environmental economist Richard Tol argued the average projection in recent work on climate change economics was that a temperature increase of 2.5 degrees Celsius "would make the average person feel as if she had lost 1.3 percent of her income." Since 1.3 percent of a person's income could be returned to them through one year of moderate growth and it would take a while to reach 2.5 degrees of warming, Tol concluded that "a century of climate change is about as good/bad for welfare as a year of economic growth."[68] As a result, the issue of climate change should be considered a matter "for those who are concerned about the distant future, faraway lands, and remote probabilities."[69]

Nordhaus has always been careful to keep his rhetoric neutral, but his findings have continued to articulate a similar message. In 2017, he argued that the costs of 3 degrees of warming would be about 1.8 percent of global income, a worthwhile price to bear for the benefits that growth would supply.[70] In 2018, while calling climate change the "ultimate challenge for economics," he still believed the economically optimal path of climate abatement would allow global warming to reach 3.5 degrees in 2100 and still increase for several more decades.[71] The next year, he determined it did not make sense to take more aggressive action to prevent the melting of the Greenland ice sheet, a development that would raise global sea levels by more than seven meters. Under all but the lowest discount rates, there was no reason to increase a carbon price to protect the ice sheets, since the benefits were too far into the future.[72]

The contrast between this vision of minor economic losses to individuals and the scenarios described by most other climate scientists is stark. Scientists' scenarios are less often quantified in dollars and cents but point to major disruptions. The IPCC argues that at 3 degrees of warming, the world will face massive extinctions of biodiversity, frequent heatwaves and droughts, and extreme rainfall events. These events will compound over time and also interact with one another: droughts and heatwaves make wildfires more likely, while wildfires consume plants that absorb rainfall. When heavy rains fall on burned landscapes, they are much more likely to produce erosion and flooding that is far more damaging than it otherwise would be. Such shifts will likely render many places unable to support traditional patterns of agriculture, potentially creating tens of millions of climate refugees. These scenarios imply major disruptions to the patterns of everyday life, even in wealthy nations, not minor dips in income.[73]

Earth scientists also fear the possibility of climatic tipping points—disruptive changes that cannot be reversed in human timescales. If ice sheets in Greenland or Antarctica melt, for example, it would take tens of thousands of years to restore them. Warming oceans might also alter the cycles of ocean circulation, thereby disrupting the Gulf Stream current that keeps Europe's climate mild or altering the Indian Ocean monsoons that provide fresh water to billions. Moreover, some of these tipping points could be self-reinforcing: melting of the Greenland ice sheets will lower the height of its glaciers, thereby subjecting them to higher temperatures at lower elevations and accelerating the process. The melting of permafrost will release huge quantities of methane, a much more potent greenhouse gas than carbon dioxide. There is great uncertainty around tipping points and whether and how fast they will occur, but scientists argue they could be nonlinear and extremely disruptive.[74]

What explains this gap between seeing climate change as a foundational threat to humanity versus an issue of "the distant future, faraway places, and remote probabilities"? One possibility is that climate economists have simply been bought off by Big Oil and their analyses represent deliberate sabotage of a consensus on climate change. There is a long history of powerful corporations funding scientists willing to shill their messages with biased research, and the economics profession has received large amounts of support from conservative donors and think tanks.[75] But such an explanation does not seem to hold much water in this case. Nordhaus, like his mentor Solow, has consistently embraced left-of-center positions and served on the CEA for Carter. Tol's synthetic study was published in a leading journal sponsored by the Association of Environmental and Resource Economists, a progressive group of economists.[76]

The more compelling answer is that their economic optimism largely derives from the discipline's enduring faith in growth, rather than its ignoring of the natural world. Analysts like Tol and Nordhaus accept that there will be negative impacts from climate change. They also acknowledge that the worst consequences will be felt by the world's poorest, many of whom work outdoors in hot zones where climate impacts may be most severe, and that they have the fewest resources to respond to environmental disruptions.[77] But this leaves a question: Is it better for the world's poor to stop climate change and remain poor, or to get wealthier while having to devote some of those additional resources to adapting to climate change? Tol and Nordhaus argue for the latter. Even with a stable climate, those in poverty face a great deal of vulnerability to issues such as political unrest and medical emergencies. Stopping climate change would not help them if they broke a leg or a civil war forced them to leave their homes. Being richer would help in those cases as well as adapting to climate change. As Nordhaus put it, if stringent climate goals "would require deep reductions in living standards in poor nations, then the policy would be the equivalent of burning down the village to save it."[78] Solving poverty, they claim, is a higher priority than addressing climate change, because it will help people address a range of threats to their well-being.

Growth has also been argued to be equally important in wealthier nations. Economists often see environmental protection as a luxury item that people will only invest in if they have surplus income: the greater the income surplus, the more consumers will be willing to dedicate to the environment. Some also invoke the idea of an "environmental Kuznets curve" based on Simon Kuznets's finding that inequality grew worse while countries were industrializing and then declined as they got wealthier. In the environmental space, countries have the worst pollution and emissions in early stages of development and then clean up their economies once they have grown wealthy. Regardless of whether people are poor or rich, then, economists frequently believe the benefits of growth outstrip the costs of climate change.[79]

But there are three major holes in this argument. The first is that this view rests on a narrow conception of the harms of climate change. Damage estimates by Nordhaus and Tol exclude many of the consequences of a warming planet. Their focus on monetized costs means that massive extinctions of biodiversity are not factored in, nor are more mundane experiences, such as decreased enjoyment of summer by those who cannot enjoy being outdoors due to extreme heat or wildfire smoke. These models assume that because 87 percent of work in industrialized nations takes place indoors, it will see no economic impact from climate change. Moreover, even these expenditures, along with money paid to repair infrastructure damaged by climate change or raise seawalls, will increase GDP, further reducing the view that climate change is a problem. Finally, the damage calculations do not take into consideration tipping points or the possibility of nonlinear effects from climate change. In these economic models, then, people on a hotter planet might have higher air conditioning bills, pay more for property insurance, and face higher taxes for infrastructure repair, but life will otherwise go on as normal.[80]

The second problem is that these assumptions do not match how many people think about quality of life or our obligations to future generations. Critics of this view have noted that the use of high discount rates fails to align with how many people value the future: looking at financial bequests to future generations shows that many implicitly employ very low discount rates by trying to maximize the wealth left for their heirs. They have demonstrated that many people are willing to pay to preserve biodiversity and access to treasured landscapes. They have warned that irreversible changes and tipping points make the warming associated with the economically optimal output far more dangerous than economists imply. And they have pointed out that issues of forced migration will represent enormous human suffering. The idea that people can simply shift to new lands when climate change renders old areas unsuited for agriculture is belied by widespread resistance to refugees and increasing nationalism across the globe. The belief that climate change will be a manageable nuisance that our wealthier children can handle only makes sense when these considerations are excluded.[81]

Finally, at the same time that these models underplay the risks of climate change, they overstate the benefits of growth. The simple assumption remains that growth increases economic welfare in a linear manner. Two more dollars are twice as good as one more dollar, and the job of the economist is to figure out how to grow the pot, not determine its distribution. A rising tide, in this view, should raise all boats. In reality, this is not how the world has worked for the last several decades: yachts have been buoyed up while rowboats have been swamped. By excluding questions of distribution, these models paint a distorted view of what actions are rational to take to protect the environment.[82]

*

On October 8, 2018, the Nobel Prize in Economics was awarded to William Nordhaus and Paul Romer. The committee hailed Nordhaus for "integrating climate change into long-run macroeconomic analysis" and credited Romer with "integrating technological innovations into long-run macroeconomic analysis."[83]

The year 2018 was notable for many other reasons as well. At the time, it was the fourth hottest year in human history and saw record high temperatures everywhere from the Arctic to Japan and from Siberia to Death Valley; most of these records have already been eclipsed. The same year, Hurricane Florence broke records for rainfall deposited in the Carolinas; intense monsoons in India led to flooding that killed hundreds and caused billions of dollars of damage; wildfires in California and Greece killed scores of people; and droughts devastated farmers in northern and central Europe, Argentina and Uruguay, South Africa, China, Australia, and the United States.

The awarding of the Nobel Prize to Nordhaus and Romer exemplifies the chasm separating economists from most other thinkers about the environment. Romer was the man who declared in 1984 that exhaustible resources could be obtained at steady or decreasing prices for all time, and who saw no meaningful environmental limits to growth. The celebration of Nordhaus as an environmental scholar was far more galling to environmentalists, since his models undermined calls to move more aggressively to curb greenhouse gas emissions. In his Nobel acceptance speech, he argued the economically optimal strategy would allow warming of as much as 3.8 degrees Celsius. The idea that Nordhaus was being celebrated for his contributions to environmental policy struck many as absurd, if not offensive.[84]

The Nobel Prize committee made a further declaration about what it considered the most important economic ideas by excluding Martin Weitzman, whom many had assumed would someday share the award with Nordhaus. Their stories had long been intertwined. Both students of Solow who entered MIT in the mid-1960s, they served on the Yale faculty together for a time and worked on climate and the environment. Weitzman drew attention to the uncertainties of climate change. Given all we do not know, he thought it would be economically rational to prepare for tipping points with high consequences. Strong action to prevent climate change in the present was a wise investment just like life insurance. For environmentalists, Weitzman offered a much more compelling message of uncertainty and caution. For Weitzman, the Nobel oversight was a bitter disappointment. He began despairing about the limited influence of his work and a decline in his mental faculties; less than a year later, he took his own life.[85]

Awarding the discipline's highest honor to two men whose models celebrated growth and either downplayed or outright rejected the idea of natural limits while overlooking a voice of caution encapsulates the enduring optimism of the dismal science. It also reveals the power of past ideas. Nordhaus and Romer's optimism was grounded in old assumptions of welfare economics. It derived from the confidence that economists felt that they won the debate over limits to growth in the 1970s. And it built on a narrow vision of the environment that excluded as much as it included.

The Nobel Prize decision reveals both the resilience and danger of the invention of infinite growth. The continuing faith that growth offers so many benefits that its costs will only be minor nuisances is one of the most significant obstacles to crafting a more sustainable future.

9 * Green Growth and Its Discontents

When world leaders gathered in Rio de Janeiro in 1992 for the Earth Summit, it was an exciting and uncertain time. The Soviet Union had broken apart the year before, ending the Cold War and raising hopes for greater international harmony. The success of "Asian tiger" economies during the previous decades provided an inspiring model for many developing nations. Yet the future of the environment looked less encouraging. The dangers of climate change were becoming clearer and environmental degradation and loss of biodiversity were threatening communities around the globe. To tackle these challenges, the United Nations organized a major event: the Conference on Environment and Development. Thousands of people and many of the world's top officials came to Rio in June to discuss biodiversity protection, Indigenous rights, and climate change. Over ten days, presidents, prime ministers, and other heads of state negotiated how to balance economic growth with environmental protections.

It was a rousing success. The conference led to the

United Nations Framework Convention on Climate Change, which helped generate the Kyoto Protocol five years later, and nations agreed to protect biodiversity and acknowledged that while global environmental questions represented a common interest, more could be expected of wealthier nations than poorer ones under the idea of common but differentiated responsibilities.[1]

Hoping to build on these successes, the UN coordinated another global conference in Rio twenty years later. This time, it did not go nearly as well. In 2012, many nations were still struggling with the economic downturn stemming from the 2008 global financial crisis, and it had become clear to most that the Kyoto Protocol no longer offered a viable response to climate change. The spirit of international collaboration that marked the end of the Cold War was waning, and several major world leaders, including Barack Obama, David Cameron, and Angela Merkel, declined to attend. Expectations going into the Rio+20 conference were low, and the three days of meetings did not achieve any major breakthroughs or agreements. It was widely considered a disappointing result.[2]

But it would be a mistake to assume the Rio+20 conference achieved nothing. It left an important legacy, though not necessarily the one environmental advocates desired. Attendees picked up and promoted a new concept that was starting to gain worldwide attention: green growth.

Since the early 2010s, green growth has offered the latest justification for infinite economic expansion. Proponents of green growth argue there is no contradiction between growth and environmental sustainability. Markets can produce a clean environment as long as price signals are properly aligned and eco-friendly innovation is encouraged. If the right market indicators can be developed for the earth's ecosystem services, then green capitalists and entrepreneurs will create clean technologies, and infinite growth will no longer threaten the planet. Green growth offers a rosy view of a boundless future with little sacrifice.[3]

Like previous invocations of infinite growth, green growth's promises have rung hollow to critics, who question whether growth is as essential to human improvement as its advocates suggest and challenge its assumptions that market forces are enough to achieve planetary sustainability. These debates have roots much deeper than the espousal of green growth. For more than half a century, economists and critics have argued over the merits of measuring growth through GDP and questioned whether alternative metrics should be used. Revisiting this history places the concept of green growth in broader context and offers substantial reason to be skeptical about its ability to deliver a sustainable future.

The Greening of GDP

It was a dream team of economists given an exciting charge: rethink the world's most powerful number. The year was 2008, and French President Nicholas Sarkozy had decided GDP was doing more harm than good. He was a surprising voice for reform. As a conservative politician and former minister of finance, most of his policy actions had sought to loosen government restrictions on the economy and boost market forces. But with the onset of a global recession in 2007, he grew increasingly concerned with the "growing gap between statistics that show continuing progress and the increasing difficulties (French people) are having in their daily lives."[4] So he pulled together a team of Nobel Prize winners, top World Bank officials, and high-level government appointees: Joseph Stiglitz as head, Amartya Sen as major adviser, and Jean-Paul Fitoussi as coordinator; notable members included Kenneth Arrow, Geoffrey Heal, Daniel Kahneman, and Nicholas Stern. A year later, they issued a report highlighting the inadequacies of GDP as a measure, emphasizing its failures to assess well-being and environmental sustainability. "What we measure affects what we do," the commission argued, concluding that "GDP is an inadequate metric."[5] It was time to prioritize statistics that emphasized well-being and sustainability rather than simply the size of economic production.

Their message found a receptive audience. In 2009, many were asking why economists had done so little to predict the bursting of housing and financial bubbles that had led to a global financial collapse. What else might economists be missing? Nor was Stiglitz's team alone in questioning GDP's prominence. In 2007, the European Union in collaboration with the Organisation for Economic Co-operation and Development (OECD), the Club of Rome, and the World Wildlife Fund had hosted a conference on "Beyond GDP" that led to a formal initiative being established. The OECD labeled the release of the Sarkozy report a "defining moment" and established a *Better Life Initiative* in 2011 to complement the organization's focus on growth with attention to well-being.[6] It asked Stiglitz, Fitoussi, and several contributors to the Sarkozy report to continue to analyze the connections between economic measurements and the quality of life. Their efforts have helped encourage many countries to collect and publish data on a much wider set of measures of well-being than is captured in GDP.[7]

Stiglitz's efforts to highlight environmental sustainability represented an evolution in his career. A student of Robert Solow and Paul Samuelson in the 1960s at MIT, he joined Solow in pushing back against the message of *The Limits to Growth*, reiterating that growth did not depend on nonrenewable resources.[8] Capital and technological progress could substitute for natural resources making "sustained growth in consumption *per capita* feasible."[9] He restated these points as late as 1997, as he was transitioning from being chairman of the Council of Economic Advisers (CEA) to chief economist of the World Bank.[10] Only after the turn of the twenty-first century did he increase the urgency of his warnings about environmental problems.

Critiquing GDP is a practice as old as the measure itself.[11] Simon Kuznets, the man who did so much to make the measure possible, offered several warnings starting in the 1930s about the danger of conflating a single number with social welfare, particularly when that number excluded many social goods, like leisure, and included many undesirable activities, such as the production of military means of war. Many other economists agreed, noting that consumption was a closer measure of what people cared about. From the 1970s to 1990s, a series of prominent economists offered suggested revisions to GDP or alternative accounting systems that sought to overcome its limitations, including William Nordhaus, James Tobin, Robert Eisner, Dale Jorgenson, John Kendrick, and Richard and Nancy Ruggles.[12]

For others, the big problem was that GDP excluded the natural world. Martin Weitzman helped pioneer one environmental critique of GDP by noting that, because it excluded depreciation, it offered a misleading view of economic sustainability. Depreciation refers to the fact that when factories produce goods, their equipment wears down and must be maintained or replaced to sustain production. A gross measure (the "G" in GDP) does not account for this, which means that a big surge in GDP might mask the fact that companies were maximizing production in the short term in ways that would curtail their ability to produce goods in the future. Weitzman noted in 1976 that this could be applied to natural resources as well, such as "pools of exhaustible natural resources."[13] A "net" calculation (NDP) that included depreciation would therefore offer a better assessment of the nation's productive capacity while also including its natural resources. However, Weitzman did not think this measure of NDP would actually make a case for significant change. He later calculated that including the depreciation of the environment might lower GDP by a couple percentage points, but technological progress would more than offset the extraction of natural resources. NDP did not suggest the logic of infinite growth needed to be reconsidered.[14]

Dissatisfied with the complacency of mainstream economics, Herman Daly pioneered the Index of Sustainable Economic Welfare (ISEW) in 1989 in collaboration with the theologian and environmentalist John Cobb.[15] Seeking to shift the dismal science's emphasis from selfish individualism to community values, they developed a measure that added uncompensated labor in homes, accounted for inequality, and deducted military expenses. But their most distinct contribution came from drawing more attention to the natural world, including the environmental damages from resource depletion, pollution control, water and noise pollution, soil erosion, and loss of wetlands. Five years later, this work culminated in the creation of the genuine progress indicator (GPI), which built on ISEW's foundation. Comparing GPI to GDP revealed the disconnect between measuring economic output and environmental sustainability. Daly and Cobb calculated that in the quarter century after 1970, GDP had been increasing steadily in the wealthy parts of the world while GPI had been flat or declining. People had been getting richer at the expense of environmental sustainability without improving their well-being.[16]

As an economist at Louisiana State University for two decades, Herman Daly knew that the state's wetlands provided numerous benefits for fish, birds, and flood control. Yet these benefits were ignored by mainstream economists and did not factor into GDP calculations. Ryan Hagerty, US Fish and Wildlife Service, via Wikimedia Commons.

In 1993, the United Nations formalized a process for green accounting to supplement GDP by establishing the System of Environmental Economic Accounting (SEEA). It advised countries to assess the consumption of exhaustible resources and the degradation of environmental systems. However, debates over how to value environmental systems meant that SEEA calculations varied widely between nations, and political resistance in nations like the United States and China meant that these numbers soon ceased to be reported.[17]

None of these alternative measures has made a major impact. Green GDP has not caught the attention of policymakers, nor has it stalled the faith in infinite growth. Quarterly reports of GDP remain front-page news and get discussed at great length, while alternative calculations are treated minimally or not at all. Politicians get voted out of office when GDP goes down, but not when carbon emissions increase. As a recent review of these alternative measures concluded, "despite efforts by some of the world's most prominent economists to integrate sustainability measures into [national accounting systems], these efforts have largely been academic."[18]

Why has GDP been so difficult to budge? Some of it, no doubt, comes down to the allure of a single number. Dashboards and arrays of figures are difficult to interpret and keep track of, while one figure is easy to grasp. Some of it is also a product of training. Those who calculate and use GDP tend to be trained in mainstream economic and statistical traditions. These defenders of GDP have been quick to label alternative measures "flawed" and "arbitrary."[19]

Others have pointed to the utility of maintaining GDP. Arthur Okun, chairman of the CEA in the late 1960s, implored the Bureau of Economic Analysis in 1971 to "resist at all costs" calls to amend GDP to include social welfare. Such a task was impossible for anyone but a "philosopher–king."[20] He insisted that GDP "is *not* a measure of total social welfare" and that if the bureau sought to impute values for leisure time, housework, or the natural world, economists would end up with a muddled measure that failed to accurately capture anything. Only by refusing to alter how GDP was calculated could economists help ensure that "no sensible person could mistake it" for a measure of well-being. It was much better to stick to things with "price tags" that offered an "objective yardstick" that could guide policymakers.[21]

For many economists, GDP retains a rightful pride of place because it does better than any of the alternatives. As a measure of production, it provides insight into the economy that policymakers can act on to prepare for war, counteract recessions, or optimize growth. And while it does not measure human well-being directly, it offers a more objective measure of how to improve human lives than anything else. GDP "is certainly better than some of the fashionable alternatives (like 'happiness')," wrote one economist recently, and that "for all its flaws, [GDP] is still a bright light shining through the mist."[22] Arguments like these have carried more weight than those of the reformers. The efforts to promote green GDP have borne little fruit and they have done little to dislodge the idea that growth as measured through ever-increasing GDP is both possible and desirable.

From Green GDP to Green Growth

During a cool and cloudy week at the end of March 2005, more than five hundred participants from over fifty countries gathered in South Korea to discuss economic growth and the environment in Asia and the Pacific. This had become a common topic in international meetings since the 1970s, but members of the United Nations Economic and Social Commission for Asia and the Pacific (ESCAP) believed they needed a new approach because their region faced a unique set of challenges and opportunities. Some of them had achieved among the highest growth rates in the world over the previous several decades, highlighted by South Korea, Hong Kong, Singapore, and Taiwan. But the region also had high levels of poverty and acute environmental problems due to its dense populations and comparatively limited natural resources. Many of the region's countries had low per capita availability of water, energy, and arable land. Creating a sustainable future required thinking in new ways.[23]

For the previous two decades, most international conferences had focused on sustainable development, which had been defined by a commission headed by the former Norwegian Prime Minister Gro Harlem Brundtland in 1987 as "development that meets the needs of the present without compromising the ability of future generations to meet their own needs." Based on the three pillars of economic development, social development, and environmental protection, sustainable development was a useful concept because it could be adapted to local considerations. But this flexibility also caused some critics to argue that it was so vague as to be meaningless.[24]

The frustrations with sustainable development bubbled up in the conference rooms at the Hotel Lotte in Seoul in 2005 as government officials, development experts, academics, and industry leaders argued that it lacked "teeth" and risked being a "roadblock" to progress. Complaining that it was a "catch-all balancing act used to trade off seemingly competing interests," they sought a narrower and more specific concept that could allow member nations to make "fundamental, concrete, and measurable changes." That new framing was green growth, which they declared to be "the way forward for Asia and the Pacific."[25]

The central appeal of green growth came from its rejection of the idea that there was an inherent antagonism between economic growth and environmental protection. The conference report approved by the member nations praised green growth as a "win-win" approach that could succeed by tapping "innovative technologies and industries" to "harmonize" growth and sustainability. Rather than seeing environmental protection as a set of social costs, they claimed that eco-friendly business models should be seen as "a driver of growth and essential for long-term economic sustainability."[26]

The key to reconciling economic growth with a healthy planet lay in better markets. Environmental degradation, the report argued, resulted from "market failure" that led to the "loss of natural capital." The answer was to "internalize environmental costs into market prices," which would encourage new businesses and incentivize eco-friendly entrepreneurs. Investments in green infrastructure and green businesses would propel a new wave of eco-friendly economic growth.[27]

By stripping away the vague category of social development, which was hard to quantify, green growth advocates could emphasize narrower projects that could be assessed numerically. A number of existing projects already fit this mold, such as a policy in South Korea that offered free recycling but required businesses and consumers to purchase special bags for waste pickup, thereby increasing the cost of using landfills. This program led to a 22 percent reduction in waste and a significant surge in recycling. The report also touted a project in Thailand that provided incentives to increase energy efficiency and decrease wastewater discharges, thereby allowing companies to save money while reducing their environmental impact. Looking forward, the member states pointed to the potential of building infrastructure for mass transit instead of highways, encouraged companies to adopt green procurement strategies that would reduce the market for unsustainably harvested materials, and advocated disclosure policies that would force companies to publish data on where they got their materials and the pollution their factories released.[28] Even the poor could benefit if green growth encouraged companies to "increase the choices available to the poor" and to "empower them to develop small-scale green businesses."[29]

It is not surprising that as the host nation of the 2005 meeting, South Korea became the first nation to adopt green growth as a central national policy. Beginning in 2008, the Lee Myung-bak administration sought to distinguish South Korea as a global leader in green growth. The administration's signature initiative focused on building an extensive network of dams and enhanced riverbanks to increase water storage and decrease flooding along the nation's four largest rivers. As an object lesson in green infrastructure, it was designed to increase efficiency while generating jobs. The second effort was to boost the nuclear power industry, aiming to enhance the electricity grid while decreasing carbon emissions. In 2011, Lee was awarded the international Zayed Sustainability Prize in recognition of his efforts.[30]

From its roots in South Korea, international interest in green growth spread rapidly. By the time the Rio+20 conference kicked off, green growth had been embraced by influential institutions, including Europe's OECD and the World Bank. In 2011, the OECD published a report that emphasized that "green and growth can go hand in hand." Decrying "misguided government policies" and praising the potential of efficiency, price signals, and innovation, the OECD encouraged European nations to focus on policies that eliminated waste and created new green markets.[31] The following year, the World Bank announced its commitment to green growth, while pledging to support "investments, analytics, data, new institutions, and financial instruments" to create a green, clean, and resilient world.[32]

Green growth quickly attracted so many adherents, in large part, because it promised economic benefits without sacrifices. Amid the disappointments of Rio in 2012, green growth was one of the few points of agreement, because it did not ask anyone to give anything up. Member nations declared their "determination" to build "a green economy" without committing to any details of what that would entail.[33]

A strong initial impetus for the development of green growth was that sustainable development was too imprecise a concept for policymaking. Yet green growth has come under considerable attack for its own limitations. Consider the case of South Korea. While the Four Rivers Project was touted as green infrastructure, an emphasis on improving shipping lanes came at the expense of facilitating natural water flows, which resulted in major algae blooms that killed fish and damaged drinking water supplies. The focus on nuclear power, while it would result in lower carbon emissions, generated significant environmental risks through the production of nuclear waste. Moreover, given that Lee Myung-bak had made his money in construction

The Four Rivers Project in South Korea was the signature green growth project of President Lee Myung-bak, one of the most outspoken advocates of green growth. Critics argued there was little green about a project that emphasized improving shipping channels and dams, such as the Daecheong Dam on the Geum River pictured here. Yoo Chung, CC BY-SA 2.5, https://creativecommons.org/licenses/by-sa/2.5, via Wikimedia Commons.

before entering politics, many wondered whether green growth was simply a gloss to justify generous government spending in a sector that would enrich his businesses.[34]

Green growth has also been critiqued for its overlap with neoliberalism. Since the 1980s, the global financial order has been heavily influenced by neoliberal policies, which have celebrated free markets and privatization while attacking government regulations. Neoliberals have celebrated entrepreneurs and capitalists as the driving forces of the economy and have claimed that social benefit is achieved through voluntary participation in markets and economic expansion. Green growth advocates often echo these arguments, celebrating green investment and urging the use of markets to solve social problems. Within the neoliberal framework, there is little room for questions of social justice and equality, and this has often been true of green growth discussions. The last several decades of neoliberalism have generated enormous wealth for some, but massive inequality and social costs for many others. These damages are rarely acknowledged, making it unclear how green growth could create a better world without explicitly correcting the problems of neoliberalism.[35]

A third critique is that most green growth discourses lean heavily on incentives for increasing efficiency while being largely silent on the question of whether there are limits to the level of economic activity that can occur while maintaining planetary sustainability. Environmental scientists point to thresholds that should not be crossed, such as a finite carbon budget, the importance of not allowing global warming to exceed 1.5 or 2 degrees Celsius, and the idea of keeping human impacts within planetary boundaries. While increasing the efficiency of economic production will undoubtedly help meet these goals, simply providing carrots for eco-friendly businesses is unlikely to be a sufficient solution.[36]

The Limits of Decoupling

At its core, the faith in green growth stems from the belief that economic activity can be decoupled from environmental impact. If a new model of a car gets 20 percent better gas mileage, for example, it will lead to a corresponding decrease in gasoline consumption while still providing the same transportation services. When such improvements are spread across the entire economy, then the environmental impacts begin to be decoupled from the economic activity. Green growth advocates envision a future where the proper deployment of market price signals shifts the overall economy enough that growth occurs without greater demands on natural ecosystems.

The fundamental question is whether the pace of decoupling is capable of delivering a sustainable future. Assessing this question requires thinking about three forms of decoupling: relative, absolute, and sufficient. Relative decoupling means each unit of economic growth has less environmental impact than the one before. Absolute decoupling signifies that economic growth occurs while overall environmental impact declines. And sufficient decoupling happens when absolute environmental declines occur at a rate sufficient to avoid exceeding planetary boundaries. The historical record demonstrates strong evidence of relative decoupling in recent decades, some indication of absolute decoupling since the turn of the twenty-first century, and very little evidence of sufficient decoupling.[37]

Relative decoupling occurred throughout the twentieth century. The global economy grew at about an average rate of 3 percent while resource use only grew 2 percent.[38] This relative improvement increased efficiency, but the absolute growth of the economy still led to about a fourteenfold increase in global greenhouse gas emissions.[39] The pace of relative decoupling accelerated beginning in the 1970s, largely in response to increases in energy prices linked to the oil crises of 1973 and 1979 and the burgeoning environmental movement. The combination of stricter environmental laws and economic incentives for companies to reduce their energy consumption helped spur significant gains in efficiency.

An absolute decoupling of economic growth from resource consumption and carbon emissions has occurred since around 2005 in a small number of advanced economies, including the United States, Britain, Germany, France, and Japan. This trend has been largely associated with the rise of renewable energy, declines in manufacturing as a percentage of the economy, and in the United States, a boom in natural gas fracking that has displaced the use of coal in electricity production. Since 2005, for example, American GDP has risen by more than 20 percent while its total emissions have declined by more than 10 percent. Some European countries like Britain and France have seen even higher rates of absolute decoupling, with growth rates of 21 percent and 15 percent, respectively, and emissions declines of more than 33 percent and 26 percent.[40]

But are these absolute levels of decoupling sufficient to avert the worst dangers of climate change and preserve sensitive ecosystems? Here the data are less sanguine. To keep climate change within safe levels, it will be necessary for fossil fuel emissions to plummet at a much faster rate than they have. To reduce greenhouse emissions to a net-zero level by 2050 will require absolute decreases of emissions of 3–5 percent per year, and more if the economy expands significantly. There is no evidence these rates are close to being achieved. In fact, at current rates of decoupling, it would take industrial economies more than two centuries to reduce their emissions to the levels needed by 2050 to keep global warming under a 2-degree threshold.[41]

A further problem with the emphasis on decoupling is that it mirrors many of the same limitations of models assessing the economics of climate change. For one thing, there are limitations to the calculations that potentially skew the results. While many measures of decoupling have included the carbon emissions associated with the goods industrialized nations import from abroad, most do not include other measures of environmental impact, including land use change, airline emissions, and methane leaks. In this way, calculations of decoupling often undercount emissions and reduce questions of planetary sustainability to issues such as material inputs to production and greenhouse gases, thereby ignoring topics such as the preservation of wilderness spaces, ocean acidification, and biodiversity. Achieving a sustainable economy will require more than just decarbonization.[42]

Recent trends in decoupling should certainly be celebrated for demonstrating that it is possible to decrease the environmental impacts of many economic activities. The increases in efficiency and renewable energy generation over the last several decades make it much more possible to imagine viable scenarios for addressing climate change. Yet they also reveal the inadequacy of green growth to achieve planetary sustainability, because the current trends are too slow and incomplete.

These data also point to the dubious logic of maintaining faith in infinite growth. It is challenging enough to decrease the environmental impacts of economic activity at a rate that will avoid the most catastrophic effects of climate change and associated planetary impacts with the economy at its current size. Aggressively pursuing growth will make the scale of the problem that much harder to address. If achieving a sustainable economy is a long-term challenging task comparable to running a marathon, then each unit of growth is the equivalent of adding a rock to one's backpack every mile, making progress increasingly difficult.

The Case for Degrowth

The limits of decoupling have led a number of thinkers to argue that planetary sustainability requires us to tackle the obsession with growth, not just the way it is calculated. New measures of growth, on this view, are like rearranging the deck chairs on the *Titanic*—a futile gesture that distracts from the urgency of abandoning a hopeless cause. The never-ending quest for growth is an unsustainable and destructive mindset that must be addressed head on. Growth must give way to degrowth.[43]

The argument for degrowth is quite straightforward. All economic activity involves some level of material transformation in the world.[44] Technological innovation may lower the environmental impacts of production or consumption, but it cannot eliminate them altogether. Moreover, over the last several decades the gains of more efficient production processes have been offset by economic expansion. The larger the economy is, the harder it is to make it sustainable.[45] Degrowth advocates argue we must take a clear view of these realities. No one likes getting old and needing to sacrifice spending today to save for additional health care and services during retirement, yet nearly everyone agrees it is irresponsible to ignore this reality. Shouldn't the same be true of the earth?

While this proposition may sound gloomy, degrowth advocates are quick to point out that the absence of growth need not result in declining social welfare. In addition to drawing on ideas of environmental limits such as Nicholas Georgescu-Roegen's entropy law or the models in *The Limits to Growth*, they also invoke a long history of recognizing that more is not always better. John Stuart Mill argued in the mid-nineteenth century that the arrival of the steady state could be an improvement as it would allow people to focus their energy on the finer things of life such as leisure, art, and community, instead of spinning on the hamster wheel of always chasing more.[46] In 1930, John Maynard Keynes calculated that in a century, the economic problem of providing enough subsistence to get by would be solved, ushering in a new world of three-hour workdays and a moral reconfiguration that recognized "the love of money . . . for what it is, a somewhat disgusting morbidity, one of those semi-criminal, semi-pathological propensities which one hands over with a shudder to the specialists in mental disease."[47] Economic growth would reach a point, he believed, where it would be possible to "value ends above means and prefer the good to the useful."[48] Infinite growth, these thinkers recognized, was not necessary for a good life.

This viewpoint has been furthered by the more recent findings of the Easterlin paradox and other well-being scholars who show that growth is often not the key to a better future. This offers a hopeful message. If wealth accumulation is not a guarantor of happiness after basic material conditions are satisfied, then achieving a sustainable economy could happen while maintaining human welfare. Herman Daly has suggested that instead of growth, which is often measured quantitatively and relies on material inputs, a steady-state economy should focus on development, which is a qualitative measure linked to mental states.[49] Given that it is possible for many types of leisure, reflection, intellectual development, and community engagement to have minimal material inputs, development could be expanded in ways that economic growth cannot. Similarly, the British sustainability analyst Tim Jackson advocated for a focus on prosperity in his widely read 2009 book *Prosperity Without Growth*. Prosperity, in his view, is only partially linked to material gain. For most people, it is much more tightly linked to notions that one lives in a good society, that the future seems bright, and that others are doing well.[50] A lasting prosperity, he claims, requires a sustainable economy.

Degrowth advocates argue that it is essential to distinguish economic activities that advance well-being from those that are unnecessary. Everyone needs to eat, so it is of course essential to prioritize the growing of food. But diets rich in red meat have a much greater impact on the environment than those based on plants along with poorer health outcomes. Most people depend on vehicles for travel, but there are enormous differences between electric motors and gasoline-powered vehicles, between scooters and large SUVs, and between public transit systems and private jets. And some parts of the economy deliver very little direct value to people, such as advertising and the manufacture of goods with planned obsolescence.

Degrowthers also seek to distinguish the conscious and planned shrinking of the economy from recessions. It has been a common critique of degrowth to point out that recessions tend to be associated with large declines in well-being, particularly among people who lose their jobs. But this argument misses the point that recessions do not involve conscious selection. Choosing which parts of the economy to contract offers the chance to make plans that provide a smooth transition for workers and minimize the impacts on well-being.[51]

In further contrast to recessions, which are short term, a just transition to a degrowth economy will take considerable time to implement. In particular, government programs that provide social safety nets will need to be redesigned so they do not depend on continual growth. And corporate systems will need time to determine ways of managing capital flows to maintain a certain profit level, not grow indefinitely. Because these are vastly complex systems, it will take many years. At the same time, since environmental degradation is happening so rapidly, degrowthers argue it is essential to begin the process as soon as possible.[52]

This tension between pessimism and optimism has led to significant debates among degrowth scholars about the most compelling way to present these ideas. Many worry that the negative implications of the word "degrowth" prevent a reasonable debate about it.[53] Some defend the term, noting that to be against something can inspire others to action. Decolonization, for instance, has been a movement with broad appeal that offers an empowering call to action to overcome injustices of the past.[54] But the more common recent trend has been toward an "agrowth" approach that shifts the conversation to topics such as development, prosperity, or well-being.

A prominent recent example of this strategy is the advocacy for a well-being economy that "pursues human and ecological well-being instead of material growth."[55] The word "well-being" is particularly compelling, proponents argue, because of its cultural adaptability. Nearly all societies have deeply rooted ideas of well-being, giving it both global and local power. Moreover, they claim the positive messaging provides a better chance to be taken up in high-level policy circles. The 2018 creation of a network of Wellbeing Economy Governments has seemed to justify this faith, with Finland, Scotland, Wales, Iceland, and New Zealand collaborating on building support and policies for a well-being economy.[56]

Degrowth supporters can point to a growing number of participants in conferences and advocacy work, particularly in Europe. In addition, the recent creation of the Wellbeing Economy Governments alliances shows some interest in moving beyond growth discourses among policymakers. However, it is extremely rare to find a mainstream economist advocating degrowth policies or politicians willing to advocate it as a cause. The idea of degrowth remains on the margins.

"This May All Be Madness"

Degrowth has achieved virtually no traction within mainstream economic communities. To the limited extent the end of growth has been discussed by neoclassical economists, it has been through the lens of secular stagnation, though even this concept has gained little purchase.

At its core, the idea of secular stagnation is that growth in a mature economy will dwindle due to structural constraints ranging from a shift from manufacturing to services, lower returns to education, weak consumer demand, increased preferences for leisure over consumption, income inequality, and an aging workforce. Very low, and sometimes even negative, interest rates are often a sign of stagnation. Alvin Hansen is credited for pioneering the term in the 1930s as he analyzed the Great Depression and considered whether rapid growth was possible in a mature economy.[57] He worried that factors such as declining population growth, unemployment, and decreased demand would trap the economy in a low-level state. During the 1940s, the concept continued to generate discussion as many economists worried that the dramatic decline in government spending after World War II would lead to a recession. But as growth accelerated during the 1950s, the topic fell out of favor. Paul Samuelson, one of Hansen's students, included several pages on secular stagnation in the first versions of his widely read introductory textbook starting in 1948. But by 1958, the discussion was reduced to two short paragraphs, and then dropped altogether in 1985.[58]

Secular stagnation attracted little attention for much of the rest of the twentieth century, with small bursts of renewed interest at moments of economic stagnation, such as the stagflation of the 1970s and the dramatic slowdown of growth in Japan since the early 1990s. The experience of Japan has stood out because its economy was so powerful in the 1980s that many in America feared Japan would become the world's economic superpower. Yet this did not happen. Japan's growth began to stall in the early 1990s when property and stock market bubbles burst. Since then, several moments of apparent recovery have faltered, despite Japan having significant capital to invest, advanced technology, and a highly educated workforce. While the aging of Japan's workforce and the nation's very low immigration rates help explain the decline, it has led some to question whether Japan is an outlier or the forerunner of what other developed nations can expect.[59]

A small revitalization of secular stagnation arose among American economists in the aftermath of the 2008 financial crisis, though even its advocates acknowledged it was a heretical concept within mainstream economic circles.[60] Lawrence Summers has been the most prominent economist to argue secular stagnation could be the future. He has had a distinguished career including positions as chief economist at the World Bank, secretary of the treasury, and president of Harvard University. While at the World Bank in the early 1990s he offered one of the clearest statements of infinite growth by declaring, "There are no limits to the carrying capacity of the earth that are likely to bind any time in the foreseeable future. There isn't a risk of apocalypse due to global warming or anything else. The idea that we should put limits on growth because of some natural limit, is a profound error and one that, were it ever to prove influential, would have staggering social costs."[61]

Summers's praise of growth was largely directed at its potential to lift billions out of poverty in the global South. In 2013, he noted that five years after the start of the 2008 Recession, economic growth in developed nations remained much lower than most had predicted. He observed that with interest rates low and sometimes even negative, there was little way to spur the economy. Zero-percent interest rates represented "a chronic and systemic inhibitor of economic activity holding our economies back below their potential." This meant that secular stagnation—a "radical idea pretty firmly rejected" in the past—might be on the horizon.[62] Five years later, Summers argued the evidence had grown stronger in favor of secular stagnation, concluding that the "issue remains very much alive."[63]

The economic historian Robert Gordon similarly raised the specter of secular stagnation in 2016, citing four headwinds in the American economy: rising inequality, decreasing gains from higher education, an aging workforce, and high levels of debt. The combination of these factors was "sufficiently strong to leave virtually no room for growth over the next twenty-five years in median disposable real income per person."[64] This is not a happy conclusion, Gordon acknowledged, but one that fit the data.

Dietrich Vollrath, by contrast, offered a rosier read of the situation. He agreed in 2020 that secular stagnation had arrived, noting that whereas American growth rates averaged 2.25 percent a year from the 1950 to 2000, they were only 1 percent from 2000 to 2016.[65] But he cast this slowdown as a sign of success. While others blamed low growth on various forces, Vollrath emphasized the choices people make when they have grown wealthier. The first is having fewer children, which lowers growth by decreasing the number of people in the workforce. But this should be celebrated because it is a choice of abundance for families. The second major factor is that once people have met most of their basic material needs, they spend their additional income on services such as entertainment, education, and healthcare. This also lowers the growth rate, because productivity improvements in these sectors are harder to achieve than in the manufacturing of goods. Factories have managed to automate many production processes, but in the service sector, there are few improvements that allow a stylist to cut hair faster or an educator to teach more students in less time. A result of a growing service sector, then, is that productivity growth will be lower, and the growth rate will decline. He argues we should see this as a logical outcome of a society in which many material needs have been met. "Slow growth," he concludes, "is the optimal response to massive economic success."[66]

Secular stagnation is reminiscent of the steady state Adam Smith and his fellow classical political economists assumed would eventually emerge. Furthermore, just as Smith thought the end of growth would be melancholy, so too do many theorists of secular stagnation, excepting Vollrath. But a crucial difference lies in the role of nature in economic analysis. For Smith and the classical political economists, the stationary state resulted from the fact that land was finite and subject to the law of diminishing returns. Among thinkers such as

Summers, Gordon, and Vollrath, the natural world is largely absent. Interest rates, population demographics, services, and technological progress are front and center; climate change, resource depletion, and tipping points do not merit attention.

Yet even if secular stagnation presents the idea of limits to growth in a package palatable to mainstream economists, it remains a controversial proposal that has far more critics than advocates. Joseph Stiglitz rebuked Summers for disingenuously invoking secular stagnation instead of taking responsibility for not acting boldly enough when he was secretary of the treasury.[67] Others have argued the concept relies on ideas that are not consistent with dominant macroeconomic theories about rational agents and intertemporal optimization.[68] Even Summers has acknowledged that "this may all be madness."[69] The reality is that any discussion of limits to growth in mainstream economic discourse is deeply unpopular and largely denounced.

*

"Growth for growth's sake is the ideology of the cancer cell," wrote the environmentalist Edward Abbey in 1977.[70] Abbey has not been alone in recognizing the troubles with growth. The past several decades have seen sustained efforts to overturn the obsessive pursuit of growth. Some of these efforts have come from the fringes and been actively kept to the sidelines by the professional gatekeepers of economics. But many others have come from distinguished mainstream economists and received support from top elected leaders and international organizations. Yet even when coming from the pens of Nobelists, calls to rethink growth have not resulted in a sustained shift in policy or blunted the quest for infinite growth.

The advocacy for green growth is just the latest trend in this long history of the invention of infinite growth. Undoubtedly, improving the efficiency of economic production and using market price signals to reduce pollution will be valuable. But green growth is not enough by itself. The logic of infinite growth fails to account for aspects of planetary sustainability that are not reduced to carbon emissions. It fails to distinguish sufficiently between relative, absolute, and sufficient decoupling. And it fails to acknowledge that more growth does not always lead to better lives. Creating a sustainable future requires moving past the logic that growth is the only avenue to a better future. As Abbey presciently observed, the ideology of the cancer cell is a poor guide for humans to follow.

Conclusion

In the late 1920s, John Maynard Keynes decided to "take wings into the future." "What can we reasonably expect the level of our economic lives to be a hundred years hence?" he mused. If the past was any guide, he reasoned, growth would continue at about 2 percent a year, making the average person somewhere between four and eight times better off than at present. This abundance would fundamentally change the human condition. Throughout world history, the vast majority of human activity had been devoted to the search for subsistence, which Keynes considered the *"permanent problem of the human race."* Surely a population several times wealthier could turn its attention to the art of living, instead of scraping by. The "Economic Possibilities for Our Grandchildren," as he titled his piece, were promising indeed.[1]

Like John Stuart Mill, who in 1848 looked forward to the arrival of a stationary state as an opportunity for leisure and moral improvement, Keynes hoped abundance would lead to better lives. With the anticipated gains, people could work as little as fifteen hours a week. Society's morals could be improved, as a wealthy society would properly celebrate "ends above means and prefer the good to the useful." It would be a happier and more fulfilling world.[2]

Keynes's optimism was muted, however, by the psychological obstacles of a world of plenty. Human societies had been built around the problem of scarcity, thereby ingraining a constant need for more in "the habits and instincts of the ordinary man . . . for countless generations." How would people learn to live in totally new ways? The wealthy elites of Keynes's day inspired little hope, casting about aimlessly for ways to fill their days. "To judge from the behavior and the achievements of the wealthy classes today in any quarter of the world," he observed, "the outlook is very depressing!" Future generations would need to figure out "how to live wisely and agreeably, and well."[3]

Keynes's economic projections were largely accurate. GDP and purchasing power in Britain and the US have increased dramatically since 1930.[4] But his vision of fifteen-hour work weeks and a release from the struggles of getting by has not come to pass. Many are much richer, but this has not generated the changes in human life Keynes hoped would follow.

Today, Keynes's question burns with greater urgency. How can we step off the hamster wheel and learn to live generously with ourselves, others, and the planet? Keynes forwarded this question to future generations, but delay is no longer an option. The pursuit of infinite growth is not living "wisely and agreeably and well." How can we do better?

The task will be hard, for while Keynes was right to recognize that the problem involved psychological dimensions, he missed three other crucial points. He did not consider planetary sustainability. He did not inquire into how to transform government systems dependent on growth, largely because much of the welfare state emerged after his essay was written. And he limited his scope to the industrialized nations, paying little heed to the global South.

The enormity of the challenge can feel overwhelming. Indeed, some call it impossible. They say that without growth, social systems would collapse. They argue abandoning the pursuit of growth would doom those in the global South to perpetual poverty. They claim that growth can be green and that it is better to focus on cleaning up pollution than on slowing economic expansion. They believe it is better to be rich than to stabilize the climate.[5]

Growth's defenders raise some valid points but fail to acknowledge the perils of the status quo. To continue the pursuit of infinite growth is to ensure dramatic environmental changes that will make the planet less habitable for humans and result in the extinction of millions of species. Productive agricultural regions will be desiccated, ice sheets will melt and raise sea levels, permafrost will thaw and release captured carbon, droughts and floods will become more frequent, and biodiversity will be drastically reduced. The amount of habitable land will decrease, with increasingly bitter fights over it. Trying to make growth green will help, but it is not happening fast enough, and it does not go far enough to secure a sustainable world.

Present trends suggest a future of increased human suffering, particularly for the most vulnerable. The world is already experiencing refugee crises in which wealthy nations react with hostility to the attempted movements of hundreds of thousands of migrants. If large swaths of land can no longer support their populations, what will happen to the tens of millions that will need to migrate? The world's governance systems are not prepared to handle such a scenario peacefully. Moreover, those who will be most devastated by droughts or floods will be the least fortunate, who have little cushion to survive bad harvests and natural disasters. When wildfires, hurricanes, and extreme weather become more common, everyone will pay a price, but the poor will be harmed the most.

At the same time, growth's benefits are consistently overstated. Economic growth in certain times and places has achieved great good, and it remains a crucial hope for billions in the global South.

But empirical evidence reveals it has achieved much less benefit in the global North for the last several decades. Americans are not reporting themselves to be happier than they were several decades before, and lifespans have been stagnant and even declining. Moreover, growth's benefits have not been equally shared, and skyrocketing inequality is eroding community bonds, lowering health outcomes, and undermining faith in political systems. Too much growth enriches global elites and too little reaches those who most need it. Too much growth fractures communities and exacerbates political polarization. Too much growth destroys ecosystems for too little benefit.[6]

Giving up growth may seem overwhelming, but the uncritical pursuit of infinite growth is worse.

The great challenge, then, is to follow Keynes and imagine a new future. How can we do this? This history suggests two starting points for moving beyond the delusion that infinite growth offers the surest path to a better future. The first is to rethink economics and the second is to move beyond an obsession with growth.

Beyond an Economics of a Golden Era

Ideas are products of specific times and places. The most important ideas in the invention of infinite growth arose in the two decades after World War II. This was a golden era of growth, different in crucial ways from what came before and after. Following nearly a generation of economic hardship during the Great Depression and World War II, the end of hostilities unleashed a remarkable wave of growth across the industrialized world. Manufacturing boomed, labor unions secured higher wages for workers, and government policies helped average citizens enter the middle class.

Growth in these years delivered much good to many. About 60 percent of the American population had entered the middle class by 1960, and growth rates were even higher in Europe and Japan. It was an era in which many people had more food on the table, higher quality housing, better medical care, greater educational opportunities, and longer lifespans.

It was also a time when environmental issues were often seen as a minor nuisance. Even if resources became scarce in one place, it appeared they could be replaced with advances in technology and newly discovered deposits in the global South. The few observers who issued warnings about how infinite growth would intersect with a finite planet were largely ignored until the 1970s. It was easy to assume that the safe climatic conditions of the Holocene that had nurtured humanity's booming populations since the end of the last Ice Age were not under threat.

The discipline of economics reflected this world of impressive growth rates, declining inequality, and lack of concern for environmental conditions. Economic growth was the marvel of the postwar era, and economists used their expertise to advance their academic prestige and access to political power. Because it seemed self-evident that growth was a rising tide that would lift all boats, the foundational work in growth theory during the 1950s and 1960s paid almost no attention to questions of inequality. In fact, Solow's theory predicted that global inequality should decrease in the future because capital would be incentivized to flow to poorer regions where returns would be higher: growth would automatically make the world a more equal place. Economists also saw little reason to include the environment in their assessments of growth. Even when the fields of environmental and natural resource economics were established in the 1970s, they treated the natural world as a set of resources to be optimized and considered pollution an issue that could be addressed with market mechanisms.

By the 1980s, however, patterns of growth had shifted in much of the global North. Due to a combination of globalization, anti-union policies, declining manufacturing, and neoliberal policies, growth began to flow primarily to the wealthiest. The rate of improvement in health outcomes, lifespans, and working hours began to decline as the working and middles classes stagnated. The decades after 1980 revealed that growth did not automatically reduce inequality—it could actually have the opposite effect. At the same time, damages to the natural world were becoming much clearer as the losses to biodiversity and increased understanding of climate change made the evidence of environmental decline much more apparent.

The great failing of economics is that ideas about infinite growth have not reflected these changes. Theories forged in an era of shared prosperity and a limited understanding of planetary ecosystems have not been sufficiently updated to reflect a world of climate change, inequality, and decreasing benefits from growth in wealthy nations.

How should economics be revised to reflect current conditions? For starters, it needs to take the natural world more seriously. Too many economic models simplistically predict linear impacts from climate change, assume that indoor activity is unaffected by global warming, and do not forecast tipping points. This creates false confidence that the consequences of climate change and biodiversity loss can be managed and optimized. Despite our air-conditioned buildings and mechanized farms, humans still depend on natural systems that allow plants to grow, insects to pollinate crops, and ocean systems to support regular rainfall patterns. Economic theories must take these realities into account.

Growth should also be targeted to those who need it most, and away from those who do not. A good human future requires enabling those living in poverty to achieve financial security. Though doing so will have environmental impacts, the benefits are high enough that it should be prioritized. Kate Raworth's idea of "doughnut economics" is an appropriate encapsulation of this concept. She suggests we imagine a doughnut where the hole in the center represents the poverty that people must be brought out of. But there is also an outer edge of the doughnut, beyond which it is inappropriate for people to accumulate more resources because doing so harms others through inequality and environmental degradation. Getting as much of the world's population as possible into the doughnut means lifting those out of poverty while constraining the excesses of global elites.[7]

An economics for the Anthropocene must also focus on well-being, not economic welfare. The vast majority of economists are well aware that economic welfare is not the same as well-being. Yet there remains a broad faith that the two are correlated well enough to justify making economic welfare the top goal of many policies. This is particularly attractive to economists because economic welfare is so much simpler to define than well-being. Unfortunately, simple answers can mask deeper truths, including evidence that after people reach middle-class incomes, increased economic welfare has a diminishing impact on their quality of life. Moreover, calculations of economic welfare too rarely account for externalities such as climate change. Growth comes with costs that should only be borne when they generate significant improvements in the lives of real people, not just when they add to a quantifiable bottom line.

A further step is to ensure that distribution, not maximization, gets prioritized. Economists have also taken the convenient shortcut of largely ignoring distribution, drawing upon the argument that as a positive science, economics should focus on efficiency and growth, not inequality. The idea of Pareto optimality is a poor guide to policy when it posits an economy that grows by 2 percent a year and concentrates 90 percent of its wealth in the hands of the top 1 percent is superior to one that grows at half that rate but distributes the gains equally. It is not enough to bake a bigger pie; there must be equal or greater attention to the size of the slices and who is invited to eat them.

Finally, we need an economics that embraces humility. There is so much we do not know about the interactions among greenhouse gas emissions, biodiversity loss, ocean acidification, and the countless other natural processes that sustain human life. Scientists recently discovered extreme heat simultaneously in the Arctic and Antarctica, a phenomenon most thought could not happen.[8] Economics should acknowledge what we cannot know, and plan cautiously to avoid the most dangerous outcomes.[9]

Beyond the Fixation with Growth

Economists may have invented infinite growth, but they no longer control its destiny. The world has been rebuilt to expect growth in everything from government programs to corporate structures to personal expectations. Economists theorize growth and its possibilities, but politicians pursue it, shareholders demand it, consumers expect it, and voters punish ruling parties that do not deliver it. Like Pandora, economists could not place the idea of infinite growth back in a box even if they desired. We need a social reckoning with growth as well as an economic one.

If the great failure of economics has been to rely on ideas formed in a golden era that no longer exists, the comparable social failure has been to allow growth to become an end, rather than a means. There is too much obsession with growth for growth's sake and too little discussion of what types of growth would best improve people's lives. There is a paucity of debate in the public sphere about whether some types of growth might actually be harmful.

It is not hard to understand why this has been the case. Establishing consensus about what constitutes a good future is hard, and in a pluralistic society, there will always be disagreement. A focus on growth has allowed many populations to bypass those debates, hoping that a growing pie will enable their preferred policies to be implemented, whether those be tax cuts or an expanded social safety net, military hardware or upgraded schools. Moreover, it can be hard to measure outcomes many people desire, such as strong community bonds, personal fulfillment, and equality of opportunity. Economic welfare measured in dollars and cents is much more straightforward.

Simplicity has its virtues, but when it comes to creating thriving human futures, its limits are glaring. The fixation with growth instead of better lives and healthy ecosystems is apparent in sky-rocketing levels of inequality. It can be felt in a shrinking American middle class and the political resentments that have come from so many feeling they have been left behind. It can be detected in the re-treat of glaciers, the decline of coral reefs, and the spread of wildfires.

The evidence is clear: growth is not a panacea. But this central fact is insufficiently recognized in public conversations. Outside of a small degrowth movement, there is almost no critical question-ing of growth as the logical aim of policy. This must change to craft a sustainable future. It is necessary for citizens and politicians to be-gin asking questions such as: What type of growth should we pur-sue? What measures are necessary to ensure it has tangible impacts on well-being? How can we minimize the environmental costs of growth? What types of growth can we do without while still hav-ing a high quality of life? And perhaps most importantly, how can we create good lives based on sufficiency instead of endlessly pur-suing more?

Debate does not, of course, change the world by itself. Ideas are only transformative when they are made material through policies, changes in corporate and government structures, and altered per-sonal actions. And given how entrenched the idea of growth has be-come, it is clear there will be deep resistance to change. Moving for-ward will not be easy.

This is a place where history offers hope. The invention of infinite growth was so successful because the concept paired with a recep-tive social context. Conditions have changed, and this provides the opportunity for new ideas to take root. Today's world is character-ized by much greater recognition of the harms of climate change and growing evidence that growth is not always the answer. Perhaps this is the fertile soil we need to nurture the invention of ideas that will allow our grandchildren to look back and say we did all we could to live wisely, agreeably, and well.

Acknowledgments

This book would not have been possible without the generous and sustained support of a large community of friends, colleagues, and family. All historians are indebted to archivists, and I am particularly grateful to the librarians at the David M. Rubenstein Rare Book and Manuscript Library at Duke University, the Rare Book and Manuscript Library at Columbia University, and the Hoover Institution Library & Archives at Stanford University. Support from the Hoover Archival Workshop on Political Economy facilitated my visit to Stanford and allowed me to get early feedback on the project from fellow participants and Jennifer Burns, the organizer. Chris Clotworthy at Resources for the Future provided access and guidance to the organization's records. Librarians at Arizona State regularly helped me track down sources via interlibrary loan. I also want to thank the many historians who have written scholarship that guided my research, the vast majority of whom I have never met. I feel I have come to know them in a small way through their works and could not have completed this project without their contributions.

Financial support for the earliest stages of this research took place at postdoctoral fellowships at the Harvard University Center for the Environment and the S. V. Ciriacy-Wantrup Fellowship in Natural Resource Economics and Political Economy at University of California, Berkeley. A fellowship from the American Council of Learned Societies enabled me to spend a year away from teaching and service at a crucial time in the book's development. The Humanities Institute at Arizona State University provided funds for a book manuscript workshop, a course release, and the research assistance of Courtney Carlisle.

The most rewarding part of writing this book has been the opportunity to engage with fellow scholars. I have received invaluable feedback on numerous chapter drafts over several years from Fredrik Albritton Jonsson, Venus Bivar, Elizabeth Chatterjee, Stephen Gross, Stephen Macekura, and Carl Wennerlind; reading each other's work over the last several years has been an honor and a privilege. Matthias Schmelzer, Tim Shenk, and Paul Warde read the entire manuscript and offered generous and incisive comments that helped me streamline and sharpen my arguments. Two anonymous reviewers for the press offered extensive critiques that have significantly improved the final project. Discussions with colleagues including Joshua Abbott, Paul Burnett, Will Deringer, Tyler DesRoches, Bart Elmore, Michael Hanemann, Daniel Immerwahr, John McNeill, Antoine Missemer, Elizabeth Popp Berman, Stephen Pyne, Adam Rome, Paul Sabin, Joseph Taylor, and too many others to mention have pointed me to valuable resources and sustained my spirits.

Arizona State has been a supportive environment for crafting this book. I thank my colleagues in history and across the university for their encouragement along the way. For the last five years, I have completed most of this book in the ASU Writing Studio. My sincere thanks to Rich Furman, whose insights into the writing process made this group possible, as well as Conevery Valencius, who has long provided encouragement and moral support. She, along with Weihong Bao, Sarah Beckjord, Maria Cruz-Torres, Francoise Mirguet, Tina Montenegro, David Mozina, María de los Ángeles Picone, and Franziska Seraphim have been gracious cohosts in this collaborative endeavor.

I am grateful to my agent Elise Capron for taking a chance on this book at an early stage and helping find the ideal publisher. Tim Mennel at University of Chicago Press has staunchly supported the project throughout and expertly helped me refine the arguments and the prose. Andrea Blatz and Lindsy Rice shepherded the work through the production process, and I am thankful to Laura Tsitlidze for copyediting assistance and June Sawyers for indexing.

My most extensive thanks go to my family, who have weathered the highs and lows of my historical obsessions. Lindsey has been a true partner through the writing of this book, a decade marked by the births of our children, parenting through COVID, and navigating both our careers. She has supported my long hours at the screen while also giving me reasons to close my laptop and step away. My children, Silas and Margo, may not yet understand why I've spent so much time studying the past, but it was thinking about their future that animated much of my desire to write this book, and that is why it is dedicated to them.

Notes

Introduction

1. Summers quoted in John Barry, "Climate Change: The 'Cancer Stage of Capitalism' and the Return of the Limits to Growth," in *Climate Change and the Crisis of Capitalism*, ed. Mark Pelling et al. (London: Routledge, 2011), 129. My thanks to Fredrik Albritton Jonsson for directing my attention to this quotation.

2. Intergovernmental Panel on Climate Change, *Synthesis Report of the IPCC Sixth Assessment Report (AR6)* (Interlaken, Switzerland, 2023), https://report.ipcc.ch/ar6syr/pdf/IPCC_AR6_SYR _LongerReport.pdf.

3. William Nordhaus, "Climate Change: The Ultimate Challenge for Economics," Prize Lecture, Stockholm, December 8, 2018, accessed October 16, 2023, https://www.nobelprize.org/prizes/economic-sciences /2018/nordhaus/lecture/. For 4 degrees Celsius by 2140, see optimal path chart displayed at 19:43 mark of video recording of lecture. On Romer and no natural limits to growth, see Paul M. Romer, "Increasing Returns and Long-Run Growth," *Journal of Political Economy* 94, no. 5 (1986): 1002–37; Paul M. Romer and Hiroo Sasaki, *Monotonically Decreasing Natural Resources Prices Under Perfect Foresight* (Rochester Center for Economic Research, 1984).

4. For a small selection of the sizable literature critical of the economics profession in recent years pointing out many of the discipline's limitations, see Elizabeth Popp Berman, *Thinking like an Economist: How Efficiency Replaced Equality in U.S. Public Policy* (Princeton, NJ:

Princeton University Press, 2022); Stephen A. Marglin, *The Dismal Science: How Thinking like an Economist Undermines Community* (Cambridge, MA: Harvard University Press, 2008); Robert Skidelsky, *What's Wrong with Economics? A Primer for the Perplexed* (New Haven, CT: Yale University Press, 2020); Nancy MacLean, *Democracy in Chains: The Deep History of the Radical Right's Stealth Plan for America* (New York: Viking, 2017); Binyamin Appelbaum, *The Economists' Hour: False Prophets, Free Markets, and the Fracture of Society* (New York: Little, Brown and Company, 2019); Marion Fourcade, Etienne Ollion, and Yann Algan, "The Superiority of Economists," *Journal of Economic Perspectives* 29, no. 1 (2015): 89–114.

5. Robert M. Solow, "Notes on 'Doomsday Models,'" *Proceedings of the National Academy of Sciences* 69, no. 12 (1972): 3832.

6. A compelling illustration of the limitations of center-left economic arguments can be found in: Popp Berman, *Thinking like an Economist.* On the use of science to obfuscate issues, see Robert N. Proctor and Londa Schiebinger, eds., *Agnotology: The Making and Unmaking of Ignorance* (Palo Alto, CA: Stanford University Press, 2008); Naomi Oreskes and Erik M. Conway, *Merchants of Doubt: How a Handful of Scientists Obscured the Truth on Issues from Tobacco Smoke to Global Warming* (London: Bloomsbury Press, 2010).

7. Two books that demonstrate the complexities of these issues are Charles C. Mann, *The Wizard and the Prophet: Two Remarkable Scientists and Their Dueling Visions to Shape Tomorrow's World* (New York: Alfred A. Knopf, 2018); and Paul Sabin, *The Bet: Paul Ehrlich, Julian Simon, and Our Gamble over Earth's Future* (New Haven, CT: Yale University Press, 2013).

8. This book draws on a recent surge of interest in the history of economic growth and seeks to extend it in two ways. Compared to most other works, I take a longer historical view, tracing the debates from the mid-eighteenth century to the present. In addition, I seek to bring together two strains of the history of economic thought that have often been studied separately: growth theory and the economics of the environment. Before the turn of the twenty-first century, historians did not make economic growth a central topic of analysis, with works by Arndt, Maier, and Collins a notable exception: Heinz Wolfgang Arndt, *The Rise and Fall of Economic Growth: A Study in Contemporary Thought* (Melbourne: Longman Cheshire, 1978); Charles S. Maier, "The Politics of Productivity: Foundations of American International Economic Policy After World War II," *International Organization* 31, no. 4 (1977): 607–33; Robert M. Collins, *More: The Politics of Economic Growth in Postwar America* (Oxford: Oxford University Press, 2000). Since 2009, there has been a surge of interest in the topic: Daniel Cohen and Jane Marie Todd, *The Infinite Desire for Growth* (Princeton, NJ: Princeton University Press, 2018); Eli Cook, *The Pricing of Progress: Economic*

Indicators and the Capitalization of American Life (Cambridge, MA: Harvard University Press, 2017); Robert J. Gordon, *The Rise and Fall of American Growth: The U.S. Standard of Living Since the Civil War* (Princeton, NJ: Princeton University Press, 2016); Kerryn Higgs, *Collision Course: Endless Growth on a Finite Planet* (Cambridge, MA: The MIT Press, 2014); Stephen Macekura, *The Mismeasure of Progress: Economic Growth and Its Critics* (Chicago: University of Chicago Press, 2020); Scott O'Bryan, *The Growth Idea: Purpose and Prosperity in Postwar Japan* (Honolulu: University of Hawaii Press, 2009); Matthias Schmelzer, *The Hegemony of Growth: The OECD and the Making of the Economic Growth Paradigm* (Cambridge, UK: Cambridge University Press, 2016); Matthias Schmelzer and Iris Borowy, eds., *History of the Future of Economic Growth: Historical Roots of Current Debates on Sustainable Degrowth* (London: Routledge, 2017); Steven Stoll, *The Great Delusion: A Mad Inventor, Death in the Tropics, and the Utopian Origins of Economic Growth* (New York: Hill and Wang, 2008); Daniel Susskind, *Growth: A History and a Reckoning* (Cambridge, MA: Harvard University Press, 2024); Donald Worster, *Shrinking the Earth: The Rise and Decline of American Abundance* (New York: Oxford University Press, 2016); Andrew L. Yarrow, *Measuring America: How Economic Growth Came to Define American Greatness in the Late Twentieth Century* (Amherst: University of Massachusetts Press, 2010). Venus Bivar has written an instructive assessment of this emerging literature: Venus Bivar, "Historicizing Economic Growth: An Overview of Recent Works," *Historical Journal* 65, no. 5 (2022): 1470–89.

9. This book builds and extends the pioneering work done on the historical and social consequences of economics by scholars including Fredrik Albritton Jonsson, Elizabeth Popp Berman, Angus Burgin, Michel Callon, Gareth Dale, Marion Fourcade, Daniel Hirschman, Donald MacKenzie, Antoine Missemer, Philip Mirowski, Timothy Mitchell, Margaret Schabas, Adam Tooze, Carl Wennerlind, and many others. See, for instance, Fredrik Albritton Jonsson and Carl Wennerlind, *Scarcity: A History from the Origins of Capitalism to the Climate Crisis* (Cambridge, MA: Harvard University Press, 2023); Popp Berman, *Thinking like an Economist;* Angus Burgin, *The Great Persuasion: Reinventing Free Markets Since the Depression* (Cambridge, MA: Harvard University Press, 2015); Michel Callon, ed., *The Laws of the Markets* (Oxford: Blackwell Publishers, 1998); Gareth Dale, "Adam Smith's Green Thumb and Malthus's Three Horsemen: Cautionary Tales from Classical Political Economy," *Journal of Economic Issues* 46, no. 4 (2012): 859–80; Marion Fourcade, *Economists and Societies: Discipline and Profession in the United States, Britain, and France, 1890s to 1990s* (Princeton, NJ: Princeton University Press, 2009); Daniel Hirschman, "Inventing the Economy, Or: How We Learned to Stop Worrying and Love the GDP" (PhD diss.,

University of Michigan, 2016); Donald MacKenzie, *An Engine, Not a Camera: How Financial Models Shape Markets* (Cambridge, MA: The MIT Press, 2006); Philip Mirowski, "Energy and Energetics in Economic Theory: A Review Essay," *Journal of Economic Issues* 22, no. 3 (1988): 811–30; Timothy Mitchell, "The Work of Economics: How a Discipline Makes Its World," *European Journal of Sociology* 46, no. 2 (2005): 297–320; Timothy Mitchell, *Carbon Democracy: Political Power in the Age of Oil* (London: Verso, 2011); Margaret Schabas, *The Natural Origins of Economics* (Chicago: University of Chicago Press, 2005); Adam Tooze, *Statistics and the German State, 1900–1945: The Making of Modern Economic Knowledge* (Cambridge, UK: Cambridge University Press, 2001); Marco P. Vianna Franco and Antoine Missemer, *A History of Ecological Economic Thought* (London: Routledge, 2023).

10. John Robert McNeill, *Something New Under the Sun: An Environmental History of the Twentieth-Century World* (New York: W. W. Norton, 2000), 336.

11. The defense of growth in this section is synthesized from the arguments of economists studied in this book, including Robert Solow, Julian Simon, Mancur Olson, Walter Heller, Paul Romer, and William Nordhaus.

12. Michael Goldman, *Imperial Nature: The World Bank and Struggles for Social Justice in the Age of Globalization* (New Haven, CT: Yale University Press, 2005); Stephen Macekura, *Of Limits and Growth: The Rise of Global Sustainable Development in the Twentieth Century* (New York: Cambridge University Press, 2015).

13. Lorenzo Fioramonti, "The World's Most Powerful Number: An Assessment of 80 Years of GDP Ideology," *Anthropology Today* 30, no. 2 (2014): 12–15; Douglas R. Fox, "GDP: One of the Great Inventions of the 20th Century," *Survey of Current Business* 80, no. 1 (January 2000): 6–8.

14. Lorenzo Fioramonti, *Gross Domestic Problem: The Politics Behind the World's Most Powerful Number* (London: Zed Books, 2013); Diane Coyle, *GDP: A Brief but Affectionate History* (Princeton, NJ: Princeton University Press, 2015); Philipp Lepenies, *The Power of a Single Number: A Political History of GDP* (New York: Columbia University Press, 2016); Ehsan Masood, *The Great Invention: The Story of GDP and the Making (and Unmaking) of the Modern World* (New York: Pegasus Books, 2016); Dirk Philipsen, *The Little Big Number: How GDP Came to Rule the World and What to Do About It* (Princeton, NJ: Princeton University Press, 2015).

15. Lepenies, *Power of a Single Number*.

16. Arndt, *Rise and Fall of Economic Growth*, 30.

17. The use of stories and narrative in economics is pervasive, as it is in all fields of study. Deirdre N. McCloskey, *The Rhetoric of Economics* (Madison: University of Wisconsin Press, 1998); Robert J. Shiller, *Narrative Economics:*

How Stories Go Viral and Drive Major Economic Events (Princeton, NJ: Princeton University Press, 2019).

18. Susskind, *Growth*, 90.
19. IPCC, "AR6 Synthesis Report." Johan Rockström et al., "A Safe Operating Space for Humanity," *Nature* 461, no. 7263 (September 2009): 472–75; John R. McNeill and Peter Engelke, *The Great Acceleration: An Environmental History of the Anthropocene Since 1945* (Cambridge, MA: Harvard University Press, 2016); Elizabeth Kolbert, *The Sixth Extinction: An Unnatural History* (New York: Picador, 2014). Over the past forty years, there has been a relative decoupling between economic growth and greenhouse gas emissions, meaning that each unit of economic growth has been more efficient than before. But there has been very little absolute decoupling, which means that the benefits of a more efficient economy have been offset by the fact that the economy has grown larger. See chap. 9 for more discussion of this point. Jason Hickel and Giorgios Kallis, "Is Green Growth Possible?," *New Political Economy* 25, no. 4 (2020): 469–86.
20. Rockström et al., "Safe Operating Space for Humanity."
21. Richard A. Easterlin, "Does Economic Growth Improve the Human Lot? Some Empirical Evidence," in *Nations and Households in Economic Growth: Essays in Honor of Moses Abramovitz*, ed. Paul David and Melvin W. Reder (New York: Academic Press, 1974); Manfred Max-Neef, "Economic Growth and Quality of Life: A Threshold Hypothesis," *Ecological Economics* 15, no. 2 (1995): 115–18; Morten Tønnessen, "Wasted GDP in the USA," *Humanities and Social Sciences Communications* 10, no. 1 (2023): 681: 1–14. Daniel Kahneman, Ed Diener, and Norbert Schwarz, eds., *Well-Being: Foundations of Hedonic Psychology* (New York: Russell Sage Foundation, 1999); Richard Layard, *Happiness: Lessons from a New Science* (New York: Penguin Books, 2006); University of Chicago General Social Survey data, available from website, https://gssdataexplorer.norc.org/trends/Gender%20&%20Marriage?measure=happy (accessed September 24, 2021).
22. Richard Wilkinson and Kate Pickett, *The Spirit Level: Why Greater Equality Makes Societies Stronger* (New York: Bloomsbury Press, 2009); Robert Putnam, *Bowling Alone: The Collapse and Revival of American Community* (New York: Simon & Schuster, 2000).
23. This trend has shifted some in the last decade with the work of Thomas Piketty, Emmanuel Sanz, and Raj Chetty. But on the whole, economists have downplayed inequality, and the work of someone such as Gregory Mankiw, who has written the most widely used introductory economics textbook is illustrative: N. Gregory Mankiw, "Defending the One Percent," *Journal of Economic Perspectives* 27, no. 3 (2013): 21–34.
24. Einar H. Dyvik, "Number of Nobel Laureates in Economics by Nationality

1969–2023," *Statista*, July 4, 2024, accessed August 19, 2024, https://www
.statista.com/statistics/262901/nobel-prize-winners-in-economics-by
-nationality.

25. On growth in other regions, see Julie Livingston, *Self-Devouring Growth: A Planetary Parable as Told from Southern Africa*, Critical Global Health: Evidence, Efficacy, Ethnography (Durham, NC: Duke University Press, 2019); Macekura, *Mismeasure of Progress*; O'Bryan, *Growth Idea*; Schmelzer, *Hegemony of Growth*.

26. Mancur Olson, "Introduction," *Daedalus* 102, no. 4, The No-Growth Society (1973): 3.

27. Veronika Dolar, "The Gender Gap in Economics Is Huge—It's Even Worse than Tech," *The Conversation*, March 12, 2021, https://theconversation.com /the-gender-gap-in-economics-is-huge-its-even-worse-than-tech-156275.

28. Robert M. Solow, "The Economics of Resources or the Resources of Economics," *American Economic Review* 64, no. 2 (1974): 1.

29. A. C. Pigou, *The Economics of Welfare* (London: Macmillan, 1920), 11.

30. Many have critiqued these positions, and the views of thinkers including Fairfield Vogt, Samuel Osborn, Kenneth Boulding, Nicholas Georgescu-Roegen, and Herman Daly will be explored in later chapters.

31. Nordhaus, "Climate Change: The Ultimate Challenge," 451.

Chapter One

1. Robert L. Heilbroner, *The Worldly Philosophers: The Lives, Times, and Ideas of the Great Economic Thinkers*, 7th ed. (New York: Touchstone, 1999), chap. 4; Alison Bashford, *The New Worlds of Thomas Robert Malthus: Rereading the Principle of Population* (Princeton, NJ: Princeton University Press, 2016).

2. William Godwin, *An Enquiry Concerning Political Justice, and Its Influence on General Virtue and Happiness* (Dublin: Luke White, 1793); Jean-Antoine-Nicolas de Caritat Condorcet, *Sketch for a Historical Picture of the Progress of the Human Mind*, Library of Ideas (Ann Arbor, MI: University Microfilms, 1795).

3. Thomas Robert Malthus, *An Essay on the Principle of Population, as It Affects the Future Improvement of Society. With Remarks on the Speculations of Mr. Godwin, M. Condorcet, and Other Writers* (London: J. Johnson, 1798).

4. Mike Davis, *Late Victorian Holocausts: El Niño Famines and the Making of the Third World* (London: Verso, 2001).

5. Heilbroner, *Worldly Philosophers*, chap. 3.

6. Adam Smith, *The Theory of Moral Sentiments* (London: Printed for A. Millar and A. Kincaid and J. Bell, 1759); Adam Smith, *An Inquiry into the Nature and Causes of the Wealth of Nations*, 3 vols. (Dublin: Whitestone, 1776).

7. John Stuart Mill, *Principles of Political Economy: Abridged, with Critical, Bibliographical, and Explanatory Notes, and a Sketch of the History of Political Economy*, ed. J. Laurence Laughlin (New York: Appleton, 1884), 131.

8. E. A. Wrigley, *Continuity, Chance and Change: The Character of the Industrial Revolution in England* (Cambridge, UK: Cambridge University Press, 1988).

9. Geoffrey G. Jones, "Globalization," in *The Oxford Handbook of Business History*, ed. Geoffrey G Jones and Jonathan Zeitlin (Oxford: Oxford University Press, 2008), 142.

10. Niall Ferguson, *The Ascent of Money: A Financial History of the World* (London: Allen Lane, 2008), 25; M. I. Finley, *The Ancient Economy* (Berkeley: University of California Press, 1999), 23.

11. Margaret Schabas, *The Natural Origins of Economics* (Chicago: University of Chicago Press, 2005).

12. It is not the intention of this project to set a starting date for the discipline, so I follow other scholars in using the mid-eighteenth century to begin. Heilbroner, *Worldly Philosophers*, chap. 2; Gareth Dale, "Rule of Nature or Rule of Capital? Physiocracy, Ecological Economics, and Ideology," *Globalizations* 18, no. 7 (2021): 1230–47; Roger Backhouse, *The Ordinary Business of Life: A History of Economics from the Ancient World to the Twenty-First Century* (Princeton, NJ: Princeton University Press, 2002); Dorothy Ross, *The Origins of American Social Science* (Cambridge, UK: Cambridge University Press, 1991).

13. Wrigley, *Continuity, Chance and Change*.

14. All economic historians are indebted to the labors of Angus Maddison, who has collected enormously helpful data on the economy throughout history. Angus Maddison, *The World Economy: A Millennial Perspective* (Paris: Organisation for Economic Co-operation and Development, 2001), 17.

15. Smith, *Wealth of Nations*, 1, 30–31.

16. Smith, *Wealth of Nations*, 1, 18.

17. Joseph Persky, "Retrospectives: Adam Smith's Invisible Hands," *Journal of Economic Perspectives* 3, no. 4 (1989): 195–201. The discussion of capital and technology is elaborated in the rest of the book, beginning in earnest in chap. 3.

18. Smith, *Wealth of Nations*, 2, 481–82.

19. Smith, *Wealth of Nations*, 2, 482.

20. Smith, *Wealth of Nations*, i, 335.

21. Smith, *Wealth of Nations*, 1, 119.

22. Smith, *Wealth of Nations*, 2, 440.

23. Fredrik Albritton Jonsson and Carl Wennerlind, *Scarcity: A History from the Origins of Capitalism to the Climate Crisis* (Cambridge, MA: Harvard University Press, 2023), chap. 2; Fredrik Albritton Jonsson, "The Origins of

Cornucopianism: A Preliminary Genealogy," *Critical Historical Studies* 1, no. 1 (2014): 151–68.

24. Pierre Samuel du Pont de Nemours, *De l'exportation et de l'importation des grains* (1764), as cited in H. Spencer Banzhaf, "Productive Nature and the Net Product: Quesnay's Economies Animal and Political," *History of Political Economy* 32, no. 3 (September 1, 2000): 519.

25. Schabas, *Natural Origins of Economics*, chap. 3; Dale, "Rule of Nature or Rule of Capital?"; Banzhaf, "Productive Nature and the Net Product"; Nathaniel Wolloch, *Nature in the History of Economic Thought: How Natural Resources Became an Economic Concept* (London: Routledge, 2017), chap. 4.

26. Heilbroner, *Worldly Philosophers*, chap. 4.

27. Gareth Dale, "Critiques of Growth in Classical Political Economy: Mill's Stationary State and a Marxian Response," *New Political Economy* 18, no. 3 (2013): 431–57; Mike Davis, *Late Victorian Holocausts: El Niño Famines and the Making of the Third World* (London: Verso, 2001).

28. There is a debate about why economics is known as the dismal science. Many scholars suggest the name was popularized because of the focus on scarcity and difficult trade-offs captured in works such as Malthus. There is a counterargument that points to a different explanation. The phrase may have originated in 1849 with the Scottish thinker Thomas Carlyle, who wrote that economics was a dismal science because it saw all humans as equal and advocated the end of slavery. On this view, the moniker should be embraced by economists as a sign that the discipline was ahead of its time in terms of equality, per Daniel Levy. Even if Levy is correct about the technical origins of the term, it appears the widespread adoption of the term had more to do with Malthus's pessimism than Carlyle's racism. David M. Levy, *How the Dismal Science Got Its Name: Classical Economics and the Ur-Text of Racial Politics* (Ann Arbor: University of Michigan Press, 2001).

29. David Ricardo, *On the Principles of Political Economy and Taxation* (London: John Murray, 1817).

30. Ricardo, *Principles of Political Economy*, 49.

31. Mary S. Morgan, *The World in the Model: How Economists Work and Think* (Cambridge, UK: Cambridge University Press, 2012), chap. 2.

32. Ricardo, *Principles of Political Economy*, chap. 5.

33. Ricardo, *Principles of Political Economy*, 142.

34. Ricardo, *Principles of Political Economy*, 56.

35. Ricardo, *Principles of Political Economy*, 141.

36. Ricardo, *Principles of Political Economy*, 133.

37. Ricardo, *Principles of Political Economy*, 134.

38. Ricardo, *Principles of Political Economy*, 134.

39. Mill, *Principles of Political Economy*, 130.

40. Mill, *Principles of Political Economy*, 130.

41. Mill, *Principles of Political Economy*, 131.

42. Mill, *Principles of Political Economy*, 514.

43. Mill, *Principles of Political Economy*, 515.

44. Mill, *Principles of Political Economy*, 516.

45. Mill, *Principles of Political Economy*, 516.

46. Paul Warde, *The Invention of Sustainability: Nature and Destiny, c. 1500–1870* (Cambridge, UK: Cambridge University Press, 2018), chap. 7; Wolloch, *Nature in the History of Economic Thought;* Gareth Dale, "Adam Smith's Green Thumb and Malthus's Three Horsemen: Cautionary Tales from Classical Political Economy," *Journal of Economic Issues* 46, no. 4 (2012): 859–80.

47. William Stanley Jevons, *The Coal Question: An Inquiry Concerning the Progress of the Nation, and the Probable Exhaustion of Our Coal-Mines*, 3rd ed. (New York: Augustus M. Kelley, Publisher, 1965), 140.

48. Jevons, *The Coal Question*, 2, 3, 460.

49. Jevons first expressed his ideas on marginal utility in an 1860 letter and then formalized them in an article in 1862. These ideas received much more attention when he published an influential textbook in 1871. Margaret Schabas, *A World Ruled by Numbers: William Stanley Jevons and the Rise of Mathematical Economics* (Princeton, NJ: Princeton University Press, 1990); Harro Maas, *William Stanley Jevons and the Making of Modern Economics* (Cambridge, UK: Cambridge University Press, 2005).

50. On the marginal revolution and the rise of neoclassical economics, see Mark Blaug, *Economic Theory in Retrospect,* 3rd ed. (Cambridge, UK: Cambridge University Press, 1978), chap. 8; R. D. Collison Black, A. W. Coats, and Craufurd D. W. Goodwin, eds., *The Marginal Revolution in Economics: Interpretation and Evaluation* (Durham, NC: Duke University Press, 1973); Backhouse, *Ordinary Business of Life*, chap. 8; Henry William Spiegel, *The Growth of Economic Thought,* 3rd ed. (Durham, NC: Duke University Press, 1991), chap. 22; Philip Mirowski, *More Heat than Light: Economics as Social Physics, Physics as Nature's Economics* (Cambridge, UK: Cambridge University Press, 1989).

51. For debates at the time, see Richard Theodore Ely et al., *Science Economic Discussion . . .* (New York: The Science Company, 1886). On Ely's trial, see Ross, *Origins of American Social Science*, 117.

52. Albritton Jonsson and Wennerlind, *Scarcity*, chap. 7.

53. Benjamin G. Rader, *The Academic Mind and Reform: The Influence of Richard T. Ely in American Life* (Lexington: University Press of Kentucky, 1966), 7, 125.

54. Richard T. Ely, *The Past and the Present of Political Economy* (Baltimore, MD: N. Murray, publication agent, Johns Hopkins university, 1884), 19.

55. Other founding members included Simon Patten, Edmund James, John Bates Clark, E. A. Seligman, and Henry C. Adams. Richard T. Ely, "Constitution and By-Laws and Resolutions of the American Economic Association," *Publications of the American Economic Association* 1 (1886): 35–46.

56. Yuval P. Yonay, *The Struggle over the Soul of Economics: Institutionalist and Neoclassical Economists in America Between the Wars* (Princeton, NJ: Princeton University Press, 1998). On the persistence of other approaches outside of neoclassical economics, also see Malcolm Rutherford, *The Institutional Movement in American Economics, 1918–1947: Science and Social Control* (Cambridge, UK: Cambridge University Press, 2011); Mary S. Morgan and Malcolm Rutherford, eds., *From Interwar Pluralism to Postwar Neoclassicism: Annual Supplement to Volume 30, History of Political Economy* (Durham, NC: Duke University Press, 1998).

57. Ross, *Origins of American Social Science*; Thomas L. Haskell, *The Emergence of Professional Social Science: The American Social Science Association and the Nineteenth-Century Crisis of Authority* (Urbana: University of Illinois Press, 1977); Mary O. Furner, *Advocacy and Objectivity: A Crisis in the Professionalization of American Social Science, 1865–1905* (Lexington: Organization of American Historians by the University Press of Kentucky, 1975).

58. Marion Fourcade, *Economists and Societies: Discipline and Profession in the United States, Britain, and France, 1890s to 1990s* (Princeton, NJ: Princeton University Press, 2009), 65.

59. A. W. Coats, "The American Economic Association and the Economics Profession," *Journal of Economic Literature* 23 (December 1985): 1699.

60. Spiegel, *Growth of Economic Thought*, chap. 18.

61. Ely et al., *Science Economic Discussion*; Mirowski, *More Heat than Light*.

62. Ely et al., *Science Economic Discussion*; Rutherford, *Institutional Movement in American Economics*; Yonay, *Struggle over the Soul of Economics*.

63. Heilbroner, *Worldly Philosophers*, chap. 8.

64. Thorstein Veblen, *The Theory of the Leisure Class: An Economic Study in the Evolution of Institutions* (New York: Macmillan, 1899).

65. Walton H. Hamilton, "The Institutional Approach to Economic Theory," *American Economic Review* 9, no. 1 (1919): 301–10.

66. Hamilton, "Institutional Approach to Economic Theory," 311.

67. Hamilton, "Institutional Approach to Economic Theory," 311, 314.

68. Rutherford, *Institutional Movement in American Economics*; Morgan and Rutherford, *From Interwar Pluralism to Postwar Neoclassicism*.

69. Rutherford, *Institutional Movement in American Economics*, 37–38.

70. Wesley C. Mitchell, *Business Cycles* (Berkeley: University of California Press, 1913); John R. Commons, *History of Labour in the United States*, vol. 1 (New York: Macmillan, 1918).

71. Harold Hotelling, "The Economics of Exhaustible Resources," *Journal of Political Economy* 39, no. 2 (1931): 137–75; Gérard Gaudet, "Natural Resource Economics Under the Rule of Hotelling," *Canadian Journal of Economics* 40, no. 4 (2007): 1033–59; Shantayanan Devarajan and Anthony C. Fisher, "Hotelling's 'Economics of Exhaustible Resources': Fifty Years Later," *Journal of Economic Literature* 19 (March 1981): 65–73.

72. Hotelling, "Economics of Exhaustible Resources," 145.

73. Gaudet, "Natural Resource Economics," 1034.

74. Harold Hotelling Papers, Columbia University Rare Book & Manuscript Library, Box 51, Folder "Biographical," biography by colleagues.

75. Ingram Olkin, *Contributions to Probability and Statistics: Essays in Honor of Harold Hotelling* (Stanford, CA: Stanford University Press, 1960); Ralph W. Pfouts, *Essays in Economics and Econometrics: A Volume in Honor of Harold Hotelling* (Chapel Hill: University of North Carolina Press, 1960).

76. Newton C. Blanchard, ed., *Proceedings of a Conference of Governors* (Washington, DC: Government Printing Office, 1909), vi.

77. Blanchard, *Proceedings of a Conference of Governors*, 3.

78. Samuel P. Hays, *Conservation and the Gospel of Efficiency: The Progressive Conservation Movement, 1890–1920* (Pittsburgh, PA: University of Pittsburgh Press, 1999); Theodore Steinberg, *Down to Earth: Nature's Role in American History* (New York: Oxford University Press, 2002), chap. 9.

79. The first major textbook for natural resource economics, when it was established in 1979, declared, "The classic articles on the economics of exhaustible resources are by Gray (1914) and Hotelling (1931)." Partha Dasgupta and G. M. Heal, *Economic Theory and Exhaustible Resources*, Cambridge Economic Handbooks (Cambridge, UK: Cambridge University Press, 1979), 192. See also Philippe J. Crabbe, "The Contribution of L. C. Gray to the Economic Theory of Exhaustible Resources," *Journal of Environmental Economics and Management* 10 (1983): 195.

80. L. C. Gray, "The Economic Possibilities of Conservation," *Quarterly Journal of Economics* 27, no. 3 (1913): 497–519; Lewis Cecil Gray, "Rent Under the Assumption of Exhaustibility," *Quarterly Journal of Economics* 28, no. 3 (1914): 466–89.

81. Gray, "Economic Possibilities of Conservation," 504.

82. "Chemical orgy of waste" quotation is from H. J. Davenport in a 1910 paper to the American Economic Association, as cited in: Gray, "Economic Possibilities of Conservation," 515.

83. Gray, "Economic Possibilities of Conservation," 509, 514.

84. Gray, "Economic Possibilities of Conservation," 514.

85. Gray, "Economic Possibilities of Conservation," 517.

86. Henry C. Taylor and Anne Dewees Taylor, *The Story of Agricultural Economics in the United States, 1840–1932: Men, Services, Ideas* (Ames: Iowa State College Press, 1952); C. Ford Runge, "Agricultural Economics: A Brief Intellectual History," Staff Paper 13649 (Department of Applied Economics, University of Minnesota, 2006).

87. Sarah Phillips, *This Land, This Nation: Conservation, Rural America, and the New Deal* (Cambridge, UK: Cambridge University Press, 2007).

88. As Nobel Prize–winning economist (and adviser to growth theory pioneer Robert Solow) Wassily Leontief observed, early agricultural economists "were among the first to make use of the advanced methods of mathematical statistics," and they did so in a way that offered "an exceptional example of a healthy balance between theoretical and empirical analysis." Wassily Leontief, "Theoretical Assumptions and Nonobserved Facts," *American Economic Review* 61, no. 1 (1971): 5. Marion Fourcade made a similar argument about the advanced nature of statistical work being done by agricultural economists at this time due to the proliferation of data. Fourcade, *Economists and Societies*, chap. 2.

89. Runge, "Agricultural Economics: A Brief Intellectual History."

90. Walton H. Hamilton and Helen R. Wright, *The Case of Bituminous Coal* (New York: The Macmillan Company, 1925), 7.

91. Hamilton and Wright, *The Case of Bituminous Coal,* 251, 256.

92. Walton H. Hamilton and Helen R. Wright, *A Way of Order for Bituminous Coal* (New York: The Macmillan Company, 1928); Rutherford, *Institutional Movement in American Economics,* 68.

93. John Ise, *The United States Oil Policy* (New Haven, CT: Yale University Press, 1926), 496, 496, 497, 507.

94. George Ward Stocking, *The Oil Industry and the Competitive System: A Study in Waste* (Boston: Houghton Mifflin Company, 1925), 309–10; "In Memoriam: George W. Stocking 1892-1975," *American Economic Review* 66, no. 3 (1976): 453.

Chapter Two

1. Moses Abramovitz, "Economics of Growth," in *A Survey of Contemporary Economics*, ed. Bernard F. Haley (Homewood, IL: American Economic Association, 1952), 132.

2. Moses Abramovitz, "Days Gone By: A Memoir for My Family," 2001, https://web.archive.org/web/20070609121742/http://www-econ.stanford.edu/abramovitz/abramovitzm.html.

3. Robert J. Gordon, *The Rise and Fall of American Growth: The U.S. Standard of Living Since the Civil War* (Princeton, NJ: Princeton University Press, 2016).

4. Heinz Wolfgang Arndt, *The Rise and Fall of Economic Growth: A Study in Contemporary Thought* (Melbourne: Longman Cheshire, 1978), 30.

5. Robert M. Collins, *More: The Politics of Economic Growth in Postwar America* (Oxford: Oxford University Press, 2000), chap. 4.

6. On the emergence of growth at this time, see Matthias Schmelzer, *The Hegemony of Growth: The OECD and the Making of the Economic Growth Paradigm* (Cambridge, UK: Cambridge University Press, 2016); Collins, *More*; Charles S. Maier, "The Politics of Productivity: Foundations of American International Economic Policy After World War II," *International Organization* 31, no. 4 (1977): 607–33; Arndt, *Rise and Fall of Economic Growth*; Daniel Hirschman, "Inventing the Economy, Or: How We Learned to Stop Worrying and Love the GDP" (PhD diss., University of Michigan, 2016); Andrew L. Yarrow, *Measuring America: How Economic Growth Came to Define American Greatness in the Late Twentieth Century* (Amherst: University of Massachusetts Press, 2010); Christophe Bonneuil and Jean-Baptiste Fressoz, "Growth Unlimited: The Idea of Infinite Growth from Fossil Capitalism to Green Capitalism," in *History of the Future of Economic Growth: Historical Roots of Current Debates on Sustainable Degrowth*, ed. Matthias Schmelzer and Iris Borowy (London: Routledge, 2017), 52–68.

7. Gordon describes the period from 1870 to 1970 as a golden century: Gordon, *Rise and Fall of American Growth*.

8. W. Arthur Lewis, *The Theory of Economic Growth* (Homewood, IL: Richard D. Irwin, Inc., 1955), 5.

9. On the rediscovery of growth in this era, see Schmelzer, *Hegemony of Growth*; Arndt, *Rise and Fall of Economic Growth*; Collins, *More*.

10. Lewis, *Theory of Economic Growth*, 5.

11. Hirschman, "Inventing the Economy"; Malcolm Rutherford, *The Institutional Movement in American Economics, 1918–1947: Science and Social Control* (Cambridge, UK: Cambridge University Press, 2011).

12. Collins, *More*, 1–16.

13. Alvin H. Hansen, "Capital Goods and the Restoration of Purchasing Power," *Proceedings of the Academy of Political Science* 16, no. 1 (1934): 11–19; Alvin H. Hansen, *Full Recovery or Stagnation?* (New York: Norton, 1938); Alvin H. Hansen, "Economic Progress and Declining Population Growth," *American Economic Review* 29, no. 1 (1939): 1–15.

14. Paul McCracken (future chairman of the Council of Economic Advisers) in a 1967 letter to Hansen, as cited in John E. Miller, "From South Dakota Farm to Harvard Seminar: Alvin H. Hansen, America's Prophet of Keynesianism," *Historian* 64, no. 3–4 (2002): 604.

15. Cook, *Pricing of Progress*, chap. 5.

16. Richard Ely's 1893 textbook was one of America's most popular at the time, and it included only one reference to growth in the table of con-

tents, which referred to population growth. Simon Newcomb, who offered a mathematical text in 1885, made no reference to growth in the table of contents and the only index reference to growth referred to cities. From 1886 to 1920, *The Quarterly Journal of Economics* and *The Journal of Political Economy* had only six articles with growth in the title, and these referred to topics such as cities, population, banks, and corporations, not the economy. Richard T. Ely, *Outlines of Economics* (New York: Flood and Vincent, 1893); Simon Newcomb, *Principles of Political Economy* (New York: Harper, 1885), http://archive.org/details/principlesofpoli00newcuoft.

17. Abramovitz, "Economics of Growth," 133.

18. Timothy Mitchell, "Fixing the Economy," *Cultural Studies* 12, no. 1 (1998): 82–101; Timothy Mitchell, "Economists and the Economy in the Twentieth Century," in *The Politics of Method in the Human Sciences: Positivism and Its Epistemological Others*, ed. George Steinmetz (Durham, NC: Duke University Press, 2005). For a helpful discussion of Mitchell's thesis, see Hirschman, "Inventing the Economy."

19. One of Ricardo's most notable contributions to economics was the idea of comparative advantage, which he described with the following thought example: imagine that ninety workers in Portugal could manufacture cloth that would take one hundred workers in England and that eighty workers in Portugal could make wine that would require 120 workers in England. Even though Portugal could make its own cloth cheaper than England, the nation would be better off importing cloth from England so that it could focus on making wine, where its comparative advantage was greater.

20. Mary S. Morgan, *The World in the Model: How Economists Work and Think* (Cambridge, UK: Cambridge University Press, 2012), chap. 2.

21. John Maynard Keynes, "The British Balance of Trade, 1925–1927," *Economic Journal* 37, no. 148 (1927): 565.

22. Frederick G. Tryon, "An Index of Consumption of Fuels and Water Power," *Journal of the American Statistical Association* 22, no. 159 (1927): 279.

23. Hirschman, "Inventing the Economy," chap. 3.

24. Lucy Sprague Mitchell, "A Personal Sketch," in *Wesley Clair Mitchell: The Economic Scientist*, ed. Arthur Burns (New York: National Bureau of Economic Research [NBER], 1951), 55–106.

25. Wesley C. Mitchell, *Business Cycles* (Berkeley: University of California Press, 1913), xv.

26. Arthur Burns, "Introductory Sketch," in *Wesley Clair Mitchell: The Economic Scientist*, ed. Arthur Burns (New York: NBER, 1951), 23.

27. Wesley C. Mitchell and NBER, *Income in the United States: Its Amount and Distribution, 1909–1919*, Publications of the National Bureau of Economic Research, no. 1–2 (New York: Harcourt, Brace and Co., 1921), ix.

28. Mitchell and NBER, *Income in the United States*, 3.

29. Mitchell and NBER, *Income in the United States*, 143–47.
30. Abramovitz, "Days Gone By," 98.
31. Dirk Philipsen, *The Little Big Number: How GDP Came to Rule the World and What to Do About It* (Princeton, NJ: Princeton University Press, 2015), chap. 4.
32. Hirschman, "Inventing the Economy"; Rutherford, *Institutional Movement in American Economics*.
33. Simon Kuznets, *National Income, 1929–32* (Washington, DC: Government Printing Office, 1934), 10, 19.
34. Kuznets, *National Income*, 19.
35. Remarks at the State Capitol, Lincoln, NE, October 10, 1936, as cited in Hirschman, "Inventing the Economy," 80–81.
36. Hirschman, "Inventing the Economy," 77.
37. Philipsen, *Little Big Number*, 108.
38. Hirschman, "Inventing the Economy," 50.
39. Yarrow, *Measuring America*, 26–27.
40. Kuznets, *National Income*, 7, 4, 5.
41. Gross national product measures the output of goods and services by a nation's citizens at home and abroad; gross domestic product measures the output of goods and services within the borders of a nation, regardless of whether the producers are citizens. Since 1991, GDP has been the preferred calculation for most governments. The difference between these two measures is typically within a couple of percentage points, making the distinction between GNP and GDP relatively unimportant for this analysis.
42. Philipp Lepenies, *The Power of a Single Number: A Political History of GDP* (New York: Columbia University Press, 2016), chap. 4.
43. Philipsen, *Little Big Number*, chap. 5.
44. Philipsen, *Little Big Number*, chap. 6; Schmelzer, *The Hegemony of Growth*.
45. John Maynard Keynes, *The General Theory of Employment, Interest and Money* (New York: Harcourt, Brace and Co., 1936).
46. Lepenies, *Power of a Single Number*, chap. 4–5.
47. Lepenies, *Power of a Single Number*, chap. 4; Philipsen, *Little Big Number*, 129–30.
48. Paul A. Samuelson, "Full Employment After the War," in *Postwar Economic Problems*, ed. Seymour E. Harris (New York: McGraw-Hill Book, 1943), 27–54; Paul A. Samuelson, "Unemployment Ahead," *The New Republic*, September 11, 1944.
49. Hirschman, "Inventing the Economy," 50.
50. Collins, *More*, chap. 2.
51. Collins, *More*, 16.
52. Collins, *More*, 30.

53. Leslie Wayne, "Leon Keyserling: Economic Aide to Truman, Dies," *New York Times*, August 11, 1987.

54. Collins, *More*, 20.

55. Council of Economic Advisers (CEA), *Business and Government: Fourth Annual Report to the President by the Council of Economic Advisers* (Washington, DC: Government Printing Office, 1949), 2, 3.

56. CEA, *Business and Government*, 5.

57. CEA, *Business and Government*, 6.

58. CEA, *Business and Government*, 4.

59. Maier, "Politics of Productivity."

60. Collins, *More*, 37.

61. Nelson Lichtenstein, "From Corporatism to Collective Bargaining: Organized Labor and the Eclipse of Social Democracy in the Postwar Era," in *The Rise and Fall of the New Deal Order, 1930–1980*, ed. Steve Fraser and Gary Gerstle (Princeton, NJ: Princeton University Press, 1989), 122–52.

62. Federal Reserve Economic Data, Federal Reserve Bank of St. Louis, "Gross National Product," accessed November 27, 2022, https://fred.stlouisfed.org/series/GNP.

63. Gordon, *Rise and Fall of American Growth*.

64. In 1929, the poorest 40 percent of Americans received 12.5 percent of national income while the top 20 percent got 54.4 percent; in 1957, the poorest 40 percent increased their share to 16.1 percent while the top 20 percent declined to 45.3 percent. Black men before the war earned 41 percent and Black women 36 percent of their White counterparts; in 1960, it had improved to 67 percent for Black men and 70 percent for Black women. Collins, *More*, 42; William Lazonick, Philip Moss, and Joshua Weitz, "The Unmaking of the Black Blue-Collar Middle Class," working paper (Institute for New Economic Thinking, New York, May 20, 2021), https://www.ineteconomics.org/research/research-papers/the-unmaking-of-the-black-blue-collar-middle-class.

65. Schmelzer, *Hegemony of Growth*; Maier, "Politics of Productivity"; Scott O'Bryan, *The Growth Idea: Purpose and Prosperity in Postwar Japan* (Honolulu: University of Hawaii Press, 2009); Lepenies, *Power of a Single Number*, chap. 5; Till Düppe and Ivan Boldyrev, "Economic Knowledge in Socialism, 1945–89: Editors' Introduction," *History of Political Economy* 51, no. S1 (2019): 1–4.

66. Maier, "Politics of Productivity"; Schmelzer, *Hegemony of Growth*.

67. Schmelzer, *Hegemony of Growth*, 171.

68. Schmelzer, *Hegemony of Growth*, chap. 1; Lepenies, *Power of a Single Number*, 118–30; Philipsen, *Little Big Number*, chap. 6.

69. Collins, *More*, 46–47.

70. Samuelson cited in Alex Tabarrok, "Soviet Growth and American

Textbooks," *Marginal Revolution Blog*, January 4, 2010, accessed July 27, 2022, https://marginalrevolution.com/marginalrevolution/2010/01/soviet -growth-american-textbooks.html.

71. Paul Warde, Libby Robin, and Sverker Sörlin, *The Environment: A History of the Idea* (Baltimore, MD: Johns Hopkins University Press, 2018), 53.

72. J. Frederick Dewhurst and Associates, *America's Needs and Resources: A New Survey* (New York: The Twentieth Century Fund, 1955), 939.

73. Scott T. Burkhardt, "Environmental Optimism in an Apocalyptic Age: The Paley Commission and Resource Scarcities at Mid-Century" (master's thesis, University of Wisconsin, 2005), chap. 2.

74. Warde, Robin, and Sörlin, *The Environment: A History of the Idea*; Yannick Mahrane et al., "From Nature to Biosphere: The Political Invention of the Global Environment, 1945–1972," *Vingtième Siècle: Revue d'Histoire* 113, no. 1 (2012): 127–41; Etienne S. Benson, *Surroundings: A History of Environments and Environmentalisms* (Chicago: University of Chicago Press, 2020).

75. Charles C. Mann, *The Wizard and the Prophet: Two Remarkable Scientists and Their Dueling Visions to Shape Tomorrow's World* (New York: Alfred A. Knopf, 2018), chap. 2.

76. William Vogt, *Road to Survival* (New York: W. Sloane Associates, 1948), 17.

77. Vogt, *Road to Survival*, 17.

78. Fairfield Osborn, *Our Plundered Planet* (Boston: Little, Brown, 1948), 4–5.

79. Osborn, *Our Plundered Planet*, ix.

80. Samuel Hanson Ordway, *Resources and the American Dream, Including a Theory of the Limit of Growth* (New York: Ronald Press Co., 1953), 8.

81. Ordway, *Resources and the American Dream*, vi.

82. Mahrane et al., "From Nature to Biosphere."

83. Harry S. Truman, "Inaugural Address," Washington, DC, January 20, 1949, Harry S. Truman Presidential Library Web Site, accessed July 27, 2018, https://trumanlibrary.org/whistlestop/50yr_archive /inagural20jan1949.htm.

84. Mahrane et al., "From Nature to Biosphere."

85. Newton C. Blanchard, ed., *Proceedings of a Conference of Governors* (Washington, DC: Government Printing Office, 1909).

86. Michael A. Bernstein, *A Perilous Progress: Economists and Public Purpose in Twentieth-Century America* (Princeton, NJ: Princeton University Press, 2001), 1–2.

87. John Kenneth Galbraith, "Surveying American Economy in Terms of American Needs: America's Needs and Resources," *New York Times*, June 1, 1947.

88. J. Frederick Dewhurst and Associates, *America's Needs and Resources* (New York: The Twentieth Century Fund, 1947), 680, 686, 685.

89. Dewhurst and Associates, *America's Needs and Resources*, 597, 598, 598.

90. Harry S. Truman, letter to William Paley, January 22, 1951. Reprinted in The President's Materials Policy Commission, *Resources for Freedom*, iv.
91. President's Materials Policy Commission, *Resources for Freedom*, 5, 6, 1.
92. President's Materials Policy Commission, *Resources for Freedom*, 3, 21, 21, 169.
93. Burkhardt, "Environmental Optimism," 45.
94. President's Materials Policy Commission, *Resources for Freedom*, 169.
95. Dewhurst and Associates, *America's Needs and Resources: A New Survey*, 942–44.
96. Abramovitz, "Economics of Growth," 177–78.

Chapter Three

1. Brian Keegan, "Oral History of Robert Solow," August 15, 2007, 4. Robert M. Solow Papers, Box 108, Duke University Archives.
2. Paul A. Samuelson, "Robert Solow: An Affectionate Portrait," *Journal of Economic Perspectives* 3, no. 3 (1989): 93.
3. Keegan, "Oral History of Robert Solow," 4–6.
4. Keegan, "Oral History of Robert Solow," 24–25.
5. Israel Shenker, "Solow on Nixon Budget," *New York Times*, February 7, 1971, F3.
6. Mauro Boianovsky and Kevin D. Hoover, "In the Kingdom of Solovia: The Rise of Growth Economics at MIT, 1956–70," *History of Political Economy* 46, Supplement 1 (2014): 198–228.
7. While this book was in production, Verena Halsmayer published a book that provides additional insight into Solow's growth model: Verena Halsmayer, *Managing Growth in Miniature: Solow's Model as an Artifact* (Cambridge, UK: Cambridge University Press, 2024).
8. Keegan, "Oral History of Robert Solow," 1–3.
9. Keegan, "Oral History of Robert Solow," 1–3.
10. Leonard Solomon Silk, *The Economists* (New York: Basic Books, 1976), chap. 4; William J. Baumol and Thijs ten Raa, "Wassily Leontief: In Appreciation," *European Journal of the History of Economic Thought* 16, no. 3 (2009): 511–22; Paul Samuelson, "Our Wassily: W. W. Leontief (1905–1999)," *International Input-Output Association Conference*, 2001, accessed September 2019, https://www.iioa.org/conferences/13th/files/SamuelsonOurWassily.pdf; Holcomb B. Noble, "Wassily Leontief, Economist Who Won a Nobel, Dies at 93," *New York Times*, February 7, 1999, 50.
11. Keegan, "Oral History of Robert Solow," 11, 11, 9.
12. "Barbara Solow Obituary" *Concord Journal*, February 28, 2014, accessed September 23, 2019, https://www.legacy.com/obituaries/wickedlocal-concordjournal/obituary.aspx?n=barbara-solow&pid=169897576.

13. Samuelson, "Robert Solow," 91.
14. Wassily Leontief, "Input-Output Analysis" (1951), reprinted in Wassily Leontief, *Input-Output Economics*, 2nd ed. (New York: Oxford University Press, 1986), 14.
15. Leontief, "Input-Output Analysis," 16.
16. Leontief, "Input-Output Analysis," 15.
17. Silk, *The Economists*, 163.
18. Erik Dietzenbacher and Michael L. Lahr, *Wassily Leontief and Input-Output Economics* (Cambridge, UK: Cambridge University Press, 2004).
19. Wassily Leontief, ed., *Studies in the Structure of the American Economy: Theoretical and Empirical Explorations in Input-Output Analysis* (New York: Oxford University Press, 1953), 13.
20. Leontief, *Studies in the Structure of the American Economy*, 13–14.
21. William Breit and Barry T. Hirsch, *Lives of the Laureates: Twenty-Three Nobel Economists*, 5th ed. (Cambridge, MA: MIT Press, 2009), 157.
22. Marion Fourcade, *Economists and Societies: Discipline and Profession in the United States, Britain, and France, 1890s to 1990s* (Princeton, NJ: Princeton University Press, 2009), chap. 2; Roger Backhouse, *The Ordinary Business of Life: A History of Economics from the Ancient World to the Twenty-First Century* (Princeton, NJ: Princeton University Press, 2002), chap. 11; Michael A. Bernstein, *A Perilous Progress: Economists and Public Purpose in Twentieth-Century America* (Princeton, NJ: Princeton University Press, 2001), chap. 3.
23. Fourcade, *Economists and Societies*, 84. On Samuelson, see Roger E. Backhouse, *Founder of Modern Economics: Paul A. Samuelson, vol. 1: Becoming Samuelson, 1915–1948* (New York: Oxford University Press, 2017); Silk, *The Economists*, chap. 1.
24. Paul A. Samuelson, *Foundations of Economic Analysis* (Cambridge, MA: Harvard University Press, 1947).
25. Lucas as cited in David Warsh, *Knowledge and the Wealth of Nations: A Story of Economic Discovery* (New York: W. W. Norton, 2006), 168.
26. Arthur F. Burns and Wesley C. Mitchell, *Measuring Business Cycles* (New York: National Bureau of Economic Research, 1946).
27. Tjalling C. Koopmans, "Measurement Without Theory," *Review of Economics and Statistics* 29, no. 3 (1947): 161–72; Burns and Mitchell, *Measuring Business Cycles*.
28. Rutledge Vining, "Methodological Issues in Quantitative Economics: Koopmans on the Choice of Variables to Be Studied and of Methods of Measurement," *Review of Economics and Statistics* 31 (1949): 77–86.
29. Moses Abramovitz, "Days Gone By: A Memoir for My Family," 2001, 93, https://web.archive.org/web/20070609121742/http://www-econ.stanford.edu/abramovitz/abramovitzm.html; Malcolm Rutherford, *The Institutional*

Movement in American Economics, 1918–1947: Science and Social Control (Cambridge, UK: Cambridge University Press, 2011).

30. Paul Samuelson, "Our Wassily: W. W. Leontief (1905–1999)," *International Input-Output Association Conference,* 2001, 7, accessed September 2019, https://www.iioa.org/conferences/13th/files/SamuelsonOurWassily.pdf.

31. Samuelson, "Our Wassily," 5.

32. Philip Mirowski, *Machine Dreams: Economics Becomes a Cyborg Science* (Cambridge, UK: Cambridge University Press, 2002); Bernstein, *Perilous Progress,* chap. 3; S. M. Amadae, *Rationalizing Capitalist Democracy: The Cold War Origins of Rational Choice Liberalism* (Chicago: University of Chicago Press, 2003); Jennifer S. Light, *From Warfare to Welfare: Defense Intellectuals and Urban Problems in Cold War America* (Baltimore, MD: Johns Hopkins University Press, 2003).

33. Philip Mirowski, *More Heat than Light: Economics as Social Physics, Physics as Nature's Economics* (Cambridge, UK: Cambridge University Press, 1989).

34. Fourcade, *Economists and Societies,* 89. For a skeptical take on whether McCarthyism was a crucial factor, see E. Roy Weintraub, "McCarthyism and the Mathematization of Economics," *Journal of the History of Economic Thought* 39, no. 4 (2017): 571–97.

35. Theodore M. Porter, *Trust in Numbers: The Pursuit of Objectivity in Science and Public Life* (Princeton, NJ: Princeton University Press, 1995).

36. John Maynard Keynes, *The General Theory of Employment, Interest and Money* (New York: Harcourt, Brace, 1936); Rutherford, *Institutional Movement in American Economics.*

37. R. E. Backhouse, "Paul A. Samuelson's Move to MIT," *History of Political Economy* 46, Supplement 1 (2014): 60–80; B. Cherrier, "Toward a History of Economics at MIT, 1940–72," *History of Political Economy* 46, Supplement 1 (2014): 15–44.

38. Keegan, "Oral History of Robert Solow," 14.

39. Angus Burgin, *The Great Persuasion: Reinventing Free Markets Since the Depression* (Cambridge, MA: Harvard University Press, 2015); Philip Mirowski and Dieter Plehwe, eds., *The Road from Mont Pelerin: The Making of the Neoliberal Thought Collective* (Cambridge, MA: Harvard University Press, 2009).

40. Yann Giraud, "Negotiating the Middle-of-the-Road Position: Paul Samuelson, MIT, and the Politics of Textbook Writing, 1945–55," *History of Political Economy* 46, Supplement 1 (2014): 134–52.

41. Nicholas Wapshott, *Samuelson Friedman: The Battle over the Free Market* (New York: Norton, 2021).

42. Robert M. Solow, "Policies for Economic Growth: The Ernest Sturc Memorial Lecture," delivered November 12, 1991 (Washington, DC: The Paul H. Nitze

School for Advanced International Studies, Johns Hopkins University, 1992), 4; V. Halsmayer, "From Exploratory Modeling to Technical Expertise: Solow's Growth Model as a Multipurpose Design," *History of Political Economy* 46, Supplement 1 (2014): 229–51; Cherrier, "Toward a History of Economics at MIT"; Halsmayer, *Managing Growth in Miniature*.

43. Dani Rodrik, *Economics Rules: The Rights and Wrongs of the Dismal Science* (New York: W. W. Norton, 2015), 10. For an excellent source on how models function in economics, see Mary S. Morgan, *The World in the Model: How Economists Work and Think* (Cambridge, UK: Cambridge University Press, 2012).

44. Paul A. Samuelson, "Abstract of a Theorem Concerning Substitutability in Open Leontief Models," in *Activity Analysis of Production and Allocation: Proceedings of a Conference*, ed. Tjalling Koopmans (New York: John Wiley & Sons, 1951).

45. Robert M. Solow and Paul Samuelson, "Balanced Growth Under Constant Returns to Scale," *Econometrica* 21, no. 3 (1953): 412–24.

46. Keegan, "Oral History of Robert Solow," 15.

47. Roy F. Harrod, "An Essay in Dynamic Theory," *Economic Journal* 49, no. 193 (1939): 14–33; Evsey Domar, "Capital Expansion, Rate of Growth, and Employment," *Econometrica* 14, no. 2 (1946): 137–47.

48. Moses Abramovitz, "Economics of Growth," in *A Survey of Contemporary Economics*, ed. Bernard F. Haley (Homewood, IL: American Economic Association, 1952), 170n78. On the ignoring of Harrod's 1939 essay, see Mauro Boianovsky and Kevin D. Hoover, "The Neoclassical Growth Model and Twentieth-Century Economics," *History of Political Economy* 41, Annual Supplement (2009): 5n3.

49. James Tobin to Robert Solow, March 19, 1959, as cited in Halsmayer, "From Exploratory Modeling to Technical Expertise," 235; Verena Halsmayer and Kevin D. Hoover, "Solow's Harrod: Transforming Macroeconomic Dynamics into a Model of Long-Run Growth," *European Journal of the History of Economic Thought* 23, no. 4 (2016): 561–96.

50. Robert M. Solow, "A Contribution to the Theory of Economic Growth," *Quarterly Journal of Economics* 70, no. 1 (1956): 65–94.

51. Solow, "Contribution to the Theory of Economic Growth," 65.

52. Solow, "Contribution to the Theory of Economic Growth," 65.

53. Solow, "Contribution to the Theory of Economic Growth," 65; italics in original.

54. Charles W. Cobb and Paul H. Douglas, "A Theory of Production," *American Economic Review* 18, no. 1 (1928): 163.

55. Cobb and Douglas, "Theory of Production," 164.

56. Roger Biles, *Crusading Liberal: Paul H. Douglas of Illinois* (DeKalb: Northern Illinois University Press, 2002).

57. Solow, "Contribution to the Theory of Economic Growth," 73.
58. Warsh, *Knowledge and the Wealth of Nations*, 148.
59. Trevor Swan, "Economic Growth and Capital Accumulation," *Economic Record* 32 (1956): 334–61.
60. Robert M. Solow, "Does Growth Have a Future? Does Growth Theory Have a Future? Are These Questions Related?," *History of Political Economy* 41, no. 5 (2009): 27–34.
61. Robert W. Dimand and Barbara J. Spencer, "Trevor Swan and the Neoclassical Growth Model," *History of Political Economy* 41 (2009): 107–26.
62. Robert M. Solow, "Technical Change and the Aggregate Production Function," *Review of Economics and Statistics* 39, no. 3 (1957): 312–20.
63. Solow, "Technical Change and the Aggregate Production Function," 320.
64. Solow, "Technical Change and the Aggregate Production Function."
65. Solow, "Policies for Economic Growth"; Cherrier, "Toward a History of Economics at MIT."
66. Joseph A. Schumpeter, *Capitalism, Socialism, and Democracy* (New York: Harper & Brothers, 1942).
67. Solow, "Contribution to the Theory of Economic Growth," 93.
68. David Warsh, "Robert Solow and His Influential Economic Growth," *Chicago Tribune*, February 20, 1994, https://www.chicagotribune.com/news/ct-xpm-1994-02-20-9402200090-story.html.
69. Robert M. Solow, "Second Thoughts on Growth Theory," in *Employment and Growth: Issues for the 1980s*, ed. Alfred Steinherr and Daniel Weiserbs (Dordrecht, Netherlands: Kluwer Academic Publishers, 1987), 27.
70. Cherrier, "Toward a History of Economics at MIT," 29.
71. From 1936–1955, 0.95 percent of all articles included "growth" in the title; from 1956–1970, 4.64 percent of articles did. Boianovsky and Hoover, "Neoclassical Growth Model," 3.
72. Andrew L. Yarrow, *Measuring America: How Economic Growth Came to Define American Greatness in the Late Twentieth Century* (Amherst: University of Massachusetts Press, 2010), 37.
73. Boianovsky and Hoover, "In the Kingdom of Solovia," 198–99.
74. Cherrier, "Toward a History of Economics at MIT," 25.
75. "Robert M. Solow—Biographical," NobelPrize.org, Nobel Media AB 2019, accessed November 1, 2019, https://www.nobelprize.org/prizes/economic-sciences/1987/solow/biographical.
76. Peter Diamond, "National Debt in a Neoclassical Growth Model," *American Economic Review* 55, no. 5 (1965): 1126–50; Peter Diamond, "Optimal Paths of Capital Accumulation Under the Minimum Time Objective: A Comment," *Econometrica* 34, no. 4 (1966): 886–87.
77. Boianovsky and Hoover, "Neoclassical Growth Model," 2. Sheshinski quoted in Warsh, *Knowledge and the Wealth of Nations*, 155.

78. Hirofumi Uzawa, "On a Two-Sector Model of Economic Growth," *Review of Economic Studies* 29, no. 1 (1961): 40–47.
79. Kenneth J. Arrow, "The Economic Implications of Learning by Doing," *Review of Economic Studies* 29, no. 3 (1962): 155–73.
80. Tjalling Koopmans, "Economic Growth at a Maximal Rate," *Quarterly Journal of Economics* 78, no. 3 (1964): 355–94; James Tobin, "Money and Economic Growth," *Econometrica* 33, no. 4 (1965): 671–84.
81. F. H. Hahn and R. C. O. Matthews, "Economic Growth: A Survey," *Economic Journal* 74, no. 296 (1964): 779–902.
82. Warsh, *Knowledge and the Wealth of Nations*, 148.
83. Andrew Yarrow offers a wonderful analysis of these efforts in Yarrow, *Measuring America*.
84. As cited in Yarrow, *Measuring America*, 21. See also Caroline Jack, *Business as Usual: How Sponsored Media Sold American Capitalism in the Twentieth Century* (Chicago: University of Chicago Press, 2024).
85. Keegan, "Oral History of Robert Solow," 16–17.
86. Alan S. Blinder, "In Honor of Robert M. Solow: Nobel Laureate in 1987," *Journal of Economic Perspectives* 3, no. 3 (1989): 100.
87. Solow, "Contribution to the Theory of Economic Growth," 66.
88. Josh Ryan-Collins, Toby Lloyd, and Laurie Macfarlane, *Rethinking the Economics of Land and Housing* (London: Zed Books, 2017).
89. E. Kula, *History of Environmental Economic Thought* (London: Routledge, 1998), 66.
90. John Bates Clark, *The Distribution of Wealth: A Theory of Wages, Interest and Profits* (New York: Kelley and Millman, 1899), chap. 13, 22.
91. Solow, "Technical Change and the Aggregate Production Function," 314.
92. Solow, "Second Thoughts on Growth Theory," 67.
93. Solow, "Contribution to the Theory of Economic Growth," 67n2.
94. Solow, "Contribution to the Theory of Economic Growth," 88.
95. Cobb and Douglas, "A Theory of Production," 165.
96. Paul H. Douglas, "The Cobb–Douglas Production Function Once Again: Its History, Its Testing, and Some New Empirical Values," *Journal of Political Economy* 84, no. 5 (1976): 903–16.
97. Hirofumi Uzawa, "On the Occasion of the Inaugural Conference on 'Environment and Development Economics,'" *Environment and Development Economics* 1, no. 1 (1996): 1.
98. Hahn and Matthews, "Economic Growth: A Survey."
99. Swan, "Economic Growth and Capital Accumulation"; Solow, "Contribution to the Theory of Economic Growth," 93.
100. Swan, "Economic Growth and Capital Accumulation," 341–42.
101. J. E. Meade, *A Neo-Classical Theory of Economic Growth* (New York: Oxford University Press, 1961), v.

102. Meade, *Neo-Classical Theory of Economic Growth*, 10.
103. Keegan, "Oral History of Robert Solow," 16–17.
104. Blinder, "In Honor of Solow," 99.

Chapter Four

1. Peter R. Odell, *An Economic Geography of Oil* (Edinburgh: Neill & Company, 1963). The inflation-adjusted cost of a barrel of West Texas Intermediate oil was $34.11 in January 1948 versus $25.33 in June 1973. Data from "Crude Oil Prices: 70 Year Trend," https://www.macrotrends.net/1369/crude-oil-price-history-chart (accessed August 26, 2024).
2. Marion Fourcade, *Economists and Societies: Discipline and Profession in the United States, Britain, and France, 1890s to 1990s* (Princeton, NJ: Princeton University Press, 2009), chap. 2.
3. Philipp Lepenies, *The Power of a Single Number: A Political History of GDP* (New York: Columbia University Press, 2016), chap. 4.
4. Simon Kuznets, *Six Lectures on Economic Growth* (New York: The Free Press, 1959), 38.
5. Simon Kuznets, "Reflections on the Economic Growth of Nations," in *Toward a Theory of Economic Growth*, ed. Simon Kuznets (New York: Norton, 1968), 87.
6. Kuznets, "Reflections on the Economic Growth of Nations," 88.
7. Kuznets, "Reflections on the Economic Growth of Nations," 89.
8. Lepenies, *Power of a Single Number*, chap. 3; Colin Clark, *Population Growth and Land Use* (London: Macmillan, 1967).
9. Joan Robinson, *The Accumulation of Capital* (London: Macmillan, 1956); Nicholas Kaldor, "A Model of Economic Growth," *Economic Journal* 67, no. 268 (1957): 591–624.
10. G. C. Harcourt, "Robinson, Joan 1903–1983," *Economic Journal* 105, no. 432 (1995): 1228–43.
11. Joan Robinson, *Accumulation of Capital*. Book VI of this work is devoted to land and acknowledges its finite character but does not elaborate a theory of limits to growth based on that fact.
12. Joan Robinson, *Essays in the Theory of Economic Growth* (New York: St. Martin's Press, 1964), 74.
13. Kaldor, "A Model of Economic Growth"; Nicholas Kaldor, "Capital Accumulation and Economic Growth," in *The Theory of Capital*, ed. F. A. Lutz and Douglas Hague (New York: St. Martin's Press, 1961), 177–222.
14. Kaldor, "Capital Accumulation and Economic Growth," 179.
15. Kaldor, "A Model of Economic Growth."
16. Kaldor, "Capital Accumulation and Economic Growth," 183–84.
17. Michele Alacevich and Mauro Boianovsky, "Writing the History of

Development Economics," *History of Political Economy* 50, no. S1 (2018): 1–14; Stephen Macekura, "Economic Growth and Development: An Intellectual History," in *History of the Future of Economic Growth: Historical Roots of Current Debates on Sustainable Degrowth*, ed. Matthias Schmelzer and Iris Borowy (London: Routledge, 2017), 110–28; Jaime Ros, "The Pioneers of Development Economics and Modern Growth Theory," in *The Origins of Development Economics: How Schools of Economic Thought Have Addressed Development*, ed. Jomo K. S. and Erik S. Reinert (London: Zed Books, 2005), 81–98; John Toye, "Solow in the Tropics," *History of Political Economy* 41, Supplement 1 (2009): 221–40; Stephen Macekura, "Whither Growth? International Development, Social Indicators, and the Politics of Measurement, 1920s-1970s," *Journal of Global History* 14, no. 2 (2019): 261–79; Michele Alacevich, "The Birth of Development Economics," *History of Political Economy* 50, no. S1 (2018): 114–32.

18. Joy Rohde, *Armed with Experience: The Militarization of American Social Science Research During the Cold War* (Ithaca, NY: Cornell University Press, 2013).

19. Robert M. Solow, "A Contribution to the Theory of Economic Growth," *Quarterly Journal of Economics* 70, no. 1 (1956): 93.

20. Albert O. Hirschman, *The Strategy of Economic Development* (New Haven, CT: Yale University Press, 1958), 33.

21. Gunnar Myrdal, *Economic Theory and Underdeveloped Regions* (New York: Harper Torchbooks, 1957), 101.

22. W. Arthur Lewis, "Economic Development with Unlimited Supplies of Labour," *Manchester School of Economic and Social Studies* 22 (1954): 40.

23. Alacevich, "Birth of Development Economics."

24. P. N. Rosenstein-Rodan, "Problems of Industrialisation of Eastern and South-Eastern Europe," *Economic Journal* 53, no. 210/211 (1943): 202.

25. Rosenstein-Rodan, "Problems of Industrialisation of Europe," 204.

26. Lewis, "Economic Development with Unlimited Supplies of Labour," 155.

27. Ragnar Nurkse, *Problems of Capital Formation in Underdeveloped Countries* (New York: Oxford University Press, 1957).

28. Hirschman, *Strategy of Economic Development.*

29. Rosenstein-Rodan, "Problems of Industrialisation of Europe," 203.

30. W. Arthur Lewis, *The Theory of Economic Growth* (Homewood, IL: Richard D. Irwin, Inc., 1955), 10–11.

31. Hirschman, *Strategy of Economic Development*, 2.

32. Nurkse, *Problems of Capital Formation*, 11.

33. H. W. Singer, "The Distribution of Gains Between Investing and Borrowing Countries," *American Economic Review* 40, no. 2 (1950): 475.

34. Singer, "Distribution of Gains," 479.

35. Singer, "Distribution of Gains," 480.

36. Nicholas Stern, "The Economics of Development: A Survey," *Economic Journal* 99, no. 397 (1989): 672.

37. Partha Dasgupta, "The Place of Nature in Economic Development," in *Handbook of Development Economics*, ed. Dani Rodrik and Mark Rosenzweig, vol. 5 (Amsterdam: Elsevier, 2010), 4984.

38. Dasgupta, "Place of Nature," 4984.

39. Dasgupta, "Place of Nature," 4982.

40. W. W. Rostow, *The Stages of Economic Growth, a Non-Communist Manifesto* (Cambridge, UK: Cambridge University Press, 1960).

41. Nils Gilman, *Mandarins of the Future: Modernization Theory in Cold War America* (Baltimore, MD: Johns Hopkins University Press, 2007); Macekura, "Economic Growth and Development"; B. Cherrier, "Toward a History of Economics at MIT, 1940–72," *History of Political Economy* 46, Supplement 1 (2014): 15–44.

42. Cherrier, "Toward a History of Economics at MIT," 22.

43. At a 1960 conference dedicated to Rostow's ideas in Germany, Solow complained that Rostow failed to identify causal mechanisms and blurred the lines between history and theory. Rostow granted the criticism but responded that trying to achieve growth in the real world required more than pure theoretical models. Boianovsky and Hoover, "In the Kingdom of Solovia: The Rise of Growth Economics at MIT, 1956–70," *History of Political Economy* 46, Supplement 1 (2014): 203–4.

44. P. Temin, "The Rise and Fall of Economic History at MIT," *History of Political Economy* 46, Supplement 1 (2014): 339.

45. Boianovsky, Mauro, "Voluminous, Repetitive, and Intractable: Samuelson on Early Development Economics," *History of Political Economy* 54, no. 1 (2022): 1–35.

46. Moses Abramovitz, "Resource and Output Trends in the United States Since 1870," *American Economic Review* 46, no. 2 (1956): 11; F. H. Hahn and R. C. O. Matthews, "Economic Growth: A Survey," *Economic Journal* 74, no. 296 (1964): 836.

47. Charles R. Hulten, "Growth Accounting," working paper (National Bureau of Economic Research, Cambridge, MA, 2009).

48. Moses Abramovitz, "Economics of Growth," in *A Survey of Contemporary Economics*, ed. Bernard F. Haley (Homewood, IL: American Economic Association, 1952), 178.

49. Abramovitz, "Economics of Growth," 178.

50. Abramovitz, "Resource and Output Trends," 11.

51. Abramovitz, "Resource and Output Trends," 11.

52. Abramovitz, "Resource and Output Trends," 14.

53. Abramovitz, "Resource and Output Trends," 13.

54. Abramovitz, "Resource and Output Trends," 12.

55. Moses Abramovitz, "Catching Up, Forging Ahead, and Falling Behind," *Journal of Economic History* 46, no. 2 (1986): 398.

56. Kaldor, "Capital Accumulation and Economic Growth," 181.

57. Edward Fulton Denison, *The Sources of Economic Growth in the United States and the Alternatives Before Us* (New York: Committee for Economic Development, 1962), 2.

58. Denison, *Sources of Economic Growth*, chap. 24.

59. Denison, *Sources of Economic Growth*, 30.

60. Denison, *Sources of Economic Growth*, 93.

61. Denison, *Sources of Economic Growth*, 93.

62. Edward Fulton Denison, *Why Growth Rates Differ: Postwar Experience in Nine Western Countries* (Washington, DC: Brookings Institution, 1967), chap. 21.

63. Denison, *Why Growth Rates Differ*, 185.

64. Moses Abramovitz, "Economic Growth in the United States: A Review Article," *American Economic Review* 52, no. 4 (1962): 762.

65. Abramovitz, "Economic Growth in the US," 781.

66. Abramovitz, "Economic Growth in the US," 781.

67. Dale W. Jorgenson and Zvi Griliches, "The Explanation of Productivity Change," *Review of Economic Studies* 34, no. 3 (1967): 249–83.

68. Hulten, "Growth Accounting," 8.

69. Dale W. Jorgenson, "The Role of Energy in the U.S. Economy," *National Tax Journal* 31, no. 3 (1978): 209–20; Dale W. Jorgenson and Peter J. Wilcoxen, "Energy, the Environment, and Economic Growth," in *Handbook of Natural Resource and Energy Economics*, ed. Allen V. Kneese and James L. Sweeney, vol. 3 (Amsterdam: Elsevier, 1993), 1278.

70. The work of Angus Maddison, another prominent growth accountant, has not been discussed here. His 1987 essay comparing several countries seems to fit the same pattern: Angus Maddison, "Growth and Slowdown in Advanced Capitalist Economies: Techniques of Quantitative Assessment," *Journal of Economic Literature* 25, no. 2 (1987): 649–98.

71. Jonathan Rauch, "Ideas Change the World—And One Think Tank Quietly Did" *Reason*, October 7, 2002, accessed October 24, 2019, https://reason.com/2002/10/07/ideas-change-the-worldand-one/.

72. Harold J. Barnett and Chandler Morse, *Scarcity and Growth: The Economics of Natural Resource Availability* (Baltimore, MD: Published for Resources for the Future [RFF] by Johns Hopkins Press, 1963), 240.

73. Barnett and Morse, *Scarcity and Growth*, 97.

74. Barnett and Morse, *Scarcity and Growth*, 2–3.

75. Marion Clawson, *From Sagebrush to Sage: The Making of a Natural Resource Economist* (Washington, DC: Ana Publications, 1987), 256.

76. *Resource Scarcity, Economic Growth and the Environment: Hearings*

Before the Subcommittee on Priorities and Economy in Government of the Joint Economic Committee, 93rd Congress, 1st session (Washington, DC: US Government Printing Office, 1974), 128.

77. The President's Materials Policy Commission, *Resources for Freedom* (Washington, DC: Government Printing Office, 1952), 3.

78. Clawson, *From Sagebrush to Sage*, 261.

79. Clawson, *From Sagebrush to Sage*, 261–62.

80. Hans H. Landsberg, Leonard L. Fischman, and Joseph L. Fisher, *Resources in America's Future: Patterns of Requirements and Availabilities, 1960–2000* (Baltimore, MD: Published for RFF by the Johns Hopkins Press, 1963), 4.

81. Landsberg, Fischman, and Fisher, *Resources in America's Future*, 5.

82. Landsberg, Fischman, and Fisher, *Resources in America's Future*, 5.

83. In the 1963 Annual Report, *Resources in America's Future* is always mentioned before *Scarcity and Growth*, and is the main topic of the opening essay by President Joseph L. Fisher ("Perspectives on Population and Resources"), an essay by Landsberg on "Technological Advance and Resource Projections," and gets a ten-paragraph description in the "Appraisals and Special Projects" section while *Scarcity and Growth* is summarized in a single paragraph (RFF, *1963 Annual Report*, Washington, DC). In RFF's outreach magazine, *Resources*, the June 1963 issue summarizes many of the findings of *Resources in America's Future* without discussing *Scarcity and Growth*.

84. Barnett and Morse, *Scarcity and Growth*, 49.

85. Barnett and Morse, *Scarcity and Growth*, chap. 8.

86. Barnett and Morse, *Scarcity and Growth*, 139.

87. Barnett and Morse, *Scarcity and Growth*, 239.

88. Barnett and Morse, *Scarcity and Growth*, 236.

89. Barnett and Morse, *Scarcity and Growth*, 248.

90. Barnett and Morse, *Scarcity and Growth*, 10.

91. RFF, *1963 Annual Report*, 11, 80.

92. "RFF on TV: FOCUS on Energy Conservation" *Resources*, September–December 1977, 5.

93. RFF, *The First 25 Years, 1952–1977* (Washington, DC: RFF, 1977).

94. Robert Solow, "The Power of Ideas in the Policy Process," RFF Lunch Talk, October 15, 2002, Robert M. Solow Papers, Box 77, Duke University Archives.

95. Though anthropology, history, sociology, and psychology would all develop subfields interested in the natural environment a decade later, there was little systematic work in the 1960s. Following Julian Steward's pioneering work in the 1950s, anthropologists began to create the subfield of ecological anthropology in the 1960s. The environmental sociology section of the American Sociological Association was established in 1977, the same year

the American Society for Environmental History was founded. Philosophers established the journal *Environmental Ethics* in 1979, and while environmental psychology has not become as well established as the other subfields, it also saw a surge of work in the 1960s and 1970s, with review articles and textbooks emerging during that period.

Chapter Five

1. "Pointless" and "interminable" from Robert M. Solow, "The Last 50 Years in Growth Theory and the Next 10," *Oxford Review of Economic Policy* 23, no. 1 (2007): 4. "Smoke and no fire" from William Breit and Barry T. Hirsch, *Lives of the Laureates: Twenty-Three Nobel Economists*, 5th ed. (Cambridge, MA: MIT Press, 2009), 167.
2. Solow, "Last 50 Years in Growth Theory," 4.
3. Joan Robinson, "The Production Function and the Theory of Capital," *Review of Economic Studies* 21, no. 2 (54 1953): 81, 84.
4. Joan Robinson, *The Accumulation of Capital* (London: Macmillan, 1956).
5. Robinson, "Production Function and Theory of Capital."
6. Capital switching or reversing involves the question of whether there was a direct correlation between the interest rate and the capital intensity of the economy. Neoclassical theory predicted it should be a unidirectional correlation, which underpinned certain findings about how capital investment would affect growth rates. But Robinson and Sraffa argued there could actually be different efficient allocations of capital versus labor based on the interest rate and type of good under consideration. In particularly, time mattered enormously. Capital or labor could be supplied at different states in the production process (early, middle, or late), and each of these stages could yield multiple efficient outcomes depending on the interest rate. Capital could therefore be switched or reversed, which Robinson and Sraffa considered another point illustrating the inadequacy of neoclassical thought. Mark Blaug, *The Cambridge Revolution, Success or Failure?: A Critical Analysis of Cambridge Theories of Value and Distribution*, Hobart Paperback No 6 (London: Institute of Economic Affairs, 1974), chap. 4.
7. On the Cambridge capital controversy, see Blaug, *Cambridge Revolution*; G. C. Harcourt and N. F. Laing, *Capital and Growth; Selected Readings*, Penguin Education (Harmondsworth, UK: Penguin Books, 1971); Harvey Gram and G. Harcourt, "Joan Robinson and MIT," *History of Political Economy* 49, no. 3 (2017): 437; Roger E. Backhouse, "MIT and the Other Cambridge," *History of Political Economy* 46, Supplement 1 (2014): 252–71.
8. John Bates Clark, *The Distribution of Wealth: A Theory of Wages, Interest and Profits* (New York: Kelley & Millman, 1899).

9. Charles W. Cobb and Paul H. Douglas, "A Theory of Production," *American Economic Review* 18, no. 1 (1928): 139–65.

10. Robinson, "Production Function and Theory of Capital."

11. Robert M. Solow, "The Production Function and the Theory of Capital," *Review of Economic Studies* 23, no. 2 (56 1955): 102, 101.

12. Blaug, *Cambridge Revolution*, chap. 2.

13. Paul A. Samuelson, "A Summing Up," *Quarterly Journal of Economics* 80, no. 4 (1966): 583.

14. Blaug, *Cambridge Revolution*, 85.

15. Avi J. Cohen and G. C. Harcourt, "Whatever Happened to the Cambridge Capital Theory Controversies?," *Journal of Economic Perspectives* 17, no. 1 (2003): 199–214.

16. Marion Fourcade, Etienne Ollion, and Yann Algan, "The Superiority of Economists," *Journal of Economic Perspectives* 29, no. 1 (2015): 96.

17. Dani Rodrik, *Economics Rules: The Rights and Wrongs of the Dismal Science* (New York: W. W. Norton, 2015), 80.

18. F. H. Hahn and R. C. O. Matthews, "Economic Growth: A Survey," *Economic Journal* 74, no. 296 (1964): 888.

19. Hahn and Matthews, "Economic Growth: A Survey," 890.

20. Hahn and Matthews, "Economic Growth: A Survey," 889–90.

21. John Hicks, *Capital and Growth* (New York: Oxford University Press, 1965), 183.

22. Amartya Sen, *Growth Economics: Selected Readings* (Harmondsworth, UK: Penguin, 1970), 9–10, 32.

23. Nicholas Georgescu-Roegen, "The Economics of Production," *American Economic Review* 60, no. 2 (1970): 1.

24. Georgescu-Roegen, "Economics of Production," 1.

25. Wassily Leontief, "Theoretical Assumptions and Nonobserved Facts," *American Economic Review* 61, no. 1 (1971): 1.

26. Leontief, "Theoretical Assumptions and Nonobserved Facts," 1–2.

27. Leontief, "Theoretical Assumptions and Nonobserved Facts," 2.

28. E. H. Phelps Brown, "The Underdevelopment of Economics," *Economic Review* 82, no. 325 (1972): 1.

29. James Tobin, "Economic Growth as an Objective of Government Policy," *American Economic Review* 54, no. 3 (1964): 1.

30. Claudia Goldin and Robert A. Margo, "The Great Compression: The Wage Structure in the United States at Mid-Century," *Quarterly Journal of Economics* 107, no. 1 (1992): 1–34.

31. As an introduction to this topic, see Jeremi Suri, "The Rise and Fall of an International Counterculture, 1960–1975," *American Historical Review* 114, no. 1 (2009): 45–68.

32. William Lazonick, Philip Moss, and Joshua Weitz, "The Unmaking of the

Black Blue-Collar Middle Class," working paper (Institute for New Economic Thinking, New York, May 20, 2021), https://www.ineteconomics.org/research/research-papers/the-unmaking-of-the-black-blue-collar-middle-class.

33. William P. Jones, *The March on Washington: Jobs, Freedom, and the Forgotten History of Civil Rights* (New York: Norton, 2013).

34. Robert M. Collins, *More: The Politics of Economic Growth in Postwar America* (Oxford: Oxford University Press, 2000), chap. 5; Andrew L. Yarrow, *Measuring America: How Economic Growth Came to Define American Greatness in the Late Twentieth Century* (Amherst: University of Massachusetts Press, 2010), chap. 7; Fredrik Albritton Jonsson and Carl Wennerlind, *Scarcity: A History from the Origins of Capitalism to the Climate Crisis* (Cambridge, MA: Harvard University Press, 2023), chap. 8.

35. Simon Kuznets, *National Income, 1929–32* (Washington, DC: Government Printing Office, 1934), 7.

36. Dirk Philipsen, *The Little Big Number: How GDP Came to Rule the World and What to Do About It* (Princeton, NJ: Princeton University Press, 2015), 230–36.

37. Samuel Hanson Ordway, *Resources and the American Dream, Including a Theory of the Limit of Growth* (New York: Ronald Press Co., 1953), 11, 40.

38. Leonard Solomon Silk, *The Economists* (New York: Basic Books, 1976), chap. 3; John Kenneth Galbraith, "How Much Should a Nation Consume?," in *Perspectives on Conservation; Essays on America's Natural Resources*, ed. Henry Jarrett (New York: Published for Resources for the Future [RFF] by Johns Hopkins University Press, 1958), 89–99; John Kenneth Galbraith, *The Affluent Society* (Boston: Houghton Mifflin, 1958).

39. Galbraith, *Affluent Society*.

40. Galbraith, "How Much Should a Nation Consume?," 94.

41. Galbraith, *Affluent Society*.

42. James Galbraith, "Wassily Leontief: An Appreciation," *Challenge* 42, no. 3 (1999): 100–103.

43. Robert Solow, "Son of Affluence: A Review of 'The New Industrial State,'" *The Public Interest* 9 (1967): 103, 107.

44. Stephen P. Dunn and Steven Pressman, "The Economic Contributions of John Kenneth Galbraith," *Review of Political Economy* 17, no. 2 (2005): 161–209.

45. E. J. Mishan, *The Costs of Economic Growth* (New York: F. A. Praeger, 1967), 8, 173, x.

46. Euston Quah, "EJ Mishan, Obituary" *Guardian*, November 7, 2014, accessed November 5, 2019, https://www.theguardian.com/books/2014/nov/07/ej-mishan; Peter Sinclair, "Ezra Mishan, Contrarian and Sage: An Appreciation," *Singapore Economic Review* 61, no. 3 (2016).

47. Mishan, *Costs of Economic Growth*, 7, 6, 6, 7.

48. Robert M. Solow, "The Failures of Economics: A Diagnostic Study (Book Review)," *Review of Economics and Statistics* 39, no. 1 (1957): 97.

49. Robert M. Solow, "Does Economics Make Progress?," *Bulletin of the American Academy of Arts and Sciences* 36, no. 3 (1982): 26.

50. Mary S. Morgan, *The World in the Model: How Economists Work and Think* (Cambridge, UK: Cambridge University Press, 2012).

51. Milton Friedman, *Essays in Positive Economics* (Chicago: University of Chicago Press, 1953).

52. Robert M. Solow, "Reflections on Macroeconomic Modelling: Confessions of a DRI Addict," *Eastern Economic Journal* 11, no. 1 (1985): 80, 81.

53. Solow, "Does Economics Make Progress?"

54. Solow, "Reflections on Macroeconomic Modelling," 80–81.

55. Robert M. Solow, "Policies for Economic Growth: The Ernest Sturc Memorial Lecture," delivered November 12, 1991 (Washington, DC: The Paul H. Nitze School for Advanced International Studies, Johns Hopkins University, 1992), 8.

56. Robert M. Solow, "Second Thoughts on Growth Theory," in *Employment and Growth: Issues for the 1980s*, ed. Alfred Steinherr and Daniel Weiserbs (Dordrecht, Netherlands: Kluwer Academic Publishers, 1987), 13, 27.

57. Solow, "Second Thoughts on Growth Theory," 13.

58. Solow, "Policies for Economic Growth," 4.

59. Robert M. Solow, "Technical Progress, Capital Formation, and Economic Growth," *American Economic Review* 52, no. 2 (1962): 76–77.

60. Tobin, "Economic Growth as an Objective of Government Policy," 17.

61. Collins, *More*, chap. 2.

62. Robert M. Solow, "Is the End of the World at Hand?," in *The Economic Growth Controversy*, ed. Andrew Weintraub, Eli Schwartz, and J. Richard Aronson (White Plains, NY: International Arts and Sciences Press, 1973), 42.

63. Solow, "Is the End of the World at Hand?," 43.

64. Flavio Comim, "On the Concept of Applied Economics: Lessons from Cambridge Economics and the History of Growth Theories," *History of Political Economy* 32 (2000): 147.

65. Marion Fourcade, *Economists and Societies: Discipline and Profession in the United States, Britain, and France, 1890s to 1990s* (Princeton, NJ: Princeton University Press, 2009), chap. 2; Fourcade, Ollion, and Algan, "Superiority of Economists."

Chapter Six

1. Anthony Lewis, "To Grow and to Die," *New York Times*, January 29, 1972. Quotes by Townsend and from *The National Observer* cited in Peter

Passell, Marc Roberts, and Leonard Ross, "The Limits to Growth," *The New York Times*, April 2, 1972.

2. Donella H. Meadows et al., *The Limits to Growth: A Report for the Club of Rome's Project on the Predicament of Mankind* (Washington, DC: Potomac Associates, 1972), 23.

3. Meadows et al., *Limits to Growth*, 51.

4. Meadows et al., *Limits to Growth*, 51.

5. Meadows et al., *Limits to Growth*, 183.

6. Adam Rome, *The Genius of Earth Day: How a 1970 Teach-In Unexpectedly Made the First Green Generation* (New York: Hill and Wang, 2013); Thomas Robertson, *The Malthusian Moment: Global Population Growth and the Birth of American Environmentalism* (New Brunswick, NJ: Rutgers University Press, 2012).

7. Passell, Roberts, and Ross, "Limits to Growth."

8. Robert Solow, testimony, December 20, 1973, in *Resource Scarcity, Economic Growth and the Environment: Hearings Before the Subcommittee on Priorities and Economy in Government of the Joint Economic Committee*, 93rd Congress, 1st session (Washington, DC: US Government Printing Office, 1974), 128.

9. Mancur Olson, "Introduction," *Daedalus* 102, no. 4, The No-Growth Society (1973): 1.

10. Meir Rinde, "Richard Nixon and the Rise of American Environmentalism," *Distillations* 3, no. 1 (2017).

11. Rinde, "Richard Nixon and the Rise of American Environmentalism."

12. James Morton Turner and Andrew C. Isenberg, *The Republican Reversal: Conservatives and the Environment from Nixon to Trump* (Cambridge, MA: Harvard University Press, 2018).

13. Theodore Steinberg, *Down to Earth: Nature's Role in American History* (New York: Oxford University Press, 2002).

14. Rachel Carson, *Silent Spring* (Boston: Houghton Mifflin Harcourt, 2002; originally published 1962), 2.

15. Carson, *Silent Spring*, 8.

16. Rome, *Genius of Earth Day*.

17. Robertson, *Malthusian Moment*.

18. Matthias Schmelzer, "'Born in the Corridors of the OECD': The Forgotten Origins of the Club of Rome, Transnational Networks, and the 1970s in Global History," *Journal of Global History* 12, no. 1 (2017): 26–48.

19. Donald Worster, *Shrinking the Earth: The Rise and Decline of American Abundance* (New York: Oxford University Press, 2016), chap. 8.

20. For "vicious circles" see Meadows et al., *Limits to Growth*, 31.

21. Meadows et al., *Limits to Growth*, 51.

22. Meadows et al., *Limits to Growth*, 61.

23. Meadows et al., *Limits to Growth*, 22.

24. Worster, *Shrinking the Earth*, chap. 8.

25. Robert M. Solow, "Notes on 'Doomsday Models,'" *Proceedings of the National Academy of Sciences* 69, no. 12 (1972): 3832.

26. Robert M. Solow, "Is the End of the World at Hand?," *Challenge* 16, no. 1 (1973): 50.

27. Robert Solow, testimony, December 20, 1973, *Resource Scarcity, Economic Growth*, 93rd Cong., 1st sess., 128.

28. On the embrace of history, see Robert M. Solow, "Economic History and Economics," *American Economic Review* 75, no. 2 (1985): 328–31. For evidence of his collaboration with the philosopher John Rawls, see Robert M. Solow, "Intergenerational Equity and Exhaustible Resources," *Review of Economic Studies* 41 (1974): 29–45.

29. Robert M. Solow, "An Almost Practical Step Toward Sustainability," *Resources Policy* 19, no. 3 (1993): 162–72.

30. Solow, "Notes on Doomsday Models," 3832.

31. Robert Solow, testimony, December 20, 1973, *Resource Scarcity, Economic Growth*, 93rd Cong., 1st sess., 128.

32. William D. Nordhaus and James Tobin, "Is Growth Obsolete?," in *Economic Research: Retrospect and Prospect, Vol. 5: Economic Growth* (New York: National Bureau of Economic Research, 1972), 16.

33. Harold J. Barnett and Chandler Morse, *Scarcity and Growth: The Economics of Natural Resource Availability* (Baltimore, MD: Published for Resources for the Future [RFF] by Johns Hopkins Press, 1963), chap. 8.

34. Robert Solow, testimony, December 20, 1973, *Resource Scarcity, Economic Growth*, 93rd Cong., 1st sess., 128.

35. Edward Fulton Denison, *The Sources of Economic Growth in the United States and the Alternatives Before Us* (New York: Committee for Economic Development, 1962). Denison cites RFF work generally and Fisher and Boorstein (Joseph L. Fisher and Edward Boorstein, "The Adequacy of Resources for Economic Growth in the United States," Study Paper 13 [Washington, DC: Government Printing Office, 1959]) in particular to defend his claim that natural resources represented a small and declining percentage of America's overall economic growth. Fisher and Boorstein, in turn, used RFF data being collected for *Resources in America's Future* for their findings.

36. Nordhaus and Tobin, "Is Growth Obsolete?," 14.

37. Nordhaus, William D., "The Allocation of Energy Resources," *Brookings Papers on Economic Activity*, no. 3 (1973): 529–76.

38. Nordhaus and Tobin, "Is Growth Obsolete?," 16.

39. Robert Reinhold, "Mankind Warned of Perils in Growth," *New York Times*, February 27, 1972.

40. Mahbub ul Haq, "Limits to Growth: A Critique," *Finance and Development* 9, no. 4 (1972): 2–8.

41. Stephen Macekura, *The Mismeasure of Progress: Economic Growth and Its Critics* (Chicago: University of Chicago Press, 2020).

42. Robert Solow, testimony, December 20, 1973, *Resource Scarcity, Economic Growth*, 93rd Cong., 1st sess., 128.

43. Joseph E. Stiglitz, "Reply: Georgescu-Roegen Versus Solow/Stiglitz," *Ecological Economics* 22 (1997): 269; italics in original.

44. Passell, Roberts, and Ross, "Limits to Growth."

45. Olson, "Introduction," 2.

46. Mancur Olson, Hans H. Lansberg, and Joseph L. Fisher, "Epilogue," *Daedalus* 102, no. 4 (1973): 235.

47. Robert M. Solow, "The Economics of Resources or the Resources of Economics," *American Economic Review* 64, no. 2 (1974): 11.

48. Solow, "Intergenerational Equity and Exhaustible Resources," 41.

49. As quoted by Mancur Olson in Olson, "Introduction," 3.

50. Thomas F Gieryn, "Boundary-Work and the Demarcation of Science from Non-Science: Strains and Interests in the Professional Ideologies of Scientists," *American Sociological Review* 48, no. 6 (1983): 781–95.

51. Leonard Solomon Silk, *The Economists* (New York: Basic Books, 1976), chap. 5; Kenneth E. Boulding, "The Application of the Pure Theory of Population Change to the Theory of Capital," *Quarterly Journal of Economics* 48, no. 4 (1934): 645–66; Kenneth E. Boulding, "The Theory of a Single Investment," *Quarterly Journal of Economics* 49, no. 3 (1935): 475–94; Kenneth E. Boulding, *Economic Analysis: Revised Edition* (London: Hamish Hamilton, 1948).

52. Kenneth E. Boulding, "Samuelson's Foundations: The Role of Mathematics in Economics," *Journal of Political Economy* 56, no. 3 (1948): 187, 199.

53. Kenneth E. Boulding, *A Reconstruction of Economics* (New York: Wiley, 1950), 4.

54. Boulding, *Reconstruction of Economics*, chap. 1.

55. Kenneth E. Boulding, *The Economics of Peace* (New York: Prentice-Hall, 1945), v.

56. Boulding, *Economics of Peace*, 127–28.

57. Kenneth E. Boulding, "Toward a General Theory of Growth," *Canadian Journal of Economics and Political Science / Revue Canadienne* 19, no. 3 (1953): 327; italics in original.

58. Kenneth E. Boulding, "The Economics of the Coming Spaceship Earth," in *Environmental Quality in a Growing Economy*, ed. Henry Jarrett (Baltimore, MD: Published for RFF by Johns Hopkins University Press, 1966), 3–14.

59. Boulding, "Economics of the Coming Spaceship Earth," 4.

60. Silk, *The Economists*, 235.

61. James S. Worley, Fred M. Westfield, and Anthony M. Tang, eds., *Evolution, Welfare, and Time in Economics: Essays in Honor of Nicholas Georgescu-Roegen* (Lexington, MA: Lexington Books, 1976), ix–xi; Sylvia Nasar, "Nicholas Georgescu-Roegen, Leading Economist, Dies at 88," *The New York Times*, November 5, 1994, sec. 1.

62. Nicholas Georgescu-Roegen, "The Economics of Production," *American Economic Review* 60, no. 2 (1970): 1.

63. Nicholas Georgescu-Roegen, *The Entropy Law and the Economic Process* (Cambridge, MA: Harvard University Press, 1971).

64. Nicholas Georgescu-Roegen, "Energy and Economic Myths," *Southern Economic Journal* 41, no. 3 (1975).

65. Georgescu-Roegen, "Energy and Economic Myths," 350.

66. Georgescu-Roegen, "Energy and Economic Myths," 365.

67. Early articles by Georgescu-Roegen appeared in *The Quarterly Journal of Economics, Econometrica*, and *The Journal of Economic Issues*. On his rejection in 1978 by *The American Economic Review*, see his appeal letter to Tjalling Koopmans on February 21, 1979, Box 21, Folder: Correspondence—Boulding, Kenneth, Nicholas Georgescu-Roegen papers, David M. Rubenstein Rare Book and Manuscript Library, Duke University. On his unsuccessful Ford Foundation grant, see letter from Ford Foundation Officer William H. Branson to Gian S. Sahota on March 8, 1974, Box 22, Folder: Correspondence—Ford Foundation, 1974–1979, Nicholas Georgescu-Roegen papers, David M. Rubenstein Rare Book and Manuscript Library, Duke University.

68. Inge Røpke, "The Early History of Modern Ecological Economics," *Ecological Economics* 50 (2004): 296.

69. Lissa Harris, "The Economic Heresy of Herman Daly," *Grist*, April 10, 2003, https://grist.org/article/bank/.

70. Herman Daly, "The Stationary-State Economy: Toward a Political Economy of Biophysical Equilibrium and Moral Growth," in *Essays Toward a Steady-State Economy*, ed. Herman Daly, vol. 70 (Cuernavaca: Centro Intercultural de Documentación, 1971), 6/2.

71. Daly, "Stationary-State Economy," 6/4.

72. Herman E. Daly, *Beyond Growth: The Economics of Sustainable Development* (Boston: Beacon Press, 1996).

73. E. F. Schumacher, *Small Is Beautiful: Economics as If People Mattered* (New York: Harper & Row, 1973).

74. Herman Daly, testimony, April 2, 1973, in *The Impact of Growth on the Environment: Hearings Before the Subcommittee on Air and Water Pollution of the Committee on Public Works of the United States Senate*, 93rd Congress, 1st session (Washington, DC: US Government Printing Office, 1973), 3.

75. Nicholas Georgescu-Roegen, testimony, November 9, 1976, in *Long-Term*

Economic Growth: Hearings Before the Joint Economic Committee, 94th Congress, 2nd session (Washington, DC: US Government Printing Office, 1977), 14.

76. Jimmy Carter, as cited in Robert M. Collins, *More: The Politics of Economic Growth in Postwar America* (Oxford: Oxford University Press, 2000), 158.

77. Heinz Wolfgang Arndt, *The Rise and Fall of Economic Growth: A Study in Contemporary Thought* (Melbourne: Longman Cheshire, 1978).

78. Solow, "Intergenerational Equity and Exhaustible Resources," 41.

Chapter Seven

1. "The Text of Jimmy Carter's First Presidential Report to the American People," *New York Times*, February 3, 1977.

2. Jimmy Carter, "Address to the Nation on Energy," April 18, 1977, The American Presidency Project, accessed January 24, 2024, https://www.presidency.ucsb.edu/documents/address-the-nation-energy.

3. Jimmy Carter, "Energy and National Goals: Address to the Nation," July 15, 1979, Jimmy Carter Presidential Library and Archive, accessed January 24, 2024, https://www.jimmycarterlibrary.gov/the-carters/selected-speeches/jimmy-carter-energy-and-national-goals-address-to-the-nation.

4. James Morton Turner and Andrew C. Isenberg, *The Republican Reversal: Conservatives and the Environment from Nixon to Trump* (Cambridge, MA: Harvard University Press, 2018).

5. Turner and Isenberg, *Republican Reversal*, 39–41, 50–53.

6. Turner and Isenberg, *Republican Reversal*, chap. 2.

7. Following Julian Steward's pioneering work in the 1950s, anthropologists began to create the subfield of ecological anthropology in the 1960s. The Environmental Sociology section of the American Sociological Association was established in 1977, the same year the American Society for Environmental History was founded. Philosophers established the journal *Environmental Ethics* in 1979, and while environmental psychology has not become as well established as the other subfields, it also saw a surge of work in the 1960s and 1970s, with review articles and textbooks emerging during that period.

8. John C. Rumm, *Interview with Allen V. Kneese*, April 20 and 29, 1999, 63, oral history accessed at Resources for the Future (RFF) Library, Washington, DC.

9. Robert M. Solow, "The Economics of Resources or the Resources of Economics," *American Economic Review* 64, no. 2 (1974): 1.

10. Solow, "Economics of Resources," 2.

11. Solow, "Economics of Resources," 2.

12. It had been mentioned only once in *Scarcity and Growth* and received no mention in Nordhaus and Tobin's 1972 article "Is Growth Obsolete?" Harold J. Barnett and Chandler Morse, *Scarcity and Growth: The Economics of Natural Resource Availability* (Baltimore, MD: Published for RFF by Johns Hopkins Press, 1963); Willam D. Nordhaus and James Tobin, "Is Growth Obsolete?," in *Economic Research: Retrospect and Prospect, Vol. 5: Economic Growth* (New York: National Bureau of Economic Research, 1972), 1–80. On Hotelling's economics more generally, see Marion Gaspard, Antoine Missemer, and Thomas Michael Mueller, "A Journey into Harold Hotelling's Economics," *Journal of Economic Literature* 62, no. 3 (2024): 1186–212.

13. Solow, "Economics of Resources," 3.

14. Harold Hotelling, "The Economics of Exhaustible Resources," *Journal of Political Economy* 39, no. 2 (1931): 145.

15. Solow, "Economics of Resources," 11.

16. William D. Nordhaus, "Resources as a Constraint on Growth," *American Economic Review* 64, no. 2 (1974): 22–26; Joseph Stiglitz, "Growth with Exhaustible Natural Resources: Efficient and Optimal Growth Paths," *Review of Economic Studies* 41, no. 1 (1974): 123–37.

17. Frederick M. Peterson and Anthony C. Fisher, "The Exploitation of Extractive Resources: A Survey," *Economic Journal* 87, no. 348 (1977): 692.

18. Peterson and Fisher, "Exploitation of Extractive Resources," 704.

19. Peterson and Fisher, "Exploitation of Extractive Resources," 705, 711; italics in original.

20. Partha Dasgupta and G. M. Heal, *Economic Theory and Exhaustible Resources*, Cambridge Economic Handbooks (Cambridge, UK: Cambridge University Press, 1979), 5.

21. Dasgupta and Heal, *Economic Theory and Exhaustible Resources*, 224.

22. Shantayanan Devarajan and Anthony C. Fisher, "Hotelling's 'Economics of Exhaustible Resources': Fifty Years Later," *Journal of Economic Literature* 19 (March 1981): 65.

23. Gérard Gaudet, "Natural Resource Economics Under the Rule of Hotelling," *Canadian Journal of Economics* 40, no. 4 (2007): 1034.

24. John Livernois, "On the Empirical Significance of the Hotelling Rule," *Review of Environmental Economics and Policy* 3, no. 1 (2009): 22.

25. Dasgupta and Heal, *Economic Theory and Exhaustible Resources*, 2.

26. John M. Hartwick, "Intergenerational Equity and the Investing of Rents from Exhaustible Resources," *American Economic Review* 67, no. 5 (1977): 972.

27. Barnett and Morse, *Scarcity and Growth*, 236, 240; Hans H. Landsberg, Leonard L. Fischman, and Joseph L. Fisher, *Resources in America's Future: Patterns of Requirements and Availabilities, 1960–2000* (Baltimore, MD: Published for RFF by the Johns Hopkins Press, 1963).

28. Barnett and Morse, *Scarcity and Growth*, 252.

29. On the history of environmental economics, see H. Spencer Banzhaf,

Pricing the Priceless: A History of Environmental Economics (Cambridge, UK: Cambridge University Press, 2023); David Pearce, "An Intellectual History of Environmental Economics," *Annual Review of Energy and the Environment* 27 (2002): 57–81; E. Kula, *History of Environmental Economic Thought* (London: Routledge, 1998); Nathaniel Wolloch, *Nature in the History of Economic Thought: How Natural Resources Became an Economic Concept* (London: Routledge, 2017).

30. Pigou has played a large role in the ways historians have told the history of economics, including in Pearce 2002. H. Spencer Banzhaf has recently argued that it was only after the field was established that Pigou began to be invoked more, and that the former traditions of land and agricultural economics were essential at the early stages. Pearce, "Intellectual History of Environmental Economics"; H. Spencer Banzhaf, "A History of Pricing Pollution (or, Why Pigouvian Taxes Are Not Necessarily Pigouvian)," NBER Working Paper 27683 (National Bureau of Economic Research, Cambridge, MA, 2020), https://www.nber.org/papers/w27683. On Pigou, see Ian Kumekawa, *The First Serious Optimist: A. C. Pigou and the Birth of Welfare Economics* (Princeton, NJ: Princeton University Press, 2017); Nahid Aslanbeigui and Guy Oakes, *Arthur Cecil Pigou* (Basingstoke: Palgrave Macmillan, 2015); A. C. Pigou, *The Economics of Welfare* (London: Macmillan, 1920), 11.

31. Theodore M. Porter, *Trust in Numbers: The Pursuit of Objectivity in Science and Public Life* (Princeton, NJ: Princeton University Press, 1995); Will Deringer, "The 'Social Rate of Discount' and the Political Economy of the Future in Postwar America," article in progress. Banzhaf, *Pricing the Priceless*, 22.

32. Pigou, *Economics of Welfare*, 11.

33. Pigou, *Economics of Welfare*, 20.

34. Pigou, *Economics of Welfare*, 20.

35. Vilfredo Pareto, *Manual of Political Economy* (New York: A. M. Kelley, 1906).

36. J. R. Hicks, "The Foundations of Welfare Economics," *Economic Journal* 49, no. 196 (1939): 696–712; Nicholas Kaldor, "Welfare Propositions of Economics and Interpersonal Comparisons of Utility," *Economic Journal* 49, no. 195 (1939): 549–52.

37. Kaldor, "Welfare Propositions of Economics," 551.

38. Hicks, "Foundations of Welfare Economics," 712.

39. Lionel Robbins, *An Essay on the Nature and Significance of Economic Science* (London: Macmillan, 1932), 15.

40. Milton Friedman, *Essays in Positive Economics* (Chicago: University of Chicago Press, 1953).

41. Banzhaf, *Pricing the Priceless*, chap. 4; Susan Howson, "The Origins of Lionel Robbins's Essay on the Nature and Significance of Economic Science,"

History of Political Economy 36, no. 3 (2004): 413–43; Roger E. Backhouse and Steve G. Medema, "Defining Economics: The Long Road to Acceptance of the Robbins Definition," *Economica* 76, no. s1 (2009): 805–20. On efficiency as the normative aim of economics, see Elizabeth Popp Berman, *Thinking like an Economist: How Efficiency Replaced Equality in U.S. Public Policy* (Princeton, NJ: Princeton University Press, 2022).

42. Harold Hotelling, letter to Newton P. Drury, June 18, 1947, reprinted in *The Economics of Public Recreation: An Economic Study of the Monetary Evaluation of Recreation in the National Parks* (Land and Recreational Planning Division, National Park Service, 1949).

43. Marion Clawson, *Methods of Measuring the Demand for and Value of Outdoor Recreation* (Washington, DC: RFF, 1959); Marion Clawson, *Economics of Outdoor Recreation* (Baltimore, MD: Published for RFF by Johns Hopkins Press, 1966).

44. Marion Clawson, *From Sagebrush to Sage: The Making of a Natural Resource Economist* (Washington, DC: Ana Publications, 1987), 256.

45. John V. Krutilla, "Conservation Reconsidered," *American Economic Review* 57, no. 4 (1967): 777–86; Banzhaf, *Pricing the Priceless*, chap. 5.

46. On the switch from regulation to efficiency in environmental economics, see Popp Berman, *Thinking like an Economist*, chap. 7.

47. Ciriacy-Wantrup's most famous publication was his 1952 book *Resource Conservation*. Early research on this book was funded in part by a generous bequest Ciriacy-Wantrup left to the University of California, Berkeley, to establish postdoctoral positions in the study of natural resource economics and political economy. S. V. Ciriacy-Wantrup, *Resource Conservation: Economics and Policies* (Berkeley: University of California Press, 1952).

48. Ronald Coase, "The Problem of Social Cost," *Journal of Law and Economics* 3 (1960): 1–44.

49. H. Scott Gordon, "The Economic Theory of a Common-Property Resource: The Fishery," *Journal of Political Economy* 62, no. 2 (1954): 124–42; Vernon L. Smith, "On Models of Commercial Fishing," *Journal of Political Economy* 77, no. 2 (1969): 181–98.

50. Volvo Environmental Prize, "1990 Laureates: John V. Krutilla, Allen V. Kneese," accessed January 24, 2024, https://www.environment-prize.com/laureates/john-v-krutilla-allen-v-kneese/.

51. Banzhaf, *Pricing the Priceless*, chap. 5; Rumm, *Interview with Allen V. Kneese*, 21.

52. Rumm, *Interview with Allen V. Kneese*, 63.

53. Rumm, *Interview with Allen V. Kneese*, 62.

54. Robert Costanza and Herman E. Daly, "Toward an Ecological Economics," *Ecological Modelling* 38, no. 1–2 (1987): 2, italics in original.

55. On the history of ecological economics, see Marco P. Vianna Franco and

Antoine Missemer, *A History of Ecological Economic Thought* (London: Routledge, 2023); Juan Martínez Alier, *Ecological Economics: Energy, Environment, and Society* (Oxford: Basil Blackwell, 1987); Kula, *History of Environmental Economic Thought*; Inge Røpke, "The Early History of Modern Ecological Economics," *Ecological Economics* 50 (2004): 293–314.

56. Martínez Alier, *Ecological Economics*.

57. Røpke, "Early History of Modern Ecological Economics."

58. Barcelona, Edinburgh, Leeds, and Vienna have recognized centers, while a collaborative program between University of Vermont and McGill is the only comparable program in North America. J. Farley and K. Kish, "Ecological Economics: The Next 30 Years," *Ecological Economics*, no. 190 (2021): 1.

59. Robert Costanza, "Ecological Economics: Reintegrating the Study of Humans and Nature," *Ecological Applications* 6, no. 4 (1996): 980.

60. Clive L. Spash, "The Development of Environmental Thinking in Economics," *Environmental Values* 8, no. 4 (1999): 425.

61. Robert Costanza, "Ecological Economics in 2049: Getting Beyond the Argument Culture to the World We All Want," *Ecological Economics* 168 (2020).

62. Solow, "Economics of Resources," 11.

63. Nicholas Georgescu-Roegen, "Energy and Economic Myths," *Southern Economic Journal* 41, no. 3 (1975): 361.

64. Herman E. Daly, *Beyond Growth: The Economics of Sustainable Development* (Boston: Beacon Press, 1996).

65. Herman E. Daly, "Georgescu-Roegen Versus Solow/Stiglitz," *Ecological Economics* 22 (1997): 265.

66. Robert M. Solow, "An Almost Practical Step Toward Sustainability," *Resources Policy* 19, no. 3 (1993): 168.

67. Daly, "Georgescu-Roegen Versus Solow/Stiglitz," 261.

68. Robert M. Solow, "Reply: Georgescu-Roegen Versus Solow/Stiglitz," *Ecological Economics* 22 (1997): 267, 68.

69. Joseph E. Stiglitz, "Reply: Georgescu-Roegen Versus Solow/Stiglitz," *Ecological Economics* 22 (1997): 269; italics in original.

70. Stiglitz, "Reply," 269.

71. J. B. Opschoor, "The Hope, Faith and Love of Neoclassical Environmental Economics," *Ecological Economics* 22 (1997): 281.

72. Herman E. Daly, "Reply to Solow/Stiglitz," *Ecological Economics* 22 (1997): 271.

73. Farley and Kish, "Ecological Economics," 6.

74. Farley and Kish, "Ecological Economics," 6.

75. Spash, "Development of Environmental Thinking in Economics," 424–25.

76. Inge Røpke, "Trends in the Development of Ecological Economics from the Late 1980s to the Early 2000s," *Ecological Economics* 55 (2005): 262–90; Clive L. Spash and Anthony Ryan, "Economic Schools of Thought on the

Environment: Investigating Unity and Division," *Cambridge Journal of Economics* 36 (2012): 1091–121.
77. Costanza, "Ecological Economics in 2049."
78. Robert Solow, "The Power of Ideas in the Policy Process," Resources for the Future Lunch Talk, October 15, 2002, Robert M. Solow Papers, Box 77, Duke University Archives.

Chapter Eight

1. This section draws heavily on Paul Sabin's wonderful book on Simon and Ehrlich's bet: *The Bet: Paul Ehrlich, Julian Simon, and Our Gamble over Earth's Future* (New Haven: Yale University Press, 2013). Julian Simon quotation from his autobiography cited on page 66 of Sabin's book, and "scholarly wager of the decade" is referenced from *The Chronicle of Higher Education*, cited on page 137 of Sabin's book.
2. Julian Lincoln Simon, *The Ultimate Resource* (Princeton, NJ: Princeton University Press, 1981), 9–10.
3. Simon, *The Ultimate Resource.*
4. As cited in Sabin, *The Bet,* 155.
5. Paul R. Ehrlich, *The Population Bomb* (New York: Ballantine Books, 1968); Sabin, *The Bet,* chap. 3.
6. Julian Simon, "Resources, Population, Environment: An Oversupply of False Bad News," *Science* 208, no. 4451 (1980): 1432.
7. Sabin, *The Bet,* 162.
8. John Tierney, "Betting on the Planet," *New York Times,* December 2, 1990.
9. Tierney, "Betting on the Planet."
10. Sabin, *The Bet,* 207.
11. Robert M. Solow, "Some Lessons from Growth Theory," in *Financial Economics: Essays in Honor of Paul Cootner,* ed. W. F. Sharpe, and C. M. Cootner (Englewood Cliffs, NJ: Prentice-Hall, 1982), 246.
12. For an elaborate and delightfully narrated explanation of the rise of endogenous growth theory, see David Warsh, *Knowledge and the Wealth of Nations: A Story of Economic Discovery* (New York: W. W. Norton, 2006).
13. Paul M. Romer, "The Origins of Endogenous Growth," *Journal of Economic Perspectives* 8, no. 1 (1994): 11.
14. Paul M. Romer, "Increasing Returns and Long-Run Growth," *Journal of Political Economy* 94, no. 5 (1986): 1002.
15. Romer, "Increasing Returns and Long-Run Growth," 1003.
16. Romer, "Increasing Returns and Long-Run Growth," 1004.
17. Romer, "Increasing Returns and Long-Run Growth," 1003.
18. Paul M. Romer, "Endogenous Technological Change," *Journal of Political Economy* 98, no. 5 (1990): S71.

19. Robert E. Lucas, "On the Mechanics of Economic Development," *Journal of Monetary Economics* 22 (1988): 5; quotation from the printed version of the lecture released a few years later.

20. Lucas won in 1995; Romer in 2018. Warsh, *Knowledge and the Wealth of Nations*, chap. 23. Daniel Susskind is an example of an economist supportive of Romer's ideas about growth: Daniel Susskind, *Growth: A History and a Reckoning* (Cambridge, MA: Harvard University Press, 2024).

21. Paul M. Romer and Hiroo Sasaki, *Monotonically Decreasing Natural Resources Prices Under Perfect Foresight* (Rochester Center for Economic Research, 1984), 1.

22. Transcript of Dr. James Hansen's testimony before the US Senate Committee on Energy and Natural Resources, June 23, 1988, accessed August 3, 2023, https://www.sealevel.info/1988_Hansen_Senate_Testimony .html.

23. James E. Hansen and Larry D. Travis, "Light Scattering in Planetary Atmospheres," *Space Science Reviews* 16, no. 4 (1974): 527–610; James E. Hansen, Wei-Chyung Wang, and Andrew A. Lacis, "Mount Agung Eruption Provides Test of a Global Climatic Perturbation," *Science* 199, no. 4333 (1978): 1065–68; James Hansen and Sergej Lebedeff, "Global Trends of Measured Surface Air Temperature," *Journal of Geophysical Research* 92, no. D11 (1987): 13345–72.

24. Spencer R. Weart, *The Discovery of Global Warming* (Cambridge, MA: Harvard University Press, 2003).

25. Willam D. Nordhaus and James Tobin, "Is Growth Obsolete?," in *Economic Research: Retrospect and Prospect, Vol. 5: Economic Growth* (New York: National Bureau of Economic Research, 1972); William D. Nordhaus, "World Dynamics: Measurement Without Data," *Economic Journal* 83, no. 332 (1973): 1156–83; William D. Nordhaus, "Resources as a Constraint on Growth," *American Economic Review* 64, no. 2 (1974): 26.

26. For Murphy as office mate, see interview with Nordhaus about time at IIASA, https://iiasa.ac.at/web/home/resources/publications/options/s19 -interview-climate-change-economics-together.html (accessed May 15, 2020).

27. William D. Nordhaus, "Strategies for the Control of Carbon Dioxide" (New Haven, CT: Cowles Foundation, 1977), 17.

28. Nordhaus, "Strategies for the Control of Carbon Dioxide," 68.

29. DICE would soon receive a sibling: RICE (the Regional Integrated Climate Economy model). RICE used similar elements, but instead of treating the world as a single system broke it into twelve regions to get a more granular analysis of the varying costs and benefits of climate mitigation.

30. William D. Nordhaus, *A Question of Balance Weighing the Options on Global Warming Policies* (New Haven, CT: Yale University Press, 2008).

31. William D. Nordhaus, "An Optimal Transition Path for Controlling Green-house Gases," *Science* 258, no. 5086 (1992): 1319.

32. Nordhaus, "Optimal Transition Path."

33. Simon, *The Ultimate Resource*, 345.

34. Pigou, *Economics of Welfare*, 20; italics in original.

35. Walter Heller L., "Coming to Terms with Growth and the Environment," in *Energy, Economic Growth, and the Environment: Papers Presented at a Forum Conducted by Resources for the Future, Inc. in Washington, D.C., 20–21 April 1971*, ed. Sam H. Schurr (Baltimore, MD: Published for Resources for the Future by Johns Hopkins Press, 1972), 12.

36. Nordhaus and Tobin, "Is Growth Obsolete?"

37. Richard A. Easterlin, "Does Economic Growth Improve the Human Lot? Some Empirical Evidence," in *Nations and Households in Economic Growth: Essays in Honor of Moses Abramovitz*, ed. Paul David and Melvin W. Reder (New York: Academic Press, 1974).

38. As described in Easterlin, "Does Economic Growth Improve," 111–12.

39. Easterlin, "Does Economic Growth Improve," 112.

40. Easterlin, "Does Economic Growth Improve," 90.

41. Daniel Cohen and Jane Marie Todd, *The Infinite Desire for Growth* (Princeton, NJ: Princeton University Press, 2018).

42. For skeptical accounts, see Philip Booth, ed., . . . *And the Pursuit of Happiness: Wellbeing and the Role of Government* (London: Institute of Economic Affairs, 2012); Daniel W. Sacks, Betsey Stevenson, and Justin Wolfers, "Subjective Wellbeing, Income, Economic Development and Growth," in Booth, *And the Pursuit of Happiness*, 59–97.

43. Richard A. Easterlin, "Paradox Lost?," *Review of Behavioral Economics* 4 (2017): 314. See also Edsel L. Beja, "Income Growth and Happiness: Reassessment of the Easterlin Paradox," *International Review of Economics* 61, no. 4 (2014): 329–46. Data from University of Chicago General Social Survey available from website, https://gssdataexplorer.norc.org/trends/Gender%20&%20Marriage?measure=happy (accessed September 24, 2021). Daniel Kahneman, Ed Diener, and Norbert Schwarz, eds., *Well-Being: Foundations of Hedonic Psychology* (New York: Russell Sage Foundation, 1999); Richard Layard, *Happiness: Lessons from a New Science* (New York: Penguin Books, 2006).

44. Robert J. Gordon, *The Rise and Fall of American Growth: The U.S. Standard of Living Since the Civil War* (Princeton, NJ: Princeton University Press, 2016).

45. Gordon, *Rise and Fall of American Growth*, chap. 17–18.

46. The bottom half of wage earners took home 21.6 percent of national income in 1971 but only 14.5 percent in 2016, whereas the top 10 percent increased their share from 30.7 percent to 47.6 percent in the same period. Moritz Kuhn, Moritz Schularick, and Ulrike I. Steins, *Income and Wealth In-*

equality in America, 1949–2016 (Minneapolis, MN: Federal Reserve Bank of Minneapolis, 2018), 22.

47. Facundo Alvaredo et al., *World Inequality Report* (Paris: World Inequality Lab, 2018), 80, https://wid.world/document/world-inequality-report-2018 -english/.

48. Alvaredo et al., *World Inequality Report*, 81.

49. Rakesh Kochhar and Stella Sechopoulos, "How the American Middle Class Has Changed in the Past Five Decades," *Pew Research Center*, April 20, 2022, https://www.pewresearch.org/short-reads/2022/04/20/how-the -american-middle-class-has-changed-in-the-past-five-decades/.

50. Richard Wilkinson and Kate Pickett, *The Spirit Level: Why Greater Equality Makes Societies Stronger* (New York: Bloomsbury Press, 2009); Robert Putnam, *Bowling Alone: The Collapse and Revival of American Community* (New York: Simon & Schuster, 2000).

51. This trend has shifted some in the last decade with the work of Thomas Piketty, Emmanuel Sanz, and Raj Chetty. See N. Gregory Mankiw, "Defending the One Percent," Journal of Economic Perspectives 27, no. 3 (2013): 21–34; Daniel Hirschman, "Rediscovering the 1%: Knowledge Infrastructures and the Stylized Facts of Inequality," *American Journal of Sociology* 127, no. 3 (2021): 739–86.

52. William D. Nordhaus, "Do Real-Output and Real-Wage Measures Capture Reality? The History of Lighting Suggests Not," In *The Economics of New Goods*, ed. Timothy F. Bresnahan and Robert J. Gordon (Chicago: University of Chicago Press, 1997), 33.

53. Nordhaus, "Do Real-Output and Real-Wage Measures Capture Reality?," 30; italics in original.

54. Diane Coyle, *GDP: A Brief but Affectionate History* (Princeton, NJ: Princeton University Press, 2015), 141.

55. Coyle, *GDP*, 145.

56. Lorenzo Fioramonti, *Gross Domestic Problem: The Politics Behind the World's Most Powerful Number* (London: Zed Books, 2013).

57. David Roberts, "Discount Rates: A Boring Thing You Should Know About (with Otters!)," *Grist*, September 24, 2012, https://grist.org/article/discount -rates-a-boring-thing-you-should-know-about-with-otters/.

58. Nicholas Stern, "Stern Review: The Economics of Climate Change" (London: UK Treasury, 2006), vi, https://webarchive.nationalarchives.gov.uk /20100407172811/http://www.hm-treasury.gov.uk/stern_review_report.htm.

59. "Expert Reaction to Stern Review," *BBC News*, October 30, 2006, http:// news.bbc.co.uk/2/hi/business/6098612.stm.

60. "Yale Symposium on the Stern Review" (New Haven, CT: Yale Center for the Study of Globalization, 2007), 112, https://ycsg.yale.edu/climate-change /yale-symposium-stern-review; William Nordhaus, "Economics: Critical Assumptions in the Stern Review on Climate Change," *Science* 317, no. 5835 (2007): 201–2.

61. William D. Nordhaus, "A Review of the 'Stern Review on the Economics of Climate Change,'" *Journal of Economic Literature* 45, no. 3 (2007): 686–702.

62. Nordhaus, "Economics. Critical Assumptions," 202.

63. "Yale Symposium on the Stern Review," 128, 118.

64. "Yale Symposium on the Stern Review," 93.

65. Partha Dasgupta, "Commentary: The Stern Review's Economics of Climate Change," *National Institute Economic Review* 199, no. 1 (2007): 7.

66. Martin L. Weitzman, "A Review of 'The Stern Review on the Economics of Climate Change,'" *Journal of Economic Literature* 45, no. 3 (2007): 705.

67. William D. Nordhaus, "Revisiting the Social Cost of Carbon," *Proceedings of the National Academy of Sciences* 114, no. 7 (2017): 1520.

68. Richard S. J. Tol, "The Economic Impacts of Climate Change," *Review of Environmental Economics and Policy* 12, no. 1 (2018): 5, 6.

69. Tol, "Economic Impacts of Climate Change," 16.

70. Nordhaus, "Revisiting the Social Cost of Carbon," 1519.

71. William Nordhaus, "Climate Change: The Ultimate Challenge for Economics," Prize Lecture, Stockholm, December 8, 2018, 453, accessed October 16, 2023, https://www.nobelprize.org/prizes/economic-sciences/2018 /nordhaus/lecture/.

72. William Nordhaus, "Economics of the Disintegration of the Greenland Ice Sheet," *Proceedings of the National Academy of Sciences* 116, no. 25 (2019): 12261–69.

73. Intergovernmental Panel on Climate Change, *Synthesis Report of the IPCC Sixth Assessment Report (AR6)* (Interlaken, Switzerland, 2023), 33–43, https://report.ipcc.ch/ar6syr/pdf/IPCC_AR6_SYR_LongerReport.pdf.

74. David I. Armstrong McKay et al., "Exceeding 1.5°C Global Warming Could Trigger Multiple Climate Tipping Points," *Science* 377, no. 6611 (2022): 1171-eabn7950; Timothy M. Lenton et al., "Climate Tipping Points - Too Risky to Bet Against," *Nature* 575, no. 7784 (2019): 592–95.

75. Robert N. Proctor and Londa Schiebinger, eds., *Agnotology: The Making and Unmaking of Ignorance* (Palo Alto, CA: Stanford University Press, 2008); Naomi Oreskes and Erik M. Conway, *Merchants of Doubt: How a Handful of Scientists Obscured the Truth on Issues from Tobacco Smoke to Global Warming* (London: Bloomsbury Press, 2010); Nancy MacLean, *Democracy in Chains: The Deep History of the Radical Right's Stealth Plan for America* (New York: Viking, 2017).

76. Timothy C. Haab and John C. Whitehead, "What Do Environmental and Resource Economists Think? Results from a Survey of AERE Members," *Review of Environmental Economics and Policy* 11, no. 1 (2017): 43–58.

77. Tol, "Economic Impacts of Climate Change," 8–10.

78. Nordhaus, "Climate Change: The Ultimate Challenge," 451.

79. Gene M. Grossman and Alan B. Krueger, "Economic Growth and the Environment," *Quarterly Journal of Economics* 110, no. 2 (1995): 353–77; Bertrand Hamaide, ed., *Sustainability and the Environmental Kuznets Curve Conjecture* (Basel: Multidisciplinary Digital Publishing Institute, 2022).

80. Steve Keen, "The Appallingly Bad Neoclassical Economics of Climate Change," *Globalizations* 18, no. 7 (2021): 1149–77.

81. Clive L. Spash, "The Brave New World of Carbon Trading," *New Political Economy* 15, no. 2 (2010): 169–95; Clive L. Spash and Clemens Gattringer, "The Ethical Failures of Climate Economics," in *The Ethical Underpinnings of Climate Economics*, ed. Adrian Walsh, Säde Hormio, and Duncan Purves (Routledge, 2017), 174–94; Keen, "Appallingly Bad Neoclassical Economics of Climate Change"; Jason Hickel, "The Nobel Prize for Climate Catastrophe," *Foreign Policy*, December 6, 2018, https://foreignpolicy.com/2018/12/06/the-nobel-prize-for-climate-catastrophe/.

82. Alvaredo et al., *World Inequality Report*; Branko Milanović, *Global Inequality: A New Approach for the Age of Globalization* (Cambridge, MA: Harvard University Press, 2016).

83. "The Prize in Economic Sciences 2018," NobelPrize.org, accessed March 6, 2020, https://www.nobelprize.org/prizes/economic-sciences/2018/summary/.

84. Hickel, "Nobel Prize for Climate Catastrophe."

85. Sam Roberts, "Martin Weitzman, Virtuoso Climate Change Economist, Dies at 77," *New York Times*, September 4, 2019, Business section, https://www.nytimes.com/2019/09/04/business/energy-environment/martin-weitzman-dead.html.

Chapter Nine

1. United Nations Conference on Environment and Development, *Report of the United Nations Conference on Environment and Development: Rio de Janeiro, 3–14 June 1992* (New York: United Nations, 1993).

2. Mark McDonald, "U.N. Report from Rio on Environment a 'Suicide Note,'" *New York Times*, June 24, 2012.

3. United Nations Economic and Social Commission for Asia and the Pacific (ESCAP), "Green Growth at a Glance: The Way Forward for Asia and the Pacific" (United Nations, 2006); OECD, *Towards Green Growth* (Paris: OECD Publishing, 2011); World Bank Group, "Toward a Green, Clean, and Resilient World for All: A World Bank Group Environmental Strategy, 2012–2022" (New York: The World Bank, 2012).

4. Raksha Arora, "A Well-Being Report Card for President Sarkozy" *Gallup News*, January 17, 2008, accessed September 7, 2022, https://news.gallup.com/poll/103795/wellbeing-report-card-president-sarkozy.aspx.

5. Joseph E. Stiglitz, Amartya Sen, and Jean-Paul Fitoussi, *Report by the Commission on the Measurement of Economic Performance and Social Progress* (Paris, 2009), 7, 8.

6. Joseph Stiglitz, Jean-Paul Fitoussi, and Martine Durand, *Beyond GDP: Measuring What Counts for Economic and Social Performance* (Paris: OECD Publishing, 2018), 7. For a detailed and compelling analysis of the centrality of growth to the OECD, see Matthias Schmelzer, *The Hegemony of Growth: The OECD and the Making of the Economic Growth Paradigm* (Cambridge, UK: Cambridge University Press, 2016).

7. Stiglitz, Fitoussi, and Durand, *Beyond GDP*, app. A.

8. Joseph Stiglitz, "Growth with Exhaustible Natural Resources: Efficient and Optimal Growth Paths," *Review of Economic Studies* 41, no. 1 (1974): 123–37; Joseph Stiglitz, "Growth with Exhaustible Natural Resources: The Competitive Economy," *Review of Economic Studies* 41, no. 1 (1974): 139–52.

9. Stiglitz, "Growth with Exhaustible Natural Resources," 136; italics in original.

10. Joseph E. Stiglitz, "Reply: Georgescu-Roegen Versus Solow/Stiglitz," *Ecological Economics* 22 (1997): 269.

11. For sake of clarity of reading, I refer to GDP (gross domestic product) throughout this section, even though most calculations before the late 1980s were of GNP (gross national product). For purposes of the argument of this book, the differences between GDP and GNP are irrelevant, so I use GDP as the consistent term.

12. Willam D. Nordhaus and James Tobin, "Is Growth Obsolete?," in *Economic Research: Retrospect and Prospect, Vol. 5: Economic Growth* (New York: National Bureau of Economic Research, 1972); John W. Kendrick, *The Formation and Stocks of Total Capital* (New York: National Bureau of Economic Research, 1976); Richard Ruggles and Nancy D. Ruggles, "Integrated Economic Accounts for the United States, 1947–1980," *Survey of Current Business* 62 (1982): 1–53; Dale Jorgenson, Frank M. Gollop, and Barbara Fraumeni, *Productivity and U.S. Economic Growth* (Amsterdam: Elsevier Science & Technology, 1988); Robert Eisner, *The Total Incomes System of Accounts* (Chicago: University of Chicago Press, 1989).

13. Martin L. Weitzman, "On the Welfare Significance of National Product in a Dynamic Economy," *Quarterly Journal of Economics* 90, no. 1 (1976): 157.

14. Martin L. Weitzman and Karl-Gustaf Löfgren, "On the Welfare Significance of Green Accounting as Taught by Parable," *Journal of Environmental Economics and Management* 32, no. 2 (1997): 139–53.

15. Herman E. Daly, John B. Cobb, and Clifford W. Cobb, *For the Common Good: Redirecting the Economy Toward Community, the Environment, and a Sustainable Future* (Boston: Beacon Press, 1989), 379.

16. Clifford W. Cobb, Ted Halstead, and Jonathan Rowe, "If the GDP Is Up, Why Is America Down?," *The Atlantic*, 1995, https://www.theatlantic

.com/magazine/archive/1995/10/if-the-gdp-is-up-why-is-america-down/415605/. Critics of GPI have noted its inconsistent inclusion of social values. It measures income distribution for example, but not racial justice, and it relies on the imputation of several values not included in the market economy.

17. Stefan Schweinfest et al., "The Rise, Fall and Rethinking of Green GDP" (United Nations System of Environmental Economic Accounting, 2021), https://seea.un.org/news/rise-fall-and-rethinking-green-gdp.

18. Carter Brandon et al., "Integrating Natural Capital into National Accounts: Three Decades of Promise and Challenge," *Review of Environmental Economics and Policy* 15, no. 1 (2021): 137.

19. Philipp Lepenies, *The Power of a Single Number: A Political History of GDP* (New York: Columbia University Press, 2016); Theodore M. Porter, *Trust in Numbers: The Pursuit of Objectivity in Science and Public Life* (Princeton, NJ: Princeton University Press, 1995). "Flawed" and "arbitrary" from Diane Coyle, *GDP: A Brief but Affectionate History* (Princeton, NJ: Princeton University Press, 2015), 142.

20. Arthur M. Okun, "Should GNP Measure Social Welfare?," *Brookings Bulletin* 8, no. 3 (1971): 4.

21. Okun, "Should GNP Measure Social Welfare?," 7.

22. Coyle, *GDP*, 6, 146.

23. UN ESCAP, "Green Growth at a Glance."

24. World Commission on Environment and Development, *Our Common Future* (Oxford: Oxford University Press, 1987); S. M. Lele, "Sustainable Development: A Critical Review," *World Development* 19, no. 6 (1991): 607–21; Gareth Dale, Manu V. Mathai, and Jose Antonio Puppim de Oliveira, *Green Growth: Ideology, Political Economy and the Alternatives* (London: Zed Books, 2016), 4–5, 117.

25. UN ESCAP, "Green Growth at a Glance," 7, 6, 8.

26. UN ESCAP, "Green Growth at a Glance," 9, 13.

27. UN ESCAP, "Green Growth at a Glance," 13, 14, 28.

28. UN ESCAP, "Green Growth at a Glance," 12, 17, 18, 33, 34.

29. UN ESCAP, "Green Growth at a Glance," 39.

30. Bettina Bluemling and Sun-Jin Yun, "Giving Green Teeth to the Tiger? A Critique of Green Growth in South Korea," in *Green Growth: Ideology, Political Economy, and the Alternatives*, ed. Gareth Dale, Manu V. Mathai, and Jose A. Puppim de Oliveira (London: Zed Books, 2016), 114–30; Vesela Todorova, "Korean Leader Wins Zayed Prize," *National News*, March 14, 2011, https://www.thenationalnews.com/uae/environment/korean-leader-wins-zayed-prize-1.605514.

31. OECD, *Towards Green Growth*, 3, 11.

32. World Bank Group, "Toward a Green, Clean, and Resilient World," 8.

33. United Nations, "Future We Want: Outcome Document," 2012, accessed September 13, 2023, https://sustainabledevelopment.un.org/futurewewant.html.

34. Kim Jeong-su, "The Environmental Fallout of the Four Major Rivers Project," *Hankyoreh*, August 3, 2013, https://english.hani.co.kr/arti/english_edition/e_national/598190.html; Bluemling and Yun, "Giving Green Teeth to the Tiger?"

35. Dale, Mathai, and Puppim de Oliveira, *Green Growth*. On neoliberalism, see Philip Mirowski and Dieter Plehwe, eds., *The Road from Mont Pelerin: The Making of the Neoliberal Thought Collective* (Cambridge, MA: Harvard University Press, 2009); David Harvey, *A Brief History of Neoliberalism* (Oxford: Oxford University Press, 2005); Quinn Slobodian, *Globalists: The End of Empire and the Birth of Neoliberalism* (Cambridge, MA: Harvard University Press, 2018).

36. Jason Hickel and Giorgios Kallis, "Is Green Growth Possible?," *New Political Economy* 25, no. 4 (2020): 469–86.

37. Timothée Parrique, et al., "Decoupling Debunked: Evidence and Arguments Against Green Growth as a Sole Strategy for Sustainability" (European Environmental Bureau, 2019), https://eeb.org/library/decoupling-debunked/.

38. Hickel and Kallis, "Is Green Growth Possible?," 472.

39. United States Environmental Protection Agency, "Global Greenhouse Gas Emissions Data," accessed November 7, 2023, https://www.epa.gov/ghgemissions/global-greenhouse-gas-emissions-data.

40. Zeke Hausfather, "Absolute Decoupling of Economic Growth and Emissions in 32 Countries," *Breakthrough Institute*, April 6, 2021, https://thebreakthrough.org/issues/energy/absolute-decoupling-of-economic-growth-and-emissions-in-32-countries.

41. Helmut Haberl et al., "A Systematic Review of the Evidence on Decoupling of GDP, Resource Use and GHG Emissions, Part II: Synthesizing the Insights," *Environmental Research Letters* 15, no. 6 (2020); Jefim Vogel and Jason Hickel, "Is Green Growth Happening? An Empirical Analysis of Achieved Versus Paris-Compliant CO_2–GDP Decoupling in High-Income Countries," *The Lancet Planetary Health* 7, no. 9 (2023): e759–69.

42. Akielly Hu and Joseph Winters, "How to 'Decouple' Emissions from Economic Growth: These Economists Say You Can't," *Grist*, March 4, 2024, https://grist.org/economics/how-to-decouple-emissions-from-economic-growth-these-economists-say-you-cant/; Vogel and Hickel, "Is Green Growth Happening?"

43. Giacomo D'Alisa, Federico Demaria, and Giorgos Kallis, *Degrowth: A Vocabulary for a New Era* (Abingdon, UK: Routledge, 2014); Hickel and Kallis, "Is Green Growth Possible?"; Tim Jackson, *Prosperity Without Growth: Economics for a Finite Planet* (London: Earthscan, 2009); Peter A. Victor,

Managing Without Growth: Slower by Design, Not Disaster (Cheltenham, UK: Edward Elgar, 2008); Herman E. Daly, *Beyond Growth: The Economics of Sustainable Development* (Boston: Beacon Press, 1996); Matthias Schmelzer, Andrea Vetter, and Aaron Vansintjan, *The Future Is Degrowth: A Guide to a World Beyond Capitalism* (London: Verso, 2022).

44. Thomas O. Wiedmann et al., "The Material Footprint of Nations," *Proceedings of the National Academy of Sciences* 112, no. 20 (May 19, 2015): 6271–76; Hickel and Kallis, "Is Green Growth Possible?"

45. Nicholas Georgescu-Roegen, *The Entropy Law and the Economic Process* (Cambridge, MA: Harvard University Press, 1971).

46. John Stuart Mill, *Principles of Political Economy: Abridged, with Critical, Bibliographical, and Explanatory Notes, and a Sketch of the History of Political Economy*, ed. J. Laurence Laughlin (New York: Appleton, 1884), 514–16.

47. John Maynard Keynes, "Economic Possibilities for Our Grandchildren," in *Essays in Persuasion* (New York: Harcourt, Brace and Co., 1932), 369.

48. Keynes, "Economic Possibilities for Our Grandchildren," 372.

49. Daly, *Beyond Growth*.

50. Jackson, *Prosperity Without Growth*.

51. Schmelzer, Vetter, and Vansintjan, *Future Is Degrowth*, 20–29.

52. Katharina Bohnenberger, "Money, Vouchers, Public Infrastructures? A Framework for Sustainable Welfare Benefits," *Sustainability* 12, no. 2 (2020): 596.

53. Stefan Drews and Miklós Antal, "Degrowth: A 'Missile Word' That Backfires?," *Ecological Economics* 126 (2016): 182–87; Schmelzer, Vetter, and Vansintjan, *Future Is Degrowth*, 27.

54. Jason Hickel, "What Does Degrowth Mean? A Few Points of Clarification," *Globalizations* 18, no. 7 (2021): 1105–11.

55. Lorenzo Fioramonti et al., "Wellbeing Economy: An Effective Paradigm to Mainstream Post-growth Policies?," *Ecological Economics* 192 (February 2022): 107261.

56. See the Wellbeing Economy Alliance website, and its page on the Wellbeing Economy Governments, https://weall.org/wego (accessed May 3, 2022). Anders Hayden and Clay Dasilva, "The Wellbeing Economy: Possibilities and Limits in Bringing Sufficiency from the Margins into the Mainstream," *Frontiers in Sustainability* 3 (2022).

57. Alvin H. Hansen, "Capital Goods and the Restoration of Purchasing Power," *Proceedings of the Academy of Political Science* 16, no. 1 (1934): 11–19; Alvin H. Hansen, *Full Recovery or Stagnation?* (New York: Norton, 1938); Alvin H. Hansen, "Economic Progress and Declining Population Growth," *American Economic Review* 29, no. 1 (1939): 1–15.

58. Roger E. Backhouse and Mauro Boianovsky, "Secular Stagnation: The

History of a Macroeconomic Heresy," *European Journal of the History of Economic Thought* 23, no. 6 (November 1, 2016): 954.

59. Radhika Desai, "Introduction: Japan's Secular Stagnation and the American Mirror," *Japanese Political Economy* 47, no. 4 (October 2, 2021): 281–302.

60. Backhouse and Boianovsky, "Secular Stagnation."

61. Summers quoted in John Barry, "Climate Change: The 'Cancer Stage of Capitalism' and the Return of the Limits to Growth," in *Climate Change and the Crisis of Capitalism*, ed. Mark Pelling et al. (London: Routledge, 2011), 129.

62. Lawrence Summers, "IMF Fourteenth Annual Research Conference in Honor of Stanley Fischer," November 8, 2013. Transcript at http://larrysummers.com/imf-fourteenth-annual-research-conference-in-honor-of-stanley-fischer/ (accessed January 20, 2022).

63. Lawrence Summers, "The Threat of Secular Stagnation Has Not Gone Away," blog, May 6, 2018, accessed May 5, 2022, http://larrysummers.com/2018/05/06/the-threat-of-secular-stagnation-has-not-gone-away/.

64. Robert J. Gordon, *The Rise and Fall of American Growth: The U.S. Standard of Living Since the Civil War* (Princeton, NJ: Princeton University Press, 2016), 642.

65. Dietrich Vollrath, *Fully Grown: Why a Stagnant Economy Is a Sign of Success* (Chicago: The University of Chicago Press, 2020), 2.

66. Vollrath, *Fully Grown*, 216.

67. Joseph Stiglitz, "The Myth of Secular Stagnation," *Project Syndicate*, August 28, 2018, accessed May 5, 2022, https://www.project-syndicate.org/commentary/secular-stagnation-excuse-for-flawed-policies-by-joseph-e-stiglitz-2018-08.

68. Backhouse and Boianovsky, "Secular Stagnation," 965.

69. Summers, "IMF Fourteenth Annual Research Conference."

70. Edward Abbey, *The Journey Home: Some Words in Defense of the American West* (Dutton, 1977), 183.

Conclusion

1. John Maynard Keynes, "Economic Possibilities for Our Grandchildren," in *Essays in Persuasion* (New York: Harcourt, Brace and Co., 1932), 360, 366; italics in original.

2. Keynes, "Economic Possibilities for Our Grandchildren," 369, 372.

3. Keynes, "Economic Possibilities for Our Grandchildren," 366–68.

4. GDP data from https://ourworldindata.org/grapher/gdp-per-capita-in-the-uk-since-1270 and https://ourworldindata.org/grapher/gdp-per-capita-maddison?tab=chart&country=~USA (accessed October 30, 2023).

5. Variations of these claims have been explored in previous chapters by

thinkers including Robert Solow, William Nordhaus, Julian Simon, Mahbub ul Haq, Mancur Olson, Richard Tol, and Lawrence Summers.

6. Data from University of Chicago General Social Survey, available from website, https://gssdataexplorer.norc.org/trends/Gender%20&%20Marriage ?measure=happy (accessed September 24, 2021). CDC National Center for Health Statistics, *Life Expectancy in the U.S. Dropped for the Second Year in a Row in 2021* (Atlanta: Centers for Disease Control and Prevention, August 31, 2022), https://www.cdc.gov/nchs/pressroom/nchs_press_releases /2022/20220831.htm; Richard Wilkinson and Kate Pickett, *The Spirit Level: Why Greater Equality Makes Societies Stronger* (New York: Bloomsbury Press, 2009).

7. Kate Raworth, *Doughnut Economics: Seven Ways to Think like a 21st Century Economist* (White River Junction, VT: Chelsea Green Publishing, 2017).

8. Fiona Harvey, "Heatwaves at Both of Earth's Poles Alarm Climate Scientists," *Guardian*, March 20, 2022, https://www.theguardian.com/environment /2022/mar/20/heatwaves-at-both-of-earth-poles-alarm-climate-scientists.

9. Sheila Jasanoff, "Technologies of Humility," *Nature* 450, no. 7166 (2007): 33; Weitzman, "GHG Targets as Insurance."

Bibliography

Abbey, Edward. *The Journey Home: Some Words in Defense of the American West.* Dutton, 1977.

Abramovitz, Moses. "Catching Up, Forging Ahead, and Falling Behind." *Journal of Economic History* 46, no. 2 (1986): 385–406.

Abramovitz, Moses. "Days Gone By: A Memoir for My Family." 2001. https://web.archive.org/web/20070609121742/http://www-econ .stanford.edu/abramovitz/abramovitzm.html.

Abramovitz, Moses. "Economic Growth in the United States: A Review Article." *American Economic Review* 52, no. 4 (1962): 762–82.

Abramovitz, Moses. "Economics of Growth." In *A Survey of Contemporary Economics,* edited by Bernard F. Haley, 132–78. Homewood, IL: American Economic Association, 1952.

Abramovitz, Moses. "Resource and Output Trends in the United States Since 1870." *American Economic Review* 46, no. 2 (1956): 5–23.

Alacevich, Michele. "The Birth of Development Economics." *History of Political Economy* 50, no. S1 (2018): 114–32.

Alacevich, Michele, and Mauro Boianovsky. "Writing the History of Development Economics." *History of Political Economy* 50, no. S1 (2018): 1–14.

Albritton Jonsson, Fredrik. "The Origins of Cornucopianism: A Preliminary Genealogy." *Critical Historical Studies* 1, no. 1 (2014): 151–68.

Albritton Jonsson, Fredrik, and Carl Wennerlind. *Scarcity: A History from the Origins of Capitalism to the Climate Crisis.* Cambridge, MA: Harvard University Press, 2023.

Alvaredo, Facundo, Lucas Chancel, Thomas Piketty, Emmanuel Saez, and Gabriel Zucman. *World Inequality Report.* Paris: World Inequality Lab, 2018. https://wid.world/document/world-inequality-report-2018-english/.

Amadae, S. M. *Rationalizing Capitalist Democracy: The Cold War Origins of Rational Choice Liberalism.* Chicago: University of Chicago Press, 2003.

Appelbaum, Binyamin. *The Economists' Hour: False Prophets, Free Markets, and the Fracture of Society.* New York: Little, Brown and Company, 2019.

Armstrong McKay, David I., Arie Staal, Jesse F. Abrams, Ricarda Winkelmann, Boris Sakschewski, Sina Loriani, Ingo Fetzer, Sarah E. Cornell, Johan Rockström, and Timothy M. Lenton. "Exceeding 1.5°C Global Warming Could Trigger Multiple Climate Tipping Points." *Science* 377, no. 6611 (2022): 1171-eabn7950.

Arndt, Heinz Wolfgang. *The Rise and Fall of Economic Growth: A Study in Contemporary Thought.* Melbourne: Longman Cheshire, 1978.

Arrow, Kenneth J. "The Economic Implications of Learning by Doing." *Review of Economic Studies* 29, no. 3 (1962): 155–73.

Aslanbeigui, Nahid, and Guy Oakes. *Arthur Cecil Pigou.* Basingstoke: Palgrave Macmillan, 2015.

Backhouse, R. E. "Paul A. Samuelson's Move to MIT." *History of Political Economy* 46, Supplement 1 (2014): 60–80.

Backhouse, Roger E. *Founder of Modern Economics: Paul A. Samuelson. Volume 1: Becoming Samuelson, 1915–1948.* New York: Oxford University Press, 2017.

Backhouse, Roger E. "MIT and the Other Cambridge." *History of Political Economy* 46, Supplement 1 (2014): 252–71.

Backhouse, Roger E. *The Ordinary Business of Life: A History of Economics from the Ancient World to the Twenty-First Century.* Princeton, NJ: Princeton University Press, 2002.

Backhouse, Roger E., and Mauro Boianovsky. "Secular Stagnation: The History of a Macroeconomic Heresy." *European Journal of the History of Economic Thought* 23, no. 6 (November 1, 2016): 946–70.

Backhouse, Roger E., and Steve G. Medema. "Defining Economics: The Long Road to Acceptance of the Robbins Definition." *Economica* 76, no. s1 (2009): 805–20.

Banzhaf, H. Spencer. "A History of Pricing Pollution (or, Why Pigouvian Taxes Are Not Necessarily Pigouvian)." NBER Working Paper 27683, National Bureau of Economic Research, Cambridge, MA, 2020. https://www.nber.org/papers/w27683.

Banzhaf, H. Spencer. *Pricing the Priceless: A History of Environmental Economics.* Cambridge, UK: Cambridge University Press, 2023.

Banzhaf, H. Spencer. "Productive Nature and the Net Product: Quesnay's Economies Animal and Political." *History of Political Economy* 32, no. 3 (September 1, 2000): 517–51.

Barnett, Harold J., and Chandler Morse. *Scarcity and Growth: The Economics of*

Natural Resource Availability. Baltimore, MD: Published for Resources for the Future by Johns Hopkins Press, 1963.

Barry, John. "Climate Change: The 'Cancer Stage of Capitalism' and the Return of the Limits to Growth." In *Climate Change and the Crisis of Capitalism*, edited by Mark Pelling, David Manuel-Navarrete, and Michael Redclift. London: Routledge, 2011.

Bashford, Alison. *The New Worlds of Thomas Robert Malthus: Rereading the Principle of Population.* Princeton, NJ: Princeton University Press, 2016.

Baumol, William J., and Thijs ten Raa. "Wassily Leontief: In Appreciation." *European Journal of the History of Economic Thought* 16, no. 3 (2009): 511–22.

BBC News. "Expert Reaction to Stern Review." October 30, 2006. http://news.bbc .co.uk/2/hi/business/6098612.stm.

Beja, Edsel L. "Income Growth and Happiness: Reassessment of the Easterlin Paradox." *International Review of Economics* 61, no. 4 (2014): 329–46.

Benson, Etienne S. *Surroundings: A History of Environments and Environmentalisms.* Chicago: University of Chicago Press, 2020.

Bernstein, Michael A. *A Perilous Progress: Economists and Public Purpose in Twentieth-Century America.* Princeton, NJ: Princeton University Press, 2001.

Biles, Roger. *Crusading Liberal: Paul H. Douglas of Illinois.* DeKalb: Northern Illinois University Press, 2002.

Bivar, Venus. "Historicizing Economic Growth: An Overview of Recent Works." *Historical Journal* 65, no. 5 (2022): 1470–89.

Black, R. D. Collison, A. W. Coats, and Craufurd D. W. Goodwin, eds. *The Marginal Revolution in Economics: Interpretation and Evaluation.* Durham, NC: Duke University Press, 1973.

Blanchard, Newton C., ed. *Proceedings of a Conference of Governors.* Washington, DC: Government Printing Office, 1909.

Blaug, Mark. *The Cambridge Revolution, Success or Failure? A Critical Analysis of Cambridge Theories of Value and Distribution.* Hobart Paperback No 6. London: Institute of Economic Affairs, 1974.

Blaug, Mark. *Economic Theory in Retrospect.* 3rd ed. Cambridge, UK: Cambridge University Press, 1978.

Blinder, Alan S. "In Honor of Robert M. Solow: Nobel Laureate in 1987." *Journal of Economic Perspectives* 3, no. 3 (1989): 99–105.

Bluemling, Bettina, and Sun-Jin Yun. "Giving Green Teeth to the Tiger? A Critique of Green Growth in South Korea." In *Green Growth: Ideology, Political Economy, and the Alternatives*, edited by Gareth Dale, Manu V. Mathai, and Jose A. Puppim de Oliveira, 114–30. London: Zed Books, 2016.

Bohnenberger, Katharina. "Money, Vouchers, Public Infrastructures? A Framework for Sustainable Welfare Benefits." *Sustainability* 12, no. 2 (2020): 596.

Boianovsky, Mauro. "Voluminous, Repetitive, and Intractable: Samuelson on Early Development Economics." *History of Political Economy* 54, no. 1 (2022): 1–35.

Boianovsky, Mauro, and Kevin D. Hoover. "In the Kingdom of Solovia: The Rise of Growth Economics at MIT, 1956–70." *History of Political Economy* 46, Supplement 1 (2014): 198–228.

Boianovsky, Mauro, and Kevin D. Hoover. "The Neoclassical Growth Model and Twentieth-Century Economics." *History of Political Economy* 41, Annual Supplement (2009): 1–23.

Bonneuil, Christophe, and Jean-Baptiste Fressoz. "Growth Unlimited: The Idea of Infinite Growth from Fossil Capitalism to Green Capitalism." In *History of the Future of Economic Growth: Historical Roots of Current Debates on Sustainable Degrowth*, edited by Matthias Schmelzer and Iris Borowy, 52–68. London: Routledge, 2017.

Booth, Philip, ed. . . . *And the Pursuit of Happiness: Wellbeing and the Role of Government.* London: Institute of Economic Affairs, 2012.

Boulding, Kenneth E. "The Application of the Pure Theory of Population Change to the Theory of Capital." *Quarterly Journal of Economics* 48, no. 4 (1934): 645–66.

Boulding, Kenneth E. *Economic Analysis: Revised Edition.* London: Hamish Hamilton, 1948.

Boulding, Kenneth E. *The Economics of Peace.* New York: Prentice-Hall, 1945.

Boulding, Kenneth E. "The Economics of the Coming Spaceship Earth." In *Environmental Quality in a Growing Economy*, edited by Henry Jarrett, 3–14. Baltimore, MD: Published for Resources for the Future by Johns Hopkins University Press, 1966.

Boulding, Kenneth E. *A Reconstruction of Economics.* New York: Wiley, 1950.

Boulding, Kenneth E. "Samuelson's Foundations: The Role of Mathematics in Economics." *Journal of Political Economy* 56, no. 3 (1948): 187–99.

Boulding, Kenneth E. "The Theory of a Single Investment." *Quarterly Journal of Economics* 49, no. 3 (1935): 475–94.

Boulding, Kenneth E. "Toward a General Theory of Growth." *Canadian Journal of Economics and Political Science / Revue Canadienne* 19, no. 3 (1953): 326–40.

Brandon, Carter, Katrina Brandon, Alison Fairbrass, and Rachel Neugarten. "Integrating Natural Capital into National Accounts: Three Decades of Promise and Challenge." *Review of Environmental Economics and Policy* 15, no. 1 (2021): 134–53.

Breit, William, and Barry T. Hirsch. *Lives of the Laureates: Twenty-Three Nobel Economists.* 5th ed. Cambridge, MA: MIT Press, 2009.

Burgin, Angus. *The Great Persuasion: Reinventing Free Markets Since the Depression.* Cambridge, MA: Harvard University Press, 2015.

Burkhardt, Scott T. "Environmental Optimism in an Apocalyptic Age: The Paley Commission and Resource Scarcities at Mid-Century." Master's thesis, University of Wisconsin, 2005.

Burns, Arthur. "Introductory Sketch." In *Wesley Clair Mitchell: The Economic Scientist*, edited by Arthur Burns. New York: National Bureau of Economic Research, 1951.

Burns, Arthur F., and Wesley C. Mitchell. *Measuring Business Cycles*. New York: National Bureau of Economic Research, 1946.

Callon, Michel, ed. *The Laws of the Markets*. Oxford: Blackwell Publishers, 1998.

Carson, Rachel. *Silent Spring*. Boston: Houghton Mifflin Harcourt, 2002. Originally published 1962.

CDC National Center for Health Statistics. "Life Expectancy in the U.S. Dropped for the Second Year in a Row in 2021." Atlanta: Centers for Disease Control and Prevention, August 31, 2022. https://www.cdc.gov/nchs/pressroom/nchs_press_releases/2022/20220831.htm.

Cherrier, B. "Toward a History of Economics at MIT, 1940–72." *History of Political Economy* 46, Supplement 1 (2014): 15–44.

Ciriacy-Wantrup, S. V. *Resource Conservation: Economics and Policies*. Berkeley: University of California Press, 1952.

Clark, Colin. *Population Growth and Land Use*. London: Macmillan, 1967.

Clark, John Bates. *The Distribution of Wealth: A Theory of Wages, Interest and Profits*. New York: Kelley and Millman, 1899.

Clawson, Marion. *Economics of Outdoor Recreation*. Baltimore, MD: Published for Resources for the Future by Johns Hopkins Press, 1966.

Clawson, Marion. *From Sagebrush to Sage: The Making of a Natural Resource Economist*. Washington, DC: Ana Publications, 1987.

Clawson, Marion. *Methods of Measuring the Demand for and Value of Outdoor Recreation*. Washington, DC: Resources for the Future, 1959.

Coase, Ronald. "The Problem of Social Cost." *Journal of Law and Economics* 3 (1960): 1–44.

Coats, A. W. "The American Economic Association and the Economics Profession." *Journal of Economic Literature* 23 (December 1985): 1697–727.

Cobb, Charles W., and Paul H. Douglas. "A Theory of Production." *American Economic Review* 18, no. 1 (1928): 139–65.

Cobb, Clifford W., Ted Halstead, and Jonathan Rowe. "If the GDP Is Up, Why Is America Down?" *The Atlantic*, 1995. https://www.theatlantic.com/magazine/archive/1995/10/if-the-gdp-is-up-why-is-america-down/415605/.

Cohen, Avi J., and G. C. Harcourt. "Whatever Happened to the Cambridge Capital Theory Controversies?" *Journal of Economic Perspectives* 17, no. 1 (2003): 199–214.

Cohen, Daniel, and Jane Marie Todd. *The Infinite Desire for Growth*. Princeton, NJ: Princeton University Press, 2018.

Collins, Robert M. *More: The Politics of Economic Growth in Postwar America*. Oxford: Oxford University Press, 2000.

Comim, Flavio. "On the Concept of Applied Economics: Lessons from Cambridge

Economics and the History of Growth Theories." *History of Political Economy* 32 (2000): 147.

Commons, John R. *History of Labour in the United States*. Vol. I. New York: Macmillan, 1918.

Condorcet, Jean-Antoine-Nicolas de Caritat. *Sketch for a Historical Picture of the Progress of the Human Mind*. Library of Ideas. Ann Arbor, MI: University Microfilms, 1795.

Cook, Eli. *The Pricing of Progress: Economic Indicators and the Capitalization of American Life*. Cambridge, MA: Harvard University Press, 2017.

Costanza, Robert. "Ecological Economics in 2049: Getting Beyond the Argument Culture to the World We All Want." *Ecological Economics* 168 (2020).

Costanza, Robert. "Ecological Economics: Reintegrating the Study of Humans and Nature." *Ecological Applications* 6, no. 4 (1996): 978–90.

Costanza, Robert, and Herman E. Daly. "Toward an Ecological Economics." *Ecological Modelling* 38, no. 1–2 (1987): 1–7.

Council of Economic Advisers. *Business and Government: Fourth Annual Report to the President by the Council of Economic Advisers*. Washington, DC: Government Printing Office, 1949.

Coyle, Diane. *GDP: A Brief but Affectionate History*. Princeton, NJ: Princeton University Press, 2015.

Crabbe, Philippe J. "The Contribution of L. C. Gray to the Economic Theory of Exhaustible Resources." *Journal of Environmental Economics and Management* 10 (1983): 195–220.

Dale, Gareth. "Adam Smith's Green Thumb and Malthus's Three Horsemen: Cautionary Tales from Classical Political Economy." *Journal of Economic Issues* 46, no. 4 (2012): 859–80.

Dale, Gareth. "Critiques of Growth in Classical Political Economy: Mill's Stationary State and a Marxian Response." *New Political Economy* 18, no. 3 (2013): 431–57.

Dale, Gareth. "Rule of Nature or Rule of Capital? Physiocracy, Ecological Economics, and Ideology." *Globalizations* 18, no. 7 (2021): 1230–47.

Dale, Gareth, Manu V. Mathai, and Jose Antonio Puppim de Oliveira. *Green Growth: Ideology, Political Economy and the Alternatives*. London: Zed Books, 2016.

D'Alisa, Giacomo, Federico Demaria, and Giorgos Kallis. *Degrowth: A Vocabulary for a New Era*. Abingdon, UK: Routledge, 2014.

Daly, Herman E. *Beyond Growth: The Economics of Sustainable Development*. Boston: Beacon Press, 1996.

Daly, Herman E. "Georgescu-Roegen Versus Solow/Stiglitz." *Ecological Economics* 22 (1997): 261–66.

Daly, Herman E. "Reply to Solow/Stiglitz." *Ecological Economics* 22 (1997): 271–73.

Daly, Herman E. "The Stationary-State Economy: Toward a Political Economy of Biophysical Equilibrium and Moral Growth." In *Essays Toward a Steady-State*

Economy, edited by Herman E. Daly, vol. 70. Cuernavaca: Centro Intercultural de Documentación, 1971.

Daly, Herman E., John B. Cobb, and Clifford W. Cobb. *For the Common Good: Redirecting the Economy Toward Community, the Environment, and a Sustainable Future*. Boston: Beacon Press, 1989.

Dasgupta, Partha. "Commentary: The Stern Review's Economics of Climate Change." *National Institute Economic Review* 199, no. 1 (2007): 4–7.

Dasgupta, Partha. "The Place of Nature in Economic Development." In *Handbook of Development Economics*, edited by Dani Rodrik and Mark Rosenzweig, vol. 5, 4977–5046. Amsterdam: Elsevier, 2010.

Dasgupta, Partha, and G. M. Heal. *Economic Theory and Exhaustible Resources*. Cambridge Economic Handbooks. Cambridge, UK: Cambridge University Press, 1979.

Davis, Mike. *Late Victorian Holocausts: El Niño Famines and the Making of the Third World*. London: Verso, 2001.

Denison, Edward Fulton. *The Sources of Economic Growth in the United States and the Alternatives Before Us*. New York: Committee for Economic Development, 1962.

Denison, Edward Fulton. *Why Growth Rates Differ: Postwar Experience in Nine Western Countries*. Washington, DC: Brookings Institution, 1967.

Desai, Radhika. "Introduction: Japan's Secular Stagnation and the American Mirror." *Japanese Political Economy* 47, no. 4 (October 2, 2021): 281–302.

Devarajan, Shantayanan, and Anthony C. Fisher. "Hotelling's 'Economics of Exhaustible Resources': Fifty Years Later." *Journal of Economic Literature* 19 (March 1981): 65–73.

Dewhurst, J. Frederick and Associates. *America's Needs and Resources*. New York: The Twentieth Century Fund, 1947.

Dewhurst, J. Frederick and Associates. *America's Needs and Resources: A New Survey*. New York: The Twentieth Century Fund, 1955.

Diamond, Peter. "National Debt in a Neoclassical Growth Model." *American Economic Review* 55, no. 5 (1965): 1126–50.

Diamond, Peter. "Optimal Paths of Capital Accumulation Under the Minimum Time Objective: A Comment." *Econometrica* 34, no. 4 (1966): 886–87.

Dietzenbacher, Erik, and Michael L. Lahr. *Wassily Leontief and Input-Output Economics*. Cambridge, UK: Cambridge University Press, 2004.

Dimand, Robert W., and Barbara J. Spencer. "Trevor Swan and the Neoclassical Growth Model." *History of Political Economy* 41 (2009): 107–26.

Dolar, Veronika. "The Gender Gap in Economics Is Huge—It's Even Worse than Tech." *The Conversation*, March 12, 2021. https://theconversation.com/the-gender-gap-in-economics-is-huge-its-even-worse-than-tech-156275.

Domar, Evsey. "Capital Expansion, Rate of Growth, and Employment." *Econometrica* 14, no. 2 (1946): 137–47.

Douglas, Paul H. "The Cobb–Douglas Production Function Once Again: Its History, Its Testing, and Some New Empirical Values." *Journal of Political Economy* 84, no. 5 (1976): 903–16.

Drews, Stefan, and Miklós Antal. "Degrowth: A 'Missile Word' That Backfires?" *Ecological Economics* 126 (2016): 182–87.

Dunn, Stephen P., and Steven Pressman. "The Economic Contributions of John Kenneth Galbraith." *Review of Political Economy* 17, no. 2 (2005): 161–209.

Düppe, Till, and Ivan Boldyrev. "Economic Knowledge in Socialism, 1945–89: Editors' Introduction." *History of Political Economy* 51, no. S1 (2019): 1–4.

Easterlin, Richard A. "Does Economic Growth Improve the Human Lot? Some Empirical Evidence." In *Nations and Households in Economic Growth: Essays in Honor of Moses Abramovitz*, edited by Paul David and Melvin W. Reder. New York: Academic Press, 1974.

Easterlin, Richard A. "Paradox Lost?" *Review of Behavioral Economics* 4 (2017): 311–39.

Ehrlich, Paul R. *The Population Bomb*. New York: Ballantine Books, 1968.

Eisner, Robert. *The Total Incomes System of Accounts*. Chicago: University of Chicago Press, 1989.

Ely, Richard T. "Constitution and By-Laws and Resolutions of the American Economic Association." *Publications of the American Economic Association* 1 (1886): 35–46.

Ely, Richard T. *Outlines of Economics*. New York: Flood and Vincent, 1893.

Ely, Richard T. *The Past and the Present of Political Economy*. Baltimore, MD: Johns Hopkins University, 1884.

Ely, Richard Theodore, Edwin Robert Anderson Seligman, Edmund J. James, F. W. Taussig, Simon Newcomb, Henry Carter Adams, Arthur Twining Hadley, Richmond Mayo-Smith, and Simon N. Patten. *Science Economic Discussion* . . . New York: The Science Company, 1886.

Farley, J., and K. Kish. "Ecological Economics: The Next 30 Years." *Ecological Economics*, no. 190 (2021): 1–10.

Ferguson, Niall. *The Ascent of Money: A Financial History of the World*. London: Allen Lane, 2008.

Finley, M. I. *The Ancient Economy*. Berkeley: University of California Press, 1999.

Fioramonti, Lorenzo. *Gross Domestic Problem: The Politics Behind the World's Most Powerful Number*. London: Zed Books, 2013.

Fioramonti, Lorenzo. "The World's Most Powerful Number: An Assessment of 80 Years of GDP Ideology." *Anthropology Today* 30, no. 2 (2014): 12–15.

Fioramonti, Lorenzo, et al., "Wellbeing Economy: an Effective Paradigm to Mainstream Post-Growth Policies" Ecological Economics, 192, February (2022), 107261.

Fisher, Joseph L., and Edward Boorstein. "The Adequacy of Resources for Economic Growth in the United States." Study Paper 13. Washington, DC: Government Printing Office, 1959.

Fourcade, Marion. *Economists and Societies: Discipline and Profession in the United States, Britain, and France, 1890s to 1990s.* Princeton, NJ: Princeton University Press, 2009.

Fourcade, Marion, Etienne Ollion, and Yann Algan. "The Superiority of Economists." *Journal of Economic Perspectives* 29, no. 1 (2015): 89–114.

Fox, Douglas R. "GDP: One of the Great Inventions of the 20th Century." *Survey of Current Business* 80, no. 1 (January 2000): 6–8.

Friedman, Milton. *Essays in Positive Economics.* Chicago: University of Chicago Press, 1953.

Furner, Mary O. *Advocacy and Objectivity: A Crisis in the Professionalization of American Social Science, 1865–1905.* Lexington: Organization of American Historians by the University Press of Kentucky, 1975.

Galbraith, James. "Wassily Leontief: An Appreciation." *Challenge* 42, no. 3 (1999): 100–103.

Galbraith, John Kenneth. *The Affluent Society.* Boston: Houghton Mifflin, 1958.

Galbraith, John Kenneth. "How Much Should a Nation Consume?" In *Perspectives on Conservation: Essays on America's Natural Resources*, edited by Henry Jarrett, 89–99. New York: Published for Resources for the Future by Johns Hopkins University Press, 1958.

Galbraith, John Kenneth. "Surveying American Economy in Terms of American Needs: America's Needs and Resources." *New York Times*, June 1, 1947.

Gaspard, Marion, Antoine Missemer, and Thomas Michael Mueller. "A Journey into Harold Hotelling's Economics." *Journal of Economic Literature* 62, no. 3 (2024): 1186–212.

Gaudet, Gérard. "Natural Resource Economics Under the Rule of Hotelling." *Canadian Journal of Economics* 40, no. 4 (2007): 1033–59.

Georgescu-Roegen, Nicholas. "The Economics of Production." *American Economic Review* 60, no. 2 (1970): 1–9.

Georgescu-Roegen, Nicholas. "Energy and Economic Myths." *Southern Economic Journal* 41, no. 3 (1975).

Georgescu-Roegen, Nicholas. *The Entropy Law and the Economic Process.* Cambridge, MA: Harvard University Press, 1971.

Gieryn, Thomas F. "Boundary-Work and the Demarcation of Science from Non-Science: Strains and Interests in the Professional Ideologies of Scientists." *American Sociological Review* 48, no. 6 (1983): 781–95.

Gilman, Nils. *Mandarins of the Future: Modernization Theory in Cold War America.* Baltimore, MD: Johns Hopkins University Press, 2007.

Giraud, Yann. "Negotiating the Middle-of-the-Road Position: Paul Samuelson, MIT, and the Politics of Textbook Writing, 1945–55." *History of Political Economy* 46, Supplement 1 (2014): 134–52.

Godwin, William. *An Enquiry Concerning Political Justice, and Its Influence on General Virtue and Happiness.* Dublin: Luke White, 1793.

Goldin, Claudia, and Robert A. Margo. "The Great Compression: The Wage Structure in the United States at Mid-Century." *Quarterly Journal of Economics* 107, no. 1 (1992): 1–34.

Goldman, Michael. *Imperial Nature: The World Bank and Struggles for Social Justice in the Age of Globalization*. New Haven, CT: Yale University Press, 2005.

Gordon, H. Scott. "The Economic Theory of a Common-Property Resource: The Fishery." *Journal of Political Economy* 62, no. 2 (1954): 124–42.

Gordon, Robert J. *The Rise and Fall of American Growth: The U.S. Standard of Living Since the Civil War*. Princeton, NJ: Princeton University Press, 2016.

Gram, Harvey, and G. Harcourt. "Joan Robinson and MIT." *History of Political Economy* 49, no. 3 (2017): 437.

Gray, L. C. "The Economic Possibilities of Conservation." *Quarterly Journal of Economics* 27, no. 3 (1913): 497–519.

Gray, Lewis Cecil. "Rent Under the Assumption of Exhaustibility." *Quarterly Journal of Economics* 28, no. 3 (1914): 466–89.

Grossman, Gene M., and Alan B. Krueger. "Economic Growth and the Environment." *Quarterly Journal of Economics* 110, no. 2 (1995): 353–77.

Haab, Timothy C. and John C. Whitehead, "What Do Environmental and Resource Economists Think? Results from a Survey of AERE Members," *Review of Environmental Economics and Policy* 11, no. 1 (2017): 43–58.

Haberl, Helmut, Dominik Wiedenhofer, Doris Virág, Gerald Kalt, Barbara Plank, Paul Brockway, Tomer Fishman, et al. "A Systematic Review of the Evidence on Decoupling of GDP, Resource Use and GHG Emissions, Part II: Synthesizing the Insights." *Environmental Research Letters* 15, no. 6 (2020).

Hahn, F. H., and R. C. O. Matthews. "Economic Growth: A Survey." *Economic Journal* 74, no. 296 (1964): 779–902.

Halsmayer, V. "From Exploratory Modeling to Technical Expertise: Solow's Growth Model as a Multipurpose Design." *History of Political Economy* 46, Supplement 1 (2014): 229–51.

Halsmayer, Verena. *Managing Growth in Miniature: Solow's Model as an Artifact*. Cambridge, UK: Cambridge University Press, 2024.

Halsmayer, Verena, and Kevin D. Hoover. "Solow's Harrod: Transforming Macroeconomic Dynamics into a Model of Long-Run Growth." *European Journal of the History of Economic Thought* 23, no. 4 (2016): 561–96.

Hamaide, Bertrand, ed. *Sustainability and the Environmental Kuznets Curve Conjecture*. Basel: Multidisciplinary Digital Publishing Institute, 2022.

Hamilton, Walton H. "The Institutional Approach to Economic Theory." *American Economic Review* 9, no. 1 (1919): 309–18.

Hamilton, Walton H., and Helen R. Wright. *The Case of Bituminous Coal*. New York: The Macmillan Company, 1925.

Hamilton, Walton H., and Helen R. Wright. *A Way of Order for Bituminous Coal*. New York: The Macmillan Company, 1928.

Hansen, Alvin H. "Capital Goods and the Restoration of Purchasing Power." *Proceedings of the Academy of Political Science* 16, no. 1 (1934): 11–19.

Hansen, Alvin H. "Economic Progress and Declining Population Growth." *American Economic Review* 29, no. 1 (1939): 1–15.

Hansen, Alvin H. *Full Recovery or Stagnation?* New York: Norton, 1938.

Hansen, James, and Sergej Lebedeff. "Global Trends of Measured Surface Air Temperature." *Journal of Geophysical Research* 92, no. D11 (1987): 13345–72.

Hansen, James E., and Larry D. Travis. "Light Scattering in Planetary Atmospheres." *Space Science Reviews* 16, no. 4 (1974): 527–610.

Hansen, James E., Wei-Chyung Wang, and Andrew A. Lacis. "Mount Agung Eruption Provides Test of a Global Climatic Perturbation." *Science* 199, no. 4333 (1978): 1065–68.

Haq, Mahbub ul. "Limits to Growth: A Critique." *Finance and Development* 9, no. 4 (1972): 2–8.

Harcourt, G. C. "Robinson, Joan 1903–1983." *Economic Journal* 105, no. 432 (1995): 1228–43.

Harcourt, G. C., and N. F. Laing. *Capital and Growth: Selected Readings*. Harmondsworth, UK: Penguin Books, 1971.

Harris, Lissa. "The Economic Heresy of Herman Daly." *Grist*, April 10, 2003. https://grist.org/article/bank/.

Harrod, Roy F. "An Essay in Dynamic Theory." *Economic Journal* 49, no. 193 (1939): 14–33.

Hartwick, John M. "Intergenerational Equity and the Investing of Rents from Exhaustible Resources." *American Economic Review* 67, no. 5 (1977): 972–74.

Harvey, David. *A Brief History of Neoliberalism*. Oxford: Oxford University Press, 2005.

Harvey, Fiona. "Heatwaves at Both of Earth's Poles Alarm Climate Scientists." *Guardian*, March 20, 2022. https://www.theguardian.com/environment/2022/mar/20/heatwaves-at-both-of-earth-poles-alarm-climate-scientists.

Haskell, Thomas L. *The Emergence of Professional Social Science: The American Social Science Association and the Nineteenth-Century Crisis of Authority*. Urbana: University of Illinois Press, 1977.

Hausfather, Zeke. "Absolute Decoupling of Economic Growth and Emissions in 32 Countries." *Breakthrough Institute*, April 6, 2021. https://thebreakthrough.org/issues/energy/absolute-decoupling-of-economic-growth-and-emissions-in-32-countries.

Hayden, Anders, and Clay Dasilva. "The Wellbeing Economy: Possibilities and Limits in Bringing Sufficiency from the Margins into the Mainstream." *Frontiers in Sustainability* 3 (2022).

Hays, Samuel P. *Conservation and the Gospel of Efficiency: The Progressive Conservation Movement, 1890–1920*. Pittsburgh, PA: University of Pittsburgh Press, 1999.

Heilbroner, Robert L. *The Worldly Philosophers: The Lives, Times, and Ideas of the Great Economic Thinkers*. 7th ed. New York: Touchstone, 1999.

Heller, Walter, L. "Coming to Terms with Growth and the Environment." In *Energy, Economic Growth, and the Environment: Papers Presented at a Forum Conducted by Resources for the Future, Inc. in Washington, D.C., 20–21 April 1971*, edited by Sam H. Schurr. Baltimore, MD: Published for Resources for the Future by Johns Hopkins Press, 1972.

Hickel, Jason. "The Nobel Prize for Climate Catastrophe." *Foreign Policy*, December 6, 2018. https://foreignpolicy.com/2018/12/06/the-nobel-prize-for-climate-catastrophe/.

Hickel, Jason. "What Does Degrowth Mean? A Few Points of Clarification." *Globalizations* 18, no. 7 (2021): 1105–11.

Hickel, Jason, and Giorgios Kallis. "Is Green Growth Possible?" *New Political Economy* 25, no. 4 (2020): 469–86.

Hicks, John. *Capital and Growth*. New York: Oxford University Press, 1965.

Hicks, John R. "The Foundations of Welfare Economics." *Economic Journal* 49, no. 196 (1939): 696–712.

Higgs, Kerryn. *Collision Course: Endless Growth on a Finite Planet*. Cambridge, MA: The MIT Press, 2014.

Hirschman, Albert O. *The Strategy of Economic Development*. New Haven, CT: Yale University Press, 1958.

Hirschman, Daniel. "Inventing the Economy, Or: How We Learned to Stop Worrying and Love the GDP." PhD diss., University of Michigan, 2016.

Hirschman, Daniel. "Rediscovering the 1%: Knowledge Infrastructures and the Stylized Facts of Inequality." *American Journal of Sociology* 127, no. 3 (2021): 739–86.

Hotelling, Harold. "The Economics of Exhaustible Resources." *Journal of Political Economy* 39, no. 2 (1931): 137–75.

Howson, Susan. "The Origins of Lionel Robbins's Essay on the Nature and Significance of Economic Science." *History of Political Economy* 36, no. 3 (2004): 413–43.

Hu, Akielly, and Joseph Winters. "How to 'Decouple' Emissions from Economic Growth: These Economists Say You Can't." *Grist*, March 4, 2024. https://grist.org/economics/how-to-decouple-emissions-from-economic-growth-these-economists-say-you-cant/.

Hulten, Charles R. "Growth Accounting." Working paper, National Bureau of Economic Research, Cambridge, MA, 2009.

The Impact of Growth on the Environment: Hearings Before the Subcommittee on Air and Water Pollution of the Committee on Public Works of the United States Senate, 93rd Congress, 1st session. Washington, DC: US Government Printing Office, 1973.

"In Memoriam: George W. Stocking 1892–1975." *American Economic Review* 66, no. 3 (1976): 453–54.

Intergovernmental Panel on Climate Change. *Synthesis Report of the IPCC Sixth Assessment Report (AR6)*. Interlaken, Switzerland, 2023. https://report.ipcc.ch /ar6syr/pdf/IPCC_AR6_SYR_LongerReport.pdf.

Ise, John. *The United States Oil Policy*. New Haven, CT: Yale University Press, 1926.

Jack, Caroline. *Business as Usual: How Sponsored Media Sold American Capitalism in the Twentieth Century*. Chicago: University of Chicago Press, 2024.

Jackson, Tim. *Prosperity Without Growth: Economics for a Finite Planet*. London: Earthscan, 2009.

Jasanoff, Sheila. "Technologies of Humility." *Nature* 450, no. 7166 (2007): 33.

Jeong-su, Kim. "The Environmental Fallout of the Four Major Rivers Project." *Hankyoreh*, August 3, 2013. https://english.hani.co.kr/arti/english_edition/e _national/598190.html.

Jevons, William Stanley. *The Coal Question; an Inquiry Concerning the Progress of the Nation, and the Probable Exhaustion of Our Coal-Mines*. 3rd ed. New York: Augustus M. Kelley, Publisher, 1965.

Jones, Geoffrey G. "Globalization." In *The Oxford Handbook of Business History*, edited by Geoffrey Jones G and Jonathan Zeitlin, 141–70. Oxford: Oxford University Press, 2008.

Jones, William P. *The March on Washington: Jobs, Freedom, and the Forgotten History of Civil Rights*. New York: Norton, 2013.

Jorgenson, Dale W. "The Role of Energy in the U.S. Economy." *National Tax Journal* 31, no. 3 (1978): 209–20.

Jorgenson, Dale W., Frank M. Gollop, and Barbara Fraumeni. *Productivity and U. S. Economic Growth*. Amsterdam: Elsevier Science & Technology, 1988.

Jorgenson, Dale W., and Zvi Griliches. "The Explanation of Productivity Change." *Review of Economic Studies* 34, no. 3 (1967): 249–83.

Jorgenson, Dale W., and Peter J. Wilcoxen. "Energy, the Environment, and Economic Growth." In *Handbook of Natural Resource and Energy Economics*, edited by Allen V. Kneese and James L. Sweeney, vol. 3. Amsterdam: Elsevier, 1993.

Kahneman, Daniel, Ed Diener, and Norbert Schwarz, eds. *Well-Being: Foundations of Hedonic Psychology*. New York: Russell Sage Foundation, 1999.

Kaldor, Nicholas. "Capital Accumulation and Economic Growth." In *The Theory of Capital*, edited by F. A. Lutz and Douglas Hague, 177–222. New York: St. Martin's Press, 1961.

Kaldor, Nicholas. "A Model of Economic Growth." *Economic Journal* 67, no. 268 (1957): 591–624.

Kaldor, Nicholas. "Welfare Propositions of Economics and Interpersonal Comparisons of Utility." *Economic Journal* 49, no. 195 (1939): 549–52.

Keen, Steve. "The Appallingly Bad Neoclassical Economics of Climate Change." *Globalizations* 18, no. 7 (2021): 1149–77.

Kendrick, John W. *The Formation and Stocks of Total Capital*. New York: National Bureau of Economic Research, 1976.

Keynes, John Maynard. "The British Balance of Trade, 1925–1927." *Economic Journal* 37, no. 148 (1927): 551–65.

Keynes, John Maynard. "Economic Possibilities for Our Grandchildren." In *Essays in Persuasion*, 358–73. New York: Harcourt, Brace and Co., 1932.

Keynes, John Maynard. *The General Theory of Employment, Interest and Money*. New York: Harcourt, Brace and Co., 1936.

Kochhar, Rakesh, and Stella Sechopoulos. "How the American Middle Class Has Changed in the Past Five Decades." *Pew Research Center*, April 20, 2022. https://www.pewresearch.org/short-reads/2022/04/20/how-the-american -middle-class-has-changed-in-the-past-five-decades/.

Kolbert, Elizabeth. *The Sixth Extinction: An Unnatural History*. New York: Picador, 2014.

Koopmans, Tjalling. "Economic Growth at a Maximal Rate." *Quarterly Journal of Economics* 78, no. 3 (1964): 355–94.

Koopmans, Tjalling C. "Measurement Without Theory." *Review of Economics and Statistics* 29, no. 3 (1947): 161–72.

Krutilla, John V. "Conservation Reconsidered." *American Economic Review* 57, no. 4 (1967): 777–86.

Kuhn, Moritz, Moritz Schularick, and Ulrike I. Steins. *Income and Wealth Inequality in America, 1949–2016*. Minneapolis, MN: Federal Reserve Bank of Minneapolis, 2018.

Kula, E. *History of Environmental Economic Thought*. London: Routledge, 1998.

Kumekawa, Ian. *The First Serious Optimist: A. C. Pigou and the Birth of Welfare Economics*. Princeton, NJ: Princeton University Press, 2017.

Kuznets, Simon. *National Income, 1929–32*. Washington, DC: Government Printing Office, 1934.

Kuznets, Simon. "Reflections on the Economic Growth of Nations." In *Toward a Theory of Economic Growth*, edited by Simon Kuznets, 82–122. New York: Norton, 1968.

Kuznets, Simon. *Six Lectures on Economic Growth*. New York: The Free Press, 1959.

Landsberg, Hans H., Leonard L. Fischman, and Joseph L. Fisher. *Resources in America's Future: Patterns of Requirements and Availabilities, 1960–2000*. Baltimore, MD: Published for Resources for the Future by the Johns Hopkins Press, 1963.

Layard, Richard. *Happiness: Lessons from a New Science*. New York: Penguin Books, 2006.

Lazonick, William, Philip Moss, and Joshua Weitz. "The Unmaking of the Black Blue-Collar Middle Class." Working paper, Institute for New Economic Thinking, New York, May 20, 2021. https://www.ineteconomics.org/research /research-papers/the-unmaking-of-the-black-blue-collar-middle-class.

Lele, S. M. "Sustainable Development: A Critical Review." *World Development* 19, no. 6 (1991): 607–21.

Lenton, Timothy M., Johan Rockström, Owen Gaffney, Stefan Rahmstorf, Katherine Richardson, Will Steffen, and Hans Joachim Schellnhuber. "Climate Tipping Points: Too Risky to Bet Against." *Nature* 575, no. 7784 (2019): 592–95.

Leontief, Wassily. *Input-Output Economics.* 2nd ed. New York: Oxford University Press, 1986.

Leontief, Wassily, ed. *Studies in the Structure of the American Economy; Theoretical and Empirical Explorations in Input-Output Analysis.* New York: Oxford University Press, 1953.

Leontief, Wassily. "Theoretical Assumptions and Nonobserved Facts." *American Economic Review* 61, no. 1 (1971): 1–7.

Lepenies, Philipp. *Power of a Single Number: A Political History of GDP.* New York: Columbia University Press, 2016.

Levy, David M. *How the Dismal Science Got Its Name: Classical Economics and the Ur-Text of Racial Politics.* Ann Arbor: University of Michigan Press, 2001.

Lewis, Anthony. "To Grow and to Die." *New York Times,* January 29, 1972.

Lewis, W. Arthur. "Economic Development with Unlimited Supplies of Labour." *Manchester School of Economic and Social Studies* 22 (1954): 139–91.

Lewis, W. Arthur. *The Theory of Economic Growth.* Homewood, IL: Richard D. Irwin, Inc., 1955.

Lichtenstein, Nelson. "From Corporatism to Collective Bargaining: Organized Labor and the Eclipse of Social Democracy in the Postwar Era." In *The Rise and Fall of the New Deal Order, 1930–1980,* edited by Steve Fraser and Gary Gerstle, 122–52. Princeton, NJ: Princeton University Press, 1989.

Light, Jennifer S. *From Warfare to Welfare: Defense Intellectuals and Urban Problems in Cold War America.* Baltimore, MD: Johns Hopkins University Press, 2003.

Livernois, John. "On the Empirical Significance of the Hotelling Rule." *Review of Environmental Economics and Policy* 3, no. 1 (2009): 22–41.

Livingston, Julie. *Self-Devouring Growth: A Planetary Parable as Told from Southern Africa.* Durham, NC: Duke University Press, 2019.

Long-Term Economic Growth: Hearings Before the Joint Economic Committee, 94th Congress, 2nd session. Washington, DC: US Government Printing Office, 1977.

Lucas, Robert E. "On the Mechanics of Economic Development." *Journal of Monetary Economics* 22 (1988): 3–42.

Maas, Harro. *William Stanley Jevons and the Making of Modern Economics.* Cambridge, UK: Cambridge University Press, 2005.

Macekura, Stephen. "Economic Growth and Development: An Intellectual History." In *History of the Future of Economic Growth: Historical Roots of Current Debates on Sustainable Degrowth,* edited by Matthias Schmelzer and Iris Borowy, 110–28. London: Routledge, 2017.

Macekura, Stephen. *Of Limits and Growth: The Rise of Global Sustainable Development in the Twentieth Century.* New York: Cambridge University Press, 2015.

Macekura, Stephen. *The Mismeasure of Progress: Economic Growth and Its Critics.* Chicago: University of Chicago Press, 2020.

Macekura, Stephen. "Whither Growth? International Development, Social Indicators, and the Politics of Measurement, 1920s–1970s." *Journal of Global History* 14, no. 2 (2019): 261–79.

MacKenzie, Donald. *An Engine, Not a Camera: How Financial Models Shape Markets.* Cambridge, MA: The MIT Press, 2006.

MacLean, Nancy. *Democracy in Chains: The Deep History of the Radical Right's Stealth Plan for America.* New York: Viking, 2017.

Maddison, Angus. "Growth and Slowdown in Advanced Capitalist Economies: Techniques of Quantitative Assessment." *Journal of Economic Literature* 25, no. 2 (1987): 649–98.

Maddison, Angus. *The World Economy: A Millennial Perspective.* Paris: Organisation for Economic Co-operation and Development, 2001.

Mahrane, Yannick, Marianna Fenzi, Céline Pessis, and Christophe Bonneuil. "From Nature to Biosphere: The Political Invention of the Global Environment, 1945–1972." *Vingtième Siècle: Revue d'Histoire* 113, no. 1 (2012): 127–41.

Maier, Charles S. "The Politics of Productivity: Foundations of American International Economic Policy After World War II." *International Organization* 31, no. 4 (1977): 607–33.

Malthus, Thomas Robert. *An Essay on the Principle of Population, as It Affects the Future Improvement of Society. With Remarks on the Speculations of Mr. Godwin, M. Condorcet, and Other Writers.* London: J. Johnson, 1798.

Mankiw, N. Gregory. "Defending the One Percent." *Journal of Economic Perspectives* 27, no. 3 (2013): 21–34.

Mann, Charles C. *The Wizard and the Prophet: Two Remarkable Scientists and Their Dueling Visions to Shape Tomorrow's World.* New York: Alfred A. Knopf, 2018.

Marglin, Stephen A. *The Dismal Science: How Thinking like an Economist Undermines Community.* Cambridge, MA: Harvard University Press, 2008.

Martínez Alier, Juan. *Ecological Economics: Energy, Environment, and Society.* Oxford: Basil Blackwell, 1987.

Marx, Karl. *Wage-Labor and Capital.* New York: New York Labor News Company, 1847.

Masood, Ehsan. *The Great Invention: The Story of GDP and the Making (and Unmaking) of the Modern World.* New York: Pegasus Books, 2016.

Max-Neef, Manfred. "Economic Growth and Quality of Life: A Threshold Hypothesis." *Ecological Economics* 15, no. 2 (1995): 115–18.

McCloskey, Deirdre N. *The Rhetoric of Economics.* Madison: University of Wisconsin Press, 1998.

McDonald, Mark. "U.N. Report from Rio on Environment a 'Suicide Note.'" *New York Times*, June 24, 2012.

McNeill, John R., and Peter Engelke. *The Great Acceleration: An Environmental History of the Anthropocene Since 1945.* Cambridge, MA: Harvard University Press, 2016.

McNeill, John Robert. *Something New Under the Sun: An Environmental History of the Twentieth-Century World.* New York: W. W. Norton, 2000.

Meade, J. E. *A Neo-Classical Theory of Economic Growth.* New York: Oxford University Press, 1961.

Meadows, Donella H., Dennis L. Meadows, Jørgen Randers, and William W. Behrens III. *The Limits to Growth: A Report for the Club of Rome's Project on the Predicament of Mankind.* Washington, DC: Potomac Associates, 1972.

Milanović, Branko. *Global Inequality: A New Approach for the Age of Globalization.* Cambridge, MA: Harvard University Press, 2016.

Mill, John Stuart. *Principles of Political Economy: Abridged, with Critical, Bibliographical, and Explanatory Notes, and a Sketch of the History of Political Economy.* Edited by J. Laurence Laughlin. New York: Appleton, 1884.

Miller, John E. "From South Dakota Farm to Harvard Seminar: Alvin H. Hansen, America's Prophet of Keynesianism." *The Historian* 64, no. 3–4 (2002): 603–22.

Mirowski, Philip. "Energy and Energetics in Economic Theory: A Review Essay." *Journal of Economic Issues* 22, no. 3 (1988): 811–30.

Mirowski, Philip. *Machine Dreams: Economics Becomes a Cyborg Science.* Cambridge, UK: Cambridge University Press, 2002.

Mirowski, Philip. *More Heat than Light: Economics as Social Physics, Physics as Nature's Economics.* Cambridge, UK: Cambridge University Press, 1989.

Mirowski, Philip, and Dieter Plehwe, eds. *The Road from Mont Pelerin: The Making of the Neoliberal Thought Collective.* Cambridge, MA: Harvard University Press, 2009.

Mishan, E. J. *The Costs of Economic Growth.* New York: F. A. Praeger, 1967.

Mitchell, Lucy Sprague. "A Personal Sketch." In *Wesley Clair Mitchell: The Economic Scientist,* edited by Arthur Burns, 55–106. New York: National Bureau of Economic Research, 1951.

Mitchell, Timothy. *Carbon Democracy: Political Power in the Age of Oil.* London: Verso, 2011.

Mitchell, Timothy. "Economists and the Economy in the Twentieth Century." In *The Politics of Method in the Human Sciences: Positivism and Its Epistemological Others,* edited by George Steinmetz. Durham, NC: Duke University Press, 2005.

Mitchell, Timothy. "Fixing the Economy." *Cultural Studies* 12, no. 1 (1998): 82–101.

Mitchell, Timothy. "The Work of Economics: How a Discipline Makes Its World." *European Journal of Sociology* 46, no. 2 (2005): 297–320.

Mitchell, Wesley C. *Business Cycles*. Berkeley: University of California Press, 1913.

Mitchell, Wesley C., and National Bureau of Economic Research. *Income in the United States: Its Amount and Distribution, 1909–1919*. 2 vols. Publications of the National Bureau of Economic Research, no. 1–2. New York: Harcourt, Brace and Co., 1921.

Morgan, Mary S. *The World in the Model: How Economists Work and Think*. Cambridge, UK: Cambridge University Press, 2012.

Morgan, Mary S., and Malcolm Rutherford, eds. *From Interwar Pluralism to Postwar Neoclassicism: Annual Supplement to Volume 30, History of Political Economy*. Durham, NC: Duke University Press, 1998.

Myrdal, Gunnar. *Economic Theory and Underdeveloped Regions*. New York: Harper Torchbooks, 1957.

Nasar, Sylvia. "Nicholas Georgescu-Roegen, Leading Economist, Dies at 88." *New York Times*, November 5, 1994, sec. 1.

National Park Service. *The Economics of Public Recreation: An Economic Study of the Monetary Evaluation of Recreation in the National Parks*. Land and Recreational Planning Division, National Park Service, 1949.

Newcomb, Simon. *Principles of Political Economy*. New York: Harper, 1885.

New York Times. "The Text of Jimmy Carter's First Presidential Report to the American People." February 3, 1977.

Nordhaus, William D. "The Allocation of Energy Resources." *Brookings Papers on Economic Activity*, no. 3 (1973): 529–76.

Nordhaus, William D. "Climate Change: The Ultimate Challenge for Economics." Prize Lecture, Stockholm, December 8, 2018. https://www.nobelprize.org/uploads/2018/10/nordhaus-lecture.pdf.

Nordhaus, William D. "Do Real-Output and Real-Wage Measures Capture Reality? The History of Lighting Suggests Not." In *The Economics of New Goods*, edited by Timothy F. Bresnahan and Robert J. Gordon. Chicago: University of Chicago Press, 1997.

Nordhaus, William. "Economics: Critical Assumptions in the Stern Review on Climate Change." *Science* 317, no. 5835 (2007): 201–2.

Nordhaus, William. "Economics of the Disintegration of the Greenland Ice Sheet." *Proceedings of the National Academy of Sciences*, From the Cover, 116, no. 25 (2019): 12261–69.

Nordhaus, William D. "An Optimal Transition Path for Controlling Greenhouse Gases." *Science* 258, no. 5086 (1992): 1315–19.

Nordhaus, William D. *A Question of Balance Weighing the Options on Global Warming Policies*. New Haven, CT: Yale University Press, 2008.

Nordhaus, William D. "Resources as a Constraint on Growth." *American Economic Review* 64, no. 2 (1974): 22–26.

Nordhaus, William D. "A Review of the 'Stern Review on the Economics of Climate Change.'" *Journal of Economic Literature* 45, no. 3 (2007): 686–702.

Nordhaus, William D. "Revisiting the Social Cost of Carbon." *Proceedings of the National Academy of Sciences* 114, no. 7 (2017): 1518–23.

Nordhaus, William D. "Strategies for the Control of Carbon Dioxide." New Haven, CT: Cowles Foundation, 1977.

Nordhaus, William D. "World Dynamics: Measurement Without Data." *Economic Journal* 83, no. 332 (1973): 1156–83.

Nordhaus, William D., and James Tobin. "Is Growth Obsolete?" In *Economic Research: Retrospect and Prospect, Vol. 5: Economic Growth*, 1–80. New York: National Bureau of Economic Research, 1972.

Nurkse, Ragnar. *Problems of Capital Formation in Underdeveloped Countries.* New York: Oxford University Press, 1957.

O'Bryan, Scott. *The Growth Idea: Purpose and Prosperity in Postwar Japan.* Honolulu: University of Hawaii Press, 2009.

Odell, Peter, R. *An Economic Geography of Oil.* Edinburgh: Neill & Company, 1963.

Okun, Arthur M. "Should GNP Measure Social Welfare?" *Brookings Bulletin* 8, no. 3 (1971): 4–7.

Olkin, Ingram. *Contributions to Probability and Statistics: Essays in Honor of Harold Hotelling.* Stanford, CA: Stanford University Press, 1960.

Olson, Mancur. "Introduction." *Daedalus* 102, no. 4, The No-Growth Society (1973): 1–13.

Olson, Mancur, Hans H. Lansberg, and Joseph L. Fisher. "Epilogue." *Daedalus* 102, no. 4 (1973): 229–41.

Opschoor, J. B. "The Hope, Faith and Love of Neoclassical Environmental Economics." *Ecological Economics* 22 (1997): 281–83.

Ordway, Samuel Hanson. *Resources and the American Dream, Including a Theory of the Limit of Growth.* New York: Ronald Press Co., 1953.

Oreskes, Naomi, and Erik M. Conway. *Merchants of Doubt: How a Handful of Scientists Obscured the Truth on Issues from Tobacco Smoke to Global Warming.* London: Bloomsbury Press, 2010.

Organisation for Economic Co-operation and Development. *Towards Green Growth.* Paris: OECD Publishing, 2011.

Osborn, Fairfield. *Our Plundered Planet.* Boston: Little, Brown, 1948.

Pareto, Vilfredo. *Manual of Political Economy.* New York: A. M. Kelley, 1906.

Passell, Peter, Marc Roberts, and Leonard Ross. "The Limits to Growth." *New York Times*, April 2, 1972.

Pearce, David. "An Intellectual History of Environmental Economics." *Annual Review of Energy and the Environment* 27 (2002): 57–81.

Persky, Joseph. "Retrospectives: Adam Smith's Invisible Hands." *Journal of Economic Perspectives* 3, no. 4 (1989): 195–201.

Peterson, Frederick M., and Anthony C. Fisher. "The Exploitation of Extractive Resources: A Survey." *Economic Journal* 87, no. 348 (1977): 681–721.

Pfouts, Ralph W. *Essays in Economics and Econometrics: A Volume in Honor of Harold Hotelling.* Chapel Hill: University of North Carolina Press, 1960.

Phelps Brown, E. H. "The Underdevelopment of Economics." *Economic Review* 82, no. 325 (1972): 1–10.

Philipsen, Dirk. *The Little Big Number: How GDP Came to Rule the World and What to Do About It.* Princeton, NJ: Princeton University Press, 2015.

Phillips, Sarah. *This Land, This Nation: Conservation, Rural America, and the New Deal.* Cambridge, UK: Cambridge University Press, 2007.

Pigou, A. C. *The Economics of Welfare.* London: Macmillan, 1920.

Popp Berman, Elizabeth. *Thinking like an Economist: How Efficiency Replaced Equality in U.S. Public Policy.* Princeton, NJ: Princeton University Press, 2022.

Porter, Theodore M. *Trust in Numbers: The Pursuit of Objectivity in Science and Public Life.* Princeton, NJ: Princeton University Press, 1995.

The President's Materials Policy Commission. *Resources for Freedom.* Washington, DC: Government Printing Office, 1952.

Proctor, Robert N., and Londa Schiebinger, eds. *Agnotology: The Making and Unmaking of Ignorance.* Palo Alto, CA: Stanford University Press, 2008.

Putnam, Robert. *Bowling Alone: The Collapse and Revival of American Community.* New York: Simon & Schuster, 2000.

Rader, Benjamin G. *The Academic Mind and Reform: The Influence of Richard T. Ely in American Life.* Lexington: University Press of Kentucky, 1966.

Raworth, Kate. *Doughnut Economics: Seven Ways to Think like a 21st Century Economist.* White River Junction, VT: Chelsea Green Publishing, 2017.

Reinhold, Robert. "Mankind Warned of Perils in Growth." *New York Times,* February 27, 1972.

Resource Scarcity, Economic Growth and the Environment: Hearings Before the Subcommittee on Priorities and Economy in Government of the Joint Economic Committee, 93rd Congress, 1st session. Washington, DC: US Government Printing Office, 1974.

Resources for the Future (RFF). *The First 25 Years, 1952–1977.* Washington, DC: RFF, 1977.

Ricardo, David. *On the Principles of Political Economy and Taxation.* London: John Murray, 1817.

Rinde, Meir. "Richard Nixon and the Rise of American Environmentalism." *Distillations* 3, no. 1 (2017).

Robbins, Lionel. *An Essay on the Nature and Significance of Economic Science.* London: Macmillan, 1932.

Roberts, David. "Discount Rates: A Boring Thing You Should Know About (with Otters!)." *Grist,* September 24, 2012. https://grist.org/article/discount-rates-a-boring-thing-you-should-know-about-with-otters/.

Roberts, Sam. "Martin Weitzman, Virtuoso Climate Change Economist, Dies at 77." *New York Times,* September 4, 2019, Business section. https://www.nytimes

.com/2019/09/04/business/energy-environment/martin-weitzman-dead
.html.

Robertson, Thomas. *The Malthusian Moment: Global Population Growth and the Birth of American Environmentalism.* New Brunswick, NJ: Rutgers University Press, 2012.

Robinson, Joan. *The Accumulation of Capital.* London: Macmillan, 1956.

Robinson, Joan. *Essays in the Theory of Economic Growth.* New York: St. Martin's Press, 1964.

Robinson, Joan. "The Production Function and the Theory of Capital." *Review of Economic Studies* 21, no. 2 (1953): 81–106.

Rockström, Johan, Will Steffen, Kevin Noone, Åsa Persson, F. Stuart Chapin, Eric F. Lambin, Timothy M. Lenton, et al. "A Safe Operating Space for Humanity." *Nature* 461, no. 7263 (September 2009): 472–75.

Rodrik, Dani. *Economics Rules: The Rights and Wrongs of the Dismal Science.* New York: W. W. Norton, 2015.

Rohde, Joy. *Armed with Experience: The Militarization of American Social Science Research During the Cold War.* Ithaca, NY: Cornell University Press, 2013.

Rome, Adam. *The Genius of Earth Day: How a 1970 Teach-In Unexpectedly Made the First Green Generation.* New York: Hill and Wang, 2013.

Romer, Paul M. "Endogenous Technological Change." *Journal of Political Economy* 98, no. 5 (1990): S71–102.

Romer, Paul M. "Increasing Returns and Long-Run Growth." *Journal of Political Economy* 94, no. 5 (1986): 1002–37.

Romer, Paul M. "The Origins of Endogenous Growth." *Journal of Economic Perspectives* 8, no. 1 (1994): 3–22.

Romer, Paul M., and Hiroo Sasaki. *Monotonically Decreasing Natural Resources Prices Under Perfect Foresight.* Rochester Center for Economic Research, 1984.

Røpke, Inge. "The Early History of Modern Ecological Economics." *Ecological Economics* 50 (2004): 293–314.

Røpke, Inge. "Trends in the Development of Ecological Economics from the Late 1980s to the Early 2000s." *Ecological Economics* 55 (2005): 262–90.

Ros, Jaime. "The Pioneers of Development Economics and Modern Growth Theory." In *The Origins of Development Economics: How Schools of Economic Thought Have Addressed Development,* edited by Jomo K. S. and Erik S. Reinert, 81–98. London: Zed Books, 2005.

Rosenstein-Rodan, P. N. "Problems of Industrialisation of Eastern and South-Eastern Europe." *Economic Journal* 53, no. 210/211 (1943): 202–11.

Ross, Dorothy. *The Origins of American Social Science.* Cambridge, UK: Cambridge University Press, 1991.

Rostow, W. W. *The Stages of Economic Growth, a Non-Communist Manifesto.* Cambridge, UK: Cambridge University Press, 1960.

Ruggles, Richard, and Nancy D. Ruggles. "Integrated Economic Accounts for the United States, 1947–1980." *Survey of Current Business* 62 (1982): 1–53.

Runge, C. Ford. "Agricultural Economics: A Brief Intellectual History." Staff Paper 13649, Department of Applied Economics, University of Minnesota, 2006.

Rutherford, Malcolm. *The Institutional Movement in American Economics, 1918–1947: Science and Social Control.* Cambridge, UK: Cambridge University Press, 2011.

Ryan-Collins, Josh, Toby Lloyd, and Laurie Macfarlane. *Rethinking the Economics of Land and Housing.* London: Zed Books, 2017.

Sabin, Paul. *The Bet: Paul Ehrlich, Julian Simon, and Our Gamble over Earth's Future.* New Haven, CT: Yale University Press, 2013.

Sacks, Daniel W., Betsey Stevenson, and Justin Wolfers. "Subjective Wellbeing, Income, Economic Development and Growth." In *. . . And the Pursuit of Happiness: Wellbeing and the Role of Government,* edited by Philip Booth, 59–97. London: Institute of Economic Affairs, 2012.

Samuelson, Paul A. "Abstract of a Theorem Concerning Substitutability in Open Leontief Models." In *Activity Analysis of Production and Allocation: Proceedings of a Conference,* edited by Tjalling Koopmans. New York: John Wiley & Sons, 1951.

Samuelson, Paul A. *Foundations of Economic Analysis.* Cambridge, MA: Harvard University Press, 1947.

Samuelson, Paul A. "Full Employment After the War." In *Postwar Economic Problems,* edited by Seymour E. Harris, 27–54. New York: McGraw-Hill Book, 1943.

Samuelson, Paul A. "Robert Solow: An Affectionate Portrait." *Journal of Economic Perspectives* 3, no. 3 (1989): 91–97.

Samuelson, Paul A. "A Summing Up." *Quarterly Journal of Economics* 80, no. 4 (1966): 568–83.

Samuelson, Paul A. "Unemployment Ahead." *The New Republic,* September 11, 1944.

Schabas, Margaret. *The Natural Origins of Economics.* Chicago: University of Chicago Press, 2005.

Schabas, Margaret. *A World Ruled by Numbers: William Stanley Jevons and the Rise of Mathematical Economics.* Princeton, NJ: Princeton University Press, 1990.

Schmelzer, Matthias. "'Born in the Corridors of the OECD': The Forgotten Origins of the Club of Rome, Transnational Networks, and the 1970s in Global History." *Journal of Global History* 12, no. 1 (2017): 26–48.

Schmelzer, Matthias. *The Hegemony of Growth: The OECD and the Making of the Economic Growth Paradigm.* Cambridge, UK: Cambridge University Press, 2016.

Schmelzer, Matthias, and Iris Borowy, eds. *History of the Future of Economic*

Growth: Historical Roots of Current Debates on Sustainable Degrowth. London: Routledge, 2017.

Schmelzer, Matthias, Andrea Vetter, and Aaron Vansintjan. *The Future Is Degrowth: A Guide to a World Beyond Capitalism*. London: Verso, 2022.

Schumacher, E. F. *Small Is Beautiful: Economics as If People Mattered*. New York: Harper & Row, 1973.

Schumpeter, Joseph A. *Capitalism, Socialism, and Democracy*. New York: Harper & Brothers, 1942.

Schweinfest, Stefan, Alessandra Alfieri, Jessica Ying Chan, and Bram Edens. "The Rise, Fall and Rethinking of Green GDP." United Nations System of Environmental Economic Accounting, 2021. https://seea.un.org/news/rise-fall-and -rethinking-green-gdp.

Sen, Amartya. *Growth Economics: Selected Readings*. Harmondsworth, UK: Penguin, 1970.

Shiller, Robert J. *Narrative Economics: How Stories Go Viral and Drive Major Economic Events*. Princeton, NJ: Princeton University Press, 2019.

Silk, Leonard Solomon. *The Economists*. New York: Basic Books, 1976.

Simon, Julian. "Resources, Population, Environment: An Oversupply of False Bad News." *Science* 208, no. 4451 (1980): 1431–37.

Simon, Julian Lincoln. *The Ultimate Resource*. Princeton, NJ: Princeton University Press, 1981.

Sinclair, Peter. "Ezra Mishan, Contrarian and Sage: An Appreciation." *Singapore Economic Review* 61, no. 3 (2016): 1.

Singer, H. W. "The Distribution of Gains Between Investing and Borrowing Countries." *American Economic Review* 40, no. 2 (1950): 473–85.

Skidelsky, Robert. *What's Wrong with Economics? A Primer for the Perplexed*. New Haven, CT: Yale University Press, 2020.

Slobodian, Quinn. *Globalists: The End of Empire and the Birth of Neoliberalism*. Cambridge, MA: Harvard University Press, 2018.

Smith, Adam. *An Inquiry into the Nature and Causes of the Wealth of Nations*. 3 vols. Dublin: Whitestone, 1776.

Smith, Adam. *The Theory of Moral Sentiments*. London: Printed for A. Millar and A. Kincaid and J. Bell, 1759.

Smith, Vernon L. "On Models of Commercial Fishing." *Journal of Political Economy* 77, no. 2 (1969): 181–98.

Solow, Robert M. "An Almost Practical Step Toward Sustainability." *Resources Policy* 19, no. 3 (1993): 162–72.

Solow, Robert M. "A Contribution to the Theory of Economic Growth." *Quarterly Journal of Economics* 70, no. 1 (1956): 65–94.

Solow, Robert M. "Does Economics Make Progress?" *Bulletin of the American Academy of Arts and Sciences* 36, no. 3 (1982): 13–31.

Solow, Robert M. "Does Growth Have a Future? Does Growth Theory Have a

Future? Are These Questions Related?" *History of Political Economy* 41, Supplement 1 (2009): 27–34.

Solow, Robert M. "Economic History and Economics." *American Economic Review* 75, no. 2 (1985): 328–31.

Solow, Robert M. "The Economics of Resources or the Resources of Economics." *American Economic Review* 64, no. 2 (1974): 1–14.

Solow, Robert M. "The Failures of Economics: A Diagnostic Study (Book Review)." *Review of Economics and Statistics* 39, no. 1 (1957): 96–98.

Solow, Robert M. "Intergenerational Equity and Exhaustible Resources." *Review of Economic Studies* 41 (1974): 29–45.

Solow, Robert M. "Is the End of the World at Hand?" *Challenge* 16, no. 1 (1973): 39–50.

Solow, Robert M. "Is the End of the World at Hand?" In *The Economic Growth Controversy*, edited by Andrew Weintraub, Eli Schwartz, and J. Richard Aronson. White Plains, NY: International Arts and Sciences Press, 1973.

Solow, Robert M. "The Last 50 Years in Growth Theory and the Next 10." *Oxford Review of Economic Policy* 23, no. 1 (2007): 3–14.

Solow, Robert M. "Notes on 'Doomsday Models.'" *Proceedings of the National Academy of Sciences* 69, no. 12 (1972): 3832–33.

Solow, Robert M. "Policies for Economic Growth: The Ernest Sturc Memorial Lecture." Delivered November 12, 1991. Washington, DC: The Paul H. Nitze School for Advanced International Studies, Johns Hopkins University, 1992.

Solow, Robert M. "The Production Function and the Theory of Capital." *Review of Economic Studies* 23, no. 2 (56 1955): 101–8.

Solow, Robert M. "Reflections on Macroeconomic Modelling: Confessions of a DRI Addict." *Eastern Economic Journal* 11, no. 1 (1985): 79–83.

Solow, Robert M. "Reply: Georgescu-Roegen Versus Solow/Stiglitz." *Ecological Economics* 22 (1997): 267–68.

Solow, Robert M. "Second Thoughts on Growth Theory." In *Employment and Growth: Issues for the 1980s*, edited by Alfred Steinherr and Daniel Weiserbs. Dordrecht, Netherlands: Kluwer Academic Publishers, 1987.

Solow, Robert M. "Some Lessons from Growth Theory." In *Financial Economics: Essays in Honor of Paul Cootner*, edited by W. F. Sharpe and C. M. Cootner. Englewood Cliffs, NJ: Prentice-Hall, 1982.

Solow, Robert. "Son of Affluence: A Review of 'The New Industrial State.'" *The Public Interest* 9 (1967): 100–108.

Solow, Robert M. "Technical Change and the Aggregate Production Function." *Review of Economics and Statistics* 39, no. 3 (1957): 312–20.

Solow, Robert M. "Technical Progress, Capital Formation, and Economic Growth." *American Economic Review* 52, no. 2 (1962): 76–86.

Solow, Robert M., and Paul Samuelson. "Balanced Growth Under Constant Returns to Scale." *Econometrica* 21, no. 3 (1953): 412–24.

Spash, Clive L. "The Brave New World of Carbon Trading." *New Political Economy* 15, no. 2 (2010): 169–95.

Spash, Clive L. "The Development of Environmental Thinking in Economics." *Environmental Values* 8, no. 4 (1999): 413–35.

Spash, Clive L., and Clemens Gattringer. "The Ethical Failures of Climate Economics." In *The Ethical Underpinnings of Climate Economics*, edited by Adrian Walsh, Säde Hormio, and Duncan Purves, 174–94. Routledge, 2017.

Spash, Clive L., and Anthony Ryan. "Economic Schools of Thought on the Environment: Investigating Unity and Division." *Cambridge Journal of Economics* 36 (2012): 1091–121.

Spiegel, Henry William. *The Growth of Economic Thought.* 3rd ed. Durham, NC: Duke University Press, 1991.

Steinberg, Theodore. *Down to Earth: Nature's Role in American History.* New York: Oxford University Press, 2002.

Stern, Nicholas. "The Economics of Development: A Survey." *Economic Journal* 99, no. 397 (1989): 597–685.

Stern, Nicholas. "Stern Review: The Economics of Climate Change." London: UK Treasury, 2006. https://webarchive.nationalarchives.gov.uk/20100407172811/http://www.hm-treasury.gov.uk/stern_review_report.htm.

Stern, Nicholas, Joseph Stiglitz, and Charlotte Taylor. "The Economics of Immense Risk, Urgent Action and Radical Change: Towards New Approaches to the Economics of Climate Change." *Journal of Economic Methodology* 29, no. 3 (2022): 181–216.

Stiglitz, Joseph. "Growth with Exhaustible Natural Resources: Efficient and Optimal Growth Paths." *Review of Economic Studies* 41, no. 1 (1974): 123–37.

Stiglitz, Joseph. "Growth with Exhaustible Natural Resources: The Competitive Economy." *Review of Economic Studies* 41, no. 1 (1974): 139–52.

Stiglitz, Joseph E. "Reply: Georgescu-Roegen Versus Solow/Stiglitz." *Ecological Economics* 22 (1997): 269–70.

Stiglitz, Joseph, Jean-Paul Fitoussi, and Martine Durand. *Beyond GDP: Measuring What Counts for Economic and Social Performance.* Paris: OECD Publishing, 2018.

Stiglitz, Joseph E., Amartya Sen, and Jean-Paul Fitoussi. *Report by the Commission on the Measurement of Economic Performance and Social Progress.* Paris, 2009.

Stocking, George Ward. *The Oil Industry and the Competitive System: A Study in Waste.* Boston: Houghton Mifflin Company, 1925.

Stoll, Steven. *The Great Delusion: A Mad Inventor, Death in the Tropics, and the Utopian Origins of Economic Growth.* New York: Hill and Wang, 2008.

Suri, Jeremi. "The Rise and Fall of an International Counterculture, 1960–1975." *American Historical Review* 114, no. 1 (2009): 45–68.

Susskind, Daniel. *Growth: A History and a Reckoning.* Cambridge, MA: Harvard University Press, 2024.

Swan, Trevor. "Economic Growth and Capital Accumulation." *Economic Record* 32 (1956): 334–61.

Taylor, Henry C., and Anne Dewees Taylor. *The Story of Agricultural Economics in the United States, 1840-1932: Men, Services, Ideas.* Ames: Iowa State College Press, 1952.

Temin, P. "The Rise and Fall of Economic History at MIT." *History of Political Economy* 46, Supplement 1 (2014): 337–50.

Tierney, John. "Betting on the Planet." *New York Times*, December 2, 1990.

Timothée Parrique, Jonathan Barth, François Briens, Christian Kerschner, Alejo Kraus-Polk, Anna Kuokkanen, and Joachim H. Spangenberg. "Decoupling Debunked: Evidence and Arguments Against Green Growth as a Sole Strategy for Sustainability." European Environmental Bureau, 2019. https://eeb.org/library/decoupling-debunked/.

Tobin, James. "Economic Growth as an Objective of Government Policy." *American Economic Review* 54, no. 3 (1964): 1–20.

Tobin, James. "Money and Economic Growth." *Econometrica* 33, no. 4 (1965): 671–84.

Todorova, Vesela. "Korean Leader Wins Zayed Prize." *National News*, March 14, 2011. https://www.thenationalnews.com/uae/environment/korean-leader-wins-zayed-prize-1.605514.

Tol, Richard S. J. "The Economic Impacts of Climate Change." *Review of Environmental Economics and Policy* 12, no. 1 (2018): 4–25.

Tønnessen, Morten. "Wasted GDP in the USA." *Humanities and Social Sciences Communications* 10, no. 1 (2023): 681: 1–14.

Tooze, Adam. *Statistics and the German State, 1900–1945: The Making of Modern Economic Knowledge.* Cambridge, UK: Cambridge University Press, 2001.

Toye, John. "Solow in the Tropics." *History of Political Economy* 41, Supplement 1 (2009): 221–40.

Tryon, Frederick G. "An Index of Consumption of Fuels and Water Power." *Journal of the American Statistical Association* 22, no. 159 (1927): 271–82.

Turner, James Morton and Isenberg, Andrew C. *The Republican Reversal: Conservatives and the Environment from Nixon to Trump.* Cambridge, MA: Harvard University Press, 2018.

United Nations Conference on Environment and Development. *Report of the United Nations Conference on Environment and Development: Rio de Janeiro, 3–14 June 1992.* New York: United Nations, 1993.

United Nations Economic and Social Commission for Asia and the Pacific (ESCAP). "Green Growth at a Glance: The Way Forward for Asia and the Pacific." United Nations, 2006.

Uzawa, Hirofumi. "On a Two-Sector Model of Economic Growth." *Review of Economic Studies* 29, no. 1 (1961): 40–47.

Uzawa, Hirofumi. "On the Occasion of the Inaugural Conference on 'Environment and Development Economics.'" *Environment and Development Economics* 1, no. 1 (1996): 1–2.

Veblen, Thorstein. *The Theory of the Leisure Class: An Economic Study in the Evolution of Institutions.* New York: Macmillan, 1899.

Vianna Franco, Marco P., and Antoine Missemer. *A History of Ecological Economic Thought.* London: Routledge, 2023.

Victor, Peter A. *Managing Without Growth: Slower by Design, Not Disaster.* Cheltenham, UK: Edward Elgar, 2008.

Vining, Rutledge. "Methodological Issues in Quantitative Economics: Koopmans on the Choice of Variables to Be Studied and of Methods of Measurement." *Review of Economics and Statistics* 31 (1949): 77–86.

Vogel, Jefim, and Jason Hickel. "Is Green Growth Happening? An Empirical Analysis of Achieved Versus Paris-Compliant CO_2–GDP Decoupling in High-Income Countries." *The Lancet Planetary Health* 7, no. 9 (2023): e759–69.

Vogt, William. *Road to Survival.* New York: W. Sloane Associates, 1948.

Vollrath, Dietrich. *Fully Grown: Why a Stagnant Economy Is a Sign of Success.* Chicago: University of Chicago Press, 2020.

Wapshott, Nicholas. *Samuelson Friedman: The Battle over the Free Market.* New York: Norton, 2021.

Warde, Paul. *The Invention of Sustainability: Nature and Destiny, c. 1500–1870.* Cambridge, UK: Cambridge University Press, 2018.

Warde, Paul, Libby Robin, and Sverker Sörlin. *The Environment: A History of the Idea.* Baltimore, MD: Johns Hopkins University Press, 2018.

Warsh, David. *Knowledge and the Wealth of Nations: A Story of Economic Discovery.* New York: W. W. Norton, 2006.

Warsh, David. "Robert Solow and His Influential Economic Growth." *Chicago Tribune*, February 20, 1994. https://www.chicagotribune.com/news/ct-xpm-1994-02-20-9402200090-story.html.

Weart, Spencer R. *The Discovery of Global Warming.* Cambridge, MA: Harvard University Press, 2003.

Weintraub, E. Roy. "McCarthyism and the Mathematization of Economics." *Journal of the History of Economic Thought* 39, no. 4 (2017): 571–97.

Weitzman, Martin L. "GHG Targets as Insurance Against Catastrophic Climate Damages." *Journal of Public Economic Theory* 14, no. 2 (2012): 221–44.

Weitzman, Martin L. "On the Welfare Significance of National Product in a Dynamic Economy." *Quarterly Journal of Economics* 90, no. 1 (1976): 156–62.

Weitzman, Martin L. "A Review of 'The Stern Review on the Economics of Climate Change.'" *Journal of Economic Literature* 45, no. 3 (2007): 703–24.

Weitzman, Martin L., and Karl-Gustaf Löfgren. "On the Welfare Significance of Green Accounting as Taught by Parable." *Journal of Environmental Economics and Management,* Journal of Environmental Economics and Management, 32, no. 2 (1997): 139–53.

Wiedmann, Thomas O., Heinz Schandl, Manfred Lenzen, Daniel Moran, Sangwon Suh, James West, and Keiichiro Kanemoto. "The Material Footprint of Nations." *Proceedings of the National Academy of Sciences* 112, no. 20 (May 19, 2015): 6271–76.

Wilkinson, Richard, and Kate Pickett. *The Spirit Level: Why Greater Equality Makes Societies Stronger.* New York: Bloomsbury Press, 2009.

Wolloch, Nathaniel. *Nature in the History of Economic Thought: How Natural Resources Became an Economic Concept.* London: Routledge, 2017.

World Bank Group. "Toward a Green, Clean, and Resilient World for All: A World Bank Group Environmental Strategy, 2012–2022." New York: The World Bank, 2012.

World Commission on Environment and Development. *Our Common Future.* Oxford: Oxford University Press, 1987.

Worley, James S., Fred M. Westfield, and Anthony M. Tang, eds. *Evolution, Welfare, and Time in Economics: Essays in Honor of Nicholas Georgescu-Roegen.* Lexington, MA: Lexington Books, 1976.

Worster, Donald. *Shrinking the Earth: The Rise and Decline of American Abundance.* New York: Oxford University Press, 2016.

Wrigley, E. A. *Continuity, Chance and Change: The Character of the Industrial Revolution in England.* Cambridge, UK: Cambridge University Press, 1988.

"Yale Symposium on the Stern Review." New Haven, CT: Yale Center for the Study of Globalization, 2007. https://ycsg.yale.edu/climate-change/yale-symposium -stern-review.

Yarrow, Andrew L. *Measuring America: How Economic Growth Came to Define American Greatness in the Late Twentieth Century.* Amherst: University of Massachusetts Press, 2010.

Yonay, Yuval P. *The Struggle over the Soul of Economics: Institutionalist and Neoclassical Economists in America Between the Wars.* Princeton, NJ: Princeton University Press, 1998.

Index

Page numbers in italics refer to figures.